W9-ACG-818

To Know
CHRIST JESUS

This is eternal life: that they may know thee, the only true God, and Jesus Christ whom thou hast sent.

(Jn 17:3)

To Know
CHRIST JESUS

F. J. SHEED

IGNATIUS PRESS   SAN FRANCISCO

Cover art: *Christ at the Home of Mary and Martha*
by Henry Ossawa Tanner, 1859–1937, Purchase, 07.3
Reproduced with the permission of The Carnegie Museum of Art

Cover design by Riz Boncan Marsella

Published in 1992 by Ignatius Press
ISBN 0–89870–419–7
Library of Congress Catalogue number 92–71935
Printed in the United States of America

Contents

Preface to the 1980 *Edition:*
EIGHTEEN YEARS LATER

I had finished writing this book before the first meeting of Pope John's Vatican Council. I remember talking at the time to Cardinal Gilroy of Sydney. He said the Pope had told him that the Council would be over in three months, so carefully had the agenda been prepared. It lasted four years; its first act had been to reject the so carefully prepared agenda. In the years that followed I never reminded the cardinal of this minor flaw in papal infallibility.

It was a different world then. I had forgotten how different. The "feel" of the period is almost impossible to recall. A kindly reviewer of the book's first edition found it too "cozy". Reviewing it today for this new edition I know what he meant. Coziness was the precise word for the generality of us. We were in the Ark; outside was the flood. There was a kind of innocence about us. The poet Gray, writing a couple of centuries earlier, might have been writing about the Catholic laity as we were then:

> Alas, regardless of their doom,
> The little victims play.

Only the rare ones sensed the explosion to come. I hadn't a notion that within five years I should be writing *Is It the Same Church?*

Changes came, a whirl of them, which to many seemed like rendings. The Catholic Church is in process of restructuring, and we do not see the end of it.

Indeed all the major churches of the West have been having their own rendings and restructurings. Pope John had said splendidly of the other Christian communions: "They bear the name of Christ on their forehead": which means that they bear the Sign of the Cross. The Cross is not cozy.

According to our temperament we can either be exhilarated by the rate of change and wish it were faster; or feel we are losing all we have ever valued. But temperament settles nothing. The test of every change is whether it brings Christ closer, and this we cannot judge unless we know him as he lived and taught among us. That is why books of this present sort are more needed now than eighteen years ago.

F. J. S.
1979

FOREWORD

This book is not a biography. There is too much of Christ's life upon which no light falls for us; and the accounts we have of the two or three luminous years are written by men not biographically-minded. It is not a Gospel commentary either, though written in light shed upon the texts by many scholars. My concern with the Gospels is to see the Face which through all the centuries has looked out from them upon men. The object is not to prove something but to meet Someone—that we should know Christ Jesus, know him as one person may know another. As Christians we love him, try to live by his law, would think it a glory to die for him. But how well do we know him?

The creeds, concerned only to give us a kind of blueprint of our redemption, go straight from his birth to his Passion and death—" . . . born of the Virgin Mary. He suffered under Pontius Pilate", says the Apostles' Creed; " . . . made man. For our sake he was crucified under Pontius Pilate", says the Nicene. That summarizes the position for a great many—a blaze of light about his birth, another about his death, but dimness in between. An occasional miracle stands out, a few parables, but there is no shape to the knowledge, no depth or connection. We seem curiously incurious about the life of One who is the life of our life.

Perhaps I exaggerate our general un-knowledge. I hope I do. Here are three quick tests. At the Transfiguration Moses and Elijah spoke with Christ: What were they talking about? Again— once, once only, we are told that our Lord was joyful: one would expect that episode to stand out like a star: Does it for most of us? Once more—one has heard unbelievers asking why we do not drop the cruel doctrine of hell and return to the simple, loving teaching of Christ in the Sermon on the Mount. It is the rarest thing to find a layman making the obvious comment that in that sermon our Lord warns his hearers of hell five separate times: nowhere else does he speak so much of hell.

Not to know these things means that we have not followed Jesus through the years of his teaching. If we would know him as he is, the infancy and the Passion are not enough. The infancy is not enough, since one baby looks much like another. The Passion is luminous, but with a special light. For by then he had yielded himself up as a victim, and we feel him different. For full knowledge we need to see him in the public ministry as well, for only then do we see him simply being himself—walking the roads of Palestine, meeting with his friends, answering his enemies. The difference is focused for us in the matter of Judas. In Gethsemane, as Judas kisses him in betrayal, Christ says, "Friend, what have you come for?" That was not at all the way he spoke of him in Capernaum—"Have I not chosen you twelve, and one of you is a devil?"

Not to know the two years or so of the public ministry, not to have lived through every incident of it, is not to know God-made-man as he dwelt among us. There are those who regard this kind of knowledge as an extra, interesting but not essential. Our salvation, they remind us, was not wrought by what he did in those years. It is by his death and Resurrection that we are saved, it is in the risen Christ that we now live.

But it is the Christ of the earthly life who is now at the right hand of the Father—that Christ, now risen, in whom we live. And, in any event, our salvation is not all that matters in religion, or even what matters most. That was the mistake of the old type of Bible Christian: he was saved, the rest was mere theology. His fellow Bible Christians might believe that God was three Persons or one only, that Christ was God and man or man only—these were secondary, the sole primary being to accept Christ as one's personal Savior. It made the self unhealthily central, unchristianly central. "This is eternal life: to know thee, the one true God, and Jesus Christ, whom thou hast sent" (Jn 17:3).

To know Christ Jesus: if we do not know him as he lived among us, acted and reacted and suffered among us, we risk not knowing him at all. For we cannot see him at the right hand of the Father as we can see him in Palestine. And we shall end either in constructing our own Christ, image of our own needs or dreams, or in having no Christ but a shadow and a name. Either way the light he might shed is not shed for us—light upon himself, light upon God.

For the kind of ignoring I have in mind cuts off a vast shaft of light into the being of God. The truth "Christ is God" is a statement not only about Christ but about God. Without it, we could still know of God, certainly, but in his own nature only— infinite, omnipotent, creating from nothing, sustaining creation in being. It would be a remote kind of knowledge, for of none of these ways of being or doing have we any personal experience. In Christ Jesus we can see God in our nature, experiencing the things we have experienced, coping with situations we have to cope with. Thereby we know God as the most devout pagan cannot know him.

The first step is to return to the Gospels to learn what the Holy Spirit has willed us to know of the coming of God the Son into our race, the infancy and boyhood, the ministry, the suffering and death, the Resurrection and Ascension into heaven. There will be words and acts in which we cannot see meaning, but the evangel- ists did not write them idly, nor the Holy Spirit idly inspire them to do so. We must read intently, growing in knowledge of his words and acts, building our intimacy with himself.

What I am attempting here is a first outline. From it, the reader who would advance in the knowledge of Christ Jesus has two ways open to him. He should take them both.

One way is to study the thrust of the Old Testament into the New—direct quotations or paraphrases, beginnings brought to their completion, whole patterns in the relation of man to God repeated at a new level. I have indicated a handful of these, but there are scores, hundreds, with light in all of them. The other way is to plunge deeper into the study of the theological roots and fruits—what is there, in the Gospels, to be learned about God, about man, about the God-Man—the doctrinal implications of all his activities and teachings.

Ancillary to both these will be a study of the four Gospels as books—manuscripts and dates; authorship; relation to one another, what can be conjectured as to the plan and purpose of the writers, and how events in the new Church may have affected their decisions about inclusion or omission, ways of thinking and writing in the first century; contemporary writings and contemporary religious movements which influenced the evangelists or were influenced by them. I have called this ancillary. I might have called it a third way of advance. For some of its practitioners it is primary.

Even to make the beginning that this book envisages will require a growth in our reading power—including the power to relate things said in different Gospels or in different parts of the same Gospel. It will require what is rare in modern readers, a total concentration of the mind. Take two examples from one of the parts of our Lord's life on which the light does fall for every one of us—his three hours on the Cross.

Saint Luke tells us he said to the repentant thief, "This day thou shalt be with me in paradise"; we tend to think the thief went straight to heaven. But Saint John reports Christ as saying to Mary Magdalen after his Resurrection, "I am not yet ascended to my Father." What, then, was paradise?

We all know, and rejoice to know, that Jesus said to Mary, "Behold thy son", and to Saint John, "Behold thy mother." But there is an intensely dramatic element that we must miss unless we remember, from Saint Matthew and Saint Mark's accounts of the Crucifixion, that John's own mother was standing there.

Nor is it only the Gospels that shed light upon the Gospels, but the whole Bible. For an example of what the Old Testament has in it to give, take one more of the Lord's seven words from the Cross—"My God, my God, why hast thou forsaken me?" It is a profoundly mysterious saying: great spiritual masters have found deep—and various—meanings in it. But these words were not new words wrenched from Jesus by the agony of the moment. They were a quotation. They are the opening words of Psalm 22. So we must find what the words mean in the Psalm. Finding this, we find something else, which must have startled every Jew within hearing, even more than the words themselves. If you do not chance to remember what this is, read the Psalm.

Besides Scripture all sorts of other things—but two, especially, the general history of the period, and the religious atmosphere at that particular moment—will help us towards the vivid seeing, which should be ours, of our Lord as he lived.

General history: we need to know, for instance, what the Romans were doing in Palestine, why the Samaritan woman was so surprised that a Jew should speak to her, who Herod the Great was—the Massacre of the Innocents is easier to believe when we know what experience he had in massacre.

For understanding, the *religious atmosphere* matters most of all. Take a single example. Jesus said, "It is not what goes into the mouth that defiles a man but what comes out." Obvious, we think, in the spiritual order; indeed we wonder why he troubled to say it: till we remember the Old Testament distinction between food clean and unclean, and learn how far beyond this the scribes had gone—argued, for instance, whether it was sinful to eat an egg if the hen had laid it on the Sabbath.

One last word. We read the Gospels, not as if no one had ever read them before, and all is still to discover. We are not exploring virgin territory, wondering what we shall come upon. From his Church we know that our Lord Jesus Christ is God, second Person of the Blessed Trinity, the Word of the Father, equal in all things to the Father, eternally God. And we know that at a point of time, the Word took to himself and made his own a human soul and body, became man. He did not temporarily cease to be God—the phrase is meaningless. The Jesus who was born of Mary was God and could do all that goes with being God, was man and could live man's life in its fullness. He was true God and true Man. But that in him which said "I"—whether he was uttering the infinite reality of his Godhead or the finite powers and limitations of his manhood—was God the Son.

With this in our mind we read the Gospels. To know Christ Jesus—which is the sole concern of this book—it does not suffice to meditate on what divinity means and what manhood means, and see how we can fit them into one picture without too much distortion of either. It is easy to turn the one Person and the two natures into a diagram, deducing all sorts of propositions from it: building up a highly intellectual devotional life from it. But Christ our Lord was not a diagram. To study him solely so would be like deriving all one's ideas about man from the definition "Man is a rational animal"—plunging deeper and deeper into the meaning of rationality and animality, and combining the two sets of findings. Of course we must examine the definition, but we must also study men. In them we find scores of things for which the definition has not prepared us—irrationality, for one, the rational animal's continuing unreasonableness!

One has met people who give their lives to the study of the theology of the Incarnation, and hardly know the Gospels at all. When they come across Gospel incidents which do not seem to fit their diagram, their tendency is to dismiss them—almost as though the Lord should have known better. But the one certain way to know what a God-Man could do is to see the one God-Man in action—not *could* a divine person have done thus or thus in a human nature, but what *did* Christ Jesus do, what *did* he say? Return from the Gospels to the dogmatic formulation, and we find it glowing with new richness.

When the apostles were choosing a man to replace fallen Judas (Acts 1:21), they stated the essential qualification: "There are men among us who have walked in our company all through the time when the Lord Jesus came and went among us, from the time when John used to baptize to the day when Jesus was taken from us. One of these ought to be added to our number as a witness of his Resurrection." Knowledge of our Lord's public ministry was an essential requirement for an apostle then. For the apostolate, it still is. Saint Matthias, pray for us.

1 ON MEETING CHRIST JESUS

The Order of Events

The temptations were over, Satan had gone his way, angels had ministered to Jesus. "After this," Saint Matthew says (4:12), "hearing of John's imprisonment, he withdrew into Galilee."

"After this": it is a tantalizing phrase; representative of a whole attitude in the evangelists. How long after? And what happened in between? The first three Gospels give us no hint of an answer. It is John (1:29–3:36) who tells us. He has not mentioned either the baptism or the temptations. These had been described by the other three evangelists, and their Gospels had been current in the Christian world for a good thirty years before John wrote his. As so often, he assumes that his readers will know what they contain. He is more concerned to tell us what they do not. From him we learn that in the two months between Satan's departure for his own place and the Baptist's departure for Herod's prison lies the beginning of what we call Jesus' public life.

How long was it to last? Three years, we say confidently. But not one of the evangelists tells us in so many words. They simply had not our interest in dates and such. Matthew and Mark and Luke give us almost no indication at all—one might be left with the impression that everything happened within one year. John, writing after the others, puts us right about that. He mentions three Paschs—three feasts of the Passover.

Jesus' baptism in the Jordan came a month or two before the Passover of the first year. He was crucified at the Passover of the third year. By our count that would be just two years and a small fraction. But by Jewish counting it reckoned as three years—most of the first, the whole of the second, and up to about Easter of the third.

But the evangelists set us another problem. Just as they have not our interest in dates, they do not mind much about the order of events.

The general sequence of the public life is clear—the baptism by John in Jordan, the ministry in Galilee, briefer missions outside Palestine, the ministry in Judea and Perea, the Passion and death. Where episodes are related to the great Jewish feasts—Passover, Pentecost, Tabernacles, Dedication—we see when they happened and the intervals between one and another; yet not always, even then. The first concern of the writers is with what Jesus did and said; but each arranges things according to the plan he had in his own mind in the construction of his Gospel.

Something said at one time reminds them of something said at a different time, so they put it in; a particular action reminds them of some word that sheds light upon it or draws light from it, so that is put in. Thus Luke has the choosing of the Twelve immediately before the Sermon on the Mount, which is so very much a plan of life for the Church they were to rule; Matthew has only Peter and Andrew, James and John called from their fishing before the sermon and mentions even his own calling after. In the sermon itself, the general opinion of scholars seems to be that Matthew weaves together things said by Jesus on many occasions in order to give a whole section of his teaching in one pattern.

Saint Augustine wrote: "Anyone can see there is no point in asking in what order our Lord uttered these words. For we cannot fail to discover, on the most excellent authority (that of the Evangelists themselves), that there is no failure of truth in giving a sermon in an order different from that in which it was first uttered: whether the order was thus or thus makes no difference to the substance of what was said" (*De consensu Evangelistarum* ii, 39, 86).

What Jesus Did and Said

The Gospels, then, do not put all the things that happened in the same order. The main lines are clear: for the points on which the Gospels seem to differ I follow the arrangement of the Dominican scholar, Père Lagrange. In our reading we should concentrate upon each thing Jesus did and said. These things are priceless whatever the order of the doing or saying.

About them, there will be differences in the detail of the recording. Think back to the first days of the Church, with hundreds already converted, thousands thronging in that they might find salvation in acceptance of Jesus. Unless they were quite monumentally incurious they must have wanted to know all that was to be known about the One to whom they had thus totally committed their lives here and hereafter, and their very selves.

They may have expected his immediate return; they would still want to know who and what he was, still cherish every scrap of information about things said and done by him. We cannot imagine their saying: "Ah yes, he rose from the dead. He'll be coming back soon to establish his Kingdom and we'll be in it. What happened before his death is no concern of ours. It really doesn't matter what he was like. We'll just wait for him to come back." That degree of incuriosity would be subhuman.

The one longing must have been: "Tell us about him. What was he like?" New Christians would ask old Christians; everybody would ask those who actually knew him, the men who had been with him from the beginning, to say nothing of the women, his Mother for instance and Mary Magdalen. For some episodes there would be three who could tell—Peter, James, and John; for some, scores; for most, over a dozen. Each would describe each episode as it had struck him, emphasizing the elements in it which had seemed to him significant.

Not only that, as time went on new significances would be seen. Partly these would come from situations arising in or confronting the Church, causing them to give new emphasis to certain elements in the original happenings. Thus the handful of episodes involving Gentiles might, in the moment of their happening, have seemed rather marginal, not in the main stream. But they would emerge into stronger light as it became progressively clearer that Gentiles were to be admitted to the Kingdom; that they were not to be second-class citizens; that they were to be the majority.

New significances would arise from another source—the guidance of the Holy Spirit as the things Jesus had said were lived and meditated on. At the Last Supper he had told the apostles that the Holy Spirit would lead them into all truth, bringing to their memory all he had taught them. This was to be no sudden flash, lighting up a whole sky: it was to be a "leading" into truth. We cannot know the stages of this leading, but it seems certain that many things Jesus said would not be repeated to the new Christians until the apostles had come to see what they meant: like our Lady earlier, they would ponder them in their hearts. It would be wonderful if we had an account of even one occasion when the Twelve—or even any two of them!—talked among themselves, as they must have talked a thousand times, over what their Master had said and done. But we have no record save of two meetings of apostles, each for a special purpose—to choose a replacement for Judas, to decide how far Gentile converts were bound by Jewish law.

Yet new light would mean new emphasis on elements already there, not the invention of things not there at all. What the Gospels show him as doing and saying, he did and said. Let us pause upon the "saying". Are we hearing *him?*

"Not Words but Things"

There is one minor problem which we can touch on lightly. The ancients did not bother about quotation marks; in the Gospel it is not always possible to tell where a speaker ends and the evangelist begins his own commentary. There are not many of these situations; the line of division is usually clear enough. Thus it seems generally to be agreed that John 3:16-21 is not part of Jesus' utterance nor John 3:31-36 part of the Baptist's. But there are larger problems, two especially.

Different Gospels will have Jesus saying the same things not only on different occasions, but differently. Any practised speaker would expect this. We find the best phrasing for particular ideas, and we stick to it; but some incident—a question asked, perhaps— may cause us to modify it or add to it: we are repeating ourselves all the time, with differences some of the time. So with Jesus, as he gave his teaching in place after place. And those who heard him might remember one or other form of the phrase, some might remember more than one. And anyhow, as we have already noted, the evangelists put things he said where they best fitted the plan according to which they were writing.

Our Lord spoke in Aramaic, the Gospels are written in Greek. There is one immediate difficulty about translation—words or phrases in the original language may have different meanings (as an example, the word "free" in English might mean either "not under constraint" or "not needing to be paid for"). Two translators may make different guesses as to the meaning intended.

Where spoken words are being translated there is another difficulty—words sound alike, or differ only by a letter or two: two translators may hear them differently.

There are instances of both sorts in the Gospels—as an instance of the latter, Matthew writes "*cleanse* the inside" and Luke "give alms of what is inside" where the Aramaic words would be *dakkav* and *zakkav* respectively. They are not numerous, these verbal differences, and involve nothing of great importance.

But there is a larger problem involved in all translation—two men may translate a sentence correctly, yet the odds are heavily against their producing the same identical version (my own quotations will be mainly from either Douay or Knox). Take four or five English translations of the Gospels—Douay, Authorized, Standard Revised, Confraternity, Knox. All strive to render the meaning accurately, yet it is rare to find a verse verbally the same in any three of them. The second language offers a variety of ways of expressing the original, and each translator makes his own choice. Not only that, each translator has his special way of writing his own language born of the special sort of person he is: the original thought will emerge clothed in speech unmistakably his. And those considerations apply even more strongly when the evangelists are summarizing longer teachings or sewing together things said at different times.

To come back to our question, when we read the Gospels are we hearing our Lord? Saint Augustine has given the answer— "Not words but things". We can unite our mind with the mind of Christ, and the thoughts in his mind can become thoughts in ours—all the more as the Holy Spirit living in his soul lives in ours.

We read the Gospels to meet Christ Jesus. We must read and reread them, if we want to come to our own personal intimacy with our Redeemer. Intimacy of that sort cannot be handed to us by anyone else, however gifted he may be, whatever the measure of his spiritual insight. We have to make it for ourselves, with Jesus as with any other friend, by constantly meeting him, experiencing him, meditating on the experience. Two men may be equally close in friendship with a third, yet each will have his own picture of him. No one can respond to every element in another's personality; one man will be moved by, fascinated by, elements in the third man which leave the other comparatively cold—he in turn will make his own responses which are not the first man's. It is a vast gain for any one of us to have made for ourselves this personal relation with our Lord.

Since all we know of his life is in the Gospels, we must read them with the closest attention. At every episode, remember that these are real people, not figures in a parable, not figures from an altarpiece. We have seen so many statues of the Lord, haloed and expressionless, on so many altars, that we can easily think of him as simply moving like an automaton through the rituals of redemption: doing thus and thus because our redemption requires it, or because the Old Testament prophecies said he would: himself not, except in the Passion and death, humanly reacting at all.

The qualities which spring to our mind when we think of him—how did we come by them? By meeting him in the Gospels for ourselves, or only by hearing great sermons about him and looking at pictures by great masters?

PART ONE

The First Thirty Years

"For this was I born, and for this came I into the world; that I should give testimony to the truth."

  (Jn 18:37)

2 *SETTING THE STAGE*

The human life of God the Son began in Nazareth when Mary, a virgin betrothed to Joseph, a carpenter, conceived. Let us pause to consider the time and the place and the people concerned—when, where, who.

When and Where

The time, we may be tempted to feel, hardly needs discussion. Everybody knows that time is either B.C. (before Christ) or A.D. (since Christ): therefore the Annunciation must have taken place at the beginning of 1 A.D. But it certainly did not.

We owe the division of B.C. from A.D. to a sixth-century monk, Dionysius Exiguus. England seems to have been the first country to adopt it, and only when Dionysius had been two centuries dead. From England it spread south—slowly; it took another two centuries to capture Rome. Dionysius placed the birth of our Lord in the year 753 after the founding of old Rome, that being the point from which everything was dated in the Roman Empire.

He overlooked one fact. Herod died in 750—which is 4 B.C. by Dionysius' reckoning. But Christ was born in the reign of Herod, whose fury at the news of his birth led to the flight of the Holy Family into Egypt. So Christ was born B.C.!—certainly by 4 B.C., perhaps as early as 8 B.C.: we do not know. Whenever the birth was, the visit of the angel Gabriel would have been nine months before that. There is an irony in the thought that the King of Kings was born a subject of so awful a king.

It is a shock to realize how small Palestine was—150 miles from end to end, 23 miles wide in the north, 90 in the south. The total area was 9700 square miles—a few more than Vermont, a few fewer than Maryland, roughly the size of Wales; and even that was never wholly held by the Jews, what with Phoenicians biting in at the north and Philistines at the south. And this pocket handkerchief of land was the homeland of the Jews. No people so small, no people at all, has ever affected world history as they have.

And not only religiously. Eighteen hundred years before Christ, the greatest world empire was Egypt's—and the prime minister was an Israelite—Joseph, son of Jacob. Eighteen hundred years after Christ, the greatest world empire was Britain's, and the prime minister was an Israelite, Benjamin Disraeli (who bought the Suez Canal for Britain!). The energy which over a space of almost four thousand years could bring this people to the top in nations not their own is matchless, unapproachable.

Round 1500 B.C. they had settled definitively in Palestine. Their history need not be outlined here, but a few points should be noted. They reached their highest point of worldly power under King David and his son Solomon (roughly 1000 B.C.) After Solomon's death they split into two kingdoms—Israel in the north, destroyed by Assyria (722 B.C.), Judah in the south, destroyed by Babylon (586 B.C.). There was a vast deportation of Jews into Babylon, and a return from exile fifty years later. We are now approaching 500 B.C. In the centuries that followed they had a varied history of conquest by one people after another, with a brief independence, and then conquest again—this time by the Romans, seventy years before our Lord.

By the time Mary of Nazareth was told of the child she was to conceive, most of Palestine was ruled by the unspeakable Herod as part of the Roman Empire. It had three major divisions (it was smaller than Maryland, remember)—Galilee in the north, Judea in the south, both Jewish; and Samaria in between, its inhabitants descended from colonists, sent in by the Assyrians in the eighth century, who intermarried with the handful of Jews who had not been deported. For four hundred years Samaria was polytheist. Its offer to help with the building of the new temple in Jerusalem was contemptuously refused. So the Samaritans built their own temple on Mount Gerizim and gradually came to see themselves as the true heirs of the patriarchs, the heirs who had stayed there all the time while the Jews were in foreign parts.

One of the least considerable villages of Galilee was Nazareth. It was just under ninety miles from Jerusalem, roughly the distance of Philadelphia from New York. It is never mentioned in the Old Testament. It was so inconsiderable that even little Cana, four miles away, could despise it. Here lived Mary, to whom God sent a message by the angel Gabriel.

Gabriel

Strange that we, to whom the Annunciation means so much, pay so little regard to the announcer. Gabriel was not the mailman, simply handing in a message; he was God's envoy, uttering the message, explaining it. His name means the "power of God". We have met him bearing earlier messages—to the prophet Daniel, to the priest Zechariah. Both shed light upon the supreme sending to Mary.

In the Book of Daniel, we read, he appeared twice, perhaps three times. It is the second appearance that concerns us most, for it reads rather like an annunciation before the Annunciation. Gabriel speaks of times that must elapse, and he expresses them mysteriously; but when they have passed—"Guilt done away, sin ended, wrong righted . . . he who is all holiness anointed. . . . Christ will come to be your leader. . . . The Christ will be done to death" (Dan 9:21ff.: but read chapters 8, 9, and 10 carefully: Gabriel is worth meeting, to say nothing of Daniel).

Mary and Joseph

Mary is our way of saying the name Myriam, which also appears as Mariam and Mariamne. In the two thousand years of Jewish history covered by the Old Testament the name occurs only once—Moses' sister was Myriam. But it had a great flowering round about this time. The New Testament gives us not only Mary of Nazareth, but Mary of Cleophas, Mary Magdalen (and Mary of Bethany, if she was not Mary Magdalen). What adds an almost macabre touch is that two of Herod's ten wives and three others of his family bore the name. Why this sudden flowering, we do not know. What makes it a shade more puzzling is that we do not even know what the name meant. Scholars have listed something like sixty guesses as to the meaning, based not only on Hebrew words, but also on Egyptian, since the first Myriam was born in Egypt. For Catholics there is no great interest in knowing what our Lady's name originally meant; she made it a totally new thing.

An old tradition calls her parents Joachim and Anna. We know only one thing about them with certainty, but this one thing outweighs libraries of biographical detail: for they were the only father and mother in all the history of mankind who had a child who was conceived immaculate. What legends could possibly gild that? Her parents did not, one imagines, know that she had sanctifying grace in her soul from the first moment of her exis-tence in her mother's womb—for the child had been conceived in the ordinary way of marriage. Nor had the Jews had any very detailed doctrine of sanctifying grace. At the time of the Annun-ciation, our Lady may not have known it herself: it is not fanciful to think that she learned it first from the Son who was conceived in her not only immaculate, but virginally as well.

She was betrothed to a man called Joseph. Of him, too, we know very little. Did he, like Mary, belong to Nazareth at the time of the betrothal? Scripture does not say. He was a carpenter, and he had in him the noblest blood that Israel knew, for he was a descendant of King David. Why should a man of that lineage have been a car-penter? We know that the house of David had fallen into obscurity, and obscurity and poverty were practically interchangeable terms. In the great revolt led by the Maccabees, which gave the Jews their last breath of independence before Rome swallowed them, the sons of David played no conspicuous part. A century or so after this, when the Roman Emperor Domitian ordered the destruc-tion of David's known descendants as possible centers of revolt against Roman rule, some at least were spared because they were so poor and insignificant that even the tyrant could not see them as a serious threat. It is all very puzzling to us, since we know that the Messiah, the expectation of Israel, was to be a son of David.

We are told that Joseph was of David's house. Was Mary? Again, Scripture is silent. Catholics, I think, take it for granted that she was. It is true that the Jews considered adoption as practically equivalent to physical generation: the acknowledgment by Joseph of Jesus as his child would have been legally sufficient to make Jesus a son of David. But the language of the Old Testament seems to demand for our Lord something more than a merely legal descent from David. In his first great sermon, Saint Peter speaks of Christ as "the fruit of David's loins" (Acts 2:30); Saint Paul speaks of him as "made of the seed of David, according to the flesh" (Rom 1:3). These would be strong terms for a purely legal relationship. We have no certain knowledge, but there is something attractive in the idea, proposed by many scholars, that Saint Joseph was a close relation of our Lady, so that her ancestry would be the same as his.

Betrothal, for the Jews of that day, was not simply an engagement to marry. After betrothal, the couple were husband and wife. Each continued to live at home—for a year if the bride was a virgin, for a month if she was a widow. Then came the wedding celebrations and the solemn entry of the bride into her husband's house. In the period between, the marriage act would have been unusual, perhaps, at any rate in Galilee; but not sinful. For the couple were husband and wife.

Mary of Nazareth came pregnant to the wedding, though the marriage act had not taken place. If we knew no more than this— that she, still a virgin, found herself pregnant—we should feel that she was at least entitled to an explanation: and only God could give it. It is Luke who tells us how God gave it. And it was not an explanation after the fact. Before the child was, by a miracle of God's power, conceived of her, there was explanation from God and consent from her. The child, our Savior and hers, was not forced upon her.

Luke

Saint Luke begins his Gospel by saying how he wrote it and why: "Many have taken in hand to set forth in order a narration of the things that have been accomplished among us, according as those have delivered them to us who from the beginning were eye-witnesses and ministers of the Word. So it seemed good to me also, having carefully [*akribos*] investigated all things from the beginning, to write to you, in order, most excellent Theophilus, that you may know the truth of those words in which you have been instructed."

"Those words in which you have been instructed"—we do not know what instruction in the Faith Theophilus or any other convert received. In Acts we have summaries of six sermon-speeches (2:14–36, 3:12–26, 4:8–12, 5:29–32, 10:34–43, 13:17–41)—very brief, the whole lot could be read aloud in ten minutes. They were all spoken to unbelievers, some fiercely hostile, some baptized afterward. But there is no account of the doctrine preached to instructed Christians inside the Christian assembly—if only we had notes of that long sermon preached by Paul at Troas, during which Eutychus, surely the patron saint of the Sunday laity, fell asleep! From what Saint Paul wrote to various churches—(beginning as early as twenty years after the Ascension)—on Father, Son, and Holy Spirit, on Christ human and divine, on the Mystical Body, and the Blessed Eucharist and marriage, above all on grace—we get the impression that our first ancestors in the Faith were very fully taught indeed. But what was the teaching a man received on entering the Church, the standard equipment of the new Christian? We have not been told.

Was Theophilus, indeed, yet in the Church? The *Bible de Jérusalem* raises the question, but does not answer. If he was not yet received, or only just received, he must occasionally have glanced back at those opening phrases to see if he had read them aright.

The Greek word *"akribos"*—it means accurately, carefully—could hardly have prepared him for what follows immediately—the angel Gabriel bringing to the priest Zechariah the announcement that his elderly wife would bear his elderly self a son; the angel going on to tell a virgin in Nazareth that she would conceive. One imagines Theophilus incredulously muttering *"akribos"* to himself—all the more if he had known Luke as a pagan in his medical student days at Tarsus.

An angel was well enough as ornament, fancy scrollwork in the margin as it were. But what was it doing after that sort of introductory guarantee of careful investigation? Had it been a matter of Socrates and his *daimon* — Plato said each man had one — Theophilus would have known where he was. The *daimon* was more an influence than a person. But this angel was not like that. He belonged with those superhuman messengers in human form, sent by gods to men, with whom Greek mythology was littered. All that was behind Theophilus, he and his sort had long outgrown it.

Gabriel must have bothered him — as he still bothers people. He does not, of course, bother those who do not believe in angels, they simply reject him out of hand. But many, whose religion tells them that angels really exist, are yet uncomfortable with them, wish they would keep their distance, feel that this particular story would be tidier without Gabriel. What need for an angel? God could have given Mary the explanation of her pregnancy without using an angel, they say — just as there are those who say God can give sinners forgiveness without using a priest.

If Theophilus had been long a Christian, if he had read the Epistles of Luke's master, Paul, he would have been prepared for the angel. For the Incarnation did not affect men only. It was of cosmic significance. No element of creation was untouched by it — from the material universe at one end, through demons and Satan himself, up to the unfallen angels who serve before the throne of God.

A second problem for Theophilus would surely have been the curious Greek of the opening chapters. Luke's own language was Greek, and the rest of his Gospel shows that he wrote it rather well. Then why two chapters of such very un-Greek Greek? This may have been the first question Theophilus asked Luke: "What language do you think you're writing?"

Luke's first answer may have been that he was not the author — apart from a few touches, he simply used the account he had received, either already translated into Greek, or Aramaic to be translated by himself. From whom had he received it? Ultimately from our Lady, perhaps through Saint John (to whose Gospel his own has so many likenesses). So careful an investigator would not have failed to question the apostle to whose sonship her own Son had committed her. He must have had many opportunities, if only in the two years he seems to have spent in Caesarea, forty miles from Jerusalem, while Paul was a prisoner there.

The Greek of these chapters, whether Luke's or some other person's, is patterned on, and directly quotes, the Greek of the Septuagint, the translation of the Old Testament which the Jews of Egypt had made for themselves a century before. And it could not be otherwise. Old Testament and New Testament are in one continuing stream of God's action in the world: God so announced the coming of the New that the oneness was utterly evident. The hopes are shown fulfilled, the prefigurings are shown realized. The perfect phrases had been formed for the prefigurings: they showed their perfection when applied to the reality.

The revelation of Christ would bring new richness of language, a new vocabulary, but that lay ahead. Mary of Nazareth, like Elizabeth and Zechariah and Simeon and Anna, knew only one book. The revelation made to them belonged to that one book as truly as it belonged to the book still to be written.

3 MARY CONCEIVES

Message to Zechariah

Zechariah had been chosen by lot that day to offer incense in the Temple sacrifice. He had gone alone into the sanctuary. There he saw an angel, "standing on the right side of the altar of incense".

"Fear not" were the angel's opening words. He told Zechariah that his wife Elizabeth should bear him a son who was to be called John: "He is to be high in the Lord's favor; he is to drink neither wine nor strong drink; from the time when he is yet a child in his mother's womb, he shall be filled with the Holy Spirit. He shall convert many of the children of Israel to the Lord their God. And he shall go before him in the spirit and power of Elijah" (Lk 1:13ff.).

For an instructed Jew the message could only be quite overwhelming. Samson and Samuel both had been bound to drink no wine or strong drink; Jeremiah had been claimed by God for his own before he was fashioned in his mother's womb. Thus the child that Zechariah was told he would beget was clearly linked with Samson and Samuel and Jeremiah, though they were not named; but the greatest of all the prophets, Elijah himself—"a hairy man with a girdle of leather about his loins" (2 Kings 1:8), who lived in the desert, preached repentance and rebuked rulers— was named by name! Yet it seemed that all these splendors did not astound Zechariah as much as the promise of a son to himself, so old, married to a wife past her menopause. He felt that it would be time enough to consider the greatness of the son he was to have, when he had settled the question of the possibility of having a son at all.

It was upon that point that he begged for a sign. Gabriel gave him a sign—he struck him dumb, to stay so till the child should be born; but he also gave one piece of information about himself—"I am Gabriel, who stand before God."

Message to Mary

Six months after the visit to Zechariah in the Temple in Jerusalem, Gabriel was sent by God to Mary in her own town of Nazareth. Unless the reader knows Saint Luke's account almost word for word, he should read Luke 1:26–38 before going on to what is written here. Few as the verses are, they contain the longest conversation anyone is recorded by Scripture as having with our Blessed Lady—she actually speaks twice! What is here is so perfect that one's first feeling is that not a word need be added. Yet without commentary, we shall miss a great deal of what is there for us.

Did the angel appear, visibly I mean? Luke does not say so this time, though he does say that Zechariah saw him. In the Book of Daniel we read of his appearing twice in the likeness of a man.

And then there is a third appearance, as a man indeed, but with angelic glory showing through: "His body was clear as topaz, his face shone like lightning, his eyes were like burning lamps; his arms and legs had the gleam of bronze; and when he spoke it was like the voice of a multitude" (Dan 10:5, 6). Mary would not have needed these outward showings of Gabriel's spiritual splendor: for her own was greater.

Evidently the story could have come only from our Lady herself, the other party to the conversation.

Gabriel's opening words are "Hail, full of grace, the Lord is with thee; blessed art thou among women." Mary made no reply. Gabriel misunderstood her silence. Perhaps remembering Zechariah, he told her not to be afraid. Clearly he did not yet know her very well. Contact with Zechariah was no preparation at all for understanding Mary of Nazareth. Her silence was not from terror, but from perplexity—she was "much perplexed at hearing him speak so, and cast about in her mind what she was to make of such a greeting."

Only the opening word "Hail" would have given her no trouble (the Greek word, used by Saint Luke, meant Joy, the corresponding salutation in Hebrew was Peace). The next word, which we translate "full of grace", was a different matter. There is no record of its ever having been addressed to anyone else: nor, indeed, can we be sure of its precise meaning. The form of the verb carries the sense of abundance; but abundance of what? Of *"charis"*, the Greek word tells us. That word has, ever since Saint Paul, meant sanctifying grace, and so it might have meant on the angel's lips; but it *might* have meant "privilege"—that she had been chosen by God for some great work. Whether it was grace or whether it was privilege, either way Mary had it in abundance. Either way she might well wonder.

The phrase that follows, "The Lord is with thee", was an immeasurable compliment. We ourselves say good-bye, which means "May God be with you". But what Gabriel said was not that. He was not expressing a desire that God might be with her. He was stating as a fact that God *was* with her! To whom had a

statement of *that* fact ever been made? Her Son was to promise to
be with his whole Church until the end of time. But as we know,
and Gabriel knew, it was about to have a meaning for Mary
which it never had had for a human being before, and never could
again.

Later we shall find Elizabeth saying, "Blessed art thou among
women." Most scholars think it is hers, not Gabriel's—a copyist
inserted it here in error. Whenever Mary heard the phrase, it
would have perplexed her, not as the other two phrases did,
because the words were unfamiliar, but because they were not.
She had met them before: they are applied in the Old Testament
to two women. One of them was Jael, who had saved God's
people by hammering a tent peg into the skull of the enemy
leader, Sisera (Jg 4). The other was Judith, who had saved God's
people by cutting the head off the enemy leader Holofernes
(Judith 13). A young girl might well have been startled at a
compliment, however splendid in itself, which linked her with
these particular heroines of her people. She did not know, as we
know and Gabriel knew, that she was to bear a son who would
crush a mightier and more malignant head than Sisera had or
Holofernes.

None of the puzzling things Gabriel had so far said to Mary of
Nazareth was any preparation for what he said next.

"Thou shalt conceive in thy womb, and shalt bear a Son, and
shalt call him Jesus. He shall be great, and men will know him for
the Son of the Most High. The Lord God will give him the
throne of his father David, and he shall reign over the house of
Jacob eternally; his kingdom shall never have an end."

A very slight knowledge of the Old Testament would have
made it clear to her that the son she was to conceive, the son to be
called Jesus (which means "God saves"), was to be the Messiah.
She may have recognized the words that the prophet Nathan had
said long ago to David—"Thy throne shall remain forever" (2
Sam 7:16); and the word of Isaiah, "He will sit on David's kingly
throne, to give it lasting foundations of justice and right" (Is 9:7);
in any event the one thing every Jew knew was that the Messiah
was to be son of David. But could she yet have known the

meaning of the phrase, "Son of the Most High"? Only if the doctrine of the Blessed Trinity had been specially revealed to her, as it is not revealed in the Old Testament.

Catholics have held from the beginning that Gabriel told Mary of God's plan for her as something to which her consent was asked, and that she did in fact give her consent. Gabriel's message has been called an invitation, and her "Be it done to me according to thy word" an acceptance. But, in the words actually quoted, there is no hint of invitation. Gabriel simply says "Thou shalt conceive." It reads like a flat statement of what is going to happen. The fact that Mary does utter her acceptance suggests that it was called for; we simply assume that this is one thing Gabriel must have said which is not recorded.

It seems probable that there is another. "Thou shalt conceive"— but when? The future tense can be used for anything from the next minute to the end of the world. Catholics believe that the Annunciation and the conception of Christ in his mother's womb belong together. The Church, celebrating Christ's birth on December 25, celebrates the Annunciation exactly nine months before, on March 25. If the conception was to happen immediately, it seems unthinkable that Gabriel would not have told her so.

Zechariah, told of a son to be conceived, was incredulous and asked for a sign. Mary was not incredulous, she asked for no sign. She simply asked how—"How shall this be done, because I know not man?" This particular use of the verb to know comes very early in Scripture—"Adam knew Eve his wife: and she conceived and brought forth Cain." Our Lady is asking how can she conceive since she is still a virgin.

Gabriel answered, "The Holy Spirit will come upon thee, and the power of the Most High will overshadow thee. Thus the Holy which shall be born of thee shall be called Son of God." Mary's question is completely answered. The child will not be conceived, as she herself had been conceived, in the usual way of marriage. That which, in any conception, is provided by the mother, she will provide. But what in every other conception the father provides will in this one case be produced by a miracle of God's power. The conception was to be virginal, an idea for which the

Old Testament (with its absence of virgins) had no more prepared her than pagan mythology (with its absence of virgin births) would later prepare Theophilus.

Our Lady said: "Behold the handmaid of the Lord; be it done to me according to thy word"—words of consecration bringing the second Person of the Blessed Trinity into her womb, into our race. Why had she held her acceptance of God's will unspoken until this moment? Not because she had to be persuaded, God's will was sufficient for her—she actually used a stronger word than "handmaid"; she said, "Behold the slave of the Lord." She waited before uttering her consent, surely, because she felt that if God sent her a message she owed it to him to understand it.

The Word Made Flesh

The conception announced by the angel Gabriel concerned two persons principally—the Mother and the Son. There is not one of us, of course, whom it does not concern more deeply than anything else that ever happened; but these two principally. Saint Luke, in the beginning of his Gospel, concentrates upon the Mother. Saint John, in the beginning of his, treats wholly of the Son: the Mother indeed is there, but not by direct reference. What John tells us of the Son makes the words of Gabriel, quoted by Luke, dazzlingly, almost dazingly, clear. If we are neither dazed nor dazzled, it can only mean that we have not been listening!

Gabriel had said, "The Holy which shall be born of thee shall be called Son of God." In Hebrew usage this meant he would *be* Son of God—God's messenger not having been sent to call someone what he is not! What did the phrase Son of God mean? We, taught by the Church Christ founded, assume that Son of God meant God the Son. But, in the first place, although the Old Testament contains gleams and hints of the Blessed Trinity, it does not actually teach the doctrine. And, in the second place, the phrase "sons of God" is used (by the prophet Hosea, for example) to mean men who are in God's grace. It is quite clear that Gabriel meant more than this. The Holy Spirit should come upon her and the power of the Most High should overshadow her—the Jews knew no mightier words to express a special presence and operation of God. Words of that splendor could not mean merely that she would give birth to one more Jew of true piety: that would have been a true anticlimax. Her child would be Son of God as no one ever had been or ever would be. But in what would that Sonship consist?

Saint John tells us. He does the actual conception in one swift stroke—"The Word was made flesh and dwelt among us." Then, in a phrase of total clarity, he tells who the Word is—"And we saw his glory, the glory as of the only-begotten of the Father." Others had been called sons of God in the Old Testament; a few phrases earlier, John himself has referred to men who become sons of God by grace. But the Word was not of these; he was the only-begotten; he did not become the Son of God, he was born so, in the timelessness of eternity. Twice in this first chapter John calls him the only-begotten; it is by the power of the only-begotten that the rest of men may be made sons of God

Saint John begins by calling the only-begotten not the Son but the Word: "In the beginning was the Word, and the Word was with God, and the Word was God." Never in the history of human speech has so much richness of reality been uttered with such brevity. All eternity will not be enough to unpack its content. God utters a Word, not a word made of air expelled from the lungs and shaped by throat and tongue and teeth and lips, for God is a spirit. It is not a word of the mouth but a word in the mind, an idea. We are given the truth about this idea in two steps. The Word has always been *with* God. The Word *is* God.

God, knowing himself with infinite knowing power, generates in the divine mind an idea of himself. We all have an idea of ourselves in our mind, not always a very accurate idea, even our dearest friends might laugh if they could know the idea we have of ourselves. But God's idea of himself is totally accurate, totally adequate. There is nothing in himself that is not in the idea that he eternally generates of himself; and whereas our idea is merely something, his is Someone as he himself is Someone, God as he is

God. And this second Someone within the Godhead is eternal as he is eternal—there never was a moment when God did not thus see himself imaged in his Son, there are no moments in eternity.

Thus the Son whom Mary conceived in her womb, the Son who received human nature in her womb, already possessed the divine nature eternally.

Mary Visits Zechariah's Wife

We have been studying the conception of our Lord as Saint Luke tells it and as Saint John tells it. Before continuing the narrative of our Lord's life, let us summarize what we have learned thus far about him. In the womb of Mary of Nazareth, through the nine months of gestation, was one who was fully human, but not solely human. The person, growing toward birth as every human baby grows, was the second Person of the Blessed Trinity, God the Son. Mary was his Mother. Possessing the divine nature eternally, he received a human nature of her: this one, divine Person now had two natures. To his humanity she contributed all that our mothers contribute to ours. She was not simply the mother of his human nature, but of himself—as my mother is not the mother of my nature but of me. She was the Mother of God the Son. That is what we learn from Saint John; that in more veiled language is what Saint Luke quotes Gabriel as telling her.

John and Luke tell the story from two different points of view. One link between them is that both bring in John the Baptist. Saint John almost seems to interrupt what he is telling us of the Word, to say, "There was a man sent from God, whose name was John. . . . he was not the light but was to give testimony of the light." And when the verses which form the Prologue of the Gospel are ended, John turns immediately to the preaching of John the Baptist. Similarly Gabriel, having delivered the supreme message, says to our Lady: "Thy cousin Elizabeth also has conceived a son in her old age . . . to prove that nothing can be impossible with God." Gabriel says nothing is impossible to God as a comment upon a woman past childbearing. Jesus was to say the same thing thirty years later with reference to the rich entering heaven.

Clearly John the Baptist had an essential part to play, since neither Gabriel nor John tells of the coming Redeemer without mentioning his forerunner. One cannot help feeling that Gabriel must have conveyed this to our Lady. For as the angel departed, Mary "went into the hill country with haste to visit Elizabeth."

Two questions are raised in our minds by this decision of our Lady to make the four-day caravan journey into Judea. One wonders first how old she was. We know that at a later period the normal age for betrothal was round thirteen for the bride, and between eighteen and twenty-four for the husband. Whether these were the usual ages at the time of the Annunciation, we cannot know with certainty. Our Lady may well have been thirteen or fourteen: we must not be surprised if among Mediterranean peoples girls married younger than among ourselves — Romeo's Juliet was fourteen. Yet it would seem strange for a child of that age to make so long a journey, seemingly on her own decision.

This brings us to the other question. Were her parents still alive? They are not mentioned in the account of the Annunciation, or of the visit to Elizabeth, or of our Lady's entry into Joseph's house. Parents, especially fathers, were far too important among the Jews to be simply ignored like this. It looks as if they had died before the mighty thing that was to happen to their daughter.

We tend to think of the visitation as the meeting of the two mothers. But far more important was the meeting of the two sons — it was for this, surely, that our Lady had gone in such haste. When Elizabeth heard her cousin's greeting, "the infant leaped in her womb". What this first meeting of the Redeemer and his forerunner, each in the womb of his mother, meant to either of them, we have no earthly means of knowing. But there is a kind of excitement in it for us — which is not diminished when we learn that the Greek verb for John's "leaping" is the same as for David's (2 Sam 6:14-16) when he danced before the Ark of the Lord — a wooden chest containing the written word of God. Our Lady was far more truly the Ark of the Lord than the one made by Moses ever was — though it too had been overshadowed by the power of the Most High. It was not the written word of God that she had within her.

Elizabeth's opening words are "Blessed art thou among women and blessed is the fruit of thy womb." The first words we have already met, said by Gabriel; but as we have said, scholars think that it was Elizabeth only who actually said them. There are two other things Elizabeth says upon which we must linger for a moment.

The first is "How have I deserved to be thus visited by the mother of my Lord?" Here the word "Lord" means at least Messiah. But in the Septuagint, the Greek translation of the Old Testament, the word was used for God; and although Elizabeth had probably never read the Septuagint, she had a special reason for using it in the same sense—for Gabriel had said to Zechariah that her son should "convert many of the children of Israel to the *Lord* their *God*". Zechariah was certainly in her mind when she uttered the second of the phrases upon which we thus briefly linger—"Blessed art thou for thy believing"—for Zechariah still suffered from the dumbness which had come upon him because of his failure to believe.

When Mary spoke, it was not to Elizabeth. The Magnificat is a cry to God and to all men. It is woven of passages from the Old Testament, especially the prayer that Hannah had prayed at the birth of Samuel (1 Sam 2:1-10). If that prayer is not familiar to you, do please read it and then reread the Magnificat. The similarities are obvious, the differences more so.

There is one phrase of Hannah which we cannot imagine on our Lady's lips—"Now can I flout my enemies!" And there are so many phrases in the Magnificat which could never have sounded on any lips but hers. Greatest of these is "All generations shall call me blessed." Spoken by a girl in her teens, from an insignificant town in Galilee, bride of a carpenter, the claim might seem monstrous: more monstrous even than the promise made by that other carpenter, her Son, that he would build his Church upon a fisherman and the gates of hell should not prevail against it. Either claim really would have been monstrous—if it had not been fulfilled.

Even to those who know that all generations *have* called her blessed, there is a kind of surprise in the way a statement of so much glory is linked to her "humility" (better, her lowliness). Here again there is an echo of something her Son was to say— "Learn of me, *because* I am meek and humble of heart."

Certainly there is no self-glorification in the Magnificat. In the reference to her humility we find her, in our English version, once more calling herself "handmaid" as she did to Gabriel, and once more Saint Luke's Greek word means "slave". The word startles us. We are more startled still to hear her, whose soul was filled with grace at the moment of her conception and never stained by sin, call God her Savior. There is a vast theological reality here. God was truly her Savior, both because it was by his power that she was conceived in sanctifying grace and saved from ever sinning; and because, sinless though she was, she was still a member of a sinful race—a race to which heaven was closed until the Savior healed the breach between it and God.

It is not quite clear whether or not Mary stayed with Elizabeth till John was actually born. But one feels that she must have. She would hardly have deprived the forerunner's birth of the glory of her own Son's presence. After this, we hear no more of John until he appears upon the scene once more—around thirty years later.

Message to Joseph

The two most immediately concerned in the conception of Christ were the Mother and the Son. Luke has told us of one, John of the other. But there was a third, Joseph, very differently but most deeply concerned: for his wife conceived a child of which he was not the father. Matthew tells of him (1:18–25).

Joseph's discovery and his reaction to it, Matthew gives in about forty closely packed words. Let us begin to unpack them. We shall not see the greatness of Joseph if we simply read them and pass swiftly on: and that was surely Matthew's reason for telling us the episode at all.

Mary was betrothed to Joseph, they had not yet begun their life together. Betrothal, as we have noted, was not with the Jews simply an engagement to marry, it was marriage. The ceremony—as we know it to have been somewhat later and as it may well have been in the time of Mary and Joseph—was very simple. Its elements are still to be found in our own marriage ceremonial. In the presence of two competent witnesses, the man handed the woman a coin—the smallest would do—or some token gift instead: and he said, "Be thou consecrated to me." The husband and wife did not set up house together at once. She remained with her family, he with his. But husband and wife they were. In this first chapter, we find Matthew calling Joseph "husband", the angel calling Mary "wife".

And now Mary "was found to be with child". Between the betrothal and the wife's entry into her husband's house, as we have noted, the marriage act was not customary among the Jews. But if it did take place—which it rarely did in Galilee, more often in Judea—it was not sinful, and a child born of it was legitimate.

How did Joseph learn that Mary was to bear a child? We remember her "Be it done unto me according to thy word"— addressed, one imagines, not to Gabriel but to God direct. She had gone immediately after saying it to Elizabeth in Judea. Three months later, she was back in Nazareth. Some time after that, it would have been evident that she was to have a child. The women of Nazareth would have noticed; and they would instantly have told their husbands. Did one of the husbands remark on it to Joseph? Whoever told him, we can feel sure that Joseph received the news in silence. He was a silent man; and, in any event, what could he say?

Why had Mary not told Joseph herself? We do not know. We do not even know where Joseph was living at the time of Gabriel's visit to Mary. He may have been in some other town of Galilee or even in Judea—we remember that when later they returned from Egypt, their first intention was to settle in Judea. Mary may not have seen him after the Annunciation. Would she, in any event, have found it so simple to tell him? She may well have felt it was for God to tell Joseph, as he had told herself.

"Joseph her husband, being a just man and not willing publicly to expose her, was minded to put her away privately." Nazareth was a small town, everybody would have known about Mary's condition. But Joseph's unwillingness to expose her to shame suggests that the townspeople saw no sin; they assumed that the child within her was the child of Joseph, her husband.

We cannot presume to read Joseph's mind, and no word of his has reached us. What emerges most clearly is his desire to protect Mary. Only his word could bring shame on her. I doubt he thought she had sinned. Indeed how could he? A saint of his greatness would have recognized a saint of her uniqueness.

There is one element that may have loomed very large in Joseph's mind—namely, the birth of a child to Zechariah's wife when she was past the age of childbearing. Mary would have brought the news back with her to her own family circle in Nazareth; indeed it might have reached the town anyhow, since the Temple in Jerusalem would have been buzzing with talk of the marvelous thing that had happened to one of the priests.

Faced with two certainties—his own conviction of Mary's purity and the plain fact that she had conceived—Joseph might well have felt that God had once more intervened miraculously. The mystery of her conceiving was still utterly beyond him; but at least it seemed to mean that God had some special design for her, a design in which he was not included. If so, he would have been ending the marriage solely in order to set her free for whatever God's design might be.

While he was pondering the mystery, "the angel of the Lord appeared to him in sleep." Who was the angel? His name is not mentioned, but surely it was Gabriel. The birth of the world's Redeemer seems to have been his special province. Observe the angel's opening words: "Joseph, son of David, do not be afraid to take thy wife Mary to thyself, for it is by the power of the Holy Spirit that she has conceived this child." So Joseph had been afraid! Now he learns something far greater than the great thing which had happened to Elizabeth—Mary had conceived the child virginally. And he, Joseph, *was* included in God's design for her. By God's command he was to take his virgin wife into his own house.

The angel goes on: "Thou shalt call his name Jesus, for he shall save his people from their sins."

The first six words had already been said to Mary. There was a special significance in their being said to Joseph, whom the angel had saluted as "Joseph, son of David". For Joseph to name the child meant that Joseph accepted him. We speak of Joseph as our Lord's "foster-father". But this is to misunderstand the family law of the Jews. For them, a man who adopted a child *was* the child's father, the word "beget" is actually used of fathers adopting sons. Acceptance by the father was the decisive thing. The accepted son legally acquired not only a father, but all the father's ancestors. For the Jew, Jesus was the son of David because he had been accepted as a son by Joseph, the son of David. (Observe that our Lord's name was Jesus. Christ came to be used as a name for him only after his death. In his lifetime the phrase used was the Christ, that is the Messiah, both phrases meaning the Anointed One.)

Matthew goes on to make his own comment—that all this was in fulfillment of the prophecy made by Isaiah seven hundred years before: "A virgin shall be with child and bring forth a son; and they shall call his name Emmanuel" (Is 7:14). The word "virgin" is only in the Septuagint translation, the Hebrew word seems to mean "a young, unmarried woman". No Jewish commentator had ever seen these words as meaning that the Messiah was to be born of a virgin mother. It is Matthew, inspired by the Holy Spirit, who tells us that they do. And we can know, as the Jews before Christ could not, how marvelously apt was the statement "They shall call his name Emmanuel." The word means "God with us". In fact it never had been given as a name to any Jew, nor was it now given as a name to Mary's child. But it was a precise statement about what Christ was and is. We compare it, not with the angel's words to Mary and to Joseph, "Thou shalt call his name Jesus", but with Gabriel's words to Mary that he "shall be called the Son of God".

"And Joseph rising up from sleep did as the angel of the Lord commanded him and took unto him his wife." In the tantalizing way of the evangelists Matthew gives us the essentials, leaving untold so many things we are longing to know—but are forced to admit that we do not strictly need to know! As we have seen, he compresses into forty words Joseph's discovery that Mary was about to bear a child and his reaction to the discovery. Now he needs only half as many to tell us that after the angel's visit Joseph completed the marriage by taking Mary into his own house. And, growing ever terser, he goes on to tell of the birth and naming of the child in some fifteen words.

I have spoken of things untold which we should long to hear. Above all, perhaps, we wonder about the first meeting with Mary after the angel's message to Joseph. At last she could break her own silence, and tell him what Gabriel had said to her; and Joseph at last could know what the child was whom he was to make legally his own. Yet, on a second thought, we see how improbable it was that she or Joseph should ever have discussed that meeting with any third person at all: it was the innermost secret of their marriage, and belonged only to them.

Wedding in Nazareth

But we cannot help feeling that Matthew—or at least Luke, who was a shade less reticent—might have told us about the wedding celebrations. We have to be content with what we know of the general pattern of weddings among the Jews. By betrothal, we remember, the couple were made husband and wife. It was the simplest of ceremonies, needing only the presence of two witnesses. The celebrations surrounding the homecoming—that is what the wedding was—were a very different matter, involving every relative and friend that either of them had.

The great day began with the bridegroom and his friends going in procession, with lights and music, to bring the bride from her house to his. Jesus is referring to this procession in the parable about the five silly girls who had no oil for their lamps (Mt 25). But what exactly was Mary's house? Saint Luke says that she returned from Judea "to her own house". She must have been living with someone. Luke does not tell us who this someone might be: nor does Matthew—he indeed does not even say that either the angel's visit to Joseph or the marriage took place in Nazareth: the first place he names is Bethlehem, where Christ was born; Nazareth he does not mention till the return from Egypt.

At the bridegroom's house there would be feasting, more or less luxurious according to his wealth or poverty. With the rich, the feast sometimes lasted for days. In the parable of the guest who had no wedding garment (Mt 22) our Lord refers to a feast of rather special magnificence—there had been a great slaying of "cattle and fatlings". But that feast was given by a king. The one given by Joseph the carpenter would not have been on that scale. It would probably have been closer to the one given thirty years later in Cana in Galilee (Jn 2): for that was given by friends of our Lady, and Cana was only a few miles from Nazareth. There we may be sure the cattle and fatlings were in no rich profusion, for the poor of Galilee hardly ever had meat on their tables; we read that the wine ran out; and we may feel reasonably sure that the group of fishermen Jesus brought with him probably wore nothing very special in the way of wedding garments.

How far the wedding feast of Mary and Joseph resembled that of Cana, we can only guess—we simply cannot see either Mary or Joseph putting on any very spectacular show. But one thing the two feasts have in common—Christ was present at both of them! No royal wedding had ever had a glory to compare with that. The poorest Catholic can have it now with a nuptial Mass.

4 BORN IN BETHLEHEM

Journey to Bethlehem

The wedding celebrations over, Mary had barely settled in Joseph's home, when the Emperor Augustus intervened startlingly in their lives. He ordered a census of his Empire.

Since Christ was born and grew to manhood under him, this Augustus is worth a glance. He had begun life as Octavius; when his great-uncle, Julius Caesar, adopted him as his heir, he added the name Caesar. In alliance with Mark Antony—Cleopatra's friend, as every reader of Shakespeare knows—he had destroyed Caesar's murderer, Brutus. Thirteen years later he defeated Antony and Cleopatra at the sea battle of Actium; Antony died by the sword and Cleopatra by snakebite, both self-administered; Augustus was left sole ruler of the Roman world. For all practical purposes the Roman Republic was at the end of its five centuries of existence, though Octavius preserved many of the old forms. The Empire had begun. The Senate conferred on Octavius the name Augustus, which means "majestic"—very much as our Lord would one day change Simon's name to Rock.

At the time of his intervention in the lives of Mary and Joseph, Caesar Augustus had been ruling Rome and its Empire for a quarter century. By all the standards men knew he was a good ruler, indeed a superb ruler. To many, especially in the provinces, it seemed that a new age had begun with him. He was not officially declared a god until after his death, but his subjects happily talked of him as one. Shortly before our Lord's birth, the proconsul of Asia proposed a new calendar, with the birthday of Augustus as New Year's Day. The loyal address welcoming the proposal uses a phrase which, applied to Augustus, seems ridiculous, but which is totally applicable to a child soon to be born: "The birth of the god was for the world the beginning of the good news."

It was Augustus, ironically perhaps, who decided that child's birthplace—he ordered a census. In Palestine a census meant that a man must—or, as some scholars say, might—register in the town of his family's origin, which for Joseph was Bethlehem. To Bethlehem Joseph went. And he took his wife with him. It was not a vast distance—ninety miles or so to Jerusalem (as it might be Philadelphia to New York, or Coventry to London), then five miles or so to Bethlehem—say four days' journey all told.

The main road linking all the great cities of the north to Jerusalem ran only a few miles from Nazareth. People usually travelled it in large groups—officials, merchants, pilgrims—for the road wound through mountains, and mountains meant bandits. But, with the census on, it was thronged with people, to say nothing of camels and donkeys. Even in so small a place as Nazareth, the carpenter would have owned a donkey, and on this journey he would have brought the donkey, and not only for their small baggage: Joseph could have walked the whole way, but not Mary, with her child so close to birth.

Why, at that moment of all moments, did Joseph take her on so arduous a journey, with the certainty that the child would be born away from home, and—as every woman in Nazareth must have warned Mary—no certainty at all where they might be at the time of birth? It is possible that the decree required wives to register in person. We do not know. But of one thing we can be sure—decree or no decree, nothing could have kept Mary from going to Bethlehem with Joseph.

Bethlehem was a town glorious with memories of the long past of her race. Genesis says that Jacob's wife Rachel was buried there, the wife he had toiled fourteen years to win—there is no love story in the Old Testament to compare with that. And Ruth, the heroine of another Old Testament love story, had gone to live there. But the chief glory of Bethlehem was not Rachel or Ruth. It was Ruth's great-grandson, David. He had been born there, and anointed king there. Gabriel had told Mary that she was to conceive and bear into the world the Son of David—not a son of David, as Joseph was and countless others, but the one who was to have the throne of David, the Messiah. It was wholly suitable, one feels, that he should be born in David's city.

But it was not mere suitability that governed her decision. To see what the profounder reason was, we must consider certain things that must have been in her mind.

What *must* have been, notice, not what may have been. There are writers on our Lady who have a tendency to tell us what she was thinking or feeling or doing; for the most part they are simply telling us what they themselves would have thought or felt or done had they been Mary, so that what they write sheds light upon themselves but not necessarily upon her. Experience teaches us that we cannot even be sure what our close friends will do in a given situation—so often we realize that we had not known what was going on in their souls' depths. And we simply have no mental equipment for reading deep into the mind of one who had never sinned and who had had sanctifying grace in her soul from the moment of her conception. Sin, original and actual, has its effect upon the mind we think with, affects our thinking therefore. It had not affected hers. We must be careful about saying what she might have done. But one thing she *must* have done.

Her mind echoing and reechoing Gabriel's message about the child she was to have, she must have studied the Scriptures as she had never studied them before, in one special sense as no one had ever studied them before. Other mothers wonder what the future holds for their child. She had the inspired word of God to tell her—not everything, but so much, so very much.

She had three months in the house of Zechariah and Elizabeth. Zechariah would have had access to the Scriptures, and never had three people intenser reason to study them. With two such sons on the way, they would not have had much time for other topics. In the light of what Mary—and Joseph—had been told, it seems certain that she must (if not as early as this, certainly in the years that followed) have observed one vast fact which had escaped the notice of the scholars of her race. Three times there is reference to the parentage of One who is to come. And every time the reference is to the woman. Back in the beginning of Genesis it is the seed of the woman that shall crush the serpent's head. The prophet Isaiah (8:14) says, "A virgin shall conceive and bear a son, and his name shall be called Emmanuel." And about the same time the prophet Micah (5:3), speaking plainly of the Messiah, uses the phrase "She that travaileth shall bring forth." Always the woman, never a hint of a male parent—and this among a people to whom the father was everything, who would not have bothered to mention the women in their own genealogical trees.

But what has all this to do with Mary's feeling that her child must be born in Bethlehem? In the verse before the one from Micah just quoted, Mary would have read: "And thou, Bethlehem Ephrata, art a little one among the clans of Judea: out of thee shall he come forth unto me that is to be the ruler in Israel: and his going forth is from the beginning, from the days of eternity." A little later when King Herod asks Jerusalem's learned men where Christ should be born, Matthew tells us that they said in Bethlehem of Judea, and quoted Micah.

Christ Is Born

When the decree of Caesar Augustus sent Joseph to Bethlehem, how could Mary have stayed behind? Augustus was not as the pagans thought a god, but Mary and Joseph must have seen the hand of God in the decree which ensured that the Son of David should be born in David's city.

But where in David's city was he to be born? Bethlehem was a village, with perhaps a thousand inhabitants. The census had crammed it with David's descendants, an uncle or two of Joseph's perhaps, countless cousins — first cousins, twentieth cousins, thirtieth cousins; for there were a thousand years and thirty generations between David and Joseph. The birth of a baby calls for privacy. Where was privacy to be had, when every available inch of space was taken?

Saint Luke does not tell us exactly where they found it. But when the child was born, he was laid in a manger. And mangers are in stables. It was probably not the kind of place the word suggests to us. Saint Justin Martyr says that it was a cave in the hillside: and, although he was writing over a century afterwards, Justin was a Palestinian himself, and in Palestine memories were long and traditions tenacious.

In our Christmas cribs there is always an ox, always an ass. Scripture does not mention them, but they were probably there — an ass because Mary must have ridden upon an ass: in her condition, she could hardly have walked; an ox, because the manger could not have been there for nothing, the cave must have been meant for some animal, almost certainly an ox. A stable would not be elegant, or even clean; but it would provide the one absolute essential, privacy, which was not at that time to be had in any building in Bethlehem.

There "Mary brought forth her firstborn son and wrapped him up in swaddling-clothes and laid him in a manger."

The word "firstborn" does not mean that there were other sons to follow. When a newly married wife had a son, he was called her firstborn, simply because there were none before him; he continued to be so called, even if there were none after him, because there were certain rights and duties attaching to the "firstborn son", whether he was an only child or not.

So now there were three in the cave, Joseph and Mary and Jesus. Soon there were more, for some shepherds were told of the child's birth by an angel (Gabriel again?). They had been "keeping the night watches over their flock" (so that we know Jesus was born in the night) when the angel appeared to them. "This day," the angel said, "in the city of David, a savior has been born for you, the Lord Christ himself. This is the sign by which you are to know him. You will find a child still in swaddling-clothes, lying in a manger" (Lk 2:10-12). A multitude of the heavenly army appeared, and there can hardly be a Christian in the world who does not know what *they* said—"Glory to God in the highest and on earth peace to men of good will."

Strange that these men should have been chosen for this revelation. To the right-minded in high places, mountain shepherds were the very scum of Israel, men of violence, thieves, perjurers, scorners of the Law: men accustomed to fighting off wolves were less likely than men of quieter lives to be in fear of scribes. To welcome Mary's son, there was one orthodox Jew, Joseph; there were those international figures, the ox and the ass; there were the shepherds, who were just about Jews; some time later there would be Gentiles, learned men from the East. But of official Jewry, not one. And this, not because they had refused to come. They had simply not been invited. They could not know who was to be born that night in Bethlehem, unless God told them. And God did not tell them.

Circumcision and Presentation

Naturally the shepherds talked of what had happened to them on the hillside. "All wondered", says Saint Luke in a masterpiece of understatement. He goes on to tell us that Mary "pondered in her heart". This is the first of four occasions on which he speaks of her pondering. Can we make even a guess at the direction of her thoughts?

Clearly much was still dark to her. At one level, she could hardly have helped asking herself why mountain shepherds—the lowest of the low in general opinion—had been chosen for an honor for which in all the Old Testament there was no precedent: a prophet and a patriarch had indeed been visited by one angel or two, but "a multitude of the heavenly host"—that was new. In the Magnificat Mary says that God "has exalted the lowly", but had she thought of anything quite as lowly as these shepherds?

More profoundly, she must have noted that the angel had described her son to them as "Christ the Lord". Just how much did the word "Lord" mean in itself? And what difference would it make—and how soon—that this particular baby should be "Christ the Lord", *her* Lord therefore? She had immensities to ponder about.

On the eighth day the child was circumcised. By that time, we may hope, they had moved out of the cave into a house, as Bethlehem emptied again after the census. The rite was probably performed by Joseph. It was a father's privilege.

By the command God gave to Abraham, every male child must undergo circumcision. It is a rite not restricted to the Jews, practised for all sorts of reasons, religious and non-religious, by many peoples. But for the Jews its meaning was wholly religious: it was the consecration to God of man's greatest power in the physical order, the power by which he shares with God in the generation of new life.

According to Jewish law, two things still remained—the buying back from God of the child, and the purification of the mother: strange to think of the Redeemer redeemed and the all-pure purified!

Since the day when the firstborn of Egypt were slain to force upon Pharaoh the liberation of God's people (Ex 13:12–16), all the firstborn of Israel were made by God his own special property, consecrated to him. Every firstborn son must be bought back. We cannot be certain, but it seems that what Joseph had to pay for the ransoming of Jesus would have been roughly the equivalent of two weeks of his earnings as a carpenter.

By the law of Moses, every mother of a son must for forty days remain in her own house, avoid contact with sacred things, and not enter the sanctuary. On the fortieth day she must offer for sacrifice a lamb and a young pigeon; but if the family was too poor to pay for a lamb, then they might offer two pigeons.

Neither for the buying back of the son, nor for the offering of the two pigeons (which was what Mary and Joseph in fact offered) was it strictly necessary to go to the Temple. But people as close to Jerusalem as these two were would have made a point of going to the Temple, and these two did. Mary would simply have dropped into the appropriate money box the price of the two pigeons for the sacrifice. What interests us in their visit was the reaction of Anna, who realized that their child was to be the Redeemer of Israel, and still more of Simeon, who took the child in his arms and uttered words which set them both "wondering".

He had come to the Temple that day—as Christ our Lord would one day go to the desert—"led by the Holy Spirit", the same Holy Spirit who had revealed to him that he should not die until he had seen the Christ. Two things strike us especially in what Simeon said as he held the child Jesus in his arms (Lk 2:29–35).

His last words were (as translated by Monsignor Knox): "This child is destined to bring about the fall of many and the rise of many in Israel; to be a sign which men will refuse to acknowledge. . . . as for thy own soul, it shall have a sword to pierce it." They are startling words to be uttered over a newborn baby. Yet we are not told that it was these words which caused Mary and Joseph to wonder. For Mary knew already, and would have discussed with Joseph, the words in the Book of Daniel (9:26)—"Christ—the Anointed One—will be done to death." The Anointed One that Daniel spoke about, who was he? Kings were anointed, so were high priests. Was Daniel talking of her child? A mother would surely have thought so. The piercing of her own soul might have begun when, after Gabriel's visit, she read that prophecy.

The words Simeon uttered, immediately before we are told that the child's parents wondered, were: "This is the light which shall give revelation to the Gentiles, this is the glory of thy people Israel." Such a naming of Gentiles before Jews, in the statement of what the Messiah was to be and do, could only be utterly shattering to the Jewish orthodox. Twice the prophet Isaiah had declared that the Messiah would be "the light of the Gentiles": as far as we can discover, the rabbis never referred to these texts of Isaiah—it was as though the prophet had committed a *faux pas* which it was politer to ignore. And now Simeon goes further, naming the Gentile first. It is almost as if he knew that the next visitors to the Holy Family would be Gentiles!

The Wise Men from the East

Luke says nothing of all that. He simply says: "After they had performed all things according to the law of the Lord they returned to Galilee." That word "after" again! Matthew tells of much that happened before they saw Galilee again.

He tells first of the visit of the magi. It is a strange episode, with no clear meaning and no sequel. The magi come for a reason we find it hard to follow, and depart leaving no trace. But Matthew does not tell it to no purpose. We cannot just give it a friendly smile and pass on.

Christian art has given us a great deal to smile at. It has produced a glowing and glorious series of pictures, in which the magi would not have recognized themselves! In the pictures, there are usually three of them: but the Gospel does not say how many they were. In the pictures, they are kings, arriving often enough with a train of camels and a horde of attendants. But magi were not kings. The name has a lower and a higher application. It was used for men who were sorcerers, astrologers, workers of magic generally—like that Simon Magus, who tried to buy the Holy Spirit from Saint Peter, and is immortalized in the sin of simony. But it was used also for men of learning, students of the stars certainly, but serious philosophers too, not magicians but sages.

Forget the notion of a procession of kings, who would have arrived in Bethlehem followed by hundreds of idlers from Jerusalem, only five miles away. Herod would not have needed to ask kings to come back and tell him where they had found the child: all Jerusalem would have known exactly where they went. It may be an exaggeration in the other direction, but closer to the truth all the same, to think of them as a group of university professors, traveling inconspicuously, as professors do to this day.

In their homeland in the East, which may have been Arabia or may have been Persia, they had seen a star, from which they concluded that one had been born who was the King of the Jews. What the star may have been, Matthew does not tell us, and there has been an immense amount of speculation by scholars ever since. The more interesting question—how did the star convey its message? —has been less discussed. What was there about it which made them so certain that it meant the birth of the King of the Jews? Again we are not told. But certain they were.

They went to Jerusalem—not led by the star, there is no suggestion that the star led them there, but because Jerusalem was the obvious place to go. If a new king of the Jews had been born, Jerusalem would be sure to know where.

That they should have gone to Jerusalem to inquire was natural. But that it should have been King Herod who answered them is one of the fiercest ironies of all history.

Naturally Jerusalem was buzzing with the news that a group of Gentiles had arrived from the East asking where they might find the King of the Jews. The Jews, of course, already had a king, Herod. But the citizens knew that the visiting sages were talking about the Messiah. At that time, the whole air was vibrant with expectation of the coming of the Messiah. When Herod died, a year or so later, three of them appeared (only a very self-deluded Messiah would have risked appearing while Herod was still there!).

The buzzing reached Herod at once—he had a superb secret police, he had to. That what the strangers were looking for was the long-prophesied Messiah was no comfort to him. Supernatural or not, another King of the Jews would mean that his own kingship was at an end. And he had worked so hard to establish it. The name Herod is from a Greek word meaning "descendant of heroes": but neither he nor anyone else knew who these heroes were. By lineage he was a nobody, the son and grandson of officials under the Hasmonean kings. His forbears were crafty men, but he was craftier. By pulling the right wires in Rome he became king himself; and king he remained till he died thirty-three years later.

In Palestine Herod was a tyrant. But in Rome he was only a courtier. He held his throne solely by the kindness of the Roman Emperor Augustus, whose little finger could have broken him. The Romans kept him in power because he was useful, and anyhow they found him on his many visits an affable and amusing person.

The Messiah of prophecy meant nothing at all to Herod. He was not a Jew by race, as the kings he succeeded had been; his father was an Idumean and his mother an Arab. He was circumcised, and in a general way avoided upsetting the religious prejudices of the Jewish people. But he did not share them. When he went to Rome to receive the kingship, he offered the proper pagan sacrifice to Jupiter Capitolinus. He built the great Jewish Temple in Jerusalem, but in other parts of Palestine he built temples to the goddess Rome and to the godlike Augustus. He was far too sophisticated a person to believe that heaven would send a Messiah; but he knew that the Jews were expecting one, and the mere rumor that one had arrived could stir them to a religious and national frenzy. The wisest course was to strangle the rumor quietly at birth.

His first step was to summon the chief priests and scribes and ask them where, according to the prophecies, the Messiah was to be born. And they quoted the text of Micah (5:2) which we have already mentioned, to show that the birth would be in Bethlehem. It is not wild to guess that he put the question, not with reference to the visit of the strangers from the East, but merely as a devout person asking information of men more learned than himself. The second step was to have the strangers brought to him privately.

It was essential that his people should not know that their story of a Messiah interested him, for that would have fanned the rumor to a blaze. He told the strangers that they should go to Bethlehem, should inquire for the child, and should return and tell him, because he too was anxious to worship. Why did he not send one of his spies after them, which might have seemed the most certain way of learning what they had discovered? We can only guess. Perhaps he felt that when there was question of a Messiah, even a spy might be carried away with excitement. He must keep the whole matter between himself and these Gentiles.

The magi seem to have swallowed Herod's story. One feels that they must have been very absorbed scholars indeed not to have raised an eyebrow at the anxiety of this bloodstained monster to worship a newborn baby, who was to take his own place and title. Had they been kings, as the legends call them, they would have understood Herod better.

So Herod sent the magi off to Bethlehem. He must have felt that he had handled what might have been a very difficult situation rather well. Bethlehem was only five miles away from Jerusalem. They would arrive there that night, would spend the next day searching. They would almost certainly find a newborn child who, they would persuade themselves, possessed whatever qualities their astrology had told them were to be expected in the Messiah. They would come back—possibly next night, since Bethlehem was so small a place—to tell him. He would kill the child. He would probably kill its parents too, lest they might, excited by the visit of the magi, be tempted to try again. He might have killed the magi too, just to close the episode.

But the magi discovered the child sooner even than Herod's optimism had thought possible. As they left Jerusalem they saw the star again. They hardly needed its guidance on their five-mile journey to Bethlehem. But in Bethlehem it "stood over the place where the child was." What was the place? Was it still the cave which had the manger in it? It seems improbable. As we have seen, with the emptying out of Joseph's cousins when the census was over, there would have been room in the town; and Saint Matthew tells us that the strangers entered the *house* (or dwelling) and "found the child". On the other hand, hill-caves in Palestine often had dwellings built above them.

"They found the child with Mary his mother." Why is Joseph not mentioned? We might very well think that he is omitted because he mattered so much less than Mary. But this is to misunderstand not only the position of a father in a Jewish family, but the position of Joseph in this particular family. After all, Matthew has been telling Joseph's story up to this moment, and continues with the visit of the angel to Joseph afterward. The simplest reason for his omission here may very well be the true one: that he was not there.

We do not know how long after the child's birth the magi appeared; but at least we may be certain that, even for the forty days before the presentation in the Temple, Joseph had to go to work. These were poor people, and could not afford long holidays. He was a carpenter, had surely brought his tools with him, and may well have been making a door or a plough on some neighboring farm.

The strangers had no doubt that they had found the child they were looking for. "Falling down, they worshipped him." The Greek word here might mean that they gave the adoration due to God; but it might mean some lesser homage. After all, the Jews had not grasped that the Messiah would be divine, and the surrounding Gentiles would hardly have known more than the chosen people. But if it was only homage, it was high homage, as to a king: they fell down before the child.

And how strange were the gifts they brought—gold, precious incense, and myrrh. If the strangers were from Arabia, they were simply bringing three of the most valuable gifts their country had to give. Gold was a gift adapted to please anyone, but it had a special suitability for a king. Incense could be offered only to gods, or the statues of gods: the Jews used it in their Temple services, Zechariah was offering it when Gabriel appeared. Myrrh was a fragrant resin, always associated with the dead—the Egyptians used it for embalming, the Jews sprinkled it on dead bodies.

Myrrh was valuable, and as such might very well be given as a present. Yet it was an odd present, perhaps, to give to a newborn baby. Herod would have chuckled, since it was his intention to slay the baby at once. Mary and Joseph may have wept a little.

Herod, we say, would have chuckled. But in fact he did not chuckle. He raged. For the learned men did not come back to Jerusalem to tell him what they had found.

We hardly think of the magi as people; indeed we picture them rather than use our minds about them. We see them as a gorgeous splash of oriental color in the dimness of the stable, but we no more think of them as saying anything than if they were the ox and the ass. There may be great paintings in which they are shown sitting and talking with our Lady, but I have never seen one. Yet conversation there must have been, one of the most thrilling conversations that ever failed to get itself written down. The magi did not simply walk in, adore, hand over their gifts, and walk out again without a word spoken.

They would at least have told the child's mother why they were there, told her more, certainly, than they had told Herod—about the star and what it had told them. And Mary would not have sat smiling but mute. Through the star it was God who had sent them; she must have told them something of what Gabriel had told her. She may perhaps have said nothing of her own virginity. But she must surely have told them of Gabriel's message that her child was to be called the Son of the Most High and that God would give him the throne of David his father. It was not merely because they happened to find a newborn baby just where a newborn baby was supposed to be that they fell down and adored.

Their coming, and the reason for it, must have been a great joy to Mary, and to Joseph when she told him of it. But there was one frightening element. They would, of course, have told her of their visit to Herod, and of his requesting them to let him know where the child was, that he too might worship. Foreigners might have swallowed such a story, especially if they came from far away, from Persia for example. But Herod had been king in his own realm for close on forty years; there could not have been a man, woman, or child among the Jews who did not know what kind of brute he was. Mary might well have shuddered at the thought of what would happen when the magi went back to him.

But the magi did not go back to Herod. They were told in sleep—a mysterious phrase, which we must simply leave as we find it—not to do so. They returned to their own country by a route which did not take them through Jerusalem. A glance at a map shows that they could have reached the eastern border of Herod's dominions in half a day or less. If they left before dawn, and slipped away as unnoticed as they had probably arrived, they could easily have reached safety before Herod woke.

Flight into Egypt

Joseph slipped away quietly too, the same night one imagines, taking Mary and the child; for an angel appeared to him in sleep to say that Herod would be seeking the child to kill him, that they must go to Egypt and stay there till the angel told him that it was safe to return. Did he and Mary remember another flight into Egypt, nine hundred years before, from a king whose word was death (1 Kings 11:40)?—Jeroboam, who had been a threat to Solomon's kingdom, fled to Egypt and stayed there till Solomon was dead.

There are legends about the Holy Family's journey into Egypt, pleasing legends but no more than that, not a fact in the lot, even a probability! They were invented by people who just couldn't wait for the miracles to start. Cana and its wedding feast were thirty years in the future, and that was too long: so they have God-made-infant working miracles. Wild beasts rush upon the group, then bow their heads reverently at sight of the child. Date-palms bend double to bring their fruit within his reach. Compared with what was actually happening— Omnipotence helpless in the arms of a creature, Omnipotence cared for as a baby by a mother—these little wonders are wholly pointless.

For we must remember that the Infant was God, the second Person of the Blessed Trinity. He did not have to wait till he was grown up enough to be God; no one is grown up enough to be God. The greatest of men at the highest point of his maturity is no closer to the Infinite than a baby in the womb—the gulf between is still measureless. In the human nature of Christ, it was always God the Son who acted and suffered. Later he would act and suffer as a grown man; on the flight into Egypt he acted and suffered as a baby—true God, real baby.

It is profoundly mysterious but utterly real that it was God who, in the humanity he had made his own, sucked milk from Mary's breast, wailed, slept in the arms of Mary or Joseph. Bowing beasts and bending date-palms are merely scribbles in the margin of that.

The Egyptian border, beyond which Herod's power did not reach, was perhaps a week's journey at the pace at which they could travel, especially as they would almost certainly have chosen the older and less frequented roads in preference to the main road, whenever possible. It must have been an appalling journey, most of it through barren country, uninhabited, with water almost impossible to find. The last part, as they approached the Egyptian border, was sheer desert, a vast sea of sand, treeless, shadeless.

It would have been a nightmare journey to any mother of a baby just born. But this was a baby whose life was sought by a powerful king. Worse than heat and sand and thirst was the terror of pursuit. How could Herod's men fail to catch them?

Massacre in Bethlehem

But they were not even pursued. Herod, in a blind rage when at last it was clear to him that the magi were not coming back, decided to kill every male baby under two in Bethlehem. As he did not know that an angel had warned Joseph (he probably did not believe in angels anyhow, certainly none of his intellectual friends did), it seemed to him that his plan was foolproof. He would have killed every newborn baby in the danger zone: by extending the slaughter to all boys born within the previous two years, he would ensure that no child would remain who could possibly be pointed at later as the one the magi meant.

Herod was a great believer in the effectiveness of murder: he owed almost everything to it, and the massacre he was now planning was quite a small-scale one—probably twenty or thirty tiny nobodies. (Strange, to learn that there is an Essene hymn telling of children slain at the birth of the Messiah.) On his accession to the throne, he had murdered fifty of the leading men in Palestine, including members of the Sanhedrin itself, the religious governing body of the Jews. He had murdered his father-in-law King Hyrcanus and his mother-in-law Alexandria: he had already murdered his first wife, Mariamne, and two of his sons, and would very soon murder a third. Given that his fear of the newborn baby could hardly have arisen from any threat to his own kingship, since he was already seventy and in appalling health, it must largely have arisen from a threat to the dynasty it was his ambition to found. Slaying his eldest three sons was an odd way of establishing a dynasty! But so long a career of murder, gluttony, and lust had left him something less than sane.

There is anguish for us, twenty centuries after, in thinking of the slain babies and their parents. For the babies, the agony was soon over; in the next world they would know Whom they had died to save and for all eternity would have that glory. For the parents, the pain would have lasted longer; but at death they too must have found that there was a special sense in which God was in their debt, as he had never been indebted to any. They and their children were the only ones who ever agonized in order to save God's life.

On December 28, three days after Christmas, we celebrate the feast of the slain children as martyrs. One thing they alone among martyrs have, they died to save God from men who would slay him.

Herod Dies

Where did the Holy Family go in Egypt, and how did they live? The second question presents no great problem. There was a large Jewish colony there—a million perhaps; and anywhere in the ancient world there was work for a carpenter. But where they lived we do not know, nor how long they stayed.

Not long, probably. They had come to Egypt to escape Herod, and in 4 B.C. Herod died. One guess is that they had barely crossed the border into Egypt, heard of the king's death within a week or two, and were back in Jerusalem in time for the presentation in the Temple. But it seems a more natural reading of Saint Luke's account and Saint Matthew's to have the visit of the magi and all that followed happen after the presentation—if only because people who had received a gift of gold would not have offered a sacrifice of the poor as Joseph and Mary did.

Herod's death was of a special horror. He was all on fire inside, "his entrails became ulcerated, every muscle ached, his feet and belly swelled up and were covered with blood. He was like a putrefying corpse, breeding worms." So the Jewish historian Josephus tells us: modern scholars think he suffered from a form of sclerosis. He had one last pleasure. Permission having arrived from Rome, he executed his son Antipater—whom he had named piously after his own father and grandfather. Five days later he was dead himself, having had two doctors of the Law burnt alive as a completion of his own preparation for death.

In his will, he divided his kingdom among the three sons he had not got round to slaying. His son Archelaus was to succeed to his throne, but to only part of his kingdom—Judea, Samaria, and the ancestral Idumea. Archelaus' full-brother, Antipas, was to be tetrarch of Galilee and Perea; his half-brother, Philip, got the rest. Rome's confirmation of the will being necessary, Archelaus went there to obtain it (Antipas, too). But the Jewish leaders sent a large deputation after them, urging Augustus not to give Herod's kingdom as Herod willed, but to make it part of the Roman province of Syria. Thus they anticipated a phrase their successors were to use a generation later against a greater than Archelaus—"We have no king but Caesar." Our Lord may have had this episode in mind when he told the parable of the nobleman who went into a far country to receive for himself a kingdom (Lk 19:12–14). In spite of the deputation, Rome confirmed the will; but it would not give Archelaus the title of king.

Nazareth Again

Once again Joseph received a message in sleep from an angel: "Take the child and his mother and go into the land of Israel." Matthew makes it clear that Joseph's first intention was to go to Judea, not to Nazareth. Where in Judea? We are not told. Possibly to the town where Zechariah and Elizabeth lived, for we know of Mary's devotion to her cousin, and she must have been passionately interested in the child who was to be her own child's forerunner. Many scholars think they would have gone to Bethlehem,

David's city. Perhaps. But would they have wanted to live in the place of the massacre? (Did they indeed yet know of the massacre? Did any of the mothers of Bethlehem know that it was for Mary's child that their own had been slain?)

They did not settle in Judea, for Archelaus was reigning there. He had begun with a massacre on his own account. Judea was no safer under him than under his unspeakable father. Joseph was told in sleep to go to Nazareth of Galilee. The small group probably took the Mediterranean coast road by Gaza (where Samson brought the temple crashing down on the Philistines who had blinded him) and Caesarea (where Pilate would later have his headquarters — it was from here that he went up to Jerusalem and sentenced our Lord to death).

The ruler in Galilee was Herod Antipas, far less savage than his brother, but destined to an immortality denied Archelaus. For Antipas was the Herod who, some thirty years later, beheaded John the Baptist, and three years after that played his own small part in the trial of Jesus. So that our Lord spent practically his whole life as a subject of the man who was to hand him back to be put to death by the Romans.

5 *NAZARETH OF GALILEE*

The Hidden Life

So the Holy Family went to Nazareth. We might almost say it vanished into Nazareth. Apart from one single episode — which did not take place in Nazareth — we hear nothing more of Christ and his Mother till he was thirty, nothing more of Joseph at all. We speak of this period as the "hidden life". The phrase is worth a look. There are two ways in which we can be wrong about it.

One way is to substitute a different meaning of the word "hidden" — as when we speak of contemplatives reliving the hidden life of the Holy Family in Nazareth. Contemplatives live their lives in their convent, unseen by the public. There is no obvious similarity to this in the life of a carpenter in Nazareth, or indeed anywhere. Joseph was a tradesman, depending for his living upon a steady stream of customers. So was Jesus when he grew to the age to be a carpenter himself. The whole town knew all three of them, saw them daily, was in and out of their home. Privacy was hardly possible in a small Eastern village, and was in any event not much valued. Their life was "hidden" only in the sense that the great world ignored them, very much as it ignores you and me, and that history carries no detail of their life, any more than it will carry details of your life or mine.

There is, of course, a profound sense in which the two sorts of hiddenness are related, but it is necessary to remember that they *are* two sorts. That the Lord of the World should have chosen the obscurity of a hill village in Galilee gives a value to obscurity which it had never had: and the contemplative lives this value in his own way.

The other way of misusing the life in Nazareth arises from forgetting that it *is* hidden. We say, for example, that we should model our own family lives upon that of the Holy Family. There are two difficulties here. The first is that the Holy Family consisted of two saints (one of them conceived immaculate), and a child who was God. It is not merely flippant to say that ordinary families are not like that. It is a plain fact that our problems must be different from theirs. When a husband is out late, his wife may find herself sick with worry as to what company he is in or in what condition he may return; the eldest boy may be neglecting his studies. . . . Imagine any hundred problems that can plague ordinary families and see how many of them could possibly have arisen for Joseph, Mary, and Jesus.

The one kind of problem we can easily imagine their sharing with many of us is lack of money. This brings us to the second difficulty in the way of the modeling of our family lives upon theirs—namely, that those years *are* hidden years, hidden from our eyes. We have not one single detail of their life in Nazareth. The only incident of those years that has come down to us took place in Jerusalem. Christ, aged twelve, deliberately went off by himself for three days, without asking Joseph and Mary or even telling them. When his Mother asked him why, his answer began, "Didn't you know?" We shall discuss this strange episode in a later chapter, but at least we can see that it is not for imitation by the children of an ordinary family. And it is quite literally the only detail we have of those years.

It is not easy to use the Holy Family as a model: we use Jesus, Mary, and Joseph as patrons—praying to them as a family to protect our family and to guide us in our relations with it. We shall do this all the better for being totally realistic about them, seeing them as they actually were—not as figures in a parable, or statues grouped about an altar, but as real people in a real family. And, in spite of Scripture's silence, there are things we can know about their life in those years—things that flow from what history tells us of events that must have affected them and from what other writings of the period tell us of everyday life in Galilee, as well as things that flow, not fancifully but necessarily, from what we know the three of them to have been in themselves.

Galilee Was Different

The Gospels give us no details about the life of the Holy Family; we should love to have them, but we do not actually need them. We know that Jesus was God the Son, born into our humanity; that Mary his Mother was conceived immaculate and conceived him virginally; that Joseph, the husband with whom she lived virginally, was a saint. There is more in that handful of truths than we shall ever exhaust; there is endless refreshment for the mind in thinking deeper into them. It would be no great enrichment to know whether the Holy Family had a cat. (They almost certainly did not: the Jews were not cat people; there is not one cat mentioned in the New Testament or in the Old—unless the "cats" of Baruch 7:21, which befouled idols, really *were* cats.) Yet God *did* become man, and anything we can know of the life he lived as man is precious. Let us glance briefly at the place where he grew through boyhood to manhood.

Galilee differed from Judea and Samaria in two ways. It was richer, and it contained a greater mixture of races. The first would not make much difference to a carpenter and his family, since the wealth would not have flowed their way, but the second could not fail to affect them, if only in their speech and their attitude to foreigners.

Judea was inhabited almost entirely by Jews, Samaria by Samaritans. But along with its Jews—fighting people, not very liturgical, not very observant of the Law's finer details, but *very* Messiah-conscious—Galilee had a great many Gentiles. The countryside was mainly Jewish, the towns were largely Gentile—Herod's Zippori, only four miles from Nazareth, was almost wholly so. The Gentiles were of many races, but Greek was the second language of them all. There are scholars who think that most Galileans could converse in Greek as well as in their own Aramaic (the language of Palestine akin to Hebrew, somewhat as Dutch is to German). It seems altogether likely that Mary and Joseph could speak Greek, and did so when talking to Gentiles or doing such shopping as could be done only in Zippori.

If the language native to them, and later to the boy Jesus, was the Aramaic of Galilee, it was as strongly marked with its own accent as any local speech in England or America today. Jews everywhere would know them for Galileans, as English people everywhere recognize the man from Lancashire or Somerset, as the servant girl in Jerusalem recognized Peter when Jesus was in the hands of the high priest. Provincial accents vary; some we admire, some we smile at. The Galilean was of this latter sort. The men of Judea mocked it, very much as Saint Augustine's African accent caused his Italian friends to mock his speaking of the Latin he wrote so superbly. In synagogue services, it was customary for a member of the congregation to give an explanation of one of the Scripture passages just read: in Judea, Galileans were discouraged from giving it: to have the congregation giggling would not have been seemly.

Galilee, we have noted, was the richest part of Palestine, with fertile soil and a lake teeming with fish. But the wealth was not for the mass of Galileans. The patches of land worked by the peasants were rented from absentee landlords, living mainly in or near Jerusalem; by the time rent had been paid to the owner, tithes to the Temple, taxes to the Roman and local authorities, the tenant had so little left that one marvels how the unskilled laborer, who worked for him, could be any poorer. There was a vast fishing industry centered on the lake; along its shores fish were salted and cured and exported in great quantities—you could have bought dried fish from Galilee in Rome. But the profits were not for the fishermen.

Joseph, as a carpenter, was not in the subhuman poverty of a tiller of the soil or a lake fisherman. By our standards the poverty of the Holy Family might seem almost destitution, but not by any standard known in Galilee.

A Carpenter and His Wife

Like all the poor in Galilee, Joseph would have lived in a small house. He probably plied his trade in a corner of it.

We get some notion of what a carpenter did from the Jewish records. From the Mishnah, a codification of Jewish law compiled a couple of centuries after Joseph's time, we get a list of the things a carpenter made then, and we can take it as giving a fair notion of how Joseph spent his days. One of a carpenter's jobs was to square off beams to support the roofs and terraces of houses. He made doors and doorframes and frames for the windows. He made the wooden ploughs the farmers used, one-handled ploughs—when Scripture speaks of putting one's *hand* to the plough, it is being literally accurate. He made winnowing forks, harrows, harnesses for the plough-animals' wear and goads for their stimulation; he made beds, bins, wooden chests, chairs, and tables for those who could afford these extras, kneading-troughs, deed-boxes—all the normal daily things, in whose making wood was used, were for Joseph to make. And a small boy would be watching him as he made them, would soon be helping him, would at last be a carpenter himself.

The small boy would be watching his Mother too. She would begin her morning's work by grinding the wheat for that day's eating in a hand-mill, stone screeching on stone. She would knead the flour in the kneading-trough Joseph had made for her, then light the oven or brazier. She would bake the bread—the daily bread of the Our Father. There would of course have been no such thing as running water in the houses of the poor. There was one well for the whole village—it is still there—and it would be Mary's task to take her pitcher to the well and wait among the women gathered there for her turn to fill it. It may have been in those daily visits to the well that the women of Nazareth had first become aware that she was to have a child. A woman might spend all the rest of her day in the house, but for water she had to leave it.

Mary would prepare and cook the family meals. With this we come to the element in the life of the Holy Family which we spoiled moderns would have found most trying. Their food lacked richness and variety to a point which would have seemed to us unbearable. Meat would not be on their table often. There would be the lamb roasted at the feast of Passover; with luck they might have meat on other great feast days, like Pentecost or Tabernacles. For the rest it would be an occasional luxury, boiled usually, pieces of lamb or mutton barely visible in a small sea of rice. Bread, which might be of wheat or might be of barley, would be the staple diet, with fish, dried or fresh, when they could get it: the nearness of the Sea of Galilee did not necessarily mean that they got it often, for it still had to be paid for.

For the most part they ate vegetables and fruit. Galilee produces grapes, raisins, pomegranates, dates, figs. Vegetables were plentiful—beans, leeks, and others of the sort which I personally find uninteresting. There were no potatoes, of course; no tea, no coffee, for drink they had the local wine; no sugar—honey was used for sweetening. One speaks of bread as the staple diet, with dried fish to flank it. But the universal food, the necessary of necessaries, the utterly indispensable, was the olive—olives eaten as fruit, olives pressed into oil. It has been called the meat and butter of the poor. A family like Joseph's probably owned its own olive tree—not growing behind the house, but one of a large cluster of trees, each tree belonging to one family. The garden of our Lord's agony was Gethsemane; the word means "olive-press".

For the rest, we can think of Mary as occupying her day like the "vigorous wife" described in the last chapter of the Book of Proverbs: "Does she not busy herself with wool and thread, plying her hand with ready skill?" She would have made all the clothes for herself and her men, covers for the beds. All that could be done in the home she did. And she never lost contact with God, God in her soul, God playing on the floor.

In the Holy Family's early years in Nazareth, what was happening in their world? Palestine, remember — Judea, Samaria, Galilee, and all the bits and pieces — was only about the size of Vermont. News did not take long to spread from end to end of it. Further, the annual pilgrimages to Jerusalem for the feasts of Passover, Pentecost, and Tabernacles meant that nothing of any consequence happened anywhere in Palestine that was not known in Nazareth. In those early years most of the news was about the shedding of blood. Herod the Great's eldest surviving son, Archelaus, had begun by killings which the Jewish historian Josephus totals at three thousand. And that was only a beginning. One sees why Joseph decided to keep Jesus out of Judea while Archelaus reigned there.

What must have gripped the attention of Mary and Joseph most was the sudden upsurge of men claiming to be the Messiah: for the carpenter and his wife knew who the Messiah was. Three men whose names are known to us were emboldened by the death of Herod the Great to claim that they were the Expected of Israel; there were others as well, whose names have not survived. The three we know about all assumed the crown, all fought hard, all were slain. The most famous of them, Judas of Gamala, called the Galilean, established himself in Zippori, only a few miles from Nazareth, and his own slayings were on a considerable scale in all the area.

As I say, the whole of those early years streamed with blood. But one single picture remains horrifyingly in the mind. The Romans crucified two thousand men in and around Zippori, and left the bodies to rot on their crosses. Our Lady and her Son could hardly have gone to the edge of the town without seeing them; no

wind could have blown from that direction without carrying
their stench.

6 JOSEPH, MARY, AND JESUS

Ever Virgin

The Holy Family *was* a family—not a mother and a son with a
man in the house. Joseph and Mary were husband and wife, and
Jesus was the son of both; Mary's son by birth, Joseph's son
because Joseph had accepted him, which for Jewish law was
decisive. Joseph was the head of the house.

Saint Matthew tells us that Joseph "took unto him his wife.
And he knew her not till she brought forth her firstborn son and
he called his name Jesus." There are two words here that might
mislead one unacquainted with Jewish law and Jewish grammatical usage. We have already noted that a son was called firstborn
whether or not there were any sons born after him. What mattered
was that there were none before him.

And the statement that "he knew her not till" Jesus was born
does not mean that they began ordinary married life afterward: it
simply tells us what the situation was before our Lord's birth and
makes no statement at all about what followed it. We read in the
Old Testament (1 Macc 5:54) that the soldiers offered burnt sacrifice in thanksgiving "because none of them had fallen until all
returned safe and sound". Saint Paul tells Timothy, "Attend unto
reading, to exhortations and to doctrine until I come" (1 Tim
4:13)—not that Timothy was to drop his reading, preaching, and
doctrine afterward. We often talk that way ourselves. "God be
with you till we meet again", a song of the First World War, was
not saying that, once the singer and his friend *did* meet, God
might bow out.

Matthew and Luke tell us that our Lady conceived Christ our Lord virginally: the Church tells us that she was "ever virgin". Later we shall find mention of "brothers and sisters" of Jesus, but as we shall see, they were not Mary's children. Whatever Mary and Joseph's original intentions had been on taking each other as husband and wife, it must have been obvious to both of them, once God the Son was conceived in her womb, that they must live together virginally. Virginity for spiritual reasons was unknown in the Old Testament, even the word virginity is not to be found there. There is one single instance of a man accepting celibacy, Jeremiah, but the reason was not that which is primary to the Catholic choice of the virgin state—it was simply that the world was too appalling to bring children into. There is no example at all of a woman choosing it. But then there had been no example of a woman conceiving God in her womb. The sense of a sacredness attaching to material things that the power of God had especially touched is strong in the Jew as it is in the Catholic. The chalice in which wine has become the blood of Christ is not for ordinary drinking. The womb in which God's only begotten Son became man is not for ordinary childbearing. A lesser saint than Joseph, indeed any man with a tinge of religion, would know that that womb was sacred and sealed.

Artists have tended to picture Joseph as an old man—apparently on the principle that since Mary had a child she had to have a husband for the sake of her reputation; and obviously, since that was her sole reason for having a husband, the older the better. But such an arrangement, with Joseph merely brought in to keep the neighbors from talking, would hardly be a marriage at all, but rather a mockery of marriage. To repeat a phrase, Joseph was not simply a man living in the house. He was the head of the house, and within the family his word was law. And he was Mary's husband. We must think of them as truly husband and wife, with a true union of personalities, each bringing completion to the other, with a profound sharing of interests, sharing of lives, enriched by the special graces from God that their virginity called for.

We must remember that Mary and Joseph were both great saints. Sanctity is the right direction of energy, and the special energy it directs is the energy of love. Both loved God supremely, and their love of God poured back in a great flood of love of each other, love so great that it made the ordinary outward manifestation unnecessary. There was more love in that virginal family, more married love, than ever a family has known.

A Child Who Was God

God the Son, possessing the divine nature eternally, became man. Not laying aside his divinity, he made a human nature his own; and this nature was not a mask, wearing which he would look like a man and act like a man; it was not a pretense of any kind. His human soul and body were real, and really his; as your soul and body are real, are really yours. True God, he became true man.

Like other men, he began at the beginning—an embryo. Like the rest of us, he was born a baby, grew into a small boy, a big boy, a youth, a man. Human bodies have laws, and his was subject to them. Human souls have laws—logical and psychological among others—and his was subject to them. He had five senses, and they really worked. The outer world came through to his brain as he saw it, as he heard and smelled and felt and tasted it. His human mind took hold of what the senses had brought to the brain, acted upon it, reacted to it, went through all the processes of human thinking upon it.

This is what the philosophers call experimental knowledge—the way human beings learn by experiencing and by reflecting upon experience. One person can get more out of soul or body than another. When the person was God, he could get incomparably more out of them than any merely human person could have gotten. But they were still a human soul and a human body. If he had gotten more out of them than was in them, then they would really have been only a kind of fiction after all.

In other words, he did not take short cuts! He did not use the divinity of his person to bypass the difficulties of his humanity. As an infant, he had to be fed from his mother's breast. He could have nourished his infant body by an act of his divine omnipotence, but that would have been to turn his humanity, not into a farce of course, but to some extent into a fiction. Miracles, when he came to work them, were for others, not to save himself trouble. He had to learn to walk, and must be helped by his parents; he had to learn to talk, with them still aiding. We must not think of him as being able to talk all the time, and merely humoring them by letting them think they were teaching him. When he said his first clear word, they were delighted and proud. With their aid he had really accomplished something which his vocal organs and the experimental powers of his human mind would not have accomplished unaided.

If Mary and Joseph had not nourished the child adequately, he would have been undernourished, and his body would have shown it. If they taught him to speak with a Galilean accent, then he spoke with a Galilean accent—at any rate until such time as schoolteachers or the meeting with men of other provinces had let him hear a more conventional utterance. Many a child ends up more learned than his parents, but there is a time when they are his only teachers. So it was with Jesus. In his human mind there were certain supernatural gifts—direct vision of God, say Catholics, and prophetic knowledge. But in the order of natural knowledge, as in the order of bodily development, he grew like other men. It was in these two orders that Mary and Joseph had to play their parental part in his growth.

What part indeed had human parents to play in the upbringing of a child who was God? This was the first stage of the question how the union of God and man in one person would work out in actual fact. There was no precedent to guide Mary and Joseph. We cannot know, and only very cautiously can we try to think out, what it meant to them. How much did they know about the child that Mary, obedient to God's will, had consented to bear virginally? Mary had her essential function in the redemption of the human race. But was she an instrument only, used by God, or an agent, intelligently and lovingly cooperating with him all the way?

In the first view, the divine plan of redemption called for a human mother and she was used, that is all: she did what she had to do, and only learned, bit by bit—from the things that happened, like everybody else—who and what the Redeemer was. In the second, God showed her, at least in the main lines, what redemption would mean, what her own function in it would be—which involved knowing that her son was divine, whether or not the doctrine of the Trinity had been revealed to her.

Scripture does not tell us which view is right. The Church does not tell us—at least explicitly. Scholarship will not settle the matter. Which view we take will depend on our idea of God, on our idea of parenthood, and ultimately on that profoundest element in our own self which decides—not, alas, infallibly—between the tolerable and the intolerable, the thinkable and the unthinkable.

It is to me improbable that she should have been simply left to find out who and what the child was that God willed on her. She is the only person, human or divine, who could say to God the Father "Your Son and mine." She was *not* just anybody—she had been drawn into what it is not fantastic to call a family relation with the Blessed Trinity. The idea is to me monstrous that God should not have told her the first thing about the Son who was his before becoming hers—the *first* thing, note.

That is how it seems to me. Yet I realize that in judging that God would have done thus or thus, I am in danger of simply deciding what I should have done had I been God! It is a danger to which all men are continually exposed, especially scholars, in love with their theory or system: the important thing is to be aware of it, to be constantly checking one's judgments in the hope of excluding it, not to be too absolute where God has not spoken.

Those may be right—though they too are fallible, and do not actually know any more about it than I—who hold that her Son's divinity was not, in the beginning, especially revealed to Mary. Yet explicit revelation is not the only way. She of all people could hardly have lived in that moment-to-moment intimacy with a child who was in fact God and not come to total certainty of his divinity, a certainty which she would have communicated to her husband. If so, her and Joseph's every instinct must have been to lie prostrate in adoration of his divinity. But that would have meant failing in their duty as parents. While they lay prostrate, the child would have died! Having God in the house like that, we feel would have kept them in a state of stricken awe, ecstasy shot through with anguish. All babies are adorable, of course, but this one was, literally.

We wonder how they could ever have gone about feeding and washing and dressing him. But in fact we have a not totally dissimilar experience ourselves: God-made-man is as truly present in the Blessed Eucharist as in the house in Nazareth. If we were so stricken with reverent awe that we could not bring ourselves to receive him into our body, we should be nullifying his whole purpose in being there sacramentally. Had Mary and Joseph simply lain prostrate in adoration of his divinity, they would have been refusing their cooperation in his plan for our redemption. If they knew him as divine, they had to adore him; because he was their child, they had to bring him up—probably with many a secret prayer to him as God's Son for guidance in bringing him up as theirs!

Let us remind ourselves what the Incarnation meant. The second Person of the Blessed Trinity, retaining his nature as God, took to himself a human nature. This one Person had two natures, divine and human. But whether he was doing the things of God in the one nature or the things of man in the other, it was always the Person who did them; and the Person was God only. Whatever was done or suffered or in any way experienced was done, suffered, experienced by God the Son. There is profound mystery here. If God had not revealed it, the human mind would never have suspected it. But he has revealed it. The actions in the human nature of Jesus were truly human, but it was God who performed them.

It may seem that I am emphasizing a truth already sufficiently clear. It can never be clear enough. As we read the Gospels, it must be continuously in our minds that it was God the Son who was doing all these things, suffering all these things. Otherwise we are not seeing what really happened. The fifth-century heretic Nestorius is said to have asserted that he could not believe that the infant at the mother's breast was God. And we ourselves may feel something of the same difficulty. But the greatest monarch ruling, the greatest poet writing, the greatest scientist discovering—these are no nearer to the infinity and omnipotence of God than a newborn baby wailing. Compared with the infinite, the mightiest of created things is less than a speck of dust. God taking our nature and being more majestic than man has ever been is not by the shadow of a hair's breadth less mysterious than God taking our nature and being an infant.

So we come back to the mystery with which Mary and Joseph had to live daily, however much or little they realized it. The child *was* God. God the Son had become *true* man, not calling upon his divinity to do what in all other men their humanity must do. That he was true man means that in the early years of Nazareth he was true child. He had to be nourished as other children are—or God would have been undernourished; washed as other children are, or God would have been left unclean; dressed as other children are, or God would have lain naked. He had to be taught to walk, taught to talk: the Word had to learn the use of words.

Small Boy in Nazareth

In all this Mary and Joseph had to help, as our parents helped us. In the order of experimental knowledge, he may well have made progress at an astounding rate, but progress he did make. He grew not only in stature but in wisdom (Lk 2:52). As God he had infinite wisdom, but in the human mind that was now his there had to be growth in wisdom. What they must have found most dazzling was teaching him his religion—*his* religion. What was it like to be teaching God about God?

Prayers would come first, the simplest prayers, using the words he had thus far mastered. Then the simpler truths. The great feasts must have helped. We Christians begin to be taught something about Christmas and Easter as tiny children. Mary and Joseph must have told him about the feasts of Passover and Pentecost. They did not yet know about a Passover thirty years away, or a Pentecost fifty days after that.

The time came when Jesus was old enough to be taken to the synagogue. The Sabbath service there began with the reading of the Shema, three passages of Scripture. We know that the devout

Jew would recite the same three passages in his morning and evening prayers. Since Jesus said them twice a day, it is worth our while to look at them ourselves.

The first passage was Deuteronomy 6:4–9, beginning, "Hear O Israel: the Lord our God is one Lord. Thou shalt love the Lord thy God with thy whole heart, and with thy whole soul, and with thy whole strength. And these words which I command thee this day shall be in thy heart. And thou shalt tell them to thy children: and thou shalt meditate upon them sitting in thy house, and walking on thy journey, sleeping and rising."

The second passage was Deuteronomy 11:13–21, beginning, "If you obey my commandments, which I command you this day, that you love the Lord your God, and serve him with all your heart, and with all your soul: he will give to your land the early and the latter rain, that you may gather in your corn, and your wine, and your oil. . . . "

The third was Numbers 15:37–41, beginning, "The Lord also said to Moses: Speak to the children of Israel, and thou shalt tell them to make to themselves fringes in the corners of their garments, putting in them ribands of blue: that when they shall see them, they may remember all the commandments of the Lord . . . may do them and be holy to their God."

All three passages are concerned with the commandments. It is fascinating to see what our Lord did with them when the time came for him to teach. The first he made the very center of his teaching, as it so evidently was of his life. When he summarized God's commands in the two commandments of love, this one he calls the first and greatest: the other, which is love of neighbor, depends wholly upon it.

But the second passage, which seems to promise earthly prosperity to those who obey God's word, and almost treats material well-being as a fruit of righteousness, is not part of his message: he carries men further and deeper: he tells them that they must be prepared for suffering and death for their obedience to him.

The third passage he never refers to at all—apart from a warning against taking the outward show of devotion as a substitute for the inner reality. Ribands of blue are not part of his message.

At six Jewish boys went to school. The class would have been held in the synagogue or, perhaps, if the weather was good, outdoors; and the children would either stand or sit on the floor. Reading and writing were taught first, though it is a reasonable guess that Jesus had learned to do both at home. The teaching was almost entirely scriptural, no mathematics worth mentioning, no geography, no history save that of Israel, no science. For the first four or five years, they were taught almost exclusively from the Torah, the five books of Moses.

Knowing the customs of the time, one wonders if Jesus was beaten at school. The Old Testament is convinced that beating is good for boys; and no one with any memory of his own school days will feel that the fact that he did not deserve to be beaten meant that he never was. Even the best of teachers suffers from his liver occasionally.

In teaching Jesus the Scriptures, his schoolteacher was spared the one major difficulty which, as we have seen, Mary and Joseph must have felt: for the schoolteacher did not know that there was anything special about this boy. What Gabriel had said of the child was one secret that they did not share with their fellow citizens of Nazareth. We know that when our Lord's public ministry began, and all Palestine was talking of his miracles and his wisdom, Nazareth was astonished. What! Jesus, the local carpenter? He had lived among them for thirty years, they knew him well, some of them had been at school with him, they had employed him often: there was simply nothing to prepare them for this!

In the year 6 A.D. there was a political happening which must have had a special meaning for the Holy Family, one that it had for no one else in Galilee, or even in Judea, which was more directly concerned. Herod's monstrous son, Archelaus, was dismissed from his rulership, after ten years of bloodshed. We have already noted that, immediately after his father's death, Archelaus had slaughtered thousands of Judeans. Compared with that, the slaughter of twenty babies in Bethlehem very shortly before seemed hardly worth remembering: some of the fathers of the slaughtered babies may well have been among these later victims. After ten years of it his subjects had had enough. Jews and Samaritans, those natural enemies, united in denouncing him to Augustus. The Emperor exiled him to Gaul and made Judea a province, under a Roman procurator. Of this province Jerusalem was not to be the capital; the procurator would rule it from Caesarea on the coast.

7 EPISODE IN THE TEMPLE

Every year, Saint Luke tells us, the parents of Jesus took the road from Nazareth to Jerusalem for the feast of the Passover. It was the greatest of Jewish feasts, commemorating the terrible night fifteen hundred years before when God forced Pharaoh to let the children of Israel go out of Egypt and their bondage. The story is told in the book of Exodus, chapters 12 and 13. The destroying angel slew every firstborn male in Egypt, animal and human, save only the firstborn of the Israelites—the angel passed over their houses. The feast was also called the Pasch from the Aramaic word meaning to pass over, Phase (two syllables!) from the similar Hebrew word.

It was only when a boy had reached the age of thirteen that he fell under the obligation laid upon all the menfolk to "present themselves before God in the place of his choice, at the three feasts of Passover, Pentecost, and Tabernacles" (Dt 16:16). Younger boys, though under no obligation, often went up to the Temple on these feasts, as did women, though they were not obliged to either. Joseph and his wife went every year.

When Jesus was twelve, they took him with them. They may have done so before, but this is the first visit of which the Holy

Spirit is concerned that we should know. This, indeed, is the only happening of which we are told anything at all in the thirty years between the return to Nazareth and the beginning of the public life. It is a mysterious episode, with great gleams of light, but a profound darkness as well. We can learn an immense amount by studying it, yet the meaning of the whole episode somehow eludes us. We can only guess why the boy did what he did.

They would have joined a large party in Nazareth at the start of the journey, and linked up with others when they reached the main road to Jerusalem from the north. In those days the road they took was about ninety miles, and they probably spread the journey over four days. Their party would not travel in any fixed formation; some would move faster, some slower; people would travel with one group of friends today, a different group tomorrow, a third group the day after. Only at the end of each day would families and friends reassemble.

They were in Jerusalem for eight days. On the first day, the fourteenth Nisan which was the first month of the Jewish year, the paschal lamb was sacrificed, either by the head of the family or by the head of the group if a number of families united for the occasion—there had to be no fewer than ten at the paschal meal and no more than twenty. On the way to the inner court of the Temple, the Holy Family passed through the outer court, and there the boy Jesus saw the moneychangers, and the men selling animals for sacrifice, whom he would one day drive out of the Temple, because they made his Father's house a den of thieves. There, perhaps, Joseph and his group bought, and were overcharged for, the lamb for their own sacrifice.

When the lamb had been slain, its blood was taken by one of the priests and sprinkled on the altar of holocausts. The lamb's body was skinned—but no bone was broken—and it was taken to the house where the family was to eat the paschal meal. The meal might last from sunset to midnight; on this day, and for the seven days following, only unleavened bread was eaten.

Next year, when he would be thirteen, Jesus, as firstborn son, would be under obligation to fast the whole day, in memory of the firstborn sons who had not perished when the angel of death passed over their houses in Egypt. We know—who of those present knew?—that the firstborn of Mary was the only-begotten of God, and that the slaying and eating of lambs at Passover were only a foreshowing of this boy who would give himself to be slain on Calvary, would give himself to be eaten in the Blessed Eucharist.

At the end of the eight days, Joseph and Mary started back for Nazareth. As we have seen, pilgrims might shift from one group to another; boys would quite certainly have darted about more than their elders; the road was so crammed with people on the move that there was no telling who was there and who wasn't. But at the end of the day when families came together again, there could be no doubt. Jesus was not there.

Mary and Joseph went looking for him among their relations and their friends, then started back for Jerusalem, asking every group—asking, surely, at every house they passed on the way. Back in the city, they knocked at every probable and improbable door. On the third day of separation "they found him in the Temple, sitting in the midst of the doctors, hearing them and asking them questions."

We have got into the way, some of us, of thinking that the twelve-year-old Jesus was teaching the most learned men of Israel. But this is not what Saint Luke says. What was happening was an example of a daily custom in the Temple. Groups would gather round a rabbi, and ask him questions, on theology or morals or ritual. He would give them the benefit of his learning, which would usually be very considerable learning. As part of his teaching, he would put questions to them. It was in one such group that his parents found Jesus.

He was not teaching the doctors, he was "hearing them, and asking them questions". It is clear that he was answering the questions put by the learned men who conducted the group: but we must realize that they were not searchers after truth asking him to enlighten them, but teachers using questions as part of their teaching method. His replies must have been brilliant, at any rate for a boy: because Luke tells us that all who heard him "were astonished at his wisdom and his answers"—and the Greek verb used is a good deal stronger than our word "astonished", they were quite "taken out of themselves"!

We, as we read the story, are not astonished, for we know who he was. Obviously he would have brilliant answers. What we should like to know is what were the *questions* he asked. Why did he pick those particular questions, whatever they were? Was it simply for the increase of his human knowledge, getting a kind of instruction that his teachers in the little school at Nazareth could not provide? Or was it to set the rabbis' minds moving in a new direction? If only Saint Luke had told us even one of the questions.

Mary and Joseph wondered too, and once again the Greek verb is stronger than the English: it was as if they had a sort of electric shock. Why? Not, one imagines, because his answers were brilliant. Most probably what startled, almost stunned them, was to see him *showing* his brilliance.

And the quality of his questions and answers was not the only variation from his normal conduct in Nazareth; there was also his behavior to themselves. As God, he had given the fourth commandment: Honor thy father and thy mother; as man he did not ignore it. We know that, when this strange episode was over, he returned to Nazareth "and was subject to them" once more. But clearly, in separating from them without even telling them in advance, he was not being "subject" to them.

That perhaps is why it was Mary who spoke to him and not Joseph. Joseph was the head of the family, and at Nazareth it was for him to make the decisions and give the commands. In any family a small boy who absents himself without permission for three days may expect to hear from his father! But both parents knew that this was no ordinary occasion: for the moment Jesus was not acting as an ordinary boy. It was his Mother who spoke to him. "Son, why hast thou done so to us? Behold, thy father and I have sought thee sorrowing." There was no rebuke here: she was not calling upon her small son for an explanation of an act of disobedience. She was simply telling him of Joseph's grief and hers.

Only twice in the Gospels is there an episode in which our Lady speaks to her Son and he replies. After this first one in the

Temple when Jesus was twelve, we must wait almost twenty years for the second, at the wedding feast of Cana. On both occasions, the Mother speaks once, the Son speaks once. And that is the whole of the reported conversation between them. We cannot afford to rush past either. Let us pause upon the first.

As we read the Gospels, we are conscious of two streams of action and utterance—our Lord sometimes acting and speaking as man simply, sometimes doing and saying things that only God could do or say. How early did this double stream begin? Did the small boy in Nazareth, normally behaving as a small boy, just occasionally remind them by word or deed that he was God?

We do not know. But the surprise his Mother expresses at his acting so entirely on his own, not consulting them or even telling them, suggests that this was the first time. She knew that there was divinity in him, because that message had come to her from heaven. From her own experience of nursing him, she knew that he was human. But how the divinity would express itself in the humanity—had she known that? Was this the first evidence?

"Son, why hast thou done so to us?" What had he done? He had let them go their way without him, separated himself from them, forsaken them. In her words we hear an echo of a cry not yet uttered: "My God, my God, why hast thou forsaken me?" Here is one sorrow of our Lady's that is not simply sorrow at her Son's sorrow, but a sorrow of her own with him as its cause.

There is a surprising thing in what she says, which leaves most of us totally unsurprised. Only the scholars would notice it. But one of them drew my attention to the strangeness of Mary's saying "thy father and I". In the language she was speaking, there was the same grammatical rule as in Latin—namely that the first personal pronoun should come first. One would expect her to have said "I and thy father". Any schoolmaster who had heard her would have been shocked at so glaring a breach of grammatical correctness. Perhaps no rule of grammar could bring her to put herself before her carpenter husband.

The boy answered her: "How is it that you sought me? Did you not know that I must be about my Father's business?" That is all. Saint Luke tells us that "they did not understand the word that he spoke to them"; and that on their return to Nazareth "his mother kept all these words in her heart." Let us look more closely at the words she found it so hard to understand.

Nineteen hundred years later, we still cannot be certain whether Jesus meant that he must be in his Father's house, or about his Father's business. In the Greek, neither word occurs, there is no noun at all, simply "my Father's". It is an idiomatic phrase which could have applied to either "house" or "business".

The earlier Fathers of the Church understood it as "house". And at any rate it reads more naturally that way, though it leaves Mary's question unanswered. The boy was not asking his parents why they had tried to find him, which would have been a ridiculous question to ask devoted parents. He was asking why they had gone searching the town for him. Didn't they know that the natural place to find him would be his Father's house? We remember a later occasion when he referred to the Temple as his Father's house—he drove out the moneychangers because they were making his Father's house "an emporium". Why hadn't Mary and Joseph come straight to the Temple?

If what he said was "about my Father's business", we *have* an answer to the question his Mother asked him. Why had he stayed behind in Jerusalem when they left? He had caused Mary and Joseph three days' anguish. Why? If there was work of his Father's that needed doing, work of which his parents could not be told, then he must do it at the cost of whatever suffering to them.

That is one problem solved. But what "business" of his Father's could he possibly be performing by joining a group gathered round a rabbi in the Temple, putting questions and answering them? We do not know. We should love to know.

There is something else. She had said "thy father", meaning Saint Joseph. The boy had answered "my Father", meaning God. We have already observed that when we are told that our Lady ponders, it is nearly always about something that the Old Testament has not told her. This was certainly an instance of that sort. In the Old Testament God is compared to a father, but the Jews did not address him as Father. In the thirty-nine books of her Old Testament the words "our Father" are not spoken to God. And her

Son, *her* Son, spoke of God as "my Father". Gabriel had said that he would be called Son of God. But how much more had he told her?

We do not know if these were some of the things our Lady pondered in her heart. Certainly Christians have been pondering them ever since; those who are given to pondering, of course. But there is one problem which must occur even to the most unreflective every time he hears the Gospel read—namely, the contrast between the anguish in her question and the cool matter-of-factness of the twelve-year-old boy's answer. "Didn't you know . . . ?" Catholic commentators think of Jesus as softening the hardness of the words with a smile, or even a caress. Whether we see it so depends on the picture we have in our minds of the Holy Family. We are safest, perhaps, when we stick to what the Gospels tell us—not how Jesus might have looked but what he actually did.

In this episode, as at the wedding feast of Cana, what he said gives an effect of brushing her words aside; but in what he did there was no brushing aside. At Cana he worked the miracle which she had so obviously asked for. From the Temple "he went down with them to Nazareth and was subject to them."

8   *CARPENTER IN NAZARETH*

After the episode in the Temple, the twelve-year-old boy went back with Joseph and Mary to Nazareth. "And he lived there in subjection to them, while his mother kept in her heart the memory of all this. And so Jesus advanced in wisdom with the years, and in favor both with God and with men" (Lk 2:51–52).

Thus Saint Luke ends his second chapter. The third begins with the emergence of John the Baptist from his desert solitude in the fifteenth year of the reign of the Roman Emperor Tiberius—

eighteen years afterwards. The words we have just had — thirty in Greek — are all Luke has to tell us of those eighteen years.

Scanty as this is, he is loquacious compared with the other three evangelists. Mark and John begin their narrative with the Baptist's mission, with no detail of what went before, save for John's marvelous "The Word was made flesh and dwelt among us." Matthew at least brings the Holy Family back from Egypt and settles them in Nazareth; but then he leaps the best part of thirty years to the Baptist, with nothing as to what happened between. Apart from Matthew's not very informative phrase, "in those days", no one of these three gives so much as a hint as to *when* John came out from his desert, the one point on which Luke spreads himself — forty whole words!

He Was Subject to Them

The last two verses of Luke's second chapter being all we have about the eighteen years in Nazareth, we must look at them closely. From them we learn four things — one about Mary, that she pondered; three about Jesus, that he was subject to his parents, that he grew in wisdom, and that God and his neighbors were pleased with him.

His Mother kept in her heart the memory of all this. Since the Immaculate Mother of God did not fully understand what had happened, it is not surprising if we do not fully understand it even now. But she kept pondering, and so must we: this is one of those things we have already noted — things that the evangelist did not relate idly, nor the Holy Spirit idly inspire. We must try to find out what it has to tell us. Observe that the episode has no sequel — no sequel, anyhow, known to us. No one mentions it again during our Lord's life, Saint Paul and the others say nothing of it in their Epistles; if it had any effect upon anyone present at it, the news has not reached us.

In this it resembles the episode Matthew tells about, the visit of the magi. One of the surprises of life in heaven may be to learn from the magi what their experience meant to them. Another may be to learn, from some person we have never heard of, the mighty things that flowed from what the boy did during the three-day separation from his parents. When they found him, he was in a crowd gathered round a rabbi in the Temple, answering questions and asking them: but obviously he had not spent three days doing that. How had he occupied the rest of the time? Was that occupation, whatever it may have been, the "business of his Father" which justified his extraordinary conduct? We do not know. It seems at least probable that Luke did not know either. Luke's story came from Mary. Did even she know? Or had Jesus kept that as a secret between his Father and himself? If so, it really would have been something for her to ponder over.

As to the scene in the Temple, the amazement probably did not spread much beyond the group actually present: it would have been a nine days' wonder for a handful of people. Nazareth, one imagines, never heard of it. The boy's schoolteacher would have been mildly surprised if some such account as Luke gives had reached him, and would certainly have dismissed it as exaggerated.

Of one thing we can be fairly sure—the boy never staged a repetition of the incident in school. If he had, the master would probably have decided that it was high time to flog some humility into him, as masters have done to brilliant boys in all ages. But Jesus did nothing so spectacular, in school or out of it. We cannot remind ourselves too often how startled his townspeople were when his public mission began. It is clear that the thirty years in Nazareth contained nothing to prepare them either for his miracles or for the incomparable power of his mind.

He lived there in subjection to them. In those dear distant days, it was normal for children to be subject to their parents. Anything else, indeed, would have been unthinkable. Why, then, does Luke bother to tell us?

One imagines two reasons. First, the author was talking about a child who was God, and one cannot lightly assume that *that* child would be obedient to parents, who after all owed to him their very existence. And, second, we have just been shown an occasion when he had not acted in subjection to them, but in total independence. Luke is now indicating how exceptional such independent action was.

When God the Son took to himself and made his own a human nature, he did really become man: as we have seen, his humanity was not a pretense. And since he had chosen to be born into our nature of a human mother, his childhood was not a pretense either. He *was* a child. By his own will he had become one of those to whom, as God, he had given the fourth commandment.

So he was subject to Mary and Joseph, but especially to Joseph, because the husband was the head of the family, and this *was* a family—not a mother and son, with Joseph there only because convention required a man. Jesus was obedient to Joseph and, to use our phrase once more, the obedience was not a pretense. He was not simply going through the motions of obedience, doing precisely what he was told because it was his duty, yet feeling all the time his own superior wisdom (as is indeed the way of lesser boys with their fathers). It was not play-acting. It was loving obedience, rich with gratitude.

Favor with God and Men

Jesus "advanced in wisdom with the years, and in favor both with God and with men". If we came upon these words in the life of a saint, we should assume, I think, that they were just a convenient way of ending off the boyhood, before coming to the adult life. We should not feel that every word must be weighed carefully by the reader, we should not feel that it had been weighed carefully by the writer. The words practically say themselves, at least of any saint who found sanctity early. They are almost a formula—as when in old ballads we come upon a stanza beginning, "When twenty years had come and gone".

The feeling that even with Luke they are primarily the ending of a period in Jesus' life, a graceful way of saying that he will tell us no more of boyhood and young manhood, is strengthened when we look back a dozen verses. For in verse forty he has already said something similar: "And so the child grew and came to his strength, full of wisdom; and the grace of God rested upon him."

It looks as if Luke thought he had finished off the first period of Jesus' life; but afterwards learned about the Finding in the Temple, inserted the episode, then once more ended with a graceful summary. (We find something similar in Saint John's Gospel where the twentieth chapter seems meant to end the story, then the twenty-first is added and similarly ended.)

But Saint Luke's phrase (like Saint John's) is not a mere formula; though the same words could be said, probably have been said, of any number of saints, we must still ask what they mean here.

Consider first the statement that *Jesus advanced in favor both with God and with men.* The Greek word used for "favor" is the word that Saint Paul uses for sanctifying grace, and with that Christ's soul was wholly filled. But it has not that meaning here, or in verse forty either. In both cases it seems to mean favor rather than sanctifying grace. Verse forty shows this by saying that the grace of God was "upon" him, not "in" him; verse fifty-two shows it by saying that he won *charis* not only from God, who can confer grace, but from men, who cannot. What the last words of the chapter mean is that the boy so behaved as to please God and men. And the men he pleased were the people of Nazareth, who would later try to slay him!

But that lay in the future. For the present they liked him. They did not see him as unique, but they saw him as excellent — one of the nicest young people in the place.

He Advanced in Wisdom

We must not think that some of Christ's actions were performed by God, some by man. All were performed by God — even those to all appearances least Godlike, as when he wept or thirsted. But the actions in his humanity were genuinely human. He did not call upon his Godhead to do for himself what in other men their humanity must do. His divinity was not a labor-saving device, his human actions being gone through for the sake of appearance. His manhood was no fiction. Our redemption depends upon its genuineness.

His human intellect was genuine too. In him as person his body and soul had their existence and the oneness of their being, as my body and soul in me. But it is not the function of the person, in me or in him, to dispense knowledge to the nature; on the contrary, knowledge comes to the person from the activities of body and soul. How an omniscient Person acts in the finite mind that he has made his own must be profoundly mysterious to us. No experience of our own sheds light here. We can only go by what the Gospels show him doing and saying, and what the Church he founded has taught us about him.

His soul, Catholic theologians tell us (cf. Decree of Holy Office, June 5, 1918), had direct vision here upon earth—the direct gaze upon God for which the rest of men must wait until they are in heaven. And Catholic theologians agree that whatever knowledge he needed as Redeemer and Teacher was directly communicated to his mind by God—the kind of knowledge we find in the prophets, though vaster, immeasurably so.

It is not possible for those who have had neither of these gifts to lay down the law about them. But at least neither seems to be a barrier to the normal processes of human knowing or to render those processes pointless. The direct vision is sheer *seeing*, not knowing by way of ideas, because God himself takes the place of the idea of God in the beatified intellect. It is not necessarily translatable into, or a substitute for, earthly knowing, which works by ideas. Indeed this non-conceptual knowing is on so different a level that it does not clearly seem to break through to earthly life. Only Christ had it while still upon earth: but we cannot trace it, or even think we trace it, with certainty in his words or acts. We do not feel, so to speak, that we ever catch him in the act of gazing upon the unveiled face of God.

On the other hand we do, again and again, find his acting or speaking in the light of knowledge, conceptual indeed but which can be in his human mind only because God "infused" it. Yet even this kind of knowledge will be all the more effective, one imagines, for the normal development of the intellect into which it is infused—no more than our Lord's Godhead is it a labor-saving device.

Luke tells us that *he advanced in wisdom.* Whatever additional lights he may have had, he had true experimental knowledge: that is, he learned by the ordinary ways of human knowledge; he meditated, as all of us should, upon what he had thus learned, and grew humanly in wisdom. In other words, his senses were not a façade but really brought the external world to his brain; his brain was there not only because he had to have a head in order to look like a man, and brains go with heads: he did not simply look like a man, his brain did what brains are meant for. Nor was his human intellect a toy, it was an instrument for use.

He learned from the people who taught him—Mary and Joseph first, then schoolteachers, and of course neighbors and friends and passing strangers—all the medley of people from whom one picks up this and that in the normal run of life. And he learned from the things that happened to him, in the house, in the town, in the countryside about him. His human mind was a more superb learning instrument and reflecting instrument than any other human being has ever had—because it came perfect from the hand of God, and the Person who used it did nothing to diminish its perfection: he perfectly used—and by using developed—every power it had. Yet it still worked by the processes proper to a human mind.

At school he was taught Scripture, first the books of Moses, then the rest of the Old Testament, and some of the great commentaries of Israel's scholars. In this matter, as always when we try to picture to ourselves what was actually happening, we are almost giddy at the thought of the boy Jesus reading the Old Testament, learning what it had to tell of the Messiah, of himself in fact. It is hard to think that he did not discuss it with his Mother: children do, naturally. And Joseph, the man of the house, would have been listening to such Scripture commentary from those two as man has never heard, listening and making his own contribution.

As the boy grew older, the talk would be freer. A time would come when he must be told that Joseph was not his father in the way of nature. Is it fanciful to think that his Mother told him not only of her own virginal conceiving but of God's message about the child himself? They were a living family, not a set piece. They were not three figures in a ritual, cataleptically rigid in their muteness about the things that mattered most, elaborately pretending that they were just like anybody else, each wondering

how much the others knew! A loving family shares everything—
shares knowledge, shares thoughts and wondering. In the beginning Mary pondered in her heart: she would have discussed her
pondering first with her husband, then with the boy, as he grew
toward manhood.

If family life means anything at all, the story of God's message
would have been gone over again and again: "The Holy Spirit
shall come upon thee, and the power of the Most High shall
overshadow thee. And therefore the Holy which shall be born of
thee shall be called Son of God." Did those words lead sooner or
later into discussion of the Trinity? I cannot pretend to know. I
can only record my own feeling that it would have been strange if
they did not. Mary was not just a convenience, to get him born,
Joseph not just a convenience, to keep the neighbors from talking.
They were the two people closest to God-made-man. If they *did*
come to talk of the Trinity or of Jesus' Godhead, we need not
assume that they used the terminology the Church has slowly
hammered out—Jesus had his own luminous experience of these
truths and may have conveyed their reality more luminously than
the Fathers of Chalcedon could have dreamed—or even comprehended! If only one knew—!

Growing up in Galilee

There are certain things we can know of Jesus' life in those
years—from looking at the countryside of Galilee, for instance,
from knowing what events in the great world would have been
talked about there, and from occasional things told us later in the
Gospels which must have had their beginnings in these years.

How did the boy spend his days? He would very early have
begun working hard, helping Joseph increasingly with the carpentry. But there were periods of holiday in every year, to say
nothing of the famous sabbatical year—every seventh year the
fields were not sown, the vineyards not pruned, all this as a way of
acknowledging that the land belonged to God. With farmers
doing the minimum in that year, carpenters would have time on
their hands. Four or five times in the thirty years before the public

ministry began, Jesus knew the easing down of labor in the sabbatical year.

As boy and young man, he must have moved about over Galilee. Very close, in the west, was Mount Carmel, sacred to every Jew for its association with the prophet Elijah. From its top, Jesus could look up and down the coast of Palestine, and far out into the Mediterranean. Fifteen miles or so to the east was the great lake, called variously the Sea of Galilee, the Lake of Gennesaret, and the Sea of Tiberias. He would have gone out in the fishing boats—a strong boy can always make himself useful. There were swarms of boys of course, strong boys and not so strong. He would not have known them all, but he may already have had his eye on a boy called Simon, with a less impulsive elder brother called Andrew, from the northern end of the lake: it is hard to imagine Simon at any age not taking whatever limelight was to be had. If he ever was out in Zebedee's boat, he would have met James and John, younger than himself probably but assertive— tempestuous men have usually been tempestuous boys.

So many places in Galilee were rich in history for one who knew the Old Testament as the boy knew it. He might sometimes have gone to the lake by way of Endor, for instance, where Saul, against his own law, visited the Witch and heard his own destruc- tion announced by dead Samuel, who so long before had anointed him. (If you have not read the passage recently, do look up 1 Samuel 28, and read it now; note especially the reason Samuel gives for objecting to being summoned back to earth.) But for us, perhaps, the main interest lies in his seeing places which would be famous forever after because of their connection with himself.

Four miles away from Nazareth was Nain, where he was to raise the widow's son to life; he may have known the widow; one cannot live thirty years in so small an area without knowing most of the people in it. On the way to the lake, he would have had to pass north or south of Mount Tabor, where one day he would be transfigured in a last gleam of glory before his death. On the shores of the lake, well to the north, was Capernaum, where he would preach the discourse on the Bread of Life which Saint John gives us in his sixth chapter. And further south, just above the

nearest point of the lakeside was Magdala. Mary, out of whom
seven devils were to be cast, and who was the first of his followers
to see him on the morning of his Resurrection, lived there; by the
time he was approaching the end of the hidden life, she may have
acquired the reputation which has caused all sinners of a particular
sort to be called Magdalens from that day to this—when they
repent, of course. If so, our Lord would have cared profoundly;
his longing to heal sinners did not grow upon him suddenly after
the public ministry started. We cannot imagine him as ever being
without it.

Nazareth was a backwater; but the yearly visits to the Temple in
Jerusalem meant that its people knew of all those happenings in
the great world which affected the Jews. One imagines the near
ecstasy with which, awhile after the Temple episode, the whole
Jewish people reacted to the crushing defeat of the Roman legions
by the Germans, far away at Teutoburg. There is always delight
for a conquered people when their conquerors suffer defeat by
anyone at all: the Jews of Palestine must have found this Roman
defeat quite peculiarly delicious, because the slain leader of the
Roman army was Varus, and it was not so long since Varus had
put down a Judean rebellion and crucified two thousand Jews.

Six years later, all Palestine, like all the world, was talking of
the death of the Emperor Augustus. He had ruled alone for
forty-four years, and by any standard then known it was good
rule. As we have seen, there were those among his subjects who
saw a new era of the world beginning with him, so that they
would even have dated it with the year One: they did not know
how nearly right they were about the new era. In his lifetime the
Roman poet Horace has Augustus reclining among the gods, his
mouth empurpled, like theirs, by the wine that makes the gods
feel more godlike. Upon his death the Roman Senate decreed that
he had become a god. We, with no axe to grind to sharper edge as
Horace had, and no experience of living under his rule, content
ourselves probably with imagining some of his merrier meetings
in the next world—with Cleopatra, for instance, who had preferred snakebite to a last earthly meeting with him.

His death had one result which was to affect Jesus. For his successor was Tiberius, who twelve years or so later was to appoint Pontius Pilate as Procurator of Judea. Jesus lived under only two Roman Emperors: by the decree of one of them he was born in Bethlehem (did dead David thank dead Augustus for that?); the official appointed by the other had him crucified on Calvary, five miles from his birthplace.

In the year 19 Tiberius expelled all Jews from Rome (Claudius was to do it again in 49—the early Church felt the effect of that later expulsion). So vast an assault upon their own people must have at once distressed and enraged the Jews of Palestine. But what must have frightened them in a personal way was that Tiberius conscripted four thousand Jewish men and sent them to the army in Sardinia. Owing to all the rituals to which Jews were subject by religion—in the matter of food, for instance, and of washing, to say nothing of the unbreakable Sabbath rest—Rome had made a practice of not conscripting Jews: but it is the first step that counts, and Jews everywhere must have had the feeling that this action of Tiberius might be the beginning of the end for their exemption.

In fact it was not. People bound by so many restrictions were more nuisance than they were worth in the army, especially the army of the Romans, who made a rule of respecting the religions of their subjects. So the young man Jesus was not called up for military service. What would he have done if he had been called upon to draw the sword in one of Caesar's wars? Would that have been one of the things of Caesar which must be rendered unto Caesar?

In the year 18 a much smaller thing happened, which was to affect our Lord more closely. Caiaphas became high priest, and worked hand-in-glove with his father-in-law Annas, who had already held the same position and had a rather touching interest in the careers of his children—he managed to have five of his sons, as well as this son-in-law, made high priest.

The men who were to crucify our Lord were moving into position. There remains to mention only Herod Antipas.

He had some of his father's gift for flattering emperors. Already he had built a wonderful new city on the shore of the lake, called it Tiberias, and moved his capital there from Zippori, which, as we remember, was only a few miles from Nazareth. In the last year of the hidden life, Herod made the one crashing mistake of his own life. He divorced his wife and stole the wife of one of his half-brothers. Her name was Herodias, and she had a daughter Salome who danced. In the end the hatred of his first wife's father lost him his tetrarchy: he died in exile.

A Larger Family Group

As the Holy Family go to live in Nazareth, darkness swallows them. When at last the darkness lifts, the family we see is not the same—one face has gone, and there are new faces.

When the hidden life ended, Joseph must have been dead. He does not figure in Jesus' public life at all, and it is unthinkable that in a Jewish family the father should go unmentioned, even more unthinkable that Mary should move about so freely with other relatives but without Joseph, if he were still alive. For Catholics, he is the patron of a happy death: he died, we feel certain, as we should all wish to die, in the presence of Jesus and Mary. Our favorite prayer to the Holy Family ends: "Jesus, Mary, and Joseph, may I breathe forth my soul in your blessed company."

But, if the family was smaller by Joseph's death, it was larger by a number of people for whom nothing so far written in the Gospels has prepared us. Immediately after Jesus worked his first public miracle at Cana, John tells us (2:12): "He went down to Capernaum with his mother, his brethren, and his disciples." Let us pause upon these brethren.

Remember that brethren simply means brothers; it is a different form of the plural, much as the word cow has two forms of the plural, cows and kine. The word kine is by now just about dead in English. The word brethren would be dead too, but for its use in the pulpit. Anyhow there is no difference between the words brethren and brothers. English has the two forms of the plural of brother, but Hebrew has not, nor has Aramaic, nor Greek, nor Latin.

So Jesus had brothers. Were they actually blood brothers, children of Mary and Joseph, conceived in the usual way of marriage after the virginal conception of Jesus?—not that that would have made them brothers, but half-brothers only, for Joseph would have been their father and he was not the father of Jesus. But in fact the word "brothers" did not necessarily mean for the Jews sons of the same parents. It could mean any close relation.

The Jewish language had no separate word for cousin, or indeed for uncle or aunt. They could of course have described a cousin as the son or daughter of a man's father's sister: it was easier to say "brother" or "sister". And so they normally did. We find plenty of instances in the Old Testament. Lot, for instance, was the son of Abraham's brother, Abraham's nephew therefore, but he is called his brother (Gen 14:14). Laban, who switched daughters on the unfortunate Jacob, was the cousin of Jacob's father, but Laban calls Jacob his brother (Gen 29:15). Later in the Old Testament (1 Chron 23:21 and 22) we find the sons of Cis (better known to readers of English as Kish) marrying their "sisters", which would have been incest if the sisters had not been in fact cousins, daughters of Cis' brother.

Thus, mention of Jesus' brothers need not mean that they were blood brothers, the word would equally have been applied to cousins. We know the names of four of our Lord's "brothers". When he was already showing the power that was in him, we remember how the people of Nazareth expressed their astonishment: "Is not this the carpenter's son? Is not his mother called Mary, and his brothers James, Joseph, and Simon and Jude? And are not all his sisters here with us?" (Mt 13:55).

Were the four thus named as his brothers, and the numerous nameless sisters, actually his blood brothers and sisters? We know that they were not. If we read the accounts of the Crucifixion—Matthew 27:56, Mark 15:40, John 19:25—we find that the mother of the first two in the list, James and Joseph, was Mary of Cleophas, called by John our Lady's "sister". So that the first two men in the list were cousins of Christ: it is hardly likely that the other two were blood brothers, relegated to numbers three and four on such a list.

Who was Mary of Cleophas? John calls her our Lady's "sister" (19:25), but that too could apply to any close female relation. Hegesippus, who was born early in the next century, says that Cleophas was Saint Joseph's brother, so that his wife would have been our Lady's sister-in-law. One of the disciples with whom Christ walked to Emmaus after the Resurrection (Lk 24:18) was named Cleophas, but no one seems to think he was the same person.

Coming back to the four "brothers"—we find among the twelve apostles two Jameses, two Simons and two Judes (Judas is the same name). As well as James the son of Zebedee, there was a James the Less, son of Alpheus; as well as Simon who became Peter, there was a Simon the Zealot; as well as Judas Iscariot, there was a Jude also called Thaddeus.

Similarity of name is not decisive with these any more than with Cleophas; but it seems fairly sure that James the son of Alpheus was the same as James "the brother of the Lord" who became bishop of the Christian body in Jerusalem, whom Paul visited in Jerusalem (Gal 1:19), and who wrote the Epistle which bears his name. And Jude, who also wrote an Epistle, calls himself brother of James. How, we may wonder, could James be both son of Alpheus and son of Mary of Cleophas? Alpheus, think some, might have been this Mary's first husband; more probably, perhaps, just as Saul took the Latin name Paul for a second name, Alpheus may have adopted the Greek name Cleophas (roughly the same name as Cleopatra, though that would hardly have been his reason for making it his own).

There is so much about all this that the evangelists do not tell us: but at least it looks as if the two families—Mary and Jesus, Mary of Cleophas and her children—were living close together, very much as one family, in Nazareth; perhaps after the deaths of Joseph and Cleophas. We note that John the Baptist, who was also a cousin, is never called a relation at all: but these others retain the title of "brothers of the Lord", and we find them acting as a family group.

Immediately after the marriage feast of Cana, as we have seen, "his mother, his brethren, and his disciples went to Capernaum"

(Jn 2:12): it looks indeed as if the whole family moved out of Nazareth, and made their home in Capernaum. After Jesus' Ascension, we find his Mother and his brethren in the Upper Room (Acts 1:14). In between they are with Mary outside the place where Jesus is preaching in Capernaum (Mk 3:31); later they are telling him why he should go up to Jerusalem for the Feast of Tabernacles (Jn 7:3).

But a couple of verses after this last reference, John almost takes our breath away by saying, "Even his brethren were without faith in him." In other words, just as he had done nothing to show the people of Nazareth how much more than man he was, so even within the closeness of the family group, he and Mary kept his secret. When he said (Mk 6:4) that a prophet was honored everywhere "except in his own country and in his own house and *among his own kindred*", he must surely have had in mind these "brothers" and "sisters" of his. For them, as for the townspeople generally, he was simply the carpenter. The cousins, of course, were to learn better: some would die as martyrs for him.

Thirty, and Not Married

We are round thirty years from Jesus' birth in Bethlehem. Very soon now his cousin, John the Baptist, will emerge from his desert and begin the mission of preaching and baptizing which brought our Lord out from his carpenter's shop and prepared the three years of teaching and miracles, at whose end he was crucified and mankind was redeemed.

There was one thing that must have struck the townspeople as singular about him: he was thirty and he was not married. Remember the rarity of virginity among the Jews—not one woman in the Old Testament, among men only the prophet Jeremiah, and he had accepted celibacy for no spiritual reason. There were eccentrics, Essenes and perhaps the sect at Qumran, withdrawn in communities of their own and remaining celibate (again for no profoundly spiritual reason—Josephus says it was because wives "give the handle to domestic quarrels"). Anyhow the carpenter was no eccentric, and he plied his trade in his own town. In Palestine men usually married round twenty. The fathers of marriageable daughters must have weighed him up and found him eligible. Those opinionated cousins of his must have asked him what he thought he was up to, still celibate when he should have been married these ten years. Mary knew why, but it was not her secret to tell.

But this was the only peculiarity (and it was not in his favor). For the rest, the town took him for granted. Even when all Palestine was ringing with his miracles and the power of his utterance, Nazareth would have none of him—they had known him all his life, been to school with him, some of them, had him do their big and small carpentry jobs—ploughs, doorframes, wooden boxes.

Their reaction to his fame was a "What, *him?*"—amused smiles perhaps to begin with, such rage when he at last came to speak in their synagogue that they tried to kill him. Imagine your own plumber suddenly turning preacher and miracle-worker after many blameless years of mending leaks in your water pipes. You would not be the first to believe, I think. Neither was Nazareth. They simply could not take all the high talk about him seriously, they knew him too well. He might fool others, but not Nazareth, never Nazareth. Not one of his apostles, apart from his own cousins, came from his own town.

They took him for granted, I say. But there is a danger that we his followers, who would as we hope die for him, may take him for granted too. All his life they had known him as a man and could not believe he was more. All *our* lives we have known him as God and have got used to the wonder of it: we can say Jesus is God and never miss a heartbeat: as the people of Nazareth could say Jesus was a carpenter and think no more of that.

It is worth our while to pause occasionally and look steadily at the mystery, so that the accustomed phrase will sound again in our mind in all its mysteriousness, almost blinding us in its wonder. We cannot be forever missing a heartbeat over the central truths of the Faith, over Trinity and Incarnation: but if we never do, it means that they have never come alive to us: religiously our pulse runs weaker than is good for us.

Let us look steadily at him. He was a carpenter in a town which, even in insignificant Galilee, was despised as insignificant. He was not playing at being a carpenter, as Marie Antoinette and her ladies played at being shepherdesses at Versailles. He *was* a carpenter; the household depended on what he made; if trade was bad his Mother had to go without. The locals hired him to make and mend in wood. He would name a price and it would be a just price. They would haggle as is the way of the East, beating him down, asking doubtless if he thought they were made of money. In a better mood (having got the price down, perhaps) they might offer him a drink.

And he was omnipotent God, the second Person of the Blessed Trinity, by whom all things were made, including the wood of his carpentry, and the drink, and the customer who was arguing with him about the price: including his own human body and human soul—that human soul which had to sustain the wonder of his divine self and not be blinded by it.

9 *THE MISSION OF JOHN THE BAPTIST*

Forerunner

All four evangelists begin Jesus' entry into public life with John the Baptist's emergence from his desert. Matthew leaps straight to John's mission after the return of the Holy Family from Egypt, Luke after the finding of the boy in the Temple. The other two actually begin their Gospel with it, nothing of our Lord's earthly life being told before, apart from John's "The Word became flesh and dwelt among us."

It is clear, then, that John the Baptist's mission was essential: Jesus' own mission needed it. In his Gospel, Saint John interrupts his breathtaking Prologue about the Incarnation of the Word (which we Catholics read as the Last Gospel at Mass) to say: "There was a man sent from God, whose name was John. This man came as a witness, to give testimony of the light, that all men might believe through him." So that the Light of the World, the Light which of all lights could surely not be hid, needed someone to give testimony to him, needed John to give testimony to him!

Little is said in the New Testament to show why John's work was thus essential. Our Lord praises him indeed: "Amongst those that are born of women there is not a greater prophet than John the Baptist" (Lk 7:28): and he was not lavish of praise; pause a moment and try to think of anyone else he praised. But although Jesus says (you will find it in the verse before) that John was to prepare his way, it is hard to find any hint from him as to why any preparation at all was necessary for a mission as powerful in word and as studded with miracles as his. We are not shown in the Gospels mighty things flowing from John's work into Christ's. And in the rest of the New Testament nothing much is made of Saint John's mission either. Saint Paul never refers to it at all, though he must have known about it, since the only description we have of John's origin is given by Paul's companion and disciple, Luke.

Thanks to Luke, all the same, the Church has been intensely aware of John ever since. He is one of that small and immeasurably select band to whom we say the Confiteor at every Mass and daily in our own prayers. Great saints have been named after him— Saint John Baptist de la Salle, for instance, who founded the Brothers of the Christian Schools in the seventeenth century; Saint John Baptist de Rossi, the eighteenth-century saint whose own instincts were rather like those of his namesake; in the nineteenth century the Curé of Ars, Jean-Marie-Baptiste Vianney, who would have loved a desert but was never allowed by God to go to one. The number of not spectacularly saintly persons who bear his name is, of course, beyond counting—the great French writer of comedy, Molière, for instance, was Jean-Baptiste Poquelin.

But all that this means is that the parents of the saints, to say nothing of the parents of the dramatist and of the unnumbered others, had a great devotion to the son of Zechariah and Elizabeth, not that they had any clear understanding of why it was essential that our Lord should have him for a forerunner, or why he should have anybody for a forerunner. What herald could *he* possibly need? Their devotion was almost certainly not to the prophet without whom Christ's mission would have lacked an essential element: it was to the child whose birth had been foretold by Gabriel, the child who had leaped in his mother's womb at the sound of Mary's voice as she entered the house of his parents with the second Person of the Blessed Trinity in her womb: it was to the man who had paid with his head for telling the truth about Salome's mother.

From John's circumcision until the day he began his great mission in preparation for Christ's greater mission, there is a gap of thirty years, and only two phrases to tell us anything about them. The first: "The child grew and was strengthened in spirit"— probably the spirit here is the Holy Spirit: the whole phrase is at once like, and not quite like, what is said of our Lord in verse 40 of Luke's second chapter. The second: "And he was in the desert until the day of his manifestation to Israel."

Zechariah and Elizabeth were both old when John was born. The general view of commentators is that they died when John was young, and that it was as a child he chose the desert rather than the priesthood to which, as his father's son, he was entitled. The whole Jewish priesthood had been a mighty thing, but a foreshadowing only. Now that the Reality it foreshadowed was itself in the world, John had a duty mightier still.

To the south of Jerusalem one finds two areas of rock and chasm, one running westward, the other eastward toward the Dead Sea, where to this day a man could live in almost total solitude. Here, probably, John the Baptist made his long novitiate. It has been suggested that he spent part of the time with the Essenes, as Josephus was to do in his late teens. They were a rigorous, ascetical sect. If he did, his teaching is in reaction against theirs.

But we have no detail of his desert life, save what he ate and what he wore. He wore a garment whose shape, if it had any shape, is not told us: it was made of camel's skin—the nomads used the same material for making tents. Round his waist was a strip of leather. He ate, so Matthew and Mark tell us, locusts and wild honey: the locust is a flying insect about two inches long: the Bedouins still eat them, dried in the sun and salted to taste. What he ate and what he wore must have mattered very little to John: it was not merely asceticism that took him into the desert, he could have been ascetical at home. Solitude was what he wanted, the solitude in which the strong soul called to it reaches maturity most surely.

Did the devil bother him? John's strange, improbable conception—of a mother past her menopause and an elderly priest—was a nine-days' wonder in and about the Temple. Satan could not have failed to know of it. The child was worth watching. And then there were the long years in the desert. There was, of course, no descent of a dove upon John, no voice from heaven: but these things had never happened to anyone, and Satan had no means of knowing that they were the sign of signs. We know that the Pharisees would later be asking themselves, and ultimately asking John, if he were the Messiah. Satan could hardly have avoided wondering too.

The Baptist Emerges from His Desert

Anyhow, devil or no devil, a time came when "the word of the Lord was made unto John, the son of Zechariah, in the desert. And he came into all the country about the Jordan, preaching the baptism of penance for the remission of sins" (Lk 3:2).

A time came, I say, but just when did it come? Luke dates it with quite extraordinary abundance, telling us who was reigning everywhere, and who was high priest. But all the people he names cover a long space of years. And the one statement that ought to pinpoint the beginning of John's ministry—"the fifteenth year of the reign of Tiberius Caesar"—turns out to be no pinpoint after all. We cannot be certain whether the first year of a Roman emperor's reign was twelve months from his accession, or merely what remained of the calendar year in which his reign began. With Tiberius, there is a further complication. Augustus had appointed him as what we should now call a coadjutor with right of succession, two years before his own death. Luke may have been counting from that appointment.

Those scholars who think that he was have one strong argument on their side. It would mean that John began his mission in the year 26, and there is reason to think that that was a sabbatical year. Every seventh year, as we have noted, there was no sowing of the fields, no pruning of the vineyards, all as a way of acknowledging that the land was God's. Farmers did the barest minimum in that year. They had time on their hands: so had the city dwellers whose work was bound up with the produce of the farms. And this would explain how it was possible for "all the country of Judea and all they of Jerusalem" to go out to see John (Mk 1:5).

John came, preaching the necessity of repentance, and urging the repentant to be baptized. His initial success was quite extraordinary. He must have baptized thousands in the river Jordan, baptizing all who asked for it—the Essene rigorists would baptize only after a long probation. He was called John the Baptist—by Jesus, by his own disciples, by Herod. It was as John the Baptist that Salome demanded his head on a platter.

None of this means that John was the inventor of baptism. He was *the* baptizer par excellence, but practically all religions had practised some form of religiously significant washing of the body. Almost all the great paganisms had it, and still have it. The Jews had it. In John's own day a Jew who had been defiled by contact with a Gentile would wash his body to cleanse himself of the defilement. In the sixteenth chapter of Leviticus, we find it united with confession of sins: the high priest must "confess all the iniquities of the children of Israel", and "shall wash his flesh in the holy place". But this is a generalized confession, not a confession of the individual's own sins.

What was special—not unique, of course, but special all the same—about John's preaching was his insistence that the individual confess his own sinfulness. And, since it is normal to men to find some bodily expression for anything they feel strongly, they would respond readily to a cleansing of the body which was so apt a symbol of the cleansing of the soul.

But what put John in the line of the very greatest of Israel's prophets was his calling upon men to repent because the Kingdom of heaven was at hand. His word for "repent" is *metanoeite,* which means literally change of mind, or more profoundly change of soul, a turning away from sin in the living depths of the being. This, indeed, in the end, was what caused the rulers of his people to turn against him. That a new kingdom should come with the Jewish people ruling the whole earth—that they expected. But they had not often been told that there must be a profound spiritual change within themselves to make the kingdom possible.

John went further. To the Pharisees, who were the spiritual vanguard of Judaism, and the Sadducees, who held the high priesthood, he used the only violent words that ever seem to have come from him: "You brood of vipers, who has shown you to flee from the wrath to come?" That was bad enough. But the unforgivable thing was to follow: "Think not to say within yourselves, We have Abraham for our father. For I tell you that God is able of these stones to raise up children to Abraham" (Mt 3:7, 9). In other words, racial descent, their special pride and glory, was not to be the test.

It is interesting to note that for John as for Christ, his cousin, it was the high ones of Judaism that called forth the most violent utterance. In general John astonishes us by his moderation. We should have expected twenty years of half-clad, half-starved life among wild beasts in a desert to produce a wild-eyed fanatic. If you had any such idea, read verses 10 to 14 of Luke's third chapter.

To people asking John what they should do, he simply said: Give your extra tunic to a man who has no tunic at all, give your surplus food to those who have not enough.

He is similarly moderate with the two classes hated most by the whole Jewish people. To tax collectors, coming for baptism and asking what they should do, he said not to extort more taxation than was due. And when the soldiers—Gentiles likely enough, with whom the Essenes would have had no contact—asked the same question, he told them not to use unnecessary violence, not to invent accusations, not to add to their pay by forcing money out of the helpless. This desert solitary could put his finger so precisely on their faults, perhaps, because so many soldiers had confessed to him. However that may be, advice of such moderation must have sounded, indeed must still sound, incredible to those who assume that an unbalanced diet must produce an unbalanced character.

The Leaders Are Not Pleased

All Judea was talking of John. Four hundred years without a prophet had left them hungry for prophecy. Prophecy, we remind ourselves, does not mean foretelling (though it can include that) but *forth*-telling, uttering the truth in the power of God. John worked no miracle. His utterance was enough.

Enough, that is, for the mass of the people. But the leaders of the Jews—with that instinct leaders so often have—saw him as dangerous. With our own enriched vocabulary, we can almost hear the word "rabble-rouser" as they discussed him among themselves. We have our Lord's word for it that they said he had a devil. If only he had confined himself to urging repentance and baptizing, he would have had their beaming approval. But he named sins, he named *their* sins. We have heard him calling them to their startled faces a brood of vipers—in the desert he must have seen many a viper with its unlovely brood.

They sent a deputation of priests and Levites to examine him: so John the Evangelist tells us (1:19). This John was one of the Baptist's disciples, and was probably there when the deputation arrived. They began by asking him who he was. He wasted no time on his genealogy—they probably knew it; anyhow, they knew that he was Zechariah's son, knew that he could have been a priest like themselves and had chosen not to be: he told them what they wanted to know—"I am not the Christ."

Was he Elijah, then? He was not.

Both questions were getting at his right to baptize. They knew from Ezekiel (36:25) that there was to be a cleansing with water in the power of God: "I will pour upon you clean water and you shall be cleansed from all your filthiness . . . and I will give you a new spirit . . . and I will take away your stony heart and give you a heart of flesh." The Messiah, then, would have a right to baptize. Elijah, too, since they believed that he would return to earth to anoint the Messiah. There remained one other possibility. Was he the Prophet?

A phrase of Deuteronomy (18:15) speaks about God raising up "a prophet of thy nation and of thy brethren, like unto me". Peter quotes this (Acts 3:22); so does Stephen (Acts 7:37) in the speech which ends in his stoning. The Jews of the first century, so long starved of prophets, saw it as promising some individual prophet, all the more special for being nameless, another Moses perhaps.

But John was not the Prophet either: he was only the voice of one crying in the wilderness, "Make straight the way of the Lord." This quotation from Isaiah the deputation brushed aside as irrelevant. They felt they could now put the question they had come to put: By what right was he baptizing at all?

John's answer contains two comparisons—of his own baptism with a mightier baptism; of himself with One mightier, already among them, for whom he was simply preparing the way. The four evangelists give each his own account of what John the Baptist had to say upon these two matters. Here I shall combine them.

As to his own right to baptize, he told the deputation nothing (but he told his own followers that it was God who had sent him to baptize with water). He said that his baptism was a cleansing of the body, not itself cleansing the soul, simply an apt symbol for the soul's cleansing. But that One was to come who would baptize with the Holy Spirit and with fire, a phrase they probably dismissed as prophetical jargon. We are not to assume that the Baptist meant more by "Holy Spirit" than the Old Testament "Spirit of God".

Of this One who was to come, who was indeed already among them, he says that he, John, is not worthy to untie the sandal strap.

Something else he says, which confirmed the suspicion the leaders had that John stood for danger to them. The mightier One to come had his winnowing fan in his hand, and would gather his wheat into the barn but would burn the chaff with unquenchable fire. They did not like this talk of wheat and chaff: they had always taken for granted that *they* were the wheat, and that the multitude ignorant of the Law were the chaff. But clearly John did not share their view: for he had called them a brood of vipers. From that time the faces of the leaders were set against him. They may not have suggested to Herod that he seize him, but they would not have been unhappy when he did.

10 *JESUS BAPTIZED BY JOHN*

Why, We Wonder

One day, while John was baptizing in the Jordan, his cousin from Nazareth presented himself for baptism. How long had John been on his mission? The evangelists, as is their way, give us no hint. Matthew says "then"; Mark says "at this time". Luke uses no phrase at all. The fourth Gospel is as "timeless" as the others; but at least it makes clear that Christ had already been baptized before the official interrogation of the Baptist.

Read what Saint Matthew says (3:13–17). John's opening words to Jesus were "I ought to be baptized by thee, and comest thou to me?" Our immediate reaction is to think that John was referring to the inferiority of his own baptism to the one he had said Christ would institute, the baptism of the Holy Spirit. But there are two reasons against this.

The first is what John the Evangelist reports the Baptist as saying *after* the baptism, that when Jesus appeared he had not known who he was. We remember the first meeting of the cousins when John in the womb of Elizabeth leaped for joy as Jesus entered the house in Mary's womb. We need not ask why the Holy Spirit did not in the first moment of this later meeting stir John to a similarly instant recognition; for the Holy Spirit had already told John by what sign he should recognize the Christ, and the sign had not yet been given. But why did one cousin not know the

other? Evidently they had not met as grown men: John had gone
to the desert as a boy; it may very well be that they never did meet
after that first meeting when each was in the womb. Certainly
nothing is made thereafter of their kinship.

What, then, did the words mean? One thing, surely. John was
baptizing sinners, in symbol of their repentance. His twenty years
of locusts and wild honey and total austerity in the desert had
given him the holiness which could recognize a holiness greater
than his own. Evidently it seemed to him monstrous that he
should be baptizing the man before him, and wholly appropriate
that he, the Baptizer, should startle the crowds he had been
baptizing by himself receiving the cleansing water at the hands of
another.

Jesus' answer to John is the second thing he is reported as
having said: the first was his answer to his Mother eighteen years
before, when she found him after a three days' search.

The second answer has the matter-of-factness of the first, and is
even briefer: "Let it be so for the present; it is well that we should
thus fulfill all due observance" (Mt 3:15, Knox version). We can
only guess why he found it due. It may well be that as John was
giving testimony to him, he felt that he must give his testimony to
John: and he chose this way of affirming John's right to baptize
which the Temple officials were to call in question. It may be
because he saw John's ministry and baptism as the high point of
the Old Testament and as a Jew wished to submit himself to it
before proceeding to the establishment of the new order. But
what matters to us, what mattered immeasurably to John, was what
followed.

The Dove and the Voice

When Jesus came up out of Jordan after being baptized by John,
"the Holy Spirit descended in a bodily shape as a dove upon him:
and a voice came from heaven: Thou art my beloved Son, in thee I
am well pleased." So says Luke (3:22).

Who saw the Dove and heard the Voice? The Baptist, certainly—
Matthew and Mark say so, the Baptist himself says so, as Saint

John tells us. But who besides? We are not told. If others present saw and heard, we must wonder what they made of the Dove, what they made of the words. There was nothing in the Old Testament to prepare them for the dove as a bodily shape for the Spirit of God: doves were offered in sacrifice, as by our Lady at the purification: but that was all the part they had in Jewish religion. To us, the dove is the symbol of symbols for the Holy Spirit; but to the crowd watching, it could have been only a bird, winging down and hovering over a youngish man, newly baptized. The Baptist knew it for more than a bird: the sign he had been promised by God was that the Holy Spirit should descend upon the One whose forerunner he was, and he tells us that he recognized the sign.

But did even he know the full meaning of the words uttered by the Voice? Other hearers, if others there were, did not. The Old Testament had not given that revelation of the Blessed Trinity in the light of which the word Son has its full meaning.

There was, of course, one other who heard the words and saw the Dove, Jesus himself. What the whole incident meant to him in his humanity we cannot know. Was its sole purpose to identify him to John the Baptist and show his uniqueness to any of the bystanders who saw it? Or had it some special significance for himself as well? He knew his own sonship, for he *was* God. Yet it must have been the same kind of thrill to his human soul as to any other creature of God to hear from the Father himself the words "in thee I am well pleased."

What of the Dove? Descending as fire, the Holy Spirit would one day open a new chapter in the life of the apostles. Descending as a dove, the Holy Spirit this day opened a new chapter in the life of their Lord. John's baptism was not the sacrament of baptism by water and the Holy Spirit, which Christ would one day establish; but when John baptized our Lord, water was there and the Holy Spirit was there.

We remind ourselves that, though Christ is God, his manhood was not merely a garment he chose to wear. He was not pretending to be a man for our redemption. He *had become* man for our redemption. His human nature was a real nature, and really human. Therefore it needed supernatural life, as ours does, if it was to do the things beyond nature which it is every man's destiny to do. As God, he knew all things and could do all things; but as man he needed the indwelling of the Holy Spirit in his soul.

This indwelling he had, in its fullness, at every moment. But there were moments when some special thing to be done called for special illumination. More than once we are told that he was acted upon, guided, by the Holy Spirit. The first occasion is the one we are now considering. It was after the descent of the Dove that he was "led by the Spirit into the desert"—the Greek word means "thrust", almost "hurled".

Why the desert? All human experience tells us that the soul should be alone with God before the beginning of any great work. Spiritual writers have written movingly upon this as a reason for the forty days of solitude. Scripture tells us nothing of that. All it says is—"Jesus was led by the Spirit into the desert *to be tempted by the devil*" (Mt 4:1).

11 *DUEL IN THE DESERT*

Forty Days' Fast

According to a very old tradition, the place of total solitude to which Jesus was led by the Spirit is a high hill, or low mountain (round 1600 feet perhaps), a little to the north of Jericho. An hour or two's walk from the place of his baptism would have taken him there. But whether or not it was in one of the many caves here, we are told that he spent forty days of complete fast.

Forty days may or may not be an exact count: forty was like seven, a kind of standard number. We are reminded of Moses and Elijah, who would one day be with him on the mount of the Transfiguration; Moses had fasted forty days on Mount Sinai before bringing down the Ten Commandments for the second time (Ex 34:28), and Elijah had fasted forty days on the journey to Mount Horeb where God spoke to him—not in the great wind or in the earthquake or in the fire but in the whisper of a gentle breeze (1 Kings 19:8). We are reminded, too, of our own less rigorous fasting in Lent. From Ash Wednesday to Holy Saturday, omitting the six Sundays of relaxed self-denial, there are forty days—by exact count!

Jesus passed the days of his fast alone with God, undistracted by people. There were wild beasts there, even an occasional lion or leopard perhaps. But they were no danger to the total innocence of Christ, and the mere noisiness of animals is not as distracting as the clatter of men's speech, uttering the muddle of men's thoughts. What his converse with his Father was we do not know, and it would be the worst kind of foolishness to try to guess. When at the age of twelve his parents lost him, we know nothing of those three days, save how they ended. So now we know nothing of the forty days, save how they ended: Satan moved in.

Satan Moves In

Modern Christians tend to see the devil as a sort of comic opera figure; they are half-ashamed of believing in him at all. Even those who know something of his deadly reality still think of him as a kind of extra, prowling about the fringes of the redemption. But in that great drama he is a principal. It was in order to be tempted by him that Jesus was led into the desert. And it was by the will of God that the three-year mission which was to end in our redemption was preceded by this conflict between the Redeemer and the Enemy. To understand why, we must see clearly who the Enemy was.

Man is not the summit of creation. He is made in God's image, but so are the angels. And they are higher in nature than man; for the spirit by which they are like God is the whole of their being, none of its energy has to go into animating a body, it does not depend upon a body for knowledge of the created universe. In nature they are, indeed, not only higher than man, they tower over him. But they too had to be tested; they had to make the choice between God and self. This test may have been given before they were admitted to the Beatific Vision—the direct seeing of God in which is all bliss. Whenever and however it happened vast numbers of them, led by one, made the wrong choice. They fell. Hell was their portion.

The leader of the revolt is the one who matters (in an old Irish phrase he is the abbot of hell). He was so constantly in Jesus' mind, that it would be foolish for us not to give him a little of ours. Jesus describes him as a murderer from the beginning, a liar, and the father of lies (Jn 8:44). The two qualities in him thus chosen for mention appear in the names given him. In Revelation he is called Apollyon, which means murderer. The commonest name for him is Devil, which means slanderer, one who lies about other people. Saint Paul is fond of the word in this meaning. In the Epistles to Timothy and Titus he warns his hearers against "devilishness" of this sort.

Jesus uses two other names. He calls him Beelzebub, which means Lord of Flies—anyone who has lived in a hot country knows what that means. The Greek has Beelzebul, Lord of the House, a Canaanite god. Most often he calls him Satan, the Enemy.

Why did he seek the conflict?

The first Adam had fallen to Satan's attack. The second Adam challenged Satan to a renewal of the conflict. The first Adam's defeat had left Satan, in fact if not in right, prince of this world— Jesus actually calls him so (Jn 12:31). If man was to be restored, Satan had personally to be overthrown. Indeed, at the time of the Fall, God's promise of a better day to come (Gen 3:14, 15) was uttered not in terms of man's restoration but only of Satan's defeat.

As punishment for causing man's fall, God would bring him even lower than his own fall had brought him: he should crawl on his belly and eat dust all the days of his life. Not only that. Man would utterly defeat him too: the seed of the woman would crush his head. We can see, dimly anyhow, why the Holy Spirit led Jesus to seek the opening battle of the decisive war. More clearly we can see why the devil accepted the challenge. Of all the persons in the drama of the redemption, he could least afford to be indifferent, for he knew that his head was to be crushed.

Very likely he did not know what the phrase meant. A pure spirit has no head for crushing. He had chosen serpent form, and God uttered his curse in serpent terms. Since then, Satan must have learned a meaning—bitter beyond our comprehending—for the phrases about going on his belly and eating dust. But he probably did not yet know, and could only torment himself with wondering, what the crushing of his head might mean. It carried the certainty of agony to be added to the agony in which he had dwelt from the time of his choice of self as against God. At least he was too intelligent to comfort himself with the possibility that what God had foretold might not happen.

He would, of course, strike at his conqueror's heel. But how should he know him? "Seed of the woman" was an odd phrase, with not much light in it for Satan. Myriads of men were born into the world, and he had lesser demons in plenty to strike at the heel of every one of them. But which was the one reserved for him? How many times had he struck at this one or that one, in the possibility that he might be *the* one, come at last?

He had good reason to investigate the carpenter of Nazareth with special closeness. We do not know how much he had seen or heard of the Annunciation and the birth in Bethlehem. But the Baptist—the first prophet in Israel for four hundred years, drawing men to repentance in their thousands—must have had Satan watching and listening. He would have heard the Baptist say that One was to come mightier than himself, and that all flesh should see the salvation of God. He would have seen Jesus coming to be baptized by John, and John urging that it should be the other way round. Had Satan seen the descent of the Dove, or heard the Voice saying: "This is my beloved Son"?

If he saw the Dove, it may have meant no more to him than to the bystanders: as we have noted, there is nothing in the Old Testament to show a dove as a symbol of God or God's power. From his twice saying to our Lord, "if you are the Son of God", we get the impression that Satan had at least heard the words. What did he make of them?

He may have never seen God. It may be that the Beatific Vision was the reward of the angels who remained faithful in the time of testing—but he had fallen. We cannot tell whether or not the doctrine of the Blessed Trinity had been revealed to the angels in their first state of grace, as our Lord has revealed it to us. If it had not, then the devil likely did not know it. He could then be only a strict unitarian; for, apart from revelation, I doubt this innermost truth about God can be known by any creature. But at least the phrase "son of God" would have struck him as having depressing possibilities.

The Duelists

"If the Son of God was revealed to us," says Saint John in his first Epistle, "it was that he might undo what the devil had done." We could not have a clearer rebuke to those who think of the devil as no more than a colorful extra in the story of our redemption, or a stronger statement of the reason why the Holy Spirit led Jesus to confront Satan at the very beginning of his public life.

Matthew and Luke describe the testing in some detail, Mark simply tells us that it happened. His Gospel, we remember, is what he has heard Peter preach; and we may imagine that Peter would find no pleasure in dwelling on the duel in the desert. For it ended with "Begone, Satan"—a phrase so close to the "Get thee behind me, Satan" which Christ later addressed to Peter himself (Mt 16:23) that the same Greek verb is used for both dismissals. Read the first eleven verses of Matthew's fourth chapter and the first thirteen verses of Luke's, weighing each incident, seeing the whole episode with your own eyes. The order of the second and third temptations is different in the two Gospels. I, like most people, follow Matthew—if only because he concludes his account (as Luke does not) with Christ's order to Satan to go away, and adds that Satan left him "until the time".

Have steadily in mind who the duelists were. One was the second Person of the Blessed Trinity, God from all eternity, yet true man in the human nature he had made his own. The other was a pure spirit, all intellect and will, the will perverted, the intellect still mighty beyond the human measure. In the three years to come, many would question and cross-question Christ: but he was never confronted by a mind comparable with Satan's. It is useful to remember that the conflict we are following involves two spirits, each of them far beyond our own mental power. We may easily be missing some of the swordplay. One other thing to remember, as we listen to Christ's answers, is that he had not eaten for a long time and his body needed food just as ours needs it.

Did Satan appear in human form, or did he tempt Christ without actually appearing, as is his way with us? We cannot know. I think most people have the feeling that Satan appeared in human form, that the reality of man in Christ was at issue with the mask of man worn by Satan. If so, it would be a figure of Satan's whole warfare, unreality assailing the real. But Satan may have tempted Jesus as he tempts you and me, with nothing to show that *he* was in action. In any event Matthew and Luke tell the story as if there had been actual confrontation, visual or mental. I shall treat it so.

We should follow the duel closely—three thrusts by Satan, three times parried by Christ. What lay behind the three thrusts? I think what principally lay behind them was Christ's sinlessness. From your past sins and mine, the devil knows where the weaknesses are, the cracks and fissures in our natures half-healed or still gaping wide open. With us, he has plenty to go on: with Christ he had nothing at all. He could only improvise. We cannot read his mind (for that matter, he may not be able to read ours): but we can look at what he did.

He made three propositions. All of them were sketched in advance—rather sketchily sketched perhaps—by the behavior of the children of Israel in the desert. Christ answered with three wholly appropriate texts, all from Deuteronomy, all dealing with the time when Israel was beginning its new life. Satan may well have been in action then too: if so, with the new Israel beginning, he was largely repeating himself. Or he may simply have taken three current views of the Messiah and tried them out in turn— that he would bring the earth wholly into the service of men's needs; that the very heavens would serve his splendor; that all the kingdoms of the world would be subject to him and to the Jewish nation whose glory he would be.

The first two temptations open with the words: "If you are the son of God". I think it was of the first urgency for Satan to find out what "son of God" meant. It had been used in the Old Testament as a name for the Messiah (Ps 2:7). But did he know what it *meant?*

"Son of God" had been variously used in the Old Testament—of the chosen people, for instance (Ex 4:22), and, in the plural, of the Jewish judges (Ps 81[82]:6). Satan knew his Old Testament, but the Book of Job he must have scrutinized with special closeness, for so much of it was about a certain Satan and the high carnival he had at Job's expense. In that book (1:6, 2:1, 38:7) "sons of God" meant the unfallen angels. Satan may well have weighed the possibility that the Messiah might be an angel, entering in some unforeseeable way into humanity for the crushing of his head.

First Testing

"When he had fasted forty days and forty nights, afterward he was hungry. And the tempter coming said to him: If thou be the Son of God, command that these stones be made bread" (Mt 4:2 and 3).

Reading quickly, we may feel that nothing could have been more natural. Our Lord must have been close to death for want of food, the nearest bakery would have been many a long mile away across the desert. Satan struck at what seemed his weakest point, urging him to turn stones into bread. But was it so natural?

So far there is nothing to tell us that Jesus had ever worked a miracle of any sort, any more than John the Baptist worked miracles—he had not yet commanded that water be made wine. It looks as if Satan was challenging him to do something he had never done. There are miracles in plenty in the Old Testament, of course, worked by God through men. But Satan does not suggest that the carpenter should ask God: he simply makes the cool suggestion: "Say to this stone that it be made bread." Stones have no ears to hear commands. Satan could only have meant that Christ should *will* that the stone be made bread.

But the wills of men have not that power over nature. The only material thing we can move by our will is our own body — we will to raise our arm, and our will sets the muscles in motion by which it is raised: through our body, we move other bodies; we cannot move them by a mere act of the will. But angels can. The whole Bible is filled with their power to produce material effects, and this can only be by their wills, since they have no bodies. Satan was calling upon the carpenter to do what a man could not do but an angel might.

Our Lord did not say whether or not he could do it. He answered with a text of Deuteronomy (8:3): "Man does not live by bread alone, but by every word that proceeds from the mouth of God." Satan, of course, knew the reference, as most of us perhaps do not. Even so, he must have wondered what it had to do with his suggestion. In Deuteronomy the words draw the moral from that earlier experience of the Israelites, when they had complained against God for bringing them to a place without food, and God had sent manna. Their meaning evidently was that, provided we do what God wants, it is for him to supply *our* wants.

Satan may well have felt that the carpenter was playing with him, parrying his thrust almost contemptuously. But the text contained one word which he may have been relieved to hear. The word was "man" — man does not live by bread alone. Christ could not possibly have quoted that text, if it had had no bearing on himself at all. It is the clearest possible statement that he is man. And if man, then presumably *only* man!

Second Testing

In his next suggestion, Satan seems to have lowered his sights: instead of urging Christ to work a miracle on his own account, he urges him to rely upon angels to work one for him.

"Then the devil took him up into the Holy City, and set him upon the pinnacle of the Temple, and said to him: If thou be the Son of God, cast thyself down, for it is written: That he has given his angels charge over thee, and in their hands shall they bear thee up, lest perhaps thou dash thy foot against a stone" (Mt 4:5, 6).

How did Satan take Jesus to Jerusalem? Did they actually go there, or did Satan use the power he has to produce images in the mind, so that our Lord would have seen himself standing on the pinnacle of the Temple? Matthew and Luke use the same Greek verb here that they and Mark use when Christ took Peter and James and John with him to the mountain of the Transfiguration, and that Matthew and Mark use of his taking the same three to be near him in Gethsemane.

One way or another, Satan took Jesus to the pinnacle of the Temple. The word pinnacle here (a diminutive of the word for wing) is thought to have been an edge of the Temple roof, overhanging the brook Kidron a good three hundred feet below: there is a tradition that Jesus' cousin, James the Less, was hurled from this spot to his death. Standing there, Jesus could look across the Kidron Valley to the Mount of Olives from which three years later he would ascend into heaven, with no need of angels to bear him up.

For the only time in this dialogue, Satan quoted Scripture— Psalm 91:11–12. From Scripture Jesus answered: "Thou shalt not tempt the Lord thy God", another quotation from Deuteronomy (6:16). For any man to challenge death to win glory for himself, at the same time challenging God to see that no harm should come to him, would be presumption and great arrogance.

Third Testing

His third thrust at Christ is totally different from the others. Let us take it piece by piece. "He took him onto a high mountain, and showed him all the kingdoms of the world in a moment of time."

The Greek verb for the "taking" of our Lord by the devil is the same as when he was taken to Jerusalem and set on the pinnacle of the Temple. But it hardly needs to be said that there was no mountain, in Palestine or anywhere else, from which all the kingdoms of the world could come within reach of a pair of human eyes. Clearly, it was by effects within our Lord's imagination that the kingdoms were made present to him. Our own experience tells us how much can happen in our mind while the hand of the clock barely moves; dreams, we are told, crammed with incident, take place in a few seconds, and our waking thoughts can throng as fast. In a mind so much more perfect than ours as Christ's was, not so dependent upon the body as sin has made ours, the question of time hardly arises at all.

Satan went on to say: "To thee will I give all this power, and the glory of them; for to me they are delivered, and to whom I will, I give them. If thou therefore wilt adore before me, all shall be thine"—or, as Matthew phrases it, "All these will I give thee, if falling down thou wilt adore me." Jesus answered with a third text from Deuteronomy: "Thou shalt adore the Lord thy God and him only shalt thou serve."

What Did Satan Want?

If we look at the three things dangled before Jesus by the devil, the direction of the temptations is upward—bread, a spectacular display, the kingdoms of this world. But in relation to the person tempted, the whole movement is downward, almost as though Satan rated him lower and lower—first he is asked to work a miracle by his own power, next to count on angels to help him through, last to prostrate himself before the tempter and call him Lord.

Did Satan expect him to be drawn by any of these suggestions? By the first, perhaps: he saw a man who had gone long hungry, he did not know what resources he might have in his soul, it seemed reasonable that hunger might dominate everything. But the second and third leave us wondering.

About the second temptation there is something puzzlingly slap-dash. In Psalm 91 there is the promise that angels will guard men who observe God's law in the ordinary living of their lives. Satan quotes this as a reason why Christ should hurl himself down from a high place in reliance on the same guardianship. The misapplication of the promise is gross enough; the actual words quoted make it almost comic. "Lest thou dash thy foot against a stone" is suited to the perils of a man walking the road of life, but simply ludicrous for a man falling from a vast height. "Just hurl yourself down," says Satan, "and God will send angels to see that you don't trip over a stone when you land." As if a man hurtling through space would be bothering about possible damage to his foot.

The third temptation has its own improbability. Even if all Satan knew about this Jesus was that he had been communing alone with God, he could hardly have expected him to fall down and adore God's enemy. But he knew more than that. He may or may not have observed the events surrounding our Lord's conception and birth, and the events surrounding his baptism by John. But of the thirty sinless years between he had a whole mass of sure knowledge.

Our Lord, we remind ourselves, was tempted in all things like us (Heb 4:15). This means that he had been subjected, as we are, to the subtlety of demons urging him to sin. But he was wholly unyielding, as we are not. Thirty years of seeing the most powerful intellects in hell getting nowhere—that was the preparation the prince of the world had for making his own effort. If he was trying to succeed where his underlings had failed, he must have met a good deal of derision from them. We have not a fraction of his mental power or experience in tempting, but we cannot help feeling that if what he wanted was to get our Lord to sin, he could have gone about it better.

There is something else we feel he must have wanted—to find out just who and what Jesus was. It seemed that he might very well be the Messiah, but of him Satan knew no more than he could find in the Old Testament; and that is mysterious darkness shot through with gleams of light, which seem to have a darkness of their own. In one sense, it would tell Satan even less than it told the holiest of the Jews, for there is, as Jesus would later say (Jn 7:17), an insight into doctrine given to those who do God's will, and Satan had not done it. There are depths in the truth clearer to the child at his first Communion than they will ever be to Satan, for all the power of his intellect.

Who was to be the one to crush his head, the one who was to overthrow the princedom of this world, which had been the one consolation to Satan's pride since his fall from heaven? Could the carpenter of Nazareth be the one? The temptations, whatever other purpose they had in his mind, surely were an effort to find out. He may or may not have hoped that the carpenter would yield to his suggestions, but he must have hoped to learn something from his answers.

The first two temptations had produced precious little, indeed nothing directly bearing on what he most wanted to know. The third temptation was a last shot: if that did not draw the information out of the carpenter, nothing would. For Satan was offering him, in return for adoration, power over all the kingdoms of the world. But this had already been promised to the Messiah—"All kings of the earth shall adore him, all nations shall serve him" (Ps 72:11). To expose the monstrousness of Satan's offer, the carpenter had but to say that he was the Messiah—if he was.

He did not say it. All that the devil got was "Begone, Satan", followed by a third text from Deuteronomy which said that only God was to be adored. The text told him nothing he did not already know about the speaker: it could have been quoted by any Jew.

Satan Moves Out

So "the devil left him: and behold angels came and ministered to him." Physically our Lord must have needed their ministrations most urgently. He may well have needed them spiritually too, for he had been in long contact with sheer evil, not abstract evil, either, but evil mighty in mind and malevolence. But did he need them as he was later to need the strengthening by an angel in Gethsemane? What had the temptations meant to him?

Observe that the word "tempt" is not always used of an evil person urging a good one to do wrong. We have already seen this when our Lord quotes Deuteronomy (6:16)—"Thou shalt not tempt the Lord thy God"—where the verb has some such meaning as "try God's patience"—almost "ask for trouble". The same sense of trying or testing is to be found when Jesus asks the apostle Philip how bread was to be bought in the wilderness for five thousand people, and John comments that he said this "to *try* him"

(Jn 6:6); and again (Rev 2:2): "Thou hast *tried* them who say they are apostles, and are not, and hast found them liars." In both these texts the same Greek verb is used (and the same Latin verb by Saint Jerome) as in the tempting of Jesus by Satan.

The trying or testing may be of the will, urging it to sin. Even then, there is a difference between the scriptural use and ours. When we say we are tempted, we mean that our will is attracted. In Scripture to be tempted meant that the will was subjected to a test: it did not mean that it was attracted: it was still a temptation even if there was no attraction whatever. In other words, the temptation was an action of the tempter, not as with us the reaction of the one tempted.

Was Christ tempted in our modern sense? The Gospels do not tell us. In Gethsemane he would cry to his Father, "Not my will but thine be done." If he had any such feeling now, the Gospels give us no hint of it. Great masters of the spiritual life have written profoundly of what the temptations meant to our Lord. I have confined myself to the words the Gospels actually use. I have written of the whole episode from Satan's end, simply because he did all the thrusting, Jesus only parried. From end to end of the episode, there are only two words of his own—"Begone, Satan." They *may* have been the cry of one in anguish of spirit, tried almost beyond bearing. But in this context they do not sound like that. It is more as if he were saying to Satan: "I've given you your chance. Now go away."

Satan did go away—"until the time". A grim little phrase, that. He came back when Jesus' Passion was about to begin.

What he thought he had learned from the duel in the desert we can only guess from what he did: he tempted Judas to betray our Lord to his enemies: thus rushing on his own defeat and exposing his head to the pierced feet which crushed it.

PART TWO

The Public Life

"I have come to call sinners to repentance."

(Lk 5:32)

"The Son of Man is come to seek and to save that which was lost."

(Lk 19:10)

"I am come to cast fire on the earth. And what will I, but that it be kindled?"

(Lk 12:49)

"I am come, a light into the world, that whoever believes in me may not remain in darkness."

(Jn 12:46)

12 *THE FIRST DISCIPLES*

With the temptations over, our Lord's public life begins.

What effect has he produced on us so far? I think it is no exaggeration to say that, in the modern sense of the word personality, he has shown very little. There is a cryptic answer to his Mother when he was twelve, and another to John at his baptism when he was thirty; there are three texts from Deuteronomy, which he quotes to Satan, adding two words of his own ("Begone, Satan"). He had impressed the learned men in the Temple as a clever boy. He was obedient to his parents and the town approved of him. He had fasted forty days in the desert.

Reread the early chapters of Luke. What picture emerges? He was devoted to his heavenly Father; he was resolute, not to be turned from his way; what he had to say he said briefly. Make a list of all the qualities you associate with him, then see how many of them he has shown so far. Very few, I think. Nothing at all to suggest the love in him.

The Lamb of God

From the desert, Matthew, Mark, and Luke take Jesus to Galilee and his ministry there. But John (1:29–3:36) tells of things he did before the definite move to the north.

First he went back to John, still baptizing in Jordan. Seeing him, the Baptist said: "Behold the Lamb of God, behold him who takes away the sin of the world."

All Catholics know the phrase. The *Agnus Dei* is a point of the Mass at which the most distracted begin to concentrate their attention. But if we are listening to what is actually said, there is one difference between what the priest says at the altar and what John said by the Jordan. The priest speaks of the Lamb of God, who takes away the *sins* of the world: John said *sin*.

There is a difference of emphasis here, no more than that. The "sins of the world" are a reminder that Christ our Lord will offer his redeeming sacrifice for all the sins that men have committed in this world. But what John actually said reminds us that there is a sin *of the world,* a sin which involves the whole human race. There are not only the sins of individual men, there is the sin of the first man, the representative man, who made a breach between the human race and God.

The angel had told Joseph that Mary's Son would save his people from their sins. John the Baptist is saying that he will redeem the whole race from the sin in which it had lain since the catastrophe of Adam. And for the first time it is clearly uttered that he will do so by suffering and dying. For this was no mere ceremonial greeting, calling only for a gracious smile of acknowledgment. It had blood in it. What must it have meant to our Lord to be greeted so?

He knew that he was the Paschal Lamb. He knew what Isaiah had said about the sheep led to the slaughter, dumb as a lamb before its shearer (53:7), what Jeremiah had said about the meek lamb led to the slaughterhouse (11:19): and he knew that the prophets were talking of himself. The Baptist's phrase told him nothing he did not already know. But he was not God only, with the humanity merely an appearance. He was flesh-and-blood man too, with tears in him to be shed over dead Lazarus and doomed Jerusalem, with a soul that could be sorrowful even unto death. Each new reminder of what lay before him would bring its own foretaste of Gethsemane.

The Baptist went on to say that this Jesus was the one to whom he had so steadily referred, the One for whom his own lesser mission was a preparation. "He is preferred before me, because he was before me." He told of the Spirit descending upon him at his baptism, and that this was the sign God promised by which he should know the Messiah. He concluded: "And I saw; and I gave testimony, that this is the Son of God."

Gabriel had told our Lady that her son should be called Son of God. Satan had said twice, "*if* you are the Son of God". Now at last a man calls him so. The Baptist had had forty days or more to meditate upon the Voice from heaven which had said, "This is my beloved Son", and he uttered the fruit of his meditation in all confidence.

Who heard the Baptist saying all this? It may be that Jesus came while the crowds were still there. It may be that he came at the end of the day when none remained save John and his disciples. We are not told. Was John the evangelist, who was to be the beloved disciple and who records the scene for us, present at it? At any rate, he was there next day when Jesus returned and the Baptist once more said, "Behold the Lamb of God" (Jn 1:36). We are even told the time of the day—it was the tenth hour, that is round four in the afternoon. The Baptist stood there with two of his disciples. One of the two was Andrew, the brother of Simon Peter. The other is not named. John never names himself; in his Gospel, the word John always means the Baptist; but whenever he pointedly avoids naming someone, that someone is himself.

As Jesus left the river bank, Andrew and John followed him. What was the Baptist thinking as he watched them go? They had been his disciples; that was now over. They had chosen the better part, and it was he himself who had shown them that it was better. He rejoiced for them; but there is always sadness when friends part. He rejoiced for them; was he longing to go with them?

"Come and See"

Jesus turned to the two and asked why they were following him, and what they wanted of him. They answered, "Rabbi, where do you live?" And he said, "Come and see."

There was something special about this interchange. It is the first wholly ordinary conversation reported of our Lord. He is asked a perfectly straight question, and he gives a perfectly normal answer, not shrouded in mystery. It might have been any three men talking.

Andrew and John called him Rabbi, which means Master. The word had not its present official meaning. A man was called Rabbi not because he held a particular position, but because other men regarded him as profoundly learned in the Law. Andrew and John had been disciples of the Baptist, had got their first apostolic training from him, knew him for the great prophet he was. Since he acknowledged Jesus as his master, they could do no less.

They went with Jesus, not of course to his home in Nazareth three days away, but to whatever shelter he had found for himself near the Jordan—a cave perhaps. There they stayed with him for what remained of the day. It is characteristic that John does not give us one word of the conversation. But it was decisive. Andrew went to find his brother Simon and said: "We have found the Christ." Simon went back with him, to be told by Jesus that whereas his name was Simon, he should be called Cephas (or, as we say, Peter). The word meant "rock". Simon must have been puzzled. At that moment he did not know, as Catholics have known these last nineteen hundred years, the point of the new name.

So far, we have seen three of the Baptist's disciples—Andrew and John and Peter—becoming Christ's instead. For the couple of months that lay between their leaving the Baptist and Herod's arresting him, our Lord's ministry was to be in Judea. Only after the arrest would he return to his own Galilee. But he did pay a flying visit there at this point. We may wonder why.

The one thing we are told that he did on this visit was to attend a wedding at Cana, a small town a few miles from Nazareth. It looks as though he had simply gone back for the wedding.

The man or girl to be married might have been one of those cousins of his, who had joined up as one family with Mary and her Son, after Joseph's death perhaps. If the whole point of the journey was in fact the wedding, he just made it in time. Cana was a three-day journey from that part of Judea where the Baptist was. And, as Saint John tells us (2:1), "On the third day, there was a marriage in Cana of Galilee."

Somewhere between leaving Judea and arriving at the wedding, the small group, Jesus and his three new disciples, collected two more, Philip and Nathanael.

To Philip, a man of Peter and Andrew's town, Bethsaida, at the north of the Sea of Galilee, our Lord said, as he was later to say to

Levi the tax collector, "Follow me." Of the winning of Philip, no more is said. He seems to have come instantly. But Nathanael, to whom Philip in his turn spoke of Christ, was a different proposition. He had to be convinced.

The Convincing of Nathanael

One gets the impression that Philip fairly exploded the great news in Nathanael's face: "We have found him of whom Moses in the Law, and the prophets did write, Jesus the son of Joseph of Nazareth" (Jn 1:45).

Nathanael was totally unimpressed. "Can any good come from Nazareth?" he asked. He may have been expressing the contempt of a biggish town for a smaller neighbor. But surely Nathanael was simply dismissing the possibility of the Messiah coming from a place which is never even mentioned in the Old Testament, and had no connection with King David, whose descendant the Messiah was to be. Had Philip bothered to say that Jesus had been born in David's city, Bethlehem, he would have eliminated one ground of scepticism. But perhaps he did not yet know about Bethlehem himself: he was a very new disciple.

Anyhow he wasted no time on argument. From his own experience, one imagines, he had learned that Jesus himself was better than any argument. He simply said: "Come and see", which was the phrase Jesus had used to Andrew and John. Nathanael let Philip take him to Jesus. As they met, Jesus said: "Behold an Israelite indeed, in whom there is no guile." At first reading, we find this a little surprising—as though an American were to say: "Good heavens, an honest American!" But what our Lord is really saying is that he was a thoroughly honest man, a true son of Israel. (How many others does one remember our Lord as praising?)

Nathanael neither accepted nor denied the compliment. What struck him was that this stranger had talked as though he knew him, and Nathanael wanted to know how. Then he got a profound shock, the profundity of which is largely lost upon us. Jesus said: "I saw you under the fig tree, before Philip called you." To us, it seems that Jesus must have seen something happening without being there—it is the first of such incidents. Knowing all that there was to follow, we do not find it very surprising.

Nathanael's reaction, however, suggests that there is more in the phrase than simply what we now call extrasensory perception. Whatever happened under the fig tree, it loomed large in his mind and he had thought it his own secret. Possibly (one man's guess being as good as another's) he had been wrestling there with a strong temptation to an act of profitable but very base dishonesty, and conscience had won. Whatever Jesus' words meant to him, he needed no more convincing.

"Rabbi," he said, "thou art the Son of God, thou art the King of Israel."

"You Shall See Heaven Opened"

From so small a thing, faith came to Nathanael. Jesus told him that it was as nothing to the great things he would yet see. And he went on to make the first statement about himself that is recorded (Jn 1:51): "Amen, amen I say to you"—it had been "thou" so far—"you shall see heaven opened, and the angels of God ascending and descending upon the Son of Man." Even an unlearned Jew would have known about Jacob's dream (Gen 28:12) of a ladder reaching up to heaven, with angels moving up and down its rungs: just as we today need be of no great learning to have heard Francis Thompson's reference to

> ... the traffic of Jacob's ladder,
> Pitched betwixt heaven and Charing Cross.

As the change from the singular "thou" to the plural "you" shows, Jesus was by now speaking not to Nathanael only but to the whole group of disciples. What he was saying grew naturally out of what had just happened, but at least the spotlight was off Nathanael. It never fell on him again. Considering that there is not one of the Twelve whose first introduction is told in anything like the same detail, it seems strange that we hear so little of him afterward. He figures among the Twelve (always linked with Philip his sponsor) by his other name, Bartholomew—son of

Talmai. To our world the name Bartholomew suggests one thing only: on his feast day in the year 1572 occurred a most appalling massacre.

The disciples would have remembered that Jacob had named the place of the dream Bethel, and a glance at the map shows us that Bethel was on one of the roads that the group might have been taking on its way to Nazareth and Cana.

Given Jesus' habit of starting some of his deepest teaching from something actually present, it is at least probable that it was their arrival at Bethel which had caused him to use the imagery of the dream that Jacob had dreamed there. If so, the group would have come due west from the river Jordan, reaching Bethel towards the end of the first day's journey. There they would have taken the main road north through Samaria. Two more days would bring them to the end of their journey—the first stage of that more-than-two-year journey whose end was Calvary. For the rest of his life, Jesus was almost continuously moving along the roads of Galilee and Samaria and Judea, always accompanied by his apostles, except on the very last mile of the road.

Who and What Was He?

One must not picture them as marching like a squad of soldiers under a corporal. They would have gone sometimes faster, sometimes slower, changing their grouping, sometimes one or two of them with the Master, the others talking to each other or to chance strangers going the same way. Among themselves, the first five would already have had plenty to talk about.

Of them all, we know Peter best. It is hard to imagine his not taking the first favorable moment to ask Nathanael what was all this about a fig tree; if Nathanael told him, the story has not come down to us. Andrew and John, too, the veterans of the party, must have told the new man Philip and the even newer man Nathanael what the Baptist had said by the side of the Jordan, and something at least of what Jesus had said in his conversation with them.

One question must have been in all their minds and on their lips pretty continuously—Who was he? or rather, since they knew he was Jesus of Nazareth, *What* was he? They were fairly sure by now that he was the Messiah, who should redeem Israel. That was his title, that was his function: but, once more, what exactly *was* he? Already they found it hard to think of him as on the human level only; he towered over other men; yet what other level was there?

One phrase uttered by the Baptist—"He was, when I was not" (Jn 1:30)—must have puzzled Andrew and John who heard him say it, and must have puzzled the other three to whom they would certainly have repeated it. *We* hardly notice it, because we know that later Jesus was to say, "Before Abraham was made, I am", and to have preexisted the Baptist strikes us as a small matter compared with preexisting Abraham. But the five disciples could not read the future. They could only wonder. After all, the Baptist was six months older than Jesus. What *could* the phrase mean?

For the moment, at any rate, they were not getting very much light from their leader upon the mystery of himself. He talked of heaven opening and angels ascending and descending. But not in a dream, as with Jacob: they themselves should see the angels. They did not know what he had in mind. Neither precisely do we: no incident quite like that is recorded.

The prophecy was an assertion of his mystery, but not an elucidation. The phrase "Son of Man" gave them no present light either. We shall talk of it again. Here note that our Lord uses it constantly—it occurs eighty times in the Gospels. But not one of his followers ever seems to have addressed him by it; they did not know what to make of it. It answered no question about him; but, by its strangeness, it was a reminder that there *was* a question to be answered.

13 *WEDDING IN CANA*

"Son, They Have No Wine"

When our Lord left Jordan for Galilee, he had three disciples—Andrew, John, and Peter. On the way he had added Philip and Nathanael. It took three days to reach Cana; and on the day of their arrival "there was a marriage in Cana of Galilee, and the mother of Jesus was there. Jesus also was invited, and his disciples" (Jn 2:1, 2). There can surely be no incident in the whole of the public life better known than the wedding feast of Cana.

Wedding feasts, we have already noted, varied in splendor. The one given in Cana by friends of our Lady, close relations perhaps, would not have been very splendid. Some small amount of meat there would have been, because a wedding was so special an occasion, but normally the poor of Galilee saw precious little meat from one year's end to another. At a wedding of their sort, everything would depend on the wine. And the wine ran out.

There can hardly be a commentator who has not connected the running out of the wine with the arrival of our Lord, who may have been expected, and his five disciples, who could hardly have been. Given that practically the whole town had probably been invited to the wedding, one cannot feel that an extra half dozen would have made all that difference. But this particular half dozen would have made a difference to the celebrations as a whole. Within a few minutes, Peter would have been holding the floor: it was his nature to. John may have attracted less notice: what matters to us is that he was meeting the woman who would be given to him as his mother on Calvary.

She it was who intervened decisively to save the miserable embarrassment of empty wine jars with a feast in full swing. It is nearly twenty years since her first recorded words to her Son—when they found him in the Temple after three days. Now for a second time we hear her speak to him: "They have no wine." She simply draws his attention to the problem, she does not tell him how to solve it. *Reading* his answer—"Woman, what is that to me and to thee? My hour is not yet come"—we would get the impression not only that he did not mean to solve it, but also that he saw no reason why he should. *Hearing* his answer, she knew that he would. She had suggested a miracle, and she knew she would get it. She said to the waiters: "Do whatever he tells you", and that is the last word we ever hear from her. If there must be a last word from her, there could hardly be a better.

Water into Wine

What her Son said to the waiters was that they should take the six stone water pots standing near the door—they would have contained something over a hundred and fifty gallons—fill them with water, draw a cup from them and carry it to the chief steward, who was simply one of the guests, given the duty of presiding over the celebrations. The water was made into wine. Tasting it, the presiding guest called the bridegroom and said to him: "Every man at first sets forth good wine, and when men have well drunk, then that which is worse. But you have kept the good wine until now."

Jesus' words, I have said, sounded like a refusal—triply so: for he not only gave two reasons why he should take no action at all, he prefaced them with the word Woman. No one today would address his mother or his wife as Woman, save in anger: and she would retort as angrily. The word Woman has become a term of contempt. One wonders why. The progress of civilization perhaps. Certainly it was not so in the time of our Lord. It was formal, rather ceremonial perhaps, not for everyday use: the Roman Emperor Augustus officially addressed Cleopatra, Queen of Egypt, as Woman. For us it is for ever consecrated by Jesus' second use of it: nailed to the Cross, he gave her Saint John for her son with the words "Woman, behold thy son." *

---

* It has been observed that we never hear Jesus address her as Mother. We have only three things he said to her, all rather special. Twice we hear her speak to him, and she does not call him Jesus. Neither do any of his friends, or the scribes and Pharisees, or the high priests—demons do, and blind Bartimeus.

The phrase "What is that to me and to thee?" is an idiomatic one, which had to take its bearing from the context in which it was spoken. But it always, it seems, contains some element of negation—at its best, something like "Let's leave it alone" or "Why should we concern ourselves?" Even without the words that follow, we should take it as a kind of brush-off—if he had not proceeded to do what she wanted!

But how could he work a miracle immediately after having said, "My hour is not yet come"? In those words is the mystery of Cana. What did he mean by his hour? Once he has begun his public teaching, it always means the time when he should die and be glorified by his Father. That meaning would not fit here. Evidently he means that the moment has not yet come to show his power to the eyes of men. Then two surprises: Mary knows that he will show it all the same. One minute his hour had not come, the next it had.

Surely the Holy Spirit was at work. We know that Jesus went into the desert to be tempted by the devil because the Holy Spirit sent him there. His certainty that his hour had not yet come would have meant that the Holy Spirit had not yet told him that he was to show his power publicly. And now, suddenly, his Mother asks him for a miracle. As we have seen, the life of the family at Nazareth had not been strewn with miracles: the cousins who had lived with them clearly had no notion what power was in him, and took a lot of convincing later that he was beyond the ordinary run of men: Nazareth did not believe in him, was indeed the only town that wanted to kill him.

Mary could have asked him to work a miracle thus publicly, only at the command of the Holy Spirit: it was not in her nature to thrust bright ideas of her own on her Son. She asked him as she was bid, and the Holy Spirit moved him to do what she asked. Thus Mary, who by her obedience had brought her Son into life, now by his obedience brought him into public life.

Improbable Miracle

The changing of water into wine—"this beginning of miracles", as Saint John calls it—must have been known all over the area by nightfall. Half the grown-ups of Cana would have been at the wedding feast: heaven knows what the hundred and fifty gallons had swollen to as they told their families.

Nazareth was only four miles off, and the fury of finding one of their own townsmen working miracles somewhere else must already have begun: If he *must* work miracles, what was wrong with Nazareth?

Then again Zippori, Herod's capital, was only about the same distance away. The king was reigning happily with the wife he had lately stolen from his brother to replace the wife he had wearied of. The new one, Herodias, was niece to both her husbands (her grandfather, the Herod of Bethlehem massacre fame, had murdered her father), and she had a daughter Salome who would have her part in a murder more famous than any that even the bloodstained herods had ever committed. We know that Herod's procurator, Chuza, had a wife, Joanna, who became one of Jesus' most devoted followers. The miracle at Cana might have been the occasion of her first hearing his name.

To the five disciples of Jesus what had happened must have been a surprise beyond words. The Baptist had won the ear of all Palestine, and the heart of most of it, without ever working a miracle at all. But what must have puzzled them was not that Jesus should be able to work miracles: they were sure he was a prophet, and miracles and prophets had gone together in Jewish history. What puzzled them was that he should have worked this particular miracle. In all the Old Testament there is no miracle worked simply to prevent a social embarrassment. Nor indeed did Jesus himself ever work such a miracle afterwards. The miracle at Cana stands solitary in being worked for the sake of a comparative trifle. If, indeed, that was all it was worked for.

It was at his Mother's suggestion that he had performed the miracle. In that single act she was giving him away, and knew she was giving him away: from now on he was public property, for miracle-workers must expect no privacy, there will always be throngs about them. Was she ever to have him to herself again? There is no mention in the Gospels of their meeting again—not till he was on the Cross, close to his death.

She knew what would be the end of the road upon which this day she started him. Once she knew that she was to be the Mother of the Messiah, she must have studied all that the Scriptures had to tell of him as it had never been studied before: for no one else had read Scripture with the immaculate intellect which went with her Immaculate Conception, no one else had ever known who it was that should have the suffering and the glory. The prophecies could not have meant so much even to the prophets who uttered them as they meant to the Mother of the One about whom they were uttered.

Why did Jesus leave Judea to spend a few days in Galilee, when he was to return there to be in the Temple for the Passover? As the only thing that is told of the Galilee visit is the wedding, our first feeling is that that must have been the reason. But one can at least imagine another reason—he might well have wanted to tell his Mother of all that had happened in the two months he had been away—the baptism in the Jordan by his kinsman and hers, God's voice from heaven and the Holy Spirit hovering over him in the form of a dove, the temptations in the desert. Especially the temptations in the desert.

Obviously Mother and Son had discussed the prophecies together. It is not easy, as I have suggested, to think of them as tight-lipped and inarticulate, each pretending not to know that the other knew what lay before the Redeemer of the world. They would hardly have missed the first of all the prophecies, the one about the seed of the woman and the crushing of Satan's head— our own minds dart back to it when we hear him address her as Woman. And now the seed of the woman had had his first confrontation with Satan: the crushing had begun. His Mother would be passionately interested. He may well have wanted to tell her.

14 MONEYCHANGERS AND NICODEMUS

The visit to Cana for the wedding feast was brief, a matter of a week or so perhaps. The Passover was approaching, and Jesus wanted to be in Jerusalem for it—as we shall see, he had a rather special reason for wanting to be there a little ahead. Yet, curiously, he traveled to Jerusalem by way of Capernaum—"he and his mother, and his brethren, and his disciples" (Jn 2:12). Capernaum took them a day's journey out of their way, and not an easy journey. It was only twenty miles from Cana, but in that distance the road descended a good sixteen hundred feet: for Cana was nine hundred feet above sea level, and Capernaum was on the edge of the lake, seven hundred feet below sea level.

We know that on the return a couple of months later to Galilee for the long Galilean ministry, Jesus used Capernaum as his headquarters. It was his town as Nazareth had been Joseph's.

They did not stay many days in Capernaum this time, but went on—at least he and the five disciples, perhaps his Mother and some of the cousins—to Jerusalem. There Jesus announced to all the Jewish world that One unlike any other was in their midst and must be reckoned with. He could hardly have announced his advent more spectacularly; what he did was at once so right and so unthinkable. It was the first of his great rages at the profaning of the sacred.

The Cleansing of God's House

One vast courtyard of the Temple had been made their own by the moneychangers and by the salesmen of sacrificial animals. Jews, coming from all over the world, had to exchange the coins they brought with them into coinage acceptable in the Temple, and could be cheated over the rate of exchange. For their burnt offerings they had to buy oxen or sheep; for the purification of mothers after childbirth, doves or pigeons; at Passover, lambs for the Paschal meal: the Temple priests lived on their share of the profits.

Jesus made "a scourge of little cords"—he was a carpenter, but this is the only thing we are ever told that he made. And he drove the moneychangers and the animal-sellers out of the Temple court. The money was scattered all over the floor, already fouled with the excrement of thousands of animals; the animals were driven out pell-mell with the profiteers who sold them; at his orders, the sellers of birds picked up their cages and ran like the rest.

One thing certain is that it was not the scourge of little cords, or even the muscles made strong by twenty years of carpentry, that drove from the courtyard scores of men hot upon money: there must have been something in the personality they could not stand against, in the blaze of the eyes or the icy condemnation in them: otherwise he would have been beaten to the ground in the first few minutes, and the moneychanging and the animal-selling would have gone on with hardly an interruption.

So far we have been following Saint John. The other three evangelists describe a very similar cleansing of the Temple, but they place it toward the end of the public life, two Passovers after this one. We cannot be certain whether it happened twice, or whether all four evangelists are describing the one incident—chronological order, as we have noted, did not matter as much to any of them as it does to us today. There is one phrase used by these three which adds something special. They tell us that Jesus justified his action by quoting two of the prophets: "My house shall be called the house of prayer"—that is Isaiah (56:7)—"but you have made it a den of thieves"—that is Jeremiah (7:11). John tells us only that he accused these people of making his Father's house an emporium.

It was sufficiently surprising that the moneychangers and the sellers of sacrificial animals should have fled before one man and his little whip. Almost as surprising is that the Temple rulers—they were Sadducees—did not arrest Jesus for so shattering a breach of the peace. They would send the Temple police to arrest him in the garden of Gethsemane: Why not now? Not only did they not arrest him; they did not even protest. They simply asked what miracle he could offer as evidence of his right to do this unparalleled thing.

We are in fact meeting for the first time an element in them which we tend to forget, so seldom do we meet anything quite like it in our world. They were profoundly worldly men, greedy for power, greedy for money; but they *did* profoundly believe in God. When self-interest made them go in for a large-scale breaking of one or other of his laws, they always built some sort of justification. A direct and unmistakable conflict with the will of the Most High they would not have dared to face. Deep in their souls lay the certainty that God *could* send a prophet; a miracle would establish that Jesus of Nazareth was in fact a prophet sent by him.

They asked Jesus what sign he would give. They did not find his answer very helpful, for the sign he offered them had not yet happened: it was his own Resurrection.

But the Temple rulers did not even know what he was saying. His actual words were: "Destroy this Temple, and in three days I will rebuild it." John tells us that the temple he meant was his body; and we who know that our own bodies are temples of the Holy Spirit are not surprised. But his questioners assumed that he was referring to the Temple out of which he had just scourged a horde of greedy men. Herod the Great had begun its building forty-six years before, they reminded him: What nonsense was this about rebuilding it in three days? The phrase stuck in their minds all the same. When he was being examined before Caiaphas, this was the one piece of evidence brought against him, misstated as a threat that he would himself destroy the Temple.

But in the week of Passover Jesus proceeded to give the kind of sign that they *would* understand, and gave it not once but many times. So that many came to "believe in his name, seeing his signs which he did" (Jn 2:23). John gives us no details of this group of miracles: but he adds a comment of his own. The miracles made many believe in Jesus; but he did not put much trust in their so-quickly-won belief, "for he knew what was in man". Miracles could move men mightily at the moment, yet their influence could fade again. And there was a surer ground than miracle for belief in him: as he would later say to Thomas—"Blessed are they that have not seen and have believed" (Jn 20:29).

Conversation with Nicodemus

John does not give us any of these miracles. He gives us something more priceless still, the name of one man brought towards belief by them and his conversation with Jesus.

Nicodemus was a man of high position, a Pharisee and a member of the Sanhedrin, the ruling Council of the Jews. He was the first of his sort to approach the carpenter. His opening words were clear affirmation: "Rabbi, we know that thou art come a teacher from God; for no man can do these signs unless God be with him" (Jn 3:2). Yet he had come by night, avoiding observation. He was a cautious man, in no haste to commit himself. He would move slowly, but that slow movement was steady progress all the same. Later (Jn 7:50) he would speak for Jesus in the Sanhedrin— mildly enough, to our taste, but it was a brave thing that he did. And it was he who provided the hundred pounds of myrrh and aloes for Jesus' burial—a vaster quantity of myrrh, we may imagine, than the wise men had brought to Bethlehem.

His visit by night is another of those occasions where we should give anything for just a little more detail than the Holy Spirit and the evangelist have given us. The conversation plunges so deep that it must have gone on far into the night. But we could read Saint John's summary of it in a few minutes. From the summary four great truths emerge.

(1) Jesus says, "Unless a man be born again of water and the Holy Spirit he cannot enter into the Kingdom of God." The Greek word John uses could mean either "born again" or "born from on high". There is no Aramaic word with both these meanings; Jesus must have said one or the other. From Saint Paul (Titus 3:5) and the chief of the apostles (1 Pet 1:3 and 23) it seems that he did say "born again". Birth means entry into life; to be born again does not mean entering the same life all over again—as Nicodemus, in true heckling vein, pretends to think: "How can a man get back into his mother's womb?" It means entering into another, higher

life, the life which gives those powers to the soul without which it would be unable to live in heaven.

Nicodemus could pretend to misunderstand the word "again"; the modern Baptists really *do* misunderstand the word "man", arguing from it against infant baptism. But that word is only in the English translation; John uses the Greek word *tis,* which is a pronoun meaning "one", anyone. By birth, all of us enter into natural life; by rebirth in baptism, we enter into the life above nature, which is our equipment for the glory God has prepared for us.

But what of the phrase "Holy Spirit"? What did Nicodemus make of that? Not the third Person of the Blessed Trinity certainly; the Trinity was not yet revealed. The Old Testament was full of the phrase "Spirit of God"—from the opening of Genesis where the Spirit moved over the waters to the prophet Ezekiel (2:24) who was sent by the Spirit of God into Chaldea. Nicodemus would simply have taken Holy Spirit as another way of saying God, especially the power of God, God acting in the world.

(2) The work of the Holy Spirit in the soul Jesus compares to the movement of the wind. We cannot see the wind; we cannot order the particular wind we happen to need but must accept whatever wind is blowing; we do not know where the wind comes from or where it goes after we have felt its breath. Grace in the soul is like that. This time Nicodemus does not pretend to misunderstand, he quite frankly does not understand at all. Jesus rebukes him: he was a master in Israel, he should have weighed such words as those of the prophet Ezekiel (2:19): "I will give them a new heart and I will put a new spirit in their breast. I will take away their heart of stone and give them a heart of flesh." For the first time Jesus is announcing one of his greatest themes, that the externals of religion are secondary. It is renewal in the very soul that matters.

(3) He tells of his own right to talk of heavenly things, saying: "No man has ever gone up into heaven; but there is One who has come down from heaven, the Son of Man who dwells in heaven" (Jn 3:13). Nicodemus could hardly have grasped at that first hearing all that the carpenter was saying of himself—that he had

preexisted as God, that he existed upon earth as man, that, in his own person as God the Son, he was in heaven still.

(4) Nor could Nicodemus have understood the words that followed: "As Moses lifted up the serpent in the desert, so must the Son of Man be lifted up: that whosoever believeth in him may not perish, but may have life everlasting." The master in Israel would have known of the brazen serpent that Moses made at God's command and set on a high pole, "bringing life to all who should look towards it as they lay wounded" (Nb 21:8). But he could not have known, nor could John who was probably there, that Jesus was foretelling that he would be lifted to his death on a cross in order to bring everlasting life to men wounded unto death by sin. To us the words are a reminder that the death he must die was steadily before him: everything he did, everything he said, was done and said in the shadow of the Cross.

15 *LEAVING JUDEA FOR GALILEE*

The conversation with Nicodemus (Jn 3) contains the fullest doctrinal statement Jesus had yet made. Saint John gets it into fewer than three hundred words. He adds half as many again of his own meditation, beginning, "God so loved the world that he gave his only begotten Son...." Reread the first twenty-one verses of Saint John's third chapter. They mean more to us than they meant to Nicodemus, who was only half-won. For the smallest Christian child knows truths—about the Holy Spirit, for instance—that the master in Israel could not know.

First Preaching about the Kingdom

Nicodemus went his way. The week of Passover was ended. That was the first Passover of Jesus' public life. Just before the second he would feed the five thousand and preach the sermon on himself as the Bread of Life. And at the third, he would be crucified.

He did not return at once to Galilee; there would be another six weeks or so in Judea before the long Galilean ministry should begin. At Ennon, a place of springs not far from the river Jordan, but much further north of Jerusalem than before, very close indeed to Herod's territory, John the Baptist was going on with his preaching about the advent of the Kingdom, and his baptizing. Somewhere in Judea, John the Evangelist tells us, Jesus and his small group of disciples seem to have been doing much the same—preaching and baptizing, though John makes it clear in the next chapter that Jesus himself did not baptize, but only his disciples: as most of them had been the Baptist's disciples first, it would have come naturally to them.

It is a mysterious period, mysterious in two ways. The Baptist was the forerunner: one wonders why he should have continued his forerunning now that Christ was there. Why indeed did he not join him as chief of disciples? And Jesus himself, having made it clear by his scourging of the moneychangers and the miracles he had worked in Passover week that he was a unique person in his own right—why, one wonders, should he spend six weeks doing the kind of work the Baptist had made his own?

We cannot pretend to know the answer to either problem: but the second, at least, is an example of Jesus' habit of not doing what *we* should have expected him to do, in fact of not doing what we should have done had we been he! It is a habit he has not abandoned in heaven. Again and again the question springs to mind, "Why doesn't he . . . ?" In this particular instance, he may have wanted to spend the time in the training of Peter and Andrew, John and James, Philip and Nathanael, meanwhile watching them and counseling them—now that, for the first time as his disciples, they were dealing with human beings.

In their minds all this must have linked up not only with the baptism administered by their first master, John, but with what their new master had said to Nicodemus about the necessity of rebirth by water and the Holy Spirit. But, whatever their perplexity about this new baptism—to which indeed they had already heard the Baptist himself refer—Jesus would hardly have left them in doubt that what they were now doing was not that mightier baptism. Yet it may have been a step beyond John's, a kind of rough sketch of the sacrament of baptism, as their later anointing the sick with oil (Mk 6:13) was of the sacrament of anointing of the sick.

Meanwhile, crowds thronged to them. Crowds thronged to the Baptist, too, at Ennon, but smaller crowds. A Jew taunted John's disciples with this, and they asked John what it all meant. There is a certain pathos and total nobility in John's answer:

"A man must be content to receive the gift which is given him from heaven, and nothing more. You yourselves are my witnesses that I told you I am not the Christ; I have been sent to go before him. The bride is for the bridegroom; but the bridegroom's friend, who stands by and listens to him, rejoices too, rejoices at hearing the bridegroom's voice; and this joy is mine now in full measure. He must become more and more, I must become less and less" (Jn 3:27–30).

Read on to the end of the chapter—six verses which may have been said by the Baptist, or may be the meditation of the evangelist.

John must become less and less: Had he any notion how soon he would be leaving the scene altogether, through the intervention of a very different bridegroom?

Arrest of the Baptist

Herod Antipas—a son of Herod the Great who was too young when his father died to excite his jealousy and therefore survived him—now ruled Galilee and Perea. On a visit to Rome he had met Herodias, the wife of one of his brothers—she was niece to both men, and seems to have had a penchant for uncles. (So indeed had her dancing daughter, Salome, who would one day marry a

great-uncle.) Antipas married Herodias, and his Arab wife fled to
her father's capital city, Petra. The whole Jewish people was
scandalized—divorce was allowed, but the book of Leviticus had
condemned the taking of a living brother's wife. In condemning
Herod's action, the Baptist spoke the mind of all Jewry.

Herod arrested him. There are two problems here. For in the
first place the Baptist was a Judean, not one of Herod's subjects.
And he had been baptizing at Ennon, near Scythopolis, which
was one of the Ten Free Cities, not therefore under Herod's
jurisdiction. Matthew and Mark tell us that John "was delivered
up" to Herod; and the Greek verb, as used in this text, always
means "betrayed" in Scripture. Ennon was in a tongue of land
lying between Herod's two provinces, Galilee and Perea; it looks
as though by some pretext the Baptist had been persuaded to cross
into one or the other.

Persuaded by whom? Agents of Herod perhaps; for Herod
certainly wanted to take the Baptist out of circulation, because of
the condemnation of his second marriage. But there is another
possibility.

Matthew and Mark say that Jesus left Judea for Galilee when he
heard of the Baptist's arrest. Why? we may wonder. Clearly it was
not fear of Herod that caused him to leave Judea, which was not
Herod's territory, and go to Galilee, which was: indeed he made
his headquarters in Capernaum, only nine miles from Herod's
new capital, Tiberias.

Saint John (4:1) alone states a reason for his leaving Judea—
namely that he "understood that the Pharisees had heard" that he
was winning more disciples than the Baptist. The Jewish historian,
Josephus, says that Herod arrested John through alarm at the crowds
he gathered. But why should Herod worry about crowds gathered
in Judea? And, if crowds bothered Herod, why should Jesus, a still
greater crowd-gatherer, put his head into Herod's mouth?

Josephus may possibly have telescoped two things—it may
have been the Pharisees who, alarmed at the crowds, betrayed
John to Herod, knowing that the tetrarch would want so powerful a critic silenced. Now that these same Pharisees realized that
Jesus' drawing-power was even greater than the Baptist's, they

were a real threat to his mission. He would die, but at his own time, not theirs.

For whatever reason, he returned to Galilee. This seems to have been in May of the first year of his public ministry. With occasional excursions, he would be in Galilee till October of the second year—fifteen or sixteen months. The four or five months already passed since his baptism in Jordan had been very full ones—the Baptism itself with the descent of the Dove and the Voice from heaven, the confrontation of Satan in the desert, the calling of John and Andrew and three more disciples, the marriage feast of Cana, the move to Capernaum, the cleansing of the Temple, the week of miracles in Jerusalem, the six weeks of preaching while his disciples baptized. At the beginning of the period he was known only in Nazareth. At the end of it, there could hardly have been a corner of Palestine that had not heard of him.

For us, it is a period of emerging personality, using the word in the ordinary way of speech. Our Lord is very strong, very resolute, no waster of words, with the possibility of vast rage in him when the sacred suffers profanation. Meekness, gentleness, compassion, have not yet shown themselves very noticeably. The bankers and the traders he scourged from the Temple would have been as much surprised as Satan, whom he dismissed with a single word, if they could have heard the hymn sung by generations of children, "Gentle Jesus, meek and mild".

His way to Galilee took him through Samaria. When the Jews returned from captivity in Babylon, we remind ourselves, the Samaritans had offered to help in the building of the Temple and been refused with insult. From that moment they and the Jews were enemies. It was with a woman of the Samaritans that Jesus was now to have one of his longest conversations.

Conversation with a Samaritan Woman

Just inside the valley which has Mount Ebal on the north, and Gerizim, the holy mountain of the Samaritans, on the south, the group came to the well where, sixteen centuries before, Jacob himself had watered his flocks. It was midday, and the disciples went on to the nearby town of Shechem to buy food. Jesus, "wearied with the journey", sat on the side of the well. A Samaritan woman came to the well to draw water and he asked her: "Give me to drink." There followed a strange conversation (Jn 4:7–26).

The woman began by expressing her amazement that he, a Jew, should talk to a Samaritan at all, above all that he should ask one of the ancestral enemy for even so small a service as a drink of water. His answer plunged into the very heart of truths not yet revealed: If she knew who he was, it was she who would be saying "give me to drink"; and he would give her "living water".

When he had spoken to Nicodemus of being "born again", Nicodemus had answered in terms of a return to, and reemergence from, his mother's womb. So now, "living water" simply suggested to the Samaritan woman the well by which they were standing. Who was this stranger, who appeared to be offering to draw more from the well than their common ancestor Jacob had drawn? Jesus answered:

"Whoever drinks of *this* water will thirst again; but he who shall drink of the water that I will give him, shall not thirst forever: the water that I will give him shall become in him a fountain of water, springing up into life everlasting."

Knowing nothing of sanctifying grace, having the sketchiest notion of the spiritual life, the woman seizes on what seems to her the marvelous element in what she had just heard—that drink would mean the end of thirst, would mean that she would never again have to carry the heavy pitcher to the well and carry it heavier still back to her home. "Give me this water", she pleads.

But because Jesus was speaking of sanctifying grace, he goes straight to the one obstacle in its way, sin.

"Go, call thy husband," he says to her, "and come back with him."

"I have no husband", she answers.

"You have said well that you have no husband. For you have had five husbands; and the one you now have is not your husband."

That a stranger should know all this about her had much the same effect upon her as Jesus' unexpected knowledge had once had upon Nathanael. It was all the proof *she* needed that he was a prophet. That being so, she would waste no time upon herself and her marital troubles; she returned to her original question as to the difference between the Samaritans with the Temple they had had on Mount Gerizim till Jews destroyed it, and the Jews with their claim that the supreme adoration of God belonged only in their own Temple on Mount Zion.

Jesus' answer would surely have had the Pharisees stoning him, could they have heard him: the time was coming, he said, when it would be known that the supreme adoration of God belonged to no one spot, not to Mount Gerizim, not even to the great Temple which he had just cleansed. Salvation, indeed, is *of* the Jews, but not only *for* the Jews: it is for all who adore God, and the place of adoration is in the depths of each soul. "God is a spirit, and they that adore him must adore him in spirit and in truth."

The prophet Jeremiah, six centuries earlier, had said that the worth of the Temple in Jerusalem lay not in itself but solely in the worthiness of the worshippers, in their souls therefore (7:4). He had said something even stronger—that in the time of the Messiah even the Ark of the Covenant would no longer hold men's hearts or minds (3:16), for God's law would be written in the spirits of men.

Yet it was no memory of Jeremiah which caused the woman to say next, "I know the Messiah is coming", but simply her feeling that he must come soon and make clear these mysterious things of which the stranger spoke. Jesus' comment upon that was the most startling thing in the whole conversation: "I am he who speaks with you" (Jn 4:26).

In every way this is startling. It is the first record of Jesus' saying that he was the Christ. Satan had tried to find out, and got no answer at all. Nathanael had said it in Jesus' presence, and had drawn no comment. In the years that followed, many people would wonder and ask. He always avoided the direct statement. Immediately after telling Peter that he was the rock upon which the Church would be founded, he warned the apostles to tell no one that he was the Christ. Even when the Baptist, from his prison, sent messengers to ask if he was the Christ, he told them to tell John that they had seen so many of the prophecies about the Messiah fulfilled in him: yet he did not say in all simplicity, "I am he." Before the Sanhedrin, faced with the direct question by the High Priest Caiaphas, he did say it. But until then, we are told of his saying it only to this woman not of his own race, a woman with five husbands behind her and living now with a man with whom she had not even bothered to go through the form of marriage, a woman from whom Caiaphas would have averted his eyes.

Indeed his disciples, returning from their shopping for food in Shechem, were as surprised, if not as shocked, as Caiaphas would have been. They did not know of her five husbands or of her present unambiguous status. But, even without that, they had two reasons for surprise: she was a Samaritan, and the two races were not on speaking terms; she was a woman, and rabbis avoided speaking to women, even their own wives, in public. They were far too much in awe of him to make any comment upon behavior so eccentric. They merely spread out the food they had bought and invited him to eat. And he said, "I have food to eat that you know not."

Like Nicodemus when our Lord spoke of being born again, like the Samaritan woman when he talked of living water, they took for granted the most literal explanation. They assumed that somebody else had arrived with food while they were away — perhaps the woman. As on the other two occasions, Jesus corrects the literalness: "My food is to do the will of him that sent me, that I may perfect his work." Obedience to his Father really was food and drink to him, no other characteristic stands out so clear in him.

But we are still by Jacob's well. The woman had left in such a hurry at seeing so many Jews bearing down upon her that she did not even take the waterpot with her. Back in Shechem, she told of the extraordinary stranger who knew all about her, and a group of the townsmen came out and asked him to stay awhile in their city. So he and his disciples stayed there two days, and many came to believe in him — not as Nathanael and the woman had, because of his miraculous knowledge of their past lives, but "because of his word"—"We ourselves have heard him, and know that this is indeed the Savior of the world." (Some years after the Ascension, two of the disciples, Peter and John, would come back to Samaria to confirm the converts Philip and the others had made there. They must have remembered those first two days.)

From Shechem the party went on to Galilee. And in Cana of the wedding feast, Jesus again worked a miracle.

16 *THE MINISTRY IN GALILEE BEGINS*

Capernaum

By a mere act of the will, our Lord in Cana healed a boy lying dangerously ill sixteen miles away in Capernaum. Thus spectacularly—for the boy's father was an official of Herod's court—the Galilean ministry opened. It would last for fifteen or sixteen months. There would be visits to Jerusalem, of course, for the feasts; and there would be other journeys outside Herod's small realm—to Tyre, for instance, a city of Phoenicia on the Mediterranean coast, where he healed the daughter of a Gentile woman after uttering what sounded like a most hurtful refusal; to Caesarea Philippi in the territory of Herod's brother Philip, where he promised Peter that he would be the rock upon which the Church should be founded. But for most of the period, he was traveling the roads and preaching in the synagogues of Galilee.

Too many of us tend to think of our Lord as moving, and acting, and speaking in a sort of luminous vacuum called Palestine, with towns in it which are names but hardly places, of which no more need be known than that they were filled with Jews and ruled by Romans. For many Christians a kind of unreality attaches to our Lord, as though he were a figure in one of his own parables. It makes his words and deeds more real to us if we see them in the place of their happening.

It is curious that we are not more aware of Capernaum. Everyone knows about Nazareth, though of our Lord's thirty years in Nazareth we have not a single detail. Yet Capernaum, which he made his headquarters during the long Galilean ministry, hardly stirs a chord. Now that we are settling down to study that ministry, it would be good to look at the map of Palestine, find Capernaum, and make for ourselves a first mental sketch of the stage of such great happenings.

We must surely be startled to see how small a stage it is. There is the lake—which we call variously the Sea of Galilee, the Sea of Tiberias, the Lake of Gennesaret—and the country round it. Most of what the Holy Spirit has moved the evangelists to record of the Galilean ministry took place within no great walking distance of its shores. Capernaum itself is to the north, three miles west of the point where the river Jordan runs into the lake; on the opposite bank of the river was Bethsaida, where Simon Peter lived until he too moved into Capernaum. On the lake itself—a small one by world standards, under seventy square miles—Jesus stilled two tempests and caused three miraculous catches of fish. A little to its northeast, he fed the five thousand with five loaves and two small fish; to the southeast, at the far end from Capernaum, occurred that strangest of episodes which ended in the drowning of two thousand pigs; to the southwest one could see Mount Tabor, which we associate with his Transfiguration; and just beyond the mountain was Nain, where he raised the widow's son to life.

In this area of a few hundred square miles, the visitor can still not only walk where Jesus walked, and stand where he stood, but can live in his very atmosphere. The rich towns that ringed the lake are gone, with only a pile of ruins here and there. The rich vegetation has gone too—centuries of neglect all but stripped the soil barren, and the thousands upon thousands of Australian gum trees planted between the two world wars would startle the Twelve, if they could return to the place of so much memory. But the sky is the same, and the lake is the same:

and that is enough. You will meet Jesus here more even than in Jerusalem.

Teaching in the Synagogues

We think of our Lord primarily as Redeemer, and rightly. But we must never forget that he was also Teacher. He was truth-giver as well as life-giver, indeed the truth-giving is an essential part of the life-giving. He began the long Galilean ministry by touring the synagogues, preaching.

At a certain point in the synagogue service, a member of the congregation would be invited by the official in charge to expound some passage in the day's reading from the Old Testament which all had heard. Jesus' fame had spread to Galilee; everyone was talking of the miracles he had worked in Jerusalem in the week of Passover, everyone who had ever felt cheated by the money-changers and the animal-sellers in the Temple must have been enchanted to hear what the carpenter of Nazareth had done to them. Once it was known that he was in the congregation, there was never any doubt that he would be called upon to expound: a congregation avid to hear the most sensational Galilean of all time might well have lynched any synagogue official who had called on anyone else.

Mark and Matthew both tell us that he preached the imminence of the Kingdom of God and the necessity of repentance. This is precisely John the Baptist's formula, so that he begins by linking up with his forerunner. We know the essential of the Baptist's teaching about repentance—that it called for a change in the very soul of the sinner—but not much beside; and of what he taught about the Kingdom of heaven, save that it was close at hand, we know nothing at all. Nor is what our Lord taught on either of these themes in his first tour of the synagogues told us—possibly because the disciples were not with him to record it: we get an impression that they had gone back to their fishing and would only be called to the apostolate a little later. But we do know what he taught about both in the months that followed; and we may assume that he began as he meant to continue.

About the Kingdom—what he had at all costs to do was destroy their confident expectation of a world conquered and the nations ruled by the Jewish people. Until he had done that, it would not be safe to announce himself as King. We have noted how he avoided saying that he was the Christ. In such a moment of effervescent nationalism the Jews might easily rise in a rebellion of the sort Rome was only too skilled at drowning in blood. What he must do, before there was any question of announcing his own messiahship, was to emphasize those elements in the Old Testament prophecies which spoke of spiritual rebirth and spiritual leadership, with Gentiles also reborn, not subjugated. We shall find him talking of his unique relation with his heavenly Father sooner than of his Christhood— for however much even the hint of a claim to divinity might madden men against himself, it would not cause a national uprising against the Romans.

What he taught about repentance—*metanoia,* change of mind, change of heart—we may gather from the Sermon on the Mount which would follow soon afterward. There, particularly, we can see why, at the very beginning of his teaching ministry, the people "were astonished at his doctrine; for he was teaching them as one having power, and not as the scribes" (Mk 1:22). The whole teaching method of the scribes was to quote some earlier authority and establish what was the traditional interpretation of the law of Moses and the teachings of the prophets. Jesus not only calls no earlier authority to show that what he is now teaching is what Moses actually meant: he assumes to himself a greater authority than even Moses had: Moses said thus and thus, "but I say to you". It was the most astonishing phrase that had ever come from Jewish lips. Either it was unspeakable arrogance— blasphemy indeed since Moses, in the passages quoted, was giving forth what God had given him; or else—what? For Galilee then and for the whole world ever since, that has been the question of questions.

First Exorcism

To make this sort of claim and not be stoned to death, he had to work miracles. In the first public miracle of this new campaign, in the Capernaum synagogue, he once more confronted the powers of hell: "There was a man with an unclean devil and he cried out with a loud voice: Let us alone, what have we to do with thee, Jesus of Nazareth? Art thou come to destroy us? I know thee who thou art, the Holy One of God" (Lk 4:33–34). For the first time we hear the carpenter called "Jesus".

It is not impossible, if God permits, for demons to take control of a man's body, using his limbs, for instance, to do what the demons will and not what he wills, using his tongue to utter not his words but theirs. Here in the synagogue, hell resumed contact with Christ. This new contact did not involve Satan himself, but one of his demons, and there was no direct tempting of Christ. But it is hard to escape the feeling that Satan was still exploring, trying to find out all he could about the miracle-worker.

A few months earlier, in the desert, Satan had said: "If thou be the Son of God", and had got no answer at all. He had been ordered to go away and he had gone; but his demons never ceased to watch and listen. They must have heard Jesus tell the Samaritan woman that he was the Christ. The carpenter might, of course, have been deluded, or he might have been simply lying: that possibility would not have escaped so practised a liar as Satan, "liar and father of lies"; others had made the same claim.

But Satan had had a long experience of studying men's characters; *and* there were the miracles. Evidently he had arrived at the conclusion that this was, at last, the Christ—Mark tells us, a little later, that the demons knew it. But what exactly was this Christ? And what plans had he against the lord of hell? Here in the synagogue, the rank-and-file demon used the possessed man's voice to cry out that he knew who Jesus was, and to put the question which mattered most of all to Satan and all hell's citizenry: "Art thou come to destroy us?" His question was not answered, any more than his leader's question had been answered. Jesus ordered him to be silent, ordered him out of the body of his victim.

As a dismissed child might slam a door, the demon flung the man to the ground in one last epileptic fit, then troubled him no more.

From the synagogue Jesus went to the house of Simon, who was to be called Peter. He and Andrew had evidently moved to Capernaum from their own city, Bethsaida; the journey was not long, they had only to cross the Jordan and travel three more miles. Simon's wife's mother lay ill with a great fever. "Standing over her, he commanded the fever, and it left her. And immediately rising, she ministered to them"—put food on the table, in fact. That is Luke's description (4:39). Mark, who, as we remember, is giving us Peter's own Gospel, adds a detail: "He lifted her up, taking her by the hand; and immediately the fever left her" (1:31). We notice that there was no question of expelling a demon this time: Jesus simply commanded the fever, as later he would command the storm.

This small miracle caused a stir among the family and neighbors; but it was as nothing to the excitement that followed upon the healing of the possessed man in all the publicity of the synagogue. Everybody with any kind of disease felt that here was healing: somehow or other they must get to the healer. It was the Sabbath day, and they could not make the journey until the Sabbath rest ended at sunset. But when that moment came "they brought to him all that were ill and that were possessed with devils; and all the city was gathered together at the door" (Mk 1:32–33).

The sick he healed, every one of them, laying his hands on them. And he cast out many devils. These also he had to order to be silent as he had ordered the one in the synagogue that morning, for they were crying out that he was the Son of God. All hell knew by now that he was the Christ.

Fishers of Men

He continued his miracle-studded way round Galilee, preaching in the synagogues. He was telling of the Kingdom of heaven, but not yet of himself as King, still less of the essential part the Kingdom would play in his own work of redeeming the world—a part so essential, indeed, that redemption and entry into the

Kingdom would be inseparable. He must still occupy himself with purifying people's expectations, cleansing these of every trace of personal or national egoism, showing them the Kingdom as essentially other-worldly—*in* this world but not of it, established by repentance, not by the sort of conquest of which they dreamed.

We get the impression that, on this preliminary journey, he traveled alone. Three months or so earlier five disciples had attached themselves to him. But they seem to have gone back to their fishing. Now he would call them definitively, beginning with Andrew and Simon Peter, John and his brother James. We should study their calling closely. It was the first stage in the actual building of the Kingdom of which he had been preaching, the Kingdom "built on the foundation of the apostles" (Eph 2:20), the Kingdom of which there should be no end.

The story is told in the fourth chapter of Matthew, the first of Mark, and the fifth of Luke. Luke tells it in fullest detail. We shall follow his account.

Jesus was standing by the lake. The crowds were thronging round him and pressing hard upon him. He had to clear a space. He adopted the only method that could possibly have worked. He got into a fishing boat—it was Simon Peter's—had it rowed out a little from the land, and preached to the crowds as he sat in the boat. To this day Catholics find pleasure in thinking of Christ's voice sounding from Peter's boat.

He told Peter to row out into the deep and lower the nets again. And now for the first time we hear Peter speak: he must have said a good deal before this, for he was almost too ready a talker; but this is the first utterance of his that the Holy Spirit thought worth recording. "Master," he said, "we have labored all the night, and have taken nothing; but at thy word I will let down the net." All Peter's discipleship was in that answer—"It seems impossible, but if *you* say so—!"

We know what followed—a haul of fish that burst the net. Peter and Andrew called to James and John, their partners, who were in another boat near by, and both boats were loaded with fish to the gunwales, nearly sinking under the weight. What was the exact nature of the miracle? Either Jesus knew that the fish would be there—if so, it was by no natural knowledge that a carpenter would read signs that the fishermen missed; or he willed them to be there.

Peter's reaction is fascinating: "Depart from me, for I am a sinful man, O Lord." After all, this was not the first miracle Peter has seen Jesus work. He had been there when his new Master spoke to Nathanael of an incident that his bodily eyes had not seen—Peter may well have thought that he was reading the other's mind. He had been at the wedding feast in Cana when the water was changed into wine, he had been there all through the week of miracles following Passover in Jerusalem. Only recently his mother-in-law had been cured of fever at a touch of Christ's hand and a word from his lips. But reading minds and healing bodies, even making wine—such things lay outside his experience: even without miracle, these were mysteries to Peter. But fish were different: he knew all about fish. This miracle hit home to him as the others had not.

So we understand the special intensity of his astonishment. But why the fear? Why was his first reaction to a vast haul of fish an overpowering sense of his own sinfulness? He had seen the money-changers scourged from the Temple—and was probably delighted to see it, feeling that they were getting what they deserved. Evidently it had not occurred to him that he was a sinner himself. This time, precisely because the miracle hit home to him in all the reality of its miraculousness, he suddenly saw Christ for the first time. Seeing Christ, he at last saw himself.

Not for the last time, Peter had said the wrong thing. He was not wrong in calling himself a sinner. It is his solitary glory that he did. Of all the sinners that ever approached our Lord, Peter is the only one we ever hear confessing himself one in so many words. Where he was wrong was in seeing his sinfulness as a reason why our Lord should depart from him. He did not yet know that Christ was the Healer—the worse one's sins, the more one needs him.

There is something rather special about the opening words of our Lord's reply: "Fear not." They are the first actual words of kindness we have heard from his lips. He did countless kind things: but we could almost count on our fingers his kind words. He was simply not given to sentimental utterance. "Fear not" were the words Gabriel had uttered, unnecessarily as he did not then know, to our Lady. This time they were necessary: Peter, aware of the glory confronting him and of his own sinful meagerness, was afraid.

So far, the story has been all Luke's. Now Matthew and Mark join in. Neither of them tells of the miracle that had just happened. Mark, we remind ourselves, was writing the Gospel that he had heard Peter preaching, and Peter was not given to telling of miracles that involved himself. Matthew was probably at that very moment harrying some poor taxpayer to the point of despair, himself sublimely unaware how soon he would hear the "Follow me" from the carpenter. In any event, a haul of fish would not have impressed Levi, the tax collector, who became the Apostle Matthew, as it did Peter the fisherman. John, who was there, does not mention any part of the incident: he was writing thirty years after the others, and could assume that what they had written did not need retelling by him.

Only Luke tells of the miraculous haul of fish and of the brief dialogue that followed. We may be certain that Luke discussed every line of his Gospel with his own master, Paul. It may be purely fanciful, yet it need not be, to think of Paul wanting this acknowledgment of something special about Peter written into the Gospel. For what Matthew and Mark tell us that Jesus says to the others in the plural, that he would make them fishers of men, we know from Luke that he said to Peter in the singular — "Henceforth *thou* shalt catch men."

In thus creating the apostles fishermen of souls, our Lord answers one question that must have occurred to the reader: What was the point of this particular miracle? Galilee was suffering from no shortage of fish; the sons of Zebedee and their partners were not facing an economic crisis which a large catch of fish might help to avert. It is always nice to catch more fish than you had expected. But it hardly calls for a miracle. The changing of water into wine did at least relieve the social embarrassment of the hosts. But what did *this* miracle do?

The answer seems to be in Jesus' way of illustrating the more important points of his teaching by some spectacular symbolic action. Later he would prove his power to heal sins by healing a paralyzed man's body. Now that he is making men fishers of souls, he shows that when they fish at his command, they do so with power far beyond their own.

Something else we learn of his teaching method: he would use comparisons of which only the precise point mentioned by him was relevant. We cannot always follow the comparison one step further than he himself took it—as when he compares his own coming to that of a thief in the night, the only point of so odd a comparison being that you don't know when. Later (Mt 13:47) he would again compare souls to fish caught in a net. One remembers that it is no advantage to the fish to be caught in a net. There is no future in it for them: they will soon be dead! In the second instance Jesus was concentrating solely on the sorting of good fish from bad, and the rejection of the bad. In this present instance his concern is solely with their catching—which, for souls, means drawing them from chaos into the hands of their Redeemer.

The incident ends with the four men leaving all things to follow Christ. All things. Including the fish.

17 MIRACLES AND EXORCISMS

The Miracles Jesus Worked

Jesus now had four disciples definitely chosen and committed, Simon Peter and Andrew, James and John. They had left the marvelous haul of fishes to the delighted Zebedee: they would not fish again until Christ's death, and then only briefly.

An improbably large catch of fish would impress fishermen. The next miracle recorded would have impressed everybody; it was a healing of a leper—"A man full of leprosy" (Lk 5:12), who said, "Lord, if thou wilt, thou canst make me clean." Jesus had compassion on him, Mark tells us (1:41), and the telling is precious—

it is the first actual mention of that compassion which is to dominate his ministry. The principal purpose of these miracles, we may presume, was to show his power and his divine mission. For that, one miracle would do as well as another. But again and again, the miracles he chose to work were those which would bring relief to suffering, solace to anguish. Let us linger awhile on his miracles.

There are Christians, people who truly love Christ all the same, who find the miracles embarrassing. At one end, the embarrassment is simply an unwillingness to mention them in the presence of their scientific friends (the God-blind ones, of course, there are plenty of others). At the other end, it is a desire to hold on to Christ while refusing to believe that the miracles ever happened. It is worth our while to glance at both ends.

To deny miracles totally is a desperate resort. They are in all four Gospels, interwoven into so much that Jesus said and did, totally accepted as fact, even by his enemies: the high priests themselves said, "The man is performing many miracles, and if we leave him to his own devices, he will find credit everywhere" (Jn 11:47). In the first centuries even adversaries did not question that the miracles happened, though they refused to see in them the work of God. If one is set against miracles, it would be simpler to write off the Gospels as fiction; take out the miracles and all that flows into them and out of them, and you have only rather tattered Gospels left.

Related to this total rejection is the view, rarer now, that these things happened, but were not really miracles—they were merely the application of physical laws, as yet unknown to the primitive science of the day. Some amiable person has said that if a monk of the Middle Ages had seen an airplane, he would have thought it a miracle. So, indeed, it would have been—if he had seen it in the Middle Ages: science and technology had not then reached the point of producing airplanes. In the matter of Jesus' miracles, the proponents of this view are demanding even more.

For in the first place, one previously undiscovered law would not do. We should need lots of them to explain the walking on the water, the calming of a tempest by a word, the changing of water into wine, the multiplication of loaves; the healing by a touch and a word of fever, leprosy, a withered hand, hemorrhage, crippled limbs, blindness, deafness; the raising from the dead not only of a girl and two men, but of Jesus himself.

And if such physical laws do exist, it would be curious if a village carpenter had stumbled upon them two thousand years ago—still more if he had left with his followers the power to do similar things, without telling any of them the scientific laws involved. He does not even hand on recipes for miracles or exorcisms of the sort we find among both Jews and pagans.

Those who accept the miracles but are bothered by the violation of natural laws and wonder why Christ saw fit to work them are under a double confusion. The laws of nature have their own sacredness, of course, but the notion that the Creator is in some way bound by them is almost comic. And in fact a miracle no more violates the laws of nature than a fielder violates the law of gravity by catching a ball on its way to the ground. He has simply brought into action another law. That is what God does: he wills to intervene in some decisive way, bringing a new force to bear either to prevent the normal effect of the laws we are all accustomed to count upon, or to bring about some effect beyond what the customary laws could by themselves produce. Whether a ball is stopped in its rush towards the ground by a fielder's hand or the will of God, the law of gravity is unaffected—the earth is still tugging at the ball exactly as before, but another force is resisting the tug. God who created nature with its laws out of nothing can introduce a new force at will. Jesus not only worked miracles himself, but he told the apostles that they should work greater miracles still. We find them working many in Jerusalem after Pentecost (Acts 2:43). And from that day to this, as Jesus promised (Mk 16:18), the Church has never been without miracles (though no Catholic is bound to believe in any miracle not recorded in Scripture).

There are four words used for them in the Gospels. They are called *wonders*—the word "miracle" is from the Latin verb "to wonder"; a miracle sets you wondering, fills you with wonder. They are called *powers* or *energies,* because divine power produces them. They are called *signs,* because they are meant to draw attention, testify, to some truth. Jesus himself likes to call them his *works*.

Apart from occasions when he worked great numbers of miracles—as during the week after Passover in Jerusalem, or that Sabbath evening in Capernaum—we are told of thirty-three individual miracles between Cana and Calvary. Some of these we shall be considering in greater detail a little further on. Here it is interesting to make a first analysis of the list as a whole.

Eight show his power over inanimate nature—he changes water into wine, calms a tempest at a word, walks upon the surface of the lake, twice causes fish to be drawn improbably from it, twice feeds large crowds with a handful of loaves and some little fish, and strikes a fig tree to barrenness with a word.

The remaining twenty-five are concerned with human beings. Six times he casts out demons, fifteen times he heals diseases or other physical defects, once he restores a severed ear, three times he brings back the dead to life—two men and a girl: the widow's son of Nain, Lazarus, and the daughter of Jairus.

Let us pause on these three, because they illustrate a feature common to all his miracles, but more spectacular in these because of what death is. There are two famous instances in the Old Testament of the dead raised to life. Elijah raised a boy, the only son of a widowed mother like the young man of Nain, at Zarephath (1 Kings 17); a few miles from Nain, Elisha raised a child at Shunem (2 Kings 4). Read the accounts. In each, we find the prophet stretched out upon the dead body, imploring God to restore it to life. Then read of the widow's son at Nain (Lk 7:11–17), the daughter of Jairus (Lk 8:40–56), Lazarus (Jn 11). In none of these is there any physical effort, simply the words: "Young man, I say to thee arise", "Maid, arise", "Lazarus, come forth." Nor is there any when, in the power of Christ, Peter raised Tabitha from the dead (Acts 9:40).

It is interesting to compare the miracles of Jesus with the sixty or so healings—no castings out of devils or raisings from death—recounted on limestone tablets, perhaps some three hundred years earlier, at Epidaurus. We know nothing of their origin—who wrote them, whose authority backed them. They are simply there. There is a sobriety in the Gospel accounts—they contain nothing comparable with the woman five years pregnant, delivered at Epidaurus of a child which ran at once to wash at a spring. Jesus healed in his own name; at Epidaurus all is the work of the god Aesculapius or the god Apollo. There is no complication of ritual or gesture in the Gospel miracles, no visit from the god in dreams, no magical formulas, simply a command.

There is an occasional bodily act—Jesus taking the victim's hand, using his saliva upon eyes or ears. Gestures of this sort were not necessary, but they did bring Christ's body into life-giving action, very much as the material order is brought into the giving of a life higher still in the sacraments.

John details fewer miracles than Matthew or Mark or Luke— seven as against nearly a score by each of the others, who, of course, are often giving their separate accounts of one same miracle. But he lays even greater stress than they on their evidential value. He most clearly shows us the special importance Jesus attached to his works as *signs,* the word John always uses.

Read John 5:18–36. Here Jesus reminded the hostile leaders of Judaism that the Baptist worked no miracles, whereas he himself worked many, and we see why he did. The Baptist's importance lay wholly in his message: but Jesus was calling on men to believe not only in his message but in himself—"The works themselves which I do give testimony of me that the Father has sent me." He returns to the same point in John's tenth chapter: "Believe the works: that you may know and believe that the Father is in me and I in the Father" (Jn 10:38).

Casting out Devils

We have spoken of modern Christians to whom the miracles cause embarrassment; but that is as nothing to their feeling about the casting out of devils. There are many Christian circles in which even to admit belief that there *is* a devil makes one an object of curiosity. In such circles Christ's casting out of devils is never mentioned voluntarily at all; if some amused unbeliever raises the matter, the answer is that Jesus himself knew better, but found it saved trouble to use the language of the people of his own day, who, to a man, were confirmed believers in the devil.

But this view can arise only out of a prolonged abstention from Gospel reading. Jesus was not that sort of person. On a matter of no importance he might have used ordinary ways of speech. But he would never have used a way of speech, however ordinary, that was based on a religious error. When his disciples assumed that a man was born blind either because of sins he would one day commit or sins his parents had already committed (Jn 9:2), he told them plainly that neither of them was the cause.

Further, when we come to read some of the accounts of expulsions of demons, we should feel that he would have been carrying the use of popular ideas and popular language rather far, if he did not believe that there were any demons there. For he spoke to them, commanded them, questioned them, granted a request made by them, ordered them to be silent about himself. Further still, when he sent the Twelve out on their first mission without him, he expressly gave them the power to cast out devils (Mt 10:8).

Let us glance at the recorded facts. Between Cana and Calvary there are thirty-three miracles mentioned individually. Of these only six are concerned with the casting out of demons.

Demons are pure spirits, more powerful *as spirits* than the souls of men, for they have no bodies (upon the animation of our bodies our own souls' energy must in part be expended), and they do not depend upon bodily senses for information about the external world. It is clear from Scripture that while they cannot create matter, they can move it about in space, rearrange its parts, work upon it in a variety of ways: they have more power over matter than we have, and need no hands or material instruments for its exercise. But great as their powers are, demons are limited in their use of them by the will of God.

It is within their power to work upon the human brain, producing images which might stimulate the desires to which a given man is already tempted; it is within their power to move a man's arms or legs, so that his gestures are really theirs not his, and he walks where they wish, not where he wishes; they can use a man's tongue and lips so that he utters their ideas not his own, or is kept from utterance altogether; they can interfere with the bodily mechanism by which he sees or hears. All these things are within their natural powers as bodiless spirits, just as it is within a snake's power to bite poisonously. But God's power is as much beyond theirs as it is beyond the snake's; and we are always under his protection against demons, unless we cast it aside.

Of the thirty-three individual miracles of our Lord's public ministry, eight manifest his power over inanimate nature. There seems to be a general impression that in the remaining twenty-five, in which he dealt with human afflictions, he did no more than use the power of his personality to heal nervous ailments of one sort or another. Further, that in a superstitious age he added to his reputation as a miracle-worker by claiming that these ailments were caused by devils and that he cast them out. Most of the symptoms of the people from whom Jesus cast out devils suggest nervous diseases which modern medicine feels itself competent to treat—deafness, dumbness, blindness, paralysis, apoplexy, lunacy.

But as we have seen, in only six of the twenty-five did he cast out devils; and while many of the other cures were of what we could now recognize as nervous diseases, many were not; death is not a nervous disease, and three times he raised the dead to life; a crippled leg is more than a nervous affliction; so are a withered hand and leprosy and a severed ear. There *is* a similarity between nervous diseases and cases of diabolical possession, for the simple reason that the devil's chosen point of entry is in the nervous system, because the nerves bring impulses to, and carry impulses from, the brain and spinal cord; when he takes control there he can prevent the commands of the will getting through to the bodily organs which normally obey them and substitute his own. Jesus often treats exactly the same symptoms without any reference to diabolic possession, healing them as physical diseases solely.

When he is sending out the Twelve on their first mission, Jesus tells them to "heal the sick, raise the dead, cleanse the lepers, cast out devils" (Mt 10:8). And in similar vein Matthew tells us (4:24) that there were brought to him "all sick people taken with different diseases and torments, *and* such as were possessed by devils, *and* lunatics, *and* those that had the palsy."

As we have said, there can be similarity between diabolic possession and nervous disease: the Catholic Church makes strenuous efforts to be sure that demons are actually present before she resorts to exorcism: it is possible even for the very skilled to be deceived—to the amusement, perhaps, of such demons as happen to be watching from the sideline. But Jesus could not be mistaken. At times we find him treating deafness, dumbness, by ordering the demon out. At other times he treats deafness, dumbness (Mk 7:32-35), blindness (Mk 8:22-26), with no mention of demons, his commands being addressed only to the afflicted body or the bodily affliction.

I have said that he orders demons out. It is fascinating to compare the speed and almost casualness of his exorcisms with the form prescribed in the Church—which occupies thirty pages of the *Rituale Romanum.* Even more fascinating is the comparison between his method and the methods of the Jewish exorcists. In the Old Testament there is no instance of the casting out of a demon—unless the spirit of melancholy from which David liberated King Saul by the music of his harp was one. But the nonscriptural writers, in the years just preceding and following the time of Jesus, have much to say on the subject.

The Jewish historian Josephus, in his *Antiquities of the Jews* (book VIII, chapter 2) describes how he himself saw a fellow countryman of his own, named Eleazar, in the presence of the Emperor Vespasian and his soldiers, draw demons out by putting to the nose of the possessed man a ring containing a root supposed to have been prescribed by Solomon for the purpose, uttering incantations composed by that same wise man! A contemporary of Josephus, Rabbi Johanan ben Zakkai, says that the evil spirit will flee if the roots of various herbs are burnt under the man's nose, and water poured round him.

Jesus used no incantations. He used no physical actions of any sort—in the Canaanite case (Mt 15:21-28), indeed, the possessed girl and her demons were not even present, only her unpossessed mother. He did not ask God to expel the evil spirits, any more than to heal the sick. He simply ordered the demons out, exactly as he had ordered their leader away after the third temptation. And they had to go. They might plead, they might abuse, but they went. Their inability to resist his word must have convinced them, as no miracle could, that he was something new in the world.

18 *"HE BLASPHEMES"*

"Thy Sins Are Forgiven Thee"

Jesus had healed diseases without calling upon God. He had cast out devils without calling upon God. Now he was to do something else in his own name alone, something that would not only startle, as the healings and exorcisms did, but scandalize as well. For the first time we are to hear the word blasphemy murmured against him.

His fame was by now enormous. There were already such masses of miracles, even before the one which must have been found quite overwhelming, the instant healing of leprosy. Jesus had told the healed leper to say nothing to anyone until he had presented himself to the priests, had undergone the ritual prescribed in the Book of Leviticus (13 and 14), and been pronounced clean. But the priests would have to be told by him how this extraordinary thing had happened; and his friends, finding him well once more, would have besieged him with questions and spread abroad his answers.

The result of all these things was that Christ "could not openly go into the city, but stayed outside in desert places" (Mk 1:45). There too, the crowds flocked to him. And when he returned to Capernaum, people thrust in to fill the house in which he was. They packed it to the doors, with more people milling outside. Among them—this we are told for the first time—Pharisees and doctors of the Law were sitting to hear what he should say. There is nothing sinister in their presence. They were the doctrinal and moral leaders of Judaism, and it was their plain duty to examine very closely the miracle-worker who seemed to be winning such attention as no one had won since Moses himself.

As he was speaking, a paralyzed man was lowered through the roof, mattress and all, the four men carrying him finding no other way to bring him to the healer through the crowd. The faith in himself that their inventiveness showed moved Jesus. He said: "Be of good heart, son, thy sins are forgiven thee" (Mt 9:2).

"Be of good heart"—that is precious to us as one of the rare instances of his using actual words of kindness to an individual. But it was the phrase which followed—"thy sins are forgiven thee"—that stunned those present in the room. Not, perhaps, the paralyzed man himself: he wanted healing for his poor body, and may easily have felt a surge of disappointment at getting only healing for his soul. But for the Pharisees and the men learned in the Law it was utterly shattering. "Why does this man speak thus? He blasphemes. Who can forgive sins, but God only?" (Mk 2:7).

Holy men of old had healed the sick, Elijah and Elisha had even raised the dead. Forgiveness of sin was different. In all the Old Testament, and in all the nonscriptural writings pouring out in such abundance just before Christ's coming, there is not so much as a hint that any man, even the Messiah, could forgive sins.

He read their minds and answered their challenge. But in his own way. Matthew tells us that he said: "Why do you think evil in your hearts?" Pause for a moment on this. He could hardly have meant that there was any sin in their thinking it blasphemy for a mere man to claim to forgive sins. "Think evil" probably means "think ill of me"—for making the claim.

The obvious answer was "I am God." But he did not give it. He did not mention God at all. He worked a miracle there and then in order, as he said, to show that "the Son of Man has power to forgive sins here on earth." He told the paralyzed man to pick up his mattress and walk home: one may imagine that this time there was no need to travel by way of the roof: the crowd would have fallen back to make a path for him. They were astonished and awed, as we are told, as indeed we hardly need to be told! They glorified God "who gave such power to men", adds Matthew (9:8). Why the plural "men"? They had seen such power in one man only. Matthew may have been thinking of the reaction not of those who saw the incident, but of those later crowds, who knew the communication of power to the apostles.

But the learned men would not all have joined in the chorus of praise. For their original point about blasphemy had not been met, unless there was more in the phrase "Son of Man" than they knew.

When he had scourged the businessmen from the Temple, the high officials only asked him by what right he did it, precisely the same question they had asked of the Baptist. In neither instance was there any suggestion that the things actually done had been in themselves sinful. Announcing that the Kingdom was at hand, calling upon men to repent, washing them with water so that the cleansing of the body might symbolize a cleansing of the soul, even taking the lash to men profaning the holy place—a mere man *might* have a right to do any of these things. It was for him to tell them what his right was.

But forgiving sins was a totally different matter. The Pharisees and the men learned in the Law had literally no alternative but to ask, "Who can forgive sins but God alone?" In the minds of Peter and Andrew, James and John, if not yet on their lips, the same question must have clamored for answer. The throng of people, dazzled by the healing of the paralytic, might go away glorifying God; but the dazzle of a miracle fades with time, and the profounder question would have returned. The word "blasphemy" uttered as an accusation by the Pharisees and the scribes would have lingered in many a mind as at least a troubling echo.

Once know that our Lord is God and the accusation vanishes. But he had not said that he was God. Even a statement that God had given him authority to forgive sins would at least have been an answer for those who believed him. But he did not say that either—at least not in words. He simply asserted that the Son of Man *had* power to forgive sins here upon earth, then effected a cure which was beyond the powers of man unaided. Some of his hearers would believe that the aid required came from God; but already the idea was forming in the minds of others, and would later be put into words, that the aid came from the lord of the demons.

We may very well ask why he did not at once say that he was God. The question arises only to be dismissed. It would be a natural enough question for unbelievers in God, even for half-believers. But if we have grasped what God is, we see two overwhelming reasons why he should not yet utter the fact of his divinity to the Jewish people.

The first is that the Jews, even those of them whose sins our Lord condemned so scathingly, did in the very depth of their being believe in God, were conscious above all of the majesty of God. If he had begun with the bald statement "I am God", only two reactions would have been possible. Those who believed him, if any did, would have been in such stricken awe of the Infinite Majesty whose presence in their midst they must accept, that all communication between him and them would have been impossible: they would have been far too terrified even to raise their eyes to his face: it was not revealed even to his closest followers till they had grown so in intimacy with him that they could not be merely terrified by it. We are so accustomed to the truth that God became man, that we do not realize how overwhelming such a fact would have seemed to people hearing it for the first time.

On the other hand, those who did not believe would have seen God blasphemed, and his majesty profaned; and the penalty was death. "A false prophet must die, who speaks in my name a thing I have not commanded" (Dt 18:20). In fact, we find that, when later Jesus said to such people, "Before Abraham was made, I AM" (Jn 8:58), they took up stones to destroy him, and he had to hide in the Temple. When he said, "I and the Father are one" (Jn 10:30), they tried to seize him and he had to make his escape to the other side of the Jordan. And in the end it was for blasphemy that he was crucified.

But there was another reason why he could not yet tell the people that he was God—not only that they would have found the truth too great to be borne or the claim too blasphemous to be tolerated, but also quite simply that they could not even have understood what he was saying about himself. For it is the second Person of the Blessed Trinity who became flesh and dwelt among us, not the Father, not the Holy Spirit, not all three. The doctrine of the Incarnation must be either meaningless or wholly misleading to people who do not know the doctrine of the Blessed Trinity. And his hearers did not know it. They knew only the solitary God.

The Son of Man

Meanwhile the name by which he refers to himself is Son of Man, Barnasha. In the Gospels he alone calls himself by that name — we find it on his lips some forty times, no one else applies it to him. After his death the name vanishes: Stephen, the first martyr, uses it in describing a vision (Acts 7:55), and it is similarly used in two visions in Revelations. But that is all. With the full revelation of his Messiahship and Godhead, it was no longer needed.

In itself the phrase is simply an idiomatic Hebrew way of saying "man". In the Book of Ezekiel, it is used ninety-four times and means no more than the plain word man. We find it likewise used in the Book of Job, and the point there is to stress the littleness of man in the face of the majesty of God. The meaning rises in the Book of Daniel. In chapter 10 the angel Gabriel appears to Daniel as "the likeness of a son of man", that is, "looking like a man".

But in chapter 7 we get the mightiest and most mysterious use of the phrase. God is upon his throne, thousands upon thousands of angels ministering to him, and ten thousand times a hundred thousand standing before him. Then "One like the son of man came with the clouds of heaven . . . and [God] gave him power and glory and a kingdom: and all peoples, tribes, and tongues shall serve him. His power is an everlasting power which shall not be taken away, and his kingdom shall not be destroyed."

When the Pharisees and the men learned in the Law accused him of blasphemy for forgiving the sins of the paralyzed man — the one who had been lowered through the roof — Jesus worked a miracle to prove that "the Son of Man" had the power to do what he had just done. This is the first time we find the phrase in the first three Gospels. John had already mentioned two uses of it. Jesus had spoken of himself as the Son of Man to Nathanael when he drew him into his company at Bethel; he had used it to Nicodemus, on that secret visit by night. What did it mean?

To us it sounds a totally unmistakable prophecy of the Messiah. But it does not seem to have caught the attention of the Jews. Round about a hundred years before the carpenter applied it to himself, we find Daniel's use of it treated in a book, the *Parables* of Enoch, and treated with great magnificence, as telling of the Messiah—before the creation of the world and for all eternity, light of the peoples, hope of the suffering, to be adored, salvation in his name, judge. But the Book of Enoch was not widely read. And the Jews who heard Jesus use the phrase could not but wonder what he meant by it. "Who is this Son of Man?" they asked. It seems that he deliberately chose a phrase which raised a question about himself, but did not give the answer; people were not yet ready for it.

But though he does not yet say, in fullness, who and what he is, he *acts* as himself. As we read the Gospels, we are conscious of two streams—episodes in which he speaks and acts as man, interwoven with episodes in which he speaks and acts as something immeasurably more. These last set both his followers and his enemies to wondering just what he was, or at least what he was claiming to be. There are times when he said things which in a man would be quite meaningless, as—"Before Abraham was made, I am"; just as now and then he said things which in a mere man would be intolerable, as—"if you love father and mother more than me, you are not worthy of me." Spoken by anyone but God, this would be monstrous. His followers knew that he was no monster. But who was he? What was he?

The Calling of Matthew

Matthew, Mark, and Luke go straight from the cure of the paralyzed man let down through the roof—and the scandal caused to the Pharisees by Jesus' claim to forgive his sins—to an episode which may strike some of us as a miracle more extraordinary still, and which struck the Pharisees as almost more scandalous. We ourselves sometimes find tax collectors a nuisance, but we do not think of them with hatred as extortioners—those feelings we reserve for the legislators who impose the taxes. It is hard for us to realize what the calling of Levi by Jesus meant to the Jews of that day.

In the Roman Empire taxes were numerous, of course; and by and large people got their money's worth in peace and security. There was an income tax—they groaned under that, it might be as much as one per cent—a property tax usually levied only when funds ran low, export taxes, death duties, purchase taxes, duties on goods leaving the district. It was the Roman custom to call for tenders for the collection of taxes in a particular province, the winner being the man who offered to collect them and retain the lowest percentage by way of commission for himself. He was the publican: he employed any number of subordinates called—one sees why—exactors. Naturally it was to the interest of the publican to get as much out of the provincials as he could manage to squeeze, because his commission would rise accordingly. He was hated, and all his officials were hated, everywhere: not least by the Jews.

On his way to the lake, Jesus passed the desk of one of these men, Levi: the Gospels call him a publican, he may have been only an exactor, but a rich one. He was at his unpleasing work when the carpenter paused in front of his desk and said, "Follow me." Levi simply followed him, leaving his cash, his account books, and the line of people who had been wondering how much he would extort from them.

In all the history of conversion, it would be hard to find one quite like this. "Follow me", the carpenter had said. Follow him where? Toward what? The carpenter had not said and the tax collector did not ask. It was enough for Levi that he was to follow the carpenter.

That Jesus should have called such a man to be a disciple must have taken everyone's breath away. Fishermen—unlearned in the Law and not very observant of it—were unlikely enough as the chosen companions of a religious leader: but a publican! Levi was to become Matthew. Only in Matthew's account is he named so. Mark in his second chapter, and Luke in his fifth, call him Levi only. After all, Matthew was an apostle and they were not. It had all happened thirty years before they wrote, still it was not for them to publish the shame that had been his.

Levi made a great feast in his own house, and invited Jesus and his disciples. There they ate with a number of Levi's colleagues— exactors, hated and despised and prosperous like himself. There were other guests too, lumped together in the Gospel accounts under the one word "sinners"—non-observers of the ritual law, Gentiles, perhaps, as well: Who else could have dined at Levi's table? One wonders what the four fishermen made of their new companion. Capernaum being his area, Levi may well have collected taxes from, and been reviled by, these very men.

What did Levi's colleagues think? And his wife? How did he break it to her that he was resigning from a highly-paid post, in order to join up with a carpenter in an enterprise that he hardly comprehended himself? Or had the carpenter, perhaps, already won her? Of all this we know nothing at all. She is simply one of those forgotten women, the wives of the apostles. Celibacy, we remember, was not held in any honor among the Jews and not practised, save by eccentrics like the Essenes. Men married at twenty or twenty-one. Saint John—traditionally unmarried—may have been still in his teens; but our Lord had not chosen a dozen boys for the foundation members of his Church. Most of them would have had wives. They are never mentioned. Curious, too, that we never hear of the children of any of the Twelve.

What went on in Levi's mind when our Lord called him from his desk, we are not told. Levi, who as Matthew wrote the story in his Gospel, could have told us, but he was not writing of himself but of his Lord—it would never have occurred to him to write this particular episode in the first person. Nor are we told what his wife thought, or his old colleagues, or his new colleagues.

But we know, from Jesus himself, what the Pharisees thought. In the parable of the Pharisee and the Publican (Lk 18:9–14) he has shown us what Pharisees felt about such as Levi. He may even have given us a glimpse of Levi's own mind—for in his only have given us a glimpse of Levi's own mind—for in his only parable about a publican he would hardly have been unmindful of the only one of that unlovely profession among the Twelve. Certainly Matthew must have listened to this parable as to no other; one can imagine the other apostles avoiding looking at him.

The Pharisee of the parable was not the best kind of Pharisee— they were not all as certain of their own perfection, there were magnificent men among them. But if his degree of complacency was not normal among Pharisees, his view of the rest of men *was*—they were "extortioners, unjust, adulterers, *even as this publican*".

Matthew must have winced. Yet think how the parable continues: "The publican, standing afar off, would not so much as lift up his eyes toward heaven; but struck his breast, saying: O God, be merciful to me a sinner." Is that a description of Levi, in the moment when he looked into the eyes of the All-Pure and saw his own uncleanness?

At least, the phrase that follows describes Levi exactly: "This man went down to his house justified, rather than the other." But what happened when Levi went down to *his* house shocked the Pharisees present even more than his summoning. For Jesus and his disciples sat at table with publicans and sinners.

The scribes had built up a great mass of ritual observance about what went into the mouth. They would not eat with, or enter the house of, Gentiles—or Jews either, if they were ritually unclean. On their lips, the word "sinners" had special reference to Jews who did not observe the rules and rituals which men learned in the Law had added to the precepts of Moses.

The Pharisees did not enter Levi's house to gaze upon a scene so degrading. They seem to have gathered outside and watched— with mounting horror—the guests as they entered. "Why does your Master eat and drink with publicans and sinners?" They had already accused him of blasphemy for forgiving a man's sins. A breach of ritual about eating was not in the same class of sinfulness. Yet it might have scandalized them more. Sins often affect us more by their impact on the imagination than by their actual grievousness.

Our Lord answered their question: "Those who are well have no need of the physician but those who are sick. I have not come to call the just but sinners to repentance."

Many, standing there, must have felt that the words settled any doubts still left. The carpenter had declared a way not their way; by every standard they had, he was a heretic about sin. For (1) he did not make ritual observance a test; (2) he claimed that he could forgive sinners; (3) he chose their company and made their conversion his first concern.

Saint Matthew — Saint Levi, that is — adds that Jesus quoted the prophet Hosea (6:6): "I will have mercy and not sacrifice", and adjured these men of learning to learn what the phrase meant. In other words, he went behind the legalities of men and appealed to a prophet inspired by God.

They could hardly object to that — which may have made them feel him to be even more objectionable. We know the fury we feel ourselves when someone quotes a text against us, and we cannot see how to answer. After that day in Capernaum, neutrality about him was no longer possible. Men must decide. We shall look more closely at the Pharisees to see why most of them decided against him. And of course there were the Sadducees.

19 *PHARISEES AND SADDUCEES*

In the Palestine of Jesus' time two groups mattered, the Sadducees and the Pharisees.

Sadducees

His first actual conflict was with the Sadducees, when he scourged the moneychangers and animal-sellers from the Temple, for the Temple was under Sadducee control. In the public life upon which he was then so spectacularly entering, most of his arguments were with Pharisees, and most of his invective was hurled at them. But it was Sadducees, under the High Priest Caiaphas and his father-in-law, the former High Priest Annas, who frightened Pilate into crucifying him (with the Pharisees in agreement). It was Sadducees who scourged Peter and John, and it was the Sadducee High Priest Ananias, the fourth of Annas' sons to hold the high priesthood, to whom Paul said, "God shall smite thee, thou whited wall" (Acts 23:3)—we remember that Jesus called the Pharisees whited sepulchres.

The Sadducees took their name from Zadok, who was high priest a thousand years before under King David and King Solomon. For centuries his descendants held the priesthood; and though this line had long ceased, the name had come to be applied to the priestly aristocracy, the group of families from whom the high priest was usually chosen and those other rich and noble families who intermarried with them. What they were by the time of Jesus it is hard to say with absolute certainty, because they have left no writings, and we must learn of them from people who naturally disliked them, like the Pharisee Josephus and the writers of the Gospels and the Acts. But there seems to be no doubt about their special characteristics.

They were believers in God, but their interests were primarily political rather than religious. As a wealthy aristocracy they tended to be more cosmopolitan than the mass of the people, priding themselves on their knowledge of the Greek authors and philosophers, able to mix in the higher levels of international society. They would have preferred to have no foreign rule, but they were skillful at negotiating, or on occasion fighting, with the ruler, whoever he happened to be. They were essentially worldly men, with a gift for worldly success. This, indeed, may be the reason for one doctrinal point upon which they differed from the Pharisees. They denied not only the resurrection, but the soul's immortality. The possibility of a life after this had no great appeal to men who had specialized in worldly success.

The high priesthood being, in the nature of things, the most powerful office in Judaism, they made it their own preserve. They were the friends of whoever made the appointments. Under the Roman procurators, Rome appointed the high priest. After fifteen years, for instance, Annas was dismissed because the Roman official of the day disliked him; but, as we have seen, he managed to have his four sons and his son-in-law appointed in their turn. The high priest appointed all the officials who mattered in the Temple, especially the ruler whom we should call the administrator, and the controller of the treasury whom we should call the chancellor.

The high priest was also president of the Sanhedrin, the governing body—under the omnipotent Romans, of course—of the Jewish people. There were local Sanhedrins, but the one that mattered was in Jerusalem, and it normally met in the Temple itself. Most of the members were Sadducees, though there were occasional Pharisees like Nicodemus, who visited Jesus by night, Joseph of Arimathea, who provided his tomb, and Gamaliel, that great spiritual leader whose pupil was Saint Paul.

Between the Sadducees and the Pharisees lay an abiding hostility. They could agree together that Jesus must be destroyed. But their reasons were different, the Pharisees having a religious ground of attack, the Sadducees mainly fearing that his success might upset the Romans, upon whom their own prosperity depended. Apart from the necessity of getting rid of the carpenter, their enmity was profound: it is curious to think that Annas' last son to hold the great office, Ananias (we have just heard what Saint Paul said to him), was stabbed to death by a member of the extreme right-wing of the Pharisees.

Both parties were quite small. According to Josephus there were about six thousand Pharisees. No one has bothered to count the Sadducees for us, but an aristocracy would not be very numerous. The Sadducees were the Establishment. The Pharisees were the vitalizing religious element.

Pharisees

The Sadducees were the rich upper class. The Pharisees in general were middle class. The mass of the people were ordinary Jews, more or less devout, more or less ritually observant, disliking the

Sadducees, revering the Pharisees. The Sadducees held the priest-hood, the great Temple in Jerusalem, and the sacrifices which could be offered only in the Temple. The Pharisees were for the most part laymen: they dominated the synagogues which were to be found in every town and village from end to end of the country. The religious life of the people took its color largely, and after the destruction of the Temple solely, from them. The special talent of the Sadducees was for the ways of the world. For the Pharisees the world was very much present, but religion came first. Without them, religion might very well have died among the Jews.

The name Pharisee means literally "separated". Separated from what? In essence from all uncleanness of soul and body, but this tended to involve keeping separate from the unclean—from those who were morally unclean, of course, but also from those who did not observe the increasingly minute rules of ritual cleanliness as well. Their rule of life was to do the will of God. But how was the will of God to be known?

In the answer to this question lay the principal difference between the Pharisees and Sadducees. The Sadducees held them-selves bound only by the books of Moses, the first five books of the Old Testament, which had for them the incidental value of saying nothing very clear about resurrection and the immortality of the soul! The Pharisees accepted not only the remainder of the Old Testament, but also the writings of the commentators, the scribes, in which they saw God as continuing to teach for man's guidance.

We do not know what man, or what body of men, made the list of inspired books in which the Jews believed that God himself was speaking. Therefore we do not know whence came the certainty that divine authority attached to them. For the Jews of our Lord's time as for the Protestant of today, the books are simply there; for the Catholic they are guaranteed by the voice of God's Church. But to centuries after centuries of men, the books have seemed to need no guarantee, their own splendor guarantees them.

The Jews of Alexandria who made the translation into Greek—the Septuagint—a century before our Lord, included seven books which are not in the Palestinian Canon or in the Protestant Bible. But substantially the Old Testament was there for the Jews Jesus met—the Law and the Prophets and the Holy Writings. Though all were the voice of God, the first five Books were special—only of *their* commands was a breach punishable by scourging. They primarily were the Torah, the Teaching, the Law.

It was Ezra who saw the Law as an instrument of instruments for the remaking of the Jewish people after their return from captivity in Babylon. From that time the Torah had a sacredness, an influence over the whole life of Judaism, unknown before. We cannot begin to understand the Jews—we cannot see how almost heartbreakingly probable was their rejection of our Lord—until we have made some effort to grasp what the Torah had come to mean to them.

One early rabbi tells us that when Moses ascended into heaven, he found God with the Torah in his hand, reading the opening verses of the nineteenth chapter of Numbers: the Torah indeed was God's daily reading! The book of *Jubilees,* written about 100 B.C., says that the angels in heaven are circumcised and observe the Sabbath. It hardly needs saying that God observed the Sabbath himself. As Dr. Abrahams tells us, in *Pharisaism and the Gospels,* "In order to be a Perfect Model for Israel's imitation, God himself sets an example of obeying his own law." Therefore God prayed—(to whom?)—God wore the fringed garment of a rabbi.

The Law, then, was everything. So far no Sadducee would have disagreed, provided one did not go beyond the books of Moses. It was the interpretations of the commentators, the scribes, the doctors, which gave Pharisaism its special quality—it was they, not Moses or any of the prophets, who showed God submitting to the laws he had made for man's governance.

After the destruction of the Temple in 70 A.D., the Sadducees disappear—no Temple meant no sacrifices, no place therefore for a priestly class; total national humiliation meant no place for a ruling class skilled in managing foreign rulers. From the crushing of Bar Kokhba's revolt in 135 A.D., the Pharisees alone have shaped the religious life of their shattered, scattered people.

We can but gaze in admiration at the courage, tenacity, determination to do God's will, with which they have brought the Jewish people through the last nineteen hundred years. If only all that energy and virtue could have been in the service of Christ! It is one of the world's tragedies that when Israel brought forth its supreme glory, the most living element in Israel rejected him. Their turning from our Lord was one of history's decisive turning points. Nothing would have been the same if they had accepted him.

To understand why they did not, we must do our best to see the Pharisees as they were at the time the great decision was made. Our first feeling is that they were arrogant, greedy for men's applause, greedy for money, hypocrites above all. And with all these faults Jesus himself charges them. His words do not mean that there were no good men among them. Some of them became Christians (Acts 15:5), and of such a man as Gamaliel, who did not, any religion might be proud. But certainly as a body they must have been passing through a bad period: it may have needed the shock of the destruction of the Temple to bring out the best in them.

When we are considering their sins, we must remember three balancing considerations. (1) The great Pharisaic writers themselves scourged the very faults in Pharisees which produced the great burst of rage from Jesus (Mt 23). (2) The same faults could be urged against ourselves: Catholics from the highest to the lowest have been guilty of them. Saint John Chrysostom was not the first or the last to say: "We imitate the hypocrites, we have even surpassed them" (*Hom. XX on Mt.*). (3) A religion—be it Pharisee or Catholic or any other—is entitled to be judged by what it actually teaches, not by the various levels of the failure of its members to live up to it. In the study of Pharisaism *at its best,* we shall find the seed of the great refusal.

Let us return to the cleavage between Pharisees and Sadducees. Both accepted the text "Fear God and keep his commandments. This is the whole meaning of man" (Qo 12:13). But for the Sadducees the commandments were to be found only in the five Books of Moses. The Pharisees held that God continued speaking through the prophets, thus bringing the inspired word on to Malachi, the last of them; and that he spoke still through the commentators, the scribes. His voice sounded clear and direct through the prophets, their key phrase was "thus saith the Lord". It came more by way of guidance through the scribes, who were content to interpret Moses and the prophets, their key phrase being "thus it is written".

The Sadducees complained that the interpretations of the scribes were frequently not in the Torah—the Teaching; and indeed the connection was often slender to vanishing point. The law of vengeance, an eye for an eye and a tooth for a tooth, emerged in rabbinic writing as a payment of money for bodily damage: indeed in all their teaching upon penalties, the Pharisees were much milder than the Sadducees. The truth is that the Pharisees saw, as their opponents did not, the need for a continuance of teaching. God had not said his last word to mankind fifteen hundred years before in the Sinai desert. Men could grow, men could learn by living. The word that God spoke to their immaturity might not be his word for them now.

Quite simply they saw the need for a development of teaching to match the development of humanity. The question was not whether some freshly minted law was in the Torah, but whether it was in harmony with the Torah. They did not say this in so many words: it seemed a matter of first urgency to show the Torah as actually teaching what the scribes now taught. But the other was in fact the principle by which their interpretation was guided. Once a new statement of the Law was accepted by the governing body of the Jewish people, it was as if it had been taught to Moses on Sinai.

Scribes

Scripture speaks of the scribes and Pharisees. In fact most of the scribes were Pharisees; they were the learned ones, and the rest of the six thousand Pharisees of Palestine accepted the scribal teaching on the law of God as authoritative. Rabbi, Master, was their title. They studied Moses and the prophets; they studied scribes who had gone before them; they analyzed, refined, applied the Law to new circumstances, multipled its precepts more and more minutely.

These precepts, running into hundreds, were derived with greater or lesser probability from the Torah, the teaching of God contained in Scripture. And they were seen as of equal authority. They were the traditions: Jesus called them "the traditions of men". Not all the Pharisees observed all of them, indeed there were recognized grades of Pharisee according to the level of observance.

The teaching office had thus passed from the priests, for most of the scribes were laymen. Jesus could say (Mt 23:2) that it is they who have occupied the chair of Moses and made it their own. Their conduct might fall far below their teaching, and their teaching may have come to have too much of man rather than of God in it, but by now they were the teachers of Israel, there were no others.

For the content of their teaching our Lord continually criticizes them — "Why do you transgress the commandments of God for your tradition?" (Mt 15:3). In truth, the "traditions", the ever-growing mass of scribal and rabbinical interpretations, had too often lost sight altogether of what God had actually commanded. And this was no new thing. Six centuries before, Jeremiah had accused the scribes as fiercely as Jesus ever did — "How do you say, 'We are wise and the law of the Lord is with us'? Indeed the lying pen of the scribes has wrought falsehood" (8:8).

Why, with all their learning, intellectual acuteness, vivid awareness of God's majesty, did the scribes so often lose the essence of God's teaching, why did they fall so deeply in love with external observance? One reason seems obvious. As teachers they lacked, and their successors in Judaism to this day lack, what we should call Theology. Judaism had, and still has, no creed. A modern scholar, Herford, notes that upon many beliefs there is "de facto agreement among Jews", but "always with the reservation that there was never any official definition of a doctrine, to be accepted under pain of excommunication".

Where this absence of theology matters most is in relation to God himself. After a thousand years of falling again and again into the worship of pagan gods, the Jewish people had returned from the Babylonian captivity magnificently and permanently monotheist. But they seem to have given hardly any mind to what God *is*. They might lie prostrate before his majesty, but they show no curiosity at all as to his nature. They did indeed see love as one of his attributes, though not the primary one: his justice was first. They labored over man's duty to obey his commands. But who and what was the Being who was just, who was loving, who must be obeyed, who must be adored? Upon that there was no teaching at all. "That they are jealous for God's honor, I can testify", says Saint Paul (Rom 10:2); "but it is with imperfect understanding."

It was this combination of adoring God and not using their mind upon him that made it possible for scribes to teach, for example, that God read the Torah daily and that he rested not only on the first Sabbath but on every Sabbath afterward; and to argue among themselves whether he was bound to this Sabbath rest or observed it from choice. It seems clear that while they could use words like "everlasting" and "almighty", could speak of God as "knowing all things", they had no real notion of what eternity and omnipotence and omniscience actually are.

And they could not have any notion because they had not sufficiently analyzed, as the great Greeks had, the meaning of "spirit". The word was constantly on their lips, both for the active power of God and for the soul of man—the element in man which accounts for all those human operations which are not of the body alone. It is invisible, it is powerful—that is about as far as they got towards saying what spirit is: though the Jews outside Palestine, like Philo, were beginning to use the Greek richness in their meditation on the vaster richness of God's revelation to his people.

Without a profounder understanding of spirit, the scribes could not advance in the knowledge of God, or even of man: they believed in man's immortality, for instance, but had hardly a notion of what life after death might be.

The Battle Is Joined

We are now in a position to see why the most religious section of the Jews decided against our Lord.

Not concerning themselves with what God in himself is, scribes and Pharisees could hardly do other than concentrate upon the commands God had given men, and upon men's duty to obey them. And as the centuries went by, this meant more and more regulations upon ritual and ceremonial generally. There were minute rules about washing—after contact with some things, before contact with others; about eating—what to eat, with whom to eat, with whom not to eat; about observance of the Sabbath, especially how much work might be done without breaking the Sabbath rest. Nothing heavier than a fig might be carried and even the distance was prescribed. There were extremists who would not allow bowels or bladders to violate the Sabbath rest.

In origin, rules were necessary, if only because their observance involved a development in self-control, especially in control of bodily instincts and appetites, which could be a most valuable discipline. And in the best of the Pharisees these rules could operate nobly for asceticism, without looming so large as to overshadow realities profounder than themselves.

Consider two incidents at the end of Rabbi Akiba's life. He was the one great Pharisee to support Bar Kokhba in his claim to be Messiah and in the rebellion which was ended so crushingly in 135 A.D. Imprisoned by the Romans and receiving the small ration of drinking water allowed by his captors, he still used part of it for ritual washing of his hands before drinking the drop that was left. He welcomed his execution by the Romans as a martyrdom in fulfillment of the text "Thou shalt love the Lord thy God with thy whole heart" (Dt 6:4, 5).

But men of that level are rare in any religion. It is easy to exaggerate the importance of ritual, and it seems that in the time of Jesus it had become for too many Pharisees almost an end in itself.

There was another danger, not inescapable but not easy to escape either. Israel was unique among peoples; the Pharisees were unique in Israel. Only heroic humility can bear its own uniqueness; and in any religion heroic humility tends to be the virtue of a minority. In too many Pharisees a misunderstanding of the nature of Israel's uniqueness led to a contempt of the Gentile. Similarly we find appalling things said about the great number of their fellow Jews, lumped together as the People of the Land, "the accursed multitude which knows not the Law". A scribe could write: "The garments of the people of the land are a source of uncleanness to the Pharisee." Not all scribes felt like this, but a sufficient number did.

We can now see how probable it was that the scribes and Pharisees should see the carpenter of Nazareth as an enemy, not only to themselves—that may have been a principal feeling among the Sadducees—but to true religion. Had he merely neglected to observe the rituals, merely failed to make due study of the Torah, they might have been charitable about him, or at worst mildly contemptuous of him. But neither upon the rituals nor upon the Torah was he simply an abstainer!

He affronted their most cherished convictions on such matters as ritual washings (the Essenes had multiplied these), eating, fasting, avoiding contact with sinners and the ritually unclean, rigorously observing the Sabbath. He made it clear in the face of the world that he regarded much of what they held dear as a barrier to religion. Even Pharisees who fully realized that the rituals were only secondary, still saw them as willed by God. As well, there was an attachment to them grown instinctive after generations of devout and devoted observance (Catholics know similar attachments). On both counts, they found Jesus' attitude to the rituals repugnant.

What was immeasurably worse was his attitude to the Torah— the Law for which, by which, with which, they lived. For Christ it was not an absolute. He himself could develop it, add to it, on no authority but his own. "Thus saith the Lord", the prophets had said. "Thus it is written", said the scribes. "It was said to them of old, *but I say unto you*", said the carpenter. No one had ever spoken like that. After all, God himself read the Torah daily!

The feeling grew that he was making himself equal to God. They had already heard him claim to forgive sins. Before long some of them would hear him say: "I and the Father are one." They must either believe him or destroy him.

We left Jesus dining in the house of Levi, the publican, who was to be Matthew the apostle. Pharisees were grouped outside. They had already been first startled and then horrified by his claim to forgive the sins of a paralyzed man, they were if anything, more horrified now to find him eating with publicans and sinners.

There followed incident after incident.

The Pharisees complained, and the disciples of John the Baptist joined in the complaint, that he did not fast as they did (Lk 5:33–35). When the bridegroom is still with you, he answered, you don't fast, you feast. This reference to himself as bridegroom did not help—for in the Old Testament God was Israel's Bridegroom.

There followed the Sabbath when his disciples, being hungry, picked ears of corn and ate them on their way through a cornfield. The Pharisees attacked this as if it were reaping, which was forbidden on the Sabbath. The point at issue was not of vast importance: scribes might well have argued learnedly among themselves whether picking corn was reaping—perhaps it was if one picked more than seven grains! Jesus wasted no time on argument of that sort. He reminded them of David and his eating ritual bread and of Sabbath activities in the Temple. (John shows him answering a question about the Sabbath by appeal to a higher law. Both answers would anger them.) Then came the two unpardonable claims—he was greater than the Temple, he was Lord even of the Sabbath (Mt 12:1–8).

A Sabbath or so later, in the synagogue, he healed a man's withered hand. The scribes allowed that work might be done on the Sabbath if it was necessary to preserve life. Jesus reminds them that if a sheep fell into a pit on the Sabbath, they would lift it out (the Essenes would not). Jesus said in effect, "Why should the man have this deformity one day longer than he need? That's not what the Sabbath rest is for."

The reaction of the Pharisees is at first sight wholly mysterious: they asked whether it was lawful for a man to heal on the Sabbath day. After all, a miracle is not worked by man, but by God. Consciously or not consciously, it was God whom they were accusing of Sabbath-breaking. We remember how the scribes taught that God himself observed the Sabbath rest scrupulously. Were they accusing the carpenter of leading God into sin? The truth is that in their fury with him (Lk 6:11), they were beyond reason.

To us whose principal motive for reading the Gospels is that we may meet Jesus, this incident is memorable for one thing specially. It is the first occasion—apart from once when he was filled with pity for a leper—on which we are told of his showing emotion. He has done things earlier in which we may in our minds see him as charged with emotion, but we are not told that he was. This time we are. And the emotion is anger. He "looked round about on them with anger, being grieved for the blindness of their hearts" (Mk 3:5).

The combination of anger and grief is a reminder that Jesus is like us not only in possessing a human nature, but in his way of being human. We, too, can be angry with someone we love, while grieving at the failure in them which rouses our anger: and who knows whether the anger is greater or the grief? Nor need we bring other people into this combination of emotions: we can be angry with ourselves and sorrowful for ourselves in one instant. From now on, we shall often see him angry with the Pharisees; let us never forget the grief which must have accompanied the anger. We shall see him shedding tears over Jerusalem: and the Pharisees were the most profoundly religious element in these, his own people.

It was the anger that the Pharisees saw, not the grief. "Going out immediately they made a consultation with the Herodians, how they might destroy him" (Mk 3:6). The Herodians were not a religious sect, making a third to Pharisees and Sadducees. They were simply men of a political cast, who wanted the kingdom of Herod the Great restored to his son Herod Antipas. This being Galilee, the Pharisees could not destroy Jesus without the cooperation of the Herod party. Not for the last time religious idealists and tough politicians worked together for tragedy.

20 THE CALLING OF THE TWELVE

The First Seven

The man with the withered hand was probably far too much excited by his nice new hand to feel the electricity in the air. Electric the air was. Jesus was angry, and sorrowful; the Pharisees were angry to slaying point.

Jesus was grieved "for the blindness of their hearts" (Mk 3:5). The Greek word, here translated "blindness", means rather "hardness" or "callousness". In the whole episode what struck these men was not the release of a fellow human from long misery, not the power of God working the miracle, but only a legal question about just what might be done on the Sabbath.

The battle was now finally joined. Just a little time before, Jesus had given his enemies an answer about new wine and old bottles, new patches and old garments (Lk 5:36–39). They may not have caught his meaning at once, but the words grew only more threatening as the meaning grew clearer. There was to be new wine better than the old—not this year's vintage compared with the vintage of years earlier: the wine itself was to be new, new grapes grown in a new soil under a new sun. There was to be a new garment—not new patches on an old garment: a new organization was needed, patching would not do. He was bringing something new into the world: the old framework would not support it.

For the new framework, he had already chosen Peter and Andrew, James and John. Now he adds eight more to complete the Twelve. "He passed the whole night offering prayer to God. And when day dawned, he called his disciples to him, choosing out twelve of them; these he called his apostles" (Lk 6:12–13).

Our Lord's human mind needed divine grace and divine guidance. It was under the direction of the Holy Spirit, we remember, that he went into the desert to be tempted by Satan. He had prayed before extending his own preaching from Capernaum to synagogues throughout Galilee (Mk 1:35). He prayed, too, before he walked on the water (Mt 14:23), and before he drew from Peter the great confession of faith and gave him the keys of the Kingdom of heaven (Lk 9:18).

So now, before completing the choice of the men who were meant to be the foundation on which his Kingdom was built (Eph 2:20), he spent the whole night in prayer. The choice was his own, as Peter tells us through Mark, but he made it with a mind illumined by God. Included in his choice were the men whom he had called to come with him in that rapid journey from the banks of Jordan to the wedding feast of Cana—Peter and Andrew, John (with James added), Philip and Nathanael. They had been much in his company since, but had not yet given up their normal work, had not yet been definitely called to the apostolate. Now they were. The seventh on the list was Levi the tax collector, Matthew to us. And there were five others of whose previous history we know nothing—Thomas, another James, another Simon, and two called Judas—Judas Iscariot, and the one whom we feel it politer to call Jude.

In this small group, there was a group smaller still. He kept Peter, James, and John specially close to him—they were the only apostles he allowed to be with him when he raised Jairus' daughter to life, they were with him at the Transfiguration, nearest to him during his agony in Gethsemane.

We know something of Peter's personality and of John's. But James never emerges: he never does anything by himself, never says anything. One solitary primacy is his, he was the first of them to be martyred. One thing we learn about these two brothers we learn from Peter: for it is Mark, his mouthpiece, who tells us that Jesus called them Sons of Thunder (3:17). The title goes well with their urging him to let them bring down fire for the destruction of the unwelcoming Samaritans (Lk 9:54). It goes well, too, with the Book of Revelation which John wrote, but not at all well with any picture one has ever seen of him.

Five Newcomers

To complete the Twelve (Mk 3), Jesus chose five men whose names we are hearing for the first time—some of them almost for the last.

James and Jude are thought to have been his cousins—we know that he had four cousins named James, Joseph, Jude, and Simon (Mk 6:3).

James, called the Less, because he was younger than the other James, was to become head of the Church in Jerusalem, and it fell to him to announce that Church's acceptance of Peter's decision not to bind Gentile converts by Jewish ritual and ceremonial law (Acts 15:13–21). He wrote the Epistle which Luther called "an epistle of straw".

Jude is usually held to be that same Jude who wrote an Epistle. At the Last Supper he asked Jesus the question which brought the answer: "If any one love me ... my Father will love him and we will make our abode with him" (Jn 14:23). There has been a recent surge of devotion to him as Help of the Hopeless.

Thomas is, apart from Peter and John, the most colorful personality among the apostles: his name is still used for people hard to convince, as Judas for traitors. The Jewish word Thomas means Twin, so does the Greek word Didymus. One wonders whose twin he was, that the fact of twinship should have given him his name—another of the Twelve, perhaps. But which? It was Thomas' glory that at the Last Supper he asked the question which was answered with "I am the Way and the Truth and the Life" (Jn 14:5–6). His glory, too, that he alone is recorded as having addressed our Lord as God—"My Lord and my God" (Jn 20:28). As glorious was his reception of Jesus' announcement that he would go to Bethany for the raising of Lazarus. They all knew that he was going to his death, for Bethany was only two miles from Jerusalem. Thomas said: "Let us go too and be killed along with him" (Jn 11:16). It is curious that he, alone of the apostles, is eclipsed by a namesake: when today we say Saint Thomas, everyone assumes that we mean Aquinas.

Simon, subtitled the Zealot, is not thought to be the Simon named in the short list of the Lord's cousins. Why the subtitle? To distinguish him, doubtless, from Simon Peter. The Zealots were the political, violently anti-Roman, wing of the Pharisees. Simon had probably been one of them. Of course the word may merely have meant that he was especially zealous: but one feels that that is hardly the adjective anybody would have chosen to distinguish him from Simon Peter, who could carry zeal to the point of embarrassment. Curious too, if Simon was of such exuberant zeal, that no single word or deed of his is recorded.

So we come to Judas, the last of the Twelve, the man from Kerioth—that is what Iscariot means. We shall be seeing more of him, alas. Here we may simply wonder why Jesus chose him: he did not have to wait for the betrayal to know that Judas was a devil (Jn 6:71). It may be that in the long night of prayer the Holy Spirit made it clear why he wanted him chosen. We observe that he was put in charge of the group's funds. Matthew, as a tax collector, had had more experience of handling money: but probably, after his conversion, the thought of money made him sick.

Our Lord called these men "apostles"—the word means "sent"—but they are called that only once in Saint Matthew's Gospel, twice in Saint Mark's, five times in Saint Luke's, never in Saint John's. The usual name for them was the Twelve. That word underlined their revolutionary importance better than the word apostles. Judaism had been built upon the twelve sons of Jacob. The similarity of number was no coincidence: Jesus told the Twelve that they would sit upon thrones judging the tribes of Israel. He was not referring to the judgment at the end of the world. The apostles were to rule the Israel of God here on earth, as judges had ruled the first Israel before the coming of the kings.

No one looking at them would have thought that at all probable! Pharisees and Sadducees alike must have been reassured to find the sort of men the carpenter had gathered round him: "ignorant nobodies", they were to call the greatest of them, Peter and John (Acts 4:13). When a leader was slain, it was a thing unheard of not to kill off his closest followers. Evidently these did not seem worth killing. They stayed on for years, unmolested in the town of Christ's slaying. Any suggestion that there was danger in leaving them alive would have been met with an amused: "Have you *seen* them?"

21 *THE SERMON ON THE MOUNT*

Rules of Life in the Kingdom

Our Lord's baptism by John had taken place in January, a cold month, even in the Jordan valley, for total immersion. The definite call of the Twelve was perhaps in June. We shall now be looking at the nine or ten months which still remained of his ministry in Galilee, ending with the vast double explosion—the feeding of the five thousand, and the sermon on the Bread of Life which cost him most of his followers.

So far his teaching seems to have followed the line of the Baptist's—that the Kingdom was at hand, and that the preparation for entry into it must be a change of soul. These last weeks had brought something new—his claim to forgive sins, to be greater than the Temple, to be Lord of the Sabbath. The Baptist had never talked like that. Nor did his hearers grasp what such talk actually meant, for he had still not said who and what he himself was. About that, they might argue and grow confused. The one thing quite clear was that he worked miracles, and that was enough to bring crowds thronging.

We learn that they had come from Judea and Galilee, Jerusalem and Herod's ancestral home Idumea, from countries away on the other side of the Jordan, from Tyre and Sidon on the Mediterranean coast. They were all trying to touch him, thrusting in on him, so much so that he told the disciples to have a small boat standing by. But this time he did not use the boat. Instead he went up onto the hillside. And there he preached.

Saint Luke gives a short account of the sermon in his chapter 6, Saint Matthew a longer account in his chapters 5, 6, and 7. It would be good to read them both before proceeding further with this chapter. Most people, I fancy, think of the Sermon on the Mount as nine verses, each beginning with the word *blessed:* if only all sermons were as short as that! In fact it takes three chapters of Saint Matthew. Even so it could be delivered at my own speaking pace in under twenty minutes, and the most sermon-resistant Catholic would hardly begin to complain so soon.

This very brevity helps us to answer one problem. There are things in one account not in the other, things in Matthew which Mark and Luke show as being said on quite other occasions. We may be quite certain that our Lord did not dismiss people who had come so far with a twenty-minute sermon. Even Matthew's account is only a tiny proportion of what he must have said; and it may have included relevant things Jesus said at other times. Of course, as we have already noted, he would have uttered the same great truths again and again, every teacher does—and very often in the same words, because when one has found the best form of words, it would be eccentric to change it.

How perfect were the words he found. Think of some of the things that everybody knows, even if he doesn't know that they are in the Sermon on the Mount—"Consider the lilies of the field", "You cannot serve God and Mammon", "By their fruits you shall know them", "Turn the other cheek", "Love your enemies, do good to them that hate you", the Our Father, the Golden Rule. Golden Rule? It was a golden sermon.

It is not quite clear whether the crowds were there for all of it. Certainly some of it could hardly have been meant for them but only for the Twelve: "You are the salt of the earth", "You are the light of the world." Much of it was of application to everyone, to everyone there, to everyone everywhere. But the whole of it is the equivalent of a special training course for the men upon whom he was going to build his Kingdom. They were not simply to be rulers wielding authority. They were to be "light", both to the darkness of the pagan world and to the dimness of the chosen people. They were to be "salt", bringing a new tang and savor to a world insipid, to a life grown dreary. The whole sermon was a commentary on the "repentance", *metanoia,* change of soul, that was at the heart of the forerunner's message. And of Christ's.

The Sermon begins with the rules of life in the Kingdom. It is blessed to be poor, provided one does not resent one's state but offers it to God; to be patient; to be hungry for justice and sorrowful; to be merciful and clean of heart; to be lovers of peace and makers of peace; to be persecuted for justice's sake, still more to be persecuted and reviled and slandered for our Lord's. It is a remarkable way of life, or program of life, here sketched. Most of these things had been spoken of, and right endurance of them praised, in the Old Testament. But they had hardly been described as adding up to blessedness, a kind of fundamental bliss, so that one would be diminished by not having them. Mercy and cleanness of heart, yes. But sorrow, persecution, reviling, and slander? Jesus is wholly uncompromising about these.

And the rewards? They practically all seem to be in a world to come. And if his followers fail? If the salt lose its savor—surely it lost a lot of its savor on the night of Gethsemane—it is fit only to be thrown out and trodden under foot. Thank God, he also will forgive unto seventy times seven. Yet for the hardened in failure, there is hell. Jesus says it again and again in these chapters.

It is an exacting standard he is setting them, reaching its climax in a phrase approached in Jewish teaching but not reached—"Be ye also perfect, as your heavenly Father is perfect." Their rigor for themselves, however, must be balanced by a total forbearance toward others. Indeed "forbearance" is too pale a word for what is demanded of them. They must not even judge others, for if they do, they will be calling upon God to judge themselves: they must be charitable, that is, not only in external act, but in judgment as well. They must treat others as they would want others to treat them.

Here again we have a phrase his hearers had never heard before. The Old Testament *does* teach negatively (Tob 4:16) that we should not treat others as we should not want to be treated by them. But phrased positively by Jesus, the Golden Rule is dazzling—and dazzlingly difficult to live up to. Which of us could keep it up for a week? To make quite clear that he means the word "others"—do unto others—in its fullness, he applies it at the extremest point: we must love our *enemies,* we must do good to those that hate us.

As well as drawing up a rule of life for his followers, he states his position with regard to the teaching already given to the Jews in the Old Testament. "Do not think that I am come to destroy the Law, or the Prophets. I am not come to destroy, but to fulfill."

Upon murder, adultery, retaliation for evil, he completes and perfects the Law given by God through Moses, always with the formula: "It was said to them of old, but *I* say to you".

His respect for the Law—which, as second Person of the Trinity, he himself had given through Moses and the prophets—is not extended to the teaching of the scribes: "I tell you, that unless your justice abound more than that of the scribes and Pharisees, you shall not enter into the Kingdom of heaven." He applies this particularly to the teaching he found in possession upon the matter of oaths. False swearing, he says, is false swearing, no matter what you swear by: you cannot evade the commandment by using some other name than God's.

What did his hearers make of all this? Some things they would have understood, and perhaps reacted against instantly—such, for example, as being told not to resent having their face slapped, but to offer the other cheek for slapping. Only slowly, perhaps, did they make their own the essence of what he was saying—namely, that no external act, however splendid, can save us; no external act, however appalling, can damn us, either. All is in the state—knowledge, will, intention—of the soul. A man is saved or damned by what he loves: God, or himself as against God. But, of course, what a man loves will tend to show itself in what he does.

At the end of the sermon Jesus had still not described the Kingdom whose founding he had already begun. Nor had he told them who he was himself. But upon this second point he had added to the claims which had already been quite sufficient to set so many of them thinking of blasphemy. Not only had he completed the law of God with a casual, unexplained "but *I* say unto you". Worse than that, he had referred (Mt 7:24) to the commands he had been giving them simply as "mine".

Group of Women

As Jesus came back into Capernaum, after the Sermon on the Mount, an episode occurred of which one phrase will surely be used until the world ends— *"Domine, non sum dignus"*, "Lord, I am not worthy." And it was uttered by a Gentile, a centurion, or company commander, in Herod's army. The leading Jews of the town asked Jesus to relieve the man's distress by healing a servant to whom he was much attached, and who was on the point of death. Their reason for intervening on behalf of a Gentile was that this particular one had built the synagogue for them: obviously—like that other centurion, Cornelius, whom Peter would one day create a precedent by baptizing (Acts 10)—he was much drawn to the Jewish religion.

As Jesus comes near the centurion's house, we hear the words we find embedded—with "I" substituted for "my servant"—in every Mass: "Lord, I am not worthy that thou shouldst enter under my roof: but only say the word, and my servant shall be healed" (Mt 13:8). The centurion was not moved by humility alone. In fact Saint Peter, who *did* enter under the roof of Cornelius, actually said, "A Jew is contaminated if he consorts with one of another race or visits him." But the man in Capernaum added a better reason why Jesus should not enter the house—it was not necessary. A mere word would be enough.

He could not have failed to hear how, only the month before, Jesus, standing in Cana, had healed the son of one of Herod's officials, twenty miles away in Capernaum (Jn 4:46–53). If he healed from as far away as Cana, why not from the next street in Capernaum? With the words "I have not found so great a faith, not even in Israel" (Mt 8 and Lk 7), Jesus willed the healing, and it took place in that instant.

It is pleasing to notice that the centurion manages to relate himself to the Blessed Sacrament in two ways: his are the words we use at Communion; and it was in the synagogue built by him that Saint John shows Jesus teaching for the first time that we must eat his flesh and drink his blood if we are to have life in us (Jn 6).

From now on, with the Pharisees in full opposition—that remark about not finding such faith in Israel must have been very bitter—Jesus, accompanied by the Twelve, travels the roads of Galilee, teaching in the synagogues and working miracles without end. Luke (8:2–3) gives us one further detail—with them went a group of women "who had been healed of evil spirits and infirmities". These not only helped in the journeying— cooking meals on the road perhaps—but they provided money as well.

Listed at this first mention by Saint Luke are Mary Magdalen, "out of whom seven devils were gone forth", Joanna, wife of Chuza, an official in Herod's administration, and Susanna. Of Susanna we hear no more. Mary Magdalen was present at the crucifixion, and she and Joanna were both at the tomb on the morning of the Resurrection. Chuza must have been an indulgent husband to allow his wife so much time out of the house. It may have been *his* son, dying in Capernaum, whom Jesus had healed in Cana.

But Mary of Magdala is the one who has had men talking from that day to this. And they have not finished talking. The devil can afflict the body, as we have seen. But "seven devils" suggests something more spectacular in the way of demonic control. She is named for the first time a few verses after the episode of the sinful woman who (Lk 7:36–50), from an alabaster box, anointed Jesus' feet as he sat at table in Simon the Pharisee's house at Capernaum in Galilee. Was Mary Magdalen this woman? Was she Lazarus' sister Mary who, as we read in Mark 14, Matthew 26, John 12, from an alabaster box anointed Jesus' feet as he sat at table in Simon the Leper's house at Bethany in Judea?

Lazarus and his family may have moved from Magdala to Bethany—perhaps because of the shameful life his sister Mary had lived before her repentance. Jesus may have made theirs the one home he was in the habit of visiting in Judea precisely because they were old friends from Galilee—Magdala is near Capernaum. *They* may—*he* may—no one knows.

22 *THREE MIRACLES*

With Capernaum as his headquarters, with the newly chosen Twelve and the handful of women helpers as his companions, Jesus spent the nine months or so that remained of his northern ministry. We shall not attempt to follow each incident in order, mainly because the evangelists have not our concern with the precise order in which one thing followed another. What matters most to us in this period is the miracle-working, the teaching, and the effect Jesus produced upon friends and enemies. We shall look first at the miracles.

Very soon after the Sermon on the Mount, we find him raising a young man from death to life, because he was moved with mercy towards his mother, a widow of Nain, a small place some eight miles from Nazareth (Lk 7:11–17). Some six months later he raised to life the daughter of Jairus. We have already talked of these miracles; but just before the second of them occur three others upon which we must pause.

Storm on the Lake

He was crossing the Lake of Galilee, dead tired, asleep in the boat. A gale of hurricane force blew down, as gales still do, from the mountains around, and the apostles were convinced that the ship would sink. Since the storm itself did not wake our Lord, they finally woke him themselves. The words they used come down to us through the centuries with all their humanity still warm in them: *"Don't you care* if we all drown?" (Mk 38).

He says, with something that sounds rather like the impatience we tend to feel ourselves when we are awakened from deep sleep: "Where is your faith?" Then—having first rebuked the Twelve for want of trust—he rebuked the wind and said to the sea, "Peace, be still." And it was still.

Demons and Swine

They came to land on the other side of the lake, further south. There they were met by a demoniac. It is worth reading Luke 8:26–39 and Mark 5:1–20, not only for the account given of the violence with which the possessing demons used the man, but also for their acceptance of Jesus' power. He asks them their name—the only time he does this—and they answer "Legion". The exorcists of the day held that a demon could be commanded if you knew his name; but Legion was not a name, it was a number! No fetish was made of exact figures in those days, and devils have made no fetish of truth in any day. So we need not assume that there were six thousand of them, that being the number of men in a Roman legion. But at any rate there were enough to make the seven devils in Mary Magdalen seem hardly worth counting.

Jesus ordered them out of the man, and they went. But they made a most curious request—that he should not send them back "into the abyss" but should send them into a vast herd of swine (Gadarene they have been called in English for centuries, but the incident seems to have happened in the territory of the Gerasenes) feeding on a slope near by. It looks as though the demons found anything preferable to going home to hell. It is a reminder that hell is all hatred, the demons torment with their hatred not only lost souls but one another. How one spirit inflicts suffering upon another less powerful than himself, we have no way of knowing. These demons, anyhow, found pigs more tolerable company than their own kind.

Jesus let them do what they asked. They entered into the pigs. Just what it meant to the pigs, again we have no way of knowing. What we do know is that they hurtled down the slope as one pig, and were drowned in the lake. So brief a reprieve did the demons obtain. They had to go home, after all.

The demons puzzle us. The pigs puzzle us. Some of the commentators puzzle us, too. Their concern is with the property rights God was infringing. One has even seen calculations of the value of two thousand pigs in that time and place, showing how gross was the injustice done to the owners. In God's defence, others urge that the owners had no business to *have* pigs since Jews were forbidden to eat them: but—the episode took place in the territory of Greek-speaking Gentiles!

God's act, of course, needs no defending: he had created all things out of nothing, and might do what he willed with his own. This, obscurely at least, the owners felt when the herdsmen told them what had happened: "It looked as if the power of God had been at work." There was no talk of prosecution. Jesus was simply asked would he please go away. The whole town feared he might do it again—or something even worse perhaps. Theirs is the only fully comprehensible reaction in the whole affair. Let the divine power be exhibited, indeed, but at someone else's expense.

The swine had plunged down a steep place into the sea. The solid citizens had asked the miracle-worker to go away. He went away. He and the Twelve got into their boat and went back to Capernaum. The demon-plagued man, now clothed and in his right mind and anxious to come with them, they left behind to tell in his own region the great things the Lord had done to him.

If only we had a record of the conversation in the boat. There are so many questions left over. Why had the demons preferred the companionship of pigs? Why had the pigs preferred drowning to the companionship of demons? Why, above all, had their Master done it? But not a word from Luke, or from Matthew who was there; not a word even from Mark, Peter's mouthpiece. It is one of those silences we find hard to bear. We could bear not knowing about the demons and their anguishes, the pigs and their panic. But we long to read deeper into the mind of our Redeemer.

By him, we know, all things were made—demons, pigs, owners, solid citizens. There is no question of his *right* to do what he did. But what was his reason? It was not his way to show his universal lordship by damaging people's property. There is only one other instance—when he willed that a fig tree should never again bear figs (Mk 11:12–14). The one instance is as puzzling as the other. Why figs? Why pigs?

One reason for working miracles at all he was to tell the Jews at the Bethesda pool after healing a cripple—"The actions which my Father has enabled me to achieve . . . bear me witness that the Father has sent me" (Jn 5:36). The incident of the pigs, the incident of the fig tree—both these show the *power* of God. But God is not only power, he is love: his miracles are for increase of life, only in these two instances for its destruction or diminution. Again God is not only power, he is wisdom: meaningless miracles would display the power but not the wisdom: meaning, therefore, his actions had: even if we, now, do not see it. Not only in the miracles but in much else that Jesus says and does are there elements of which we can make nothing. God's ways are unsearchable. So, often enough, are the God-Man's. We should never dismiss any act of his as improbable, merely because we cannot see any point in it.

"Power Is Gone out from Me"

Back on his own side of the lake there occurred the episode of the woman with the uncontrollable flux of blood. Read the accounts in Matthew 9, Mark 5, Luke 8. Her affliction had been with her for twelve years, she had spent all she had on physicians. "She was nothing the better but rather the worse", says Mark, talking as the rest of men have talked about doctors from the beginning. "She could not be healed", says Luke more soberly. Luke was a doctor.

The woman touched the hem of the carpenter's robe and was healed in that instant. We are pleased, of course, that she was healed; but what really holds our attention is the healer's reaction. He asked who had touched him; and when they said that the whole crowd was brushing and bumping against him, he insisted: "Somebody has touched me; *for I know that power is gone out from me*"—the Greek word is *dynamis,* which gives us "dynamism" and "dynamic".

It is a mysterious phrase. We have heard already that "power went out from him and healed all" (Lk 6:19). We tend, naturally, to think merely that by the power within him, his will worked upon beings outside him. Now we learn not only that power went out from him, but that he felt it going. His miracles, then, cost him something. There was effort in them.

He told the woman that *her faith* had healed her. So, leaving us pondering on the two elements whose union made his miracles—men's faith and his own power—he went on to the house of Jairus, a ruler of the synagogue. There a girl lay dead. And there once more faith—not hers but her father's—called his power into action. She lived again.

23 *REACTIONS IN GALILEE*

We have been telling of miracles—such a stream of miracles pouring out of one man as the world had never known and never would again know. Teaching poured out of him too. It was still mainly moral, with direct statement and parable urging his hearers to a change of heart—that fundamentally was what repentance was to be. We have seen, in our study of the Sermon on the Mount, how profound a change he was demanding. He talked of the coming of the Kingdom, but of its structure he gave no detail: here too he was concerned principally with the change of heart, a turning of the heart from the kingdom of the national dream, a preparation of the heart for the Kingdom he was in fact to found. And he was, as yet, casting no light upon his own self. He had made vast claims—to be greater than the Temple, to be Lord of the Sabbath, to be Master of the Law, to forgive sins. But he had not said who he was. The name by which he called himself, Son of Man, by its very mysteriousness, raised the question; but it did not answer it.

In this chapter we shall consider some of the ways in which people—Pharisees, sinners, the family in Nazareth, the Baptist's disciples—reacted to the miracles and the teaching, to the personality above all.

"Because She Has Loved Much"

At one end there was already formed a group among the Pharisees who were planning his death. At the other were men like the scribe to whom he would say, "You are not far from the kingdom of God" (Mk 12:34). In between were those whose minds were hardening against him, but not yet set in hardness. Of such was Simon, who invited Jesus to a meal in his house (Lk 7:36–50). This one treated his guest with a strict correctness but nothing beyond—

no water for his feet or oil for his head, no kiss of greeting. As they sat at table, "a woman that was in the city, a sinner", entered the room carrying an alabaster box of ointment and "began to wash his feet, with tears, and wiped them with the hairs of her head, and kissed his feet, and anointed his feet with the ointment."

Simon and the others assumed that a prophet of God would have known that the woman was a sinner and have drawn away from contact with her: therefore the carpenter had proved himself no prophet. It is not easy to follow the detail of Jesus' answer, beginning with the question about the two debtors forgiven by their creditor. His mind darts on a path of its own, by rhythm of its own, back and forth between love causing forgiveness, and forgiveness causing love. Nineteen hundred years afterwards we do not find it easy to understand all that he is saying. Simon and his friends would not have found it any easier. But though the detail may have mystified them, the main point was clear.

"Many sins are forgiven her, because she has loved much." The word "love" may sound strange to us because love had been her trade! But this love was different: it *was* love, in fact. What was really strange was the relation, now made so dazzlingly clear, between love and forgiveness. Forgiveness had been bound up with justice, just as obedience to the Law had been required by justice. To be forgiven because one has loved was the other side of "If you love me, keep my commandments." The guests at table with him were not ready for either.

Nazareth Grows Murderous

What did Nazareth think of the citizen who would not stay in it? It must have been displeased that he chose Cana, four miles away, for his first miracle, and Capernaum for his second.

On his way back from Judea to Galilee after the Baptist's arrest, he passed through Nazareth, and that time he *did* preach in the synagogue there. In this fourth chapter Luke tells us of the sermon, with its wonderful beginning. Jesus read from Isaiah (the opening of chapter 61): "The spirit of the Lord is upon me; he has anointed me, and sent me out to preach the gospel to the poor, to restore the broken-hearted; to bid the prisoners go free, and the blind have sight; to set the oppressed at liberty. . . . " As he finished the reading he said: "This Scripture is today fulfilled." Those present were overwhelmed, we are told, that such splendor should come from the mouth of the son of their own town carpenter.

As Luke's description continues, there is so complete a change of mood from admiration to murderous rage that many think he has chosen to insert here an account of the second sermon in the same synagogue, which Matthew (chapter 13) and Mark (chapter 6) describe as happening later—after he had raised the daughter of Jairus from death to life in Capernaum. Luke, indeed, has Jesus actually saying at this point that they must be wanting to know why he had not done in his own town the things he had done in Capernaum. Matthew and Mark give us the reason—he could work very few miracles in Nazareth because he found there so little of the faith which called his healing power into action.

The congregation in the synagogue still marveled at his wisdom and his miracles; but the emphasis is now stronger on the improbability of it all. "Is not this the carpenter, the son of Mary, the brother of James and Joseph and Jude and Simon? Are not also his sisters here with us?" They felt they knew all about him—the carpenter's shop, the quiet mother, the cousins brought up as one family with him. They were, Mark and Matthew tell us, "scandalized". It was almost as though they felt that God had no business giving such powers to one of whom they thought so little.

Besides, Capernaum, where so many of these miracles happened, was only twenty miles away. They must have heard accounts of the astonishing claims he had been making about himself, and the repeated offences he had given to the Pharisees, the religious leaders of the people. Was he still a true Jew, and not rather an apostate and a rebel?

If that last doubt was in their minds, he did nothing to allay it. Indeed he touched to inflammation one of their tenderest spots: for he reminded them of instances in the Old Testament where Gentiles had been preferred to Jews. With all the widows of Israel suffering in the famine, Elijah had been sent to Zarephath, to a Phoenician. With all the lepers in Israel, Elisha had cleansed only Naaman, a Syrian.

Enraged, the men of the congregation thrust him out of the synagogue, and "they brought him to the brow of the hill, on which their city was built", meaning to cast him down headlong to his death. But he passed through the midst of them. How? Perhaps with the majesty which had had the moneychangers running in panic before him. Nazareth was not to see him again.

His own comment was: "A prophet is honored everywhere, save in his own country, and his house, and among his own kindred." A totally natural comment, one feels, but for the last word. He never wastes words. What was the point of this one? What had his kindred done, thus to be included?

"Who Is My Mother?"

There would, of course, have been cousins of his in the congregation. Obviously they had not joined the mob that wanted to murder him. But in ending with "kindred" the list of those who did not honor him as a prophet, he must have had his own in mind. Not all of them, of course. James and Jude were among the twelve apostles. But some of the cousins—probably those who had stayed on in Nazareth—held out longer against conviction. Seven or eight months later, Saint John tells us (7:5): "Even his brethren were without faith in him." These were the cousins who were urging him to go up to Jerusalem for the Feast of Tabernacles, on the ground that Galilee was very much of a hole-and-corner scene for the display of his power, and that he ought to go up to make contact again with the disciples he had made over a year earlier in Judea, especially in Jerusalem. The same feeling that he really ought to be making a more spectacular use of his gifts was evident even in one of the cousins who *did* believe in him. For at the Last Supper Jude said to him: "Lord, how is it that thou wilt manifest thyself to us, *and not to the world?*" (Jn 14:22).

But to return to the unconvinced cousins. Jesus was in a house in Capernaum so thronged about with people that there was no possibility of pausing even for a meal. It seems to have been some of these relations of his who "went out to lay hold on him. For they said: He is become mad" (Mk 3:21). The Greek word for "lay hold on" is the word used of Herod when he arrested John the Baptist. "Mad" is perhaps too strong a translation, the word means rather that they thought their cousin was beside himself, strained beyond danger point, in need of care and attention. But the scribes who had come down from Jerusalem put it more viciously: "He is possessed by Beelzebub."

Then comes one of the most moving episodes in the Gospel story. "His mother and his brethren came; and standing outside"— they could not get near him because of the crowd, says Luke (8:19)—"they sent unto him, calling him" (Mk 3:31). Peter seems to be telling us, through the mouth of Mark, that these were the relations who had come to restrain him, in his own interest; and that Mary had come with them, to be near her Son in a moment even crueler than the one in which his own town had tried to slay him.

When the message was brought in, Jesus gave an answer which startles us still: and must have been gleefully retailed by any who didn't like the family: "Who is my mother and who are my brethren?" And "stretching forth his hand towards his disciples", he said: "Behold my mother and my brethren. For whosoever shall do the will of my Father, who is in heaven, he is my brother, and sister, and mother" (Mt 12:49, 50).

We are in presence here of the same element in his teaching that we find in his retort to the man who addressed him as Good Master—"Why do you call me good? None is good but one, that is God" (Mk 10:17–18). On that occasion he was not denying either that he was good or that he was God: on this, he was not denying either that he had a mother or that Mary of Nazareth was she. In each instance he went from a peripheral question to the very heart and center of reality, leaving undiscussed the peripheral question which had been the starting point. Hearing the casual, largely conventional use of the word "good", he was suddenly on fire with the sense of the infinite goodness of God. Hearing his relatives mentioned, his mind turned to the simple truth that any relation by grace is closer than the closest relation by nature. We can pick up the answer to the questions I have called peripheral from what he says in other parts of the Gospels.

Yet we can see that, for the cousins, it must have been the last straw—he had abandoned his own town, now he was disowning them, worse still he was disowning his Mother. Of all those who heard the words it may be that only she knew better.

For she knew the profound truth he was uttering. She had not to wait for Saint Augustine to tell her that she was more blessed for having received God in her soul than for having conceived God in her flesh. Just as by nature she was closest of all to him, so also in the higher relationship of grace, none equaled her; for none had ever done or ever would do the will of the Father as she had done it.

She did not see him this time. Did she see him again before Calvary? When she had asked him to work his first miracle at Cana, she knew she was ending their earthly life together: miracle-workers have no private life. He was the world's property now. She had counted the cost. Yet there must have been moments when the cost seemed to soar beyond her counting.

Messengers from the Baptist

One other cousin of Jesus, far more important than any of those brought up with him, we have not mentioned for a long time—John the Baptist. At the beginning of this year he had baptized Jesus. In March he had told of the sign by which God had shown that the carpenter was Son of God and Lamb of God. A couple of months later Herod had arrested him and imprisoned him in the fortress Machaerus, at the furthest edge of Herod's other province of Perea, on the far side of the Dead Sea. In the March following, John would be beheaded to please Herodias.

The principal object in imprisoning the Baptist was to withdraw him from circulation, because of his attacks on Herod's marriage. But some of his disciples were allowed to visit him, and he was kept informed, in a general way if not precisely, about what Christ was doing and saying. Because of the small concern the evangelists have about the order of things, we cannot be certain just at what point in the ten months of the Baptist's imprisonment two of his disciples arrived to question Jesus. Luke

(7:18-23) places the incident immediately after the raising to life of the widow's son at Nain, which would make it fairly early.

Their message was: "John the Baptist hath sent us to thee, saying: Art thou he that art to come: or look we for another?" Was this the Baptist's own question? we wonder. Or had his disciples been bothering him to the point where he said, "Go and ask him yourselves"? The second seems the more probable. John had seen the sign from God, and uttered his own certainty without the shadow of a perhaps. He had seen disciples of his own taking him at his word, leaving him to follow Jesus. It is hard to think that, even in the long silences of the fortress Machaerus, doubts had been born in him. Whereas we know that the disciples who remained with him were troubled by the success of the new prophet if only because of their love for the forerunner; troubled, too, to find him less austere than their own master.

In the weeks before John's arrest his disciples had told him (Jn 3:22-30) that all men were coming to Jesus. John answered that Jesus was the bridegroom, himself only the bridegroom's friend. A month or so later, after the famous banquet in Levi's house, John's disciples joined with the Pharisees in criticizing Jesus because his disciples did not fast as they did. Our Lord answered that while the bridegroom was there, people should feast: fasting could wait till he was gone. *Bridegroom,* we have already noted: that is what he called himself, that was what the Baptist had called him, that was what the Old Testament had called God, with Israel for God's bride.

Whether or not the question now raised was the Baptist's own, there *was* a problem. Jesus had worked miracles and given profound moral teaching. But he had so far given no hint of what he was going to do, no hint indeed that he was going to do anything at all. John had spoken of him (Lk 3:17) as bearing a great winnowing fan, separating the chaff of Israel from the wheat, burning the chaff with unquenchable fire. He had seen him as laying the axe to the root of the tree. There was as yet not much evidence of winnowing fan or axe. The forerunner might well have wondered what exactly he had forerun.

Was Jesus the Messiah? As so often, he did not answer his interrogators with a plain yes. His very first act—*in that same hour,* says Luke (7:21)—was to work a series of miracles. Then he spoke: "Go and relate to John what you have heard and seen—the blind see, the lame walk, the lepers are made clean, the deaf hear, the dead rise again, the poor have the gospel preached to them." There was one other sentence in the message. We shall glance at it in a moment. Meanwhile pause upon what he had said thus far.

Apart from the lepers, all these things had been spoken by Isaiah as linked with a new order and the One who should establish it. But we are left with two questions.

The first applies to Isaiah as well as to Jesus. What exactly was the force of the *poor* having the good news preached to them? The spiritual leaders of Israel did not bar anyone on account of material poverty, some of the most esteemed Pharisees were very poor indeed. It seems that the reference was to the illiterate, those who neither studied nor rigidly observed the Law, in general the unregarded, the despised.

The second applies to Jesus only. He had been working miracles in Judea well before John's arrest, John certainly knew all about them then, and his informants would have told him about the miracles in Galilee too. It does not seem that Jesus was telling him anything that he had not known before he dispatched the messengers with their question. It might have helped if we knew what the messengers made of the carpenter's reply. But we are not told. There is perhaps a hint in Jesus' last sentence to them: "Blessed is he that shall not be scandalized in me." We are only guessing. All we are actually told is that they went their way! We do not know what John made of the reply either, or if he even heard it. Herod may have beheaded him before they got back.

It is a pity that they did not stay long enough to hear Jesus' praise of his forerunner. To the people round him he posed the question of the Baptist's significance in the history of Israel and of the world. When they had thronged out into the desert where John was preaching, what had they gone to see? Not the wind blowing through the reeds, they could have seen that anywhere. Not a man richly clad, the courts of kings are the place for that sort. They had gone to see a prophet, one who should speak out reality under the inspiration of God.

But even then, though this prophet came after so long a famine of prophecy, they did not grasp that he was the greatest of all the prophets: for, Jesus told them, John was the angel of whom Malachi had spoken, who should make the way ready for the coming of the Messiah — the last, therefore, of that great line and the highest in function.

The Baptist's disciples would surely have been enchanted to hear that, but perhaps less so as they saw what Jesus was actually saying — that *he himself* was the One for whom John had prepared the way. We get the feeling that their devotion to John would not lightly bear the preeminence of the carpenter.

The next words would have disenchanted them totally. Great as John was, mightier even than Moses and Elijah, "the lesser in the Kingdom of God is greater than he". Had they heard this, they could hardly have borne to repeat it to their own imprisoned master. Would John himself have understood all that lay in the words? He had said that the One who was to follow him should baptize "with the Holy Spirit and with fire", so that everyone who received the new baptism would receive something greater than God had given John.

But did he know, had he the faintest conception even, how much greater? Until Jesus had revealed not only the doctrine of the Blessed Trinity (which gives the fullness of meaning to the Holy Spirit), but also the doctrine of the Mystical Body, men could not know what dignity lies in incorporation with God-made-man. The Baptist, to say nothing of Moses and Elijah, may have made an immeasurably greater use of his lesser gift: but lesser his gift was than what is given to us, the least of us.

24 *FIRST SENDING OF THE TWELVE*

Day of Parables

Quite suddenly Jesus burst into parable. From the thirteenth chapter of Matthew and the fourth of Mark we are told of one particular day on which he created this new way of teaching. By the lakeside he began with the story of the sower whose seed fell so variously—on good ground, on stony ground, among thorns, right outside the field; and went on to half a dozen others, which must have sounded to his more learned hearers like a lot of agricultural small talk, with a fisherman's net and a pearl thrown in.

It truly was a new thing that came into the world that day. The word parable merely means "comparison". But in Jesus' use it means the illustration of spiritual truths by comparison with happenings in ordinary life—happenings with a plot like the prodigal son or the good Samaritan, in a single incident like a farmer sowing seed, or a natural process like leaven working in meal: but always natural happenings, with no animals talking or fish flying. The elements in the spiritual process are shown related to one another like the elements in the natural process: our familiarity with the natural process helps us to familiarity with the spiritual.

Jesus seems to have uttered no parables earlier. In the whole of the Old Testament there are none, rudimentary sketches only. Their introduction marks a new stage in the teaching on the Kingdom.

In the Sermon on the Mount he had talked of the change of heart required in those who should enter the Kingdom. In the parables he taught certain of the inner principles of the Kingdom itself. Observe that he still says nothing of its external structure, what officers it should have or what functions—not the faintest sketch of a blueprint. Men's expectations were too far from the reality; he must reshape their minds, not by violently imposing a new shape but by bringing to life the deepest elements in themselves.

At this stage, we are told, he taught the multitude about the Kingdom in parables only, explaining to his apostles apart. There were certain depths of truths for which only the few were ready. He makes it quite clear that the parables have different levels of meaning. There was one meaning, plain on the surface and of high spiritual value, which all could see and profit by. But we have his own word for it that below the surface there were hidden truths about the Kingdom, and that he told the stories in such a way that those who would be revolted by these and would certainly misuse them to the peril of their own souls and other people's, should not understand what he was saying.

The first and most famous—about the sower and the seed that fell so variously—does not use the word Kingdom: that appears in the explanation Jesus gave the disciples (and then only in Matthew's rendering). The overall meaning of the parable is that the establishment of the Kingdom would not mean an elevation *en masse* of the chosen people—it would depend for each individual on the response he himself made to the truth revealed to him: those who made the right response would themselves bear spiritual fruit beyond all measure: in spite of all the wastage there would be a rich harvest. But wastage there would be. The overall meaning was clear enough as Christ uttered it, and clear beyond any question by the time the Gospels came to be written. It was an unpleasant shock to the listeners, but it needed no elucidation.

Christ in his explanation assumed that it needed none. He went straight to the various ways of receiving the Word, for this is one parable where every detail matters vitally to every listener. The four ways were at the heart of practicality when Jesus taught them; they are at its heart now and at all times. It looks as if the explanation already existed in a standardized version which the evangelists used, for scholars tell us its Greek differs rather from theirs. It is an unrivalled summary of spiritual attitudes, and of itself elucidates what I have called the parable's overall meaning.

So the chosen people would not, as they had expected, be taken into the Kingdom in a body.

Again, they had expected the Kingdom to come suddenly, but the parable of the mustard seed says that it will grow slowly, gradually, beginning very small. They had expected it to come spectacularly, with a whole world cowering before it, but the parable of the leaven says that it will come silently, secretly, attracting no attention. They had assumed that entry into the Kingdom would be final, a goal achieved, but the parables of the wheat and the weeds and of the fishing net with good fish in it and bad, both show that upon this earth the Kingdom itself will contain not the perfect only, and that ultimately those who are evil will be cast from it, into the fire or into the sea.

Two other tiny parables which we read as spoken on that day—the pearl of great price and the treasure hidden in a field—were a reminder of the vastness of what is at stake. Compared with that, all other successes are meaningless; men will make the Kingdom their own only if they are willing to sacrifice everything else for it.

After that first rich group of parables by the lakeside, there would be many more—two dozen or so up to that story of the wise and foolish virgins which Jesus told in Jerusalem three days before his death. They are all concerned with the Kingdom of God—the Kingdom in the world, the Kingdom in the soul.

As we read the first outpouring of parables whether or not they were all told on one day (Mt 13, Mk 4), we may find it puzzling that the hearers found *them* puzzling. With an occasional exception—like the unjust steward—all the parables, these first and those that came after, seem so clear to us. We have known them all our lives. Yet we may be missing the principal meaning in our Lord's mind as he spoke them.

They are about the Kingdom of God. We remind ourselves, quite correctly, that the Kingdom of God is wherever God is King, wherever his law is obeyed—in the soul of each believer, for instance. So, I think, most of us read the parables—as magnificent spiritual and moral lessons about God's action in the soul, our own soul, and about our duties to him and to one another.

The parables are indeed about God's Kingdom in souls. But as a totality they were primarily about the Kingdom Jesus was to found in the world. That this is their primary meaning is perhaps the reason for our finding them only in the first three Gospels, written within a generation of his death. There are none in Saint John's Gospel, written thirty or forty years afterward. They are never alluded to in the remainder of the New Testament. For the Church was already in existence, with every characteristic foretold by the parables more and more plainly to be seen. Later they would return to the Christian consciousness, but in their second significance, their meaning for us individually.

The Twelve Sent to Preach and Heal

At last we see Jesus following up the promise he made when he called the Twelve six months earlier, that they should be fishers of men, drawing men into his Kingdom. So far we have seen the apostles only as a dozen men who went about with him. All the light has fallen upon *him*. *They* are simply there. Since their calling, no one of them has said or done anything much, or anything at all. They plucked corn as they passed through a cornfield, but there was nothing particularly apostolic in that. Now they ask Jesus why he teaches in parables. That is all, so far.

A reader coming to the Gospels for the first time and knowing nothing of the history of the Church would be totally unprepared to find Jesus saying to these faceless, voiceless, men: "To you it is given to know the mystery of the Kingdom of God" (Mk 4:11). Nor does anything spectacular seem to follow, not immediately at any rate. The darkness closes on them again. Once more they are simply there. They cross the lake with Jesus, see the demon-possessed swine hurl themselves to their drowning, return for the healing of the woman with an issue of blood, the raising of Jairus' daughter, the rejection of their Master by his own townspeople. But they do not do or say anything very notable, they seem to contribute nothing at all. They were in a panic at the probability of drowning. But who would not be?

They had been called to the apostolate about the June of the first year of the public ministry. We cannot be certain of the precise order of things or the precise dates, because the evangelists, as we have noted, had not our modern concern with such matters. But it seems probable that the incident of the drowned pigs took place in the December, and the day of parables just before that. The months that followed are given a single verse by Saint Mark, and four verses by Saint Matthew. We learn that Jesus spent them going from town to town, "teaching in the synagogues, preaching the gospel of the kingdom, healing every disease" (Mt 9:35). And in March, he sent out his twelve apostles on their first mission without him. "He gave them power and authority over all devils and to cure diseases." And he sent them to preach the Kingdom of God.

The word "apostle" means one who is sent. This is the only time we are told that Jesus "sent" the Twelve. He prefaced their sending most movingly: "Seeing the multitudes, he had compassion on them, because they were distressed, and lying like sheep that had no shepherd. Then he said to his disciples: The harvest indeed is great, but the laborers are few. Pray ye therefore the lord of the harvest, that he send forth laborers into his harvest" (Mt 9:35-38).

They were to go to the Jews only—not to the Gentiles, not even to the Samaritans, but "to the lost sheep of the house of Israel" (Mt 10:6)—the sheep distressed and shepherdless.

They were to go in pairs (Mk 6:7). One wonders which of them went with Judas—that other Simon, perhaps, whom Matthew pairs with him in the list of the Twelve. The mind reels at the thought of Judas preaching a sermon. What, indeed, did the mission mean to him? Was his first zeal still in him? We may doubt it, for it was only a month or so later that Jesus said of him "one of you is a devil" (Jn 6:71). There would have been excitement for him, of course, in casting out devils—and ironical amusement for the devils, if they knew the way he was going. But what did he teach?

What, indeed, did any of them teach? They must have been thronged about by people wanting to know who and what their Master was, still more what he meant to do. The Twelve could not have said very much in answer. Not only did they not as yet know that the carpenter was God, they were not even certain that he was the Messiah. It would be some months still before Peter's assertion and Jesus' acceptance of it settled that question for them, and indeed went far beyond. But when the assertion and the acceptance did come, Jesus commanded (Mt 16:20) that they should tell no man that he was the Christ—they themselves did not understand his Christhood sufficiently to enlighten others: they were more likely to mislead, and that might have meant rioting and bloodshed. So this was not part of their message on the first mission—whatever else people wanted to know, the apostles were in no position to tell them *that*. We may assume, also, that had they gone round two by two saying, "Moses says but Jesus says", that Jesus was greater than the Temple, Lord of the Sabbath—then two by two they would have been stoned to death.

Their message was about the Kingdom and its near approach. But even here we are left wondering. They had heard the Sermon on the Mount, they had heard the parables of the first day and received instruction about them given to themselves alone. But how much, *at this time,* did they really understand of the Kingdom? They were not quick learners, and they were not learned to start with. If only Jesus had chosen twelve scribes—

Even after Jesus had said that he would build his Church upon Peter, we find the apostles arguing among themselves on the road to Capernaum as to which of them should be greatest in the Kingdom. Months after that, actually at the Last Supper, the argument was still raging. And, in between, James and John tried to preempt the highest places for themselves. None of this suggests any very profound grasp on the nature of the Kingdom. The very last words we hear from them before the Ascension are: "Will you at this time restore the Kingdom *to Israel?*" And indeed it would be years after the Ascension before the Holy Spirit brought them to grasp, what the later parables taught so insistently, that within the Kingdom Gentile and Jew should be all one.

We are left wondering, I say, whether they would have been very good at answering questions even about the Kingdom. They did not know when it would come, or how, or what it would look like. But at least they knew the change of heart that entry into the Kingdom would require. They had been told to *preach,* and this would probably be mainly at the services in the synagogues where there would be no heckling to bother them. With the service over, they would work their miracles—"heal the sick" (anointing many of them with oil, as Saint Mark adds, a kind of sacrament in embryo perhaps), "raise the dead, cleanse the lepers, cast out devils" (Mt 10:8). Questioners would get no chance. Their subtleties would be lost in the clamor of sick men made well, dead men brought back to life, devils growling resentment at their own impotence to refuse the commands of these insignificant ones.

Anyhow the problem does not seem to have troubled the apostles. Later Jesus sent out not twelve only but seventy-two of his followers—who would hardly have been better equipped—on a similar mission. And when these returned all their talk was of devils they had cast out, with never a word of questions they could not answer.

Matthew and John and Peter (whose Gospel Mark wrote) were among the six pairs of apostles sent out on that first mission (Mt 10). No one of them gives us a single detail. Yet it may well have been the most nerve-racking experience any of them had yet had. To begin with, they had been ordered to take the road with no money and no food, wearing nothing but what they stood up in—they went out as mendicant friars would later go. They were to live on what they were given, and for men not rich indeed but respectably brought up, this could have been trying.

Yet it was as nothing to what they had been told they must *do*. We can imagine the cold pain in the back and the gulp as they steeled themselves to their first miracle—would the disease obey them? Would the devils? Their first sermon might have meant a chiller pain, a more sickening gulp—anyone who remembers his own first speech will know about that. And preaching was such a long way away from fishing, or even tax collecting. Fishermen had no training as prophets, tax collectors still less.

Their instructions were so very exacting (some indeed envisaged a wider apostolate than this first one). They were to be wise as serpents—considering the part that the serpent's cunning had played in the Fall of man, it is interesting that our Lord mentions its wisdom. It is faintly surprising that he offers his apostles the serpent for their imitation at all.

The dove also is held up for their imitation. Yet there is nothing dovelike in what they must do if any house or city will not receive them or hear their words: "Going forth out of that house or city, shake off the dust from your feet" (Mt 10:14). This shaking the dust from the feet was an exclusively Jewish gesture— Jews used it, for instance, when returning to the Holy Land from the lands of the Gentiles. The apostles must have been startled to be instructed to use it against their fellow Jews.

The Baptist Murdered

What was Jesus doing while the Twelve were out on their mission? We cannot be sure, but it seems at least probable that he paid that visit to Nazareth which ended so hatefully for him. We may be certain that the Twelve were not with him that day. Peter, who would later slice off the ear of the high priest's servant, would not have stood quietly by while his Master was hustled to the edge of a high cliff. But wherever he was, the return of the Twelve with their stories of what they had done and taught must have occurred about the same time as the murder of John the Baptist at the command of Herod Antipas, tetrarch of Galilee and Perea (Mk 6:21–29).

There is hardly a better-known story in the Bible. The Baptist had been imprisoned in the fortress-palace of Machaerus, principally because of his attacks upon the marriage of Herod and Herodias. The point of the attack was, not that Herod was her uncle—for her first husband was her uncle too—but that Herod had taken her from his brother Philip (a colorless man, who lived on quietly in Rome after the loss of his wife as before). John must have known that to rouse the anger both of a son and a granddaughter of Herod the Great (who had slain the infants in Bethlehem) was to ask for death.

In the end, it was not Herod who wanted the Baptist's death, only Herodias. He had promised the dancing daughter, Salome, anything she asked; her mother had her ask for the Baptist's head. This Herod was not a great murderer, he would kill for policy, but not merely to relieve his feelings. And he knew that such a killing would infuriate both the Jewish people, who had a vast reverence for John, and, what was possibly even more dangerous, the Roman governor of Judea, Pontius Pilate: for the Baptist was a man of Judea, not a Galilean, and the ruler of Galilee had no rights over him. Herod was driven to a murder he did not want by Herodias—who felt about John the Baptist as perhaps Anne Boleyn felt about John Fisher.

25 *MAINLY ABOUT BREAD*

Just a year earlier, with the Passover approaching, John had hailed Jesus as Lamb of God, reminding him of the death he must die for the sin of the world. Now, with a second Passover approaching, John's death was another reminder of his own: at the third Passover he himself would die by a slaying even more violent. Christ lived always in the knowledge of the death he would die. He was God, of course. But he was true man too, with a soul that could be sorrowful even unto death. Each new reminder would be a foretaste of Gethsemane.

The evangelists do not tell us how Jesus reacted to the Baptist's death—not specifically, that is. But the reaction is there all the same. Saint John tells us (chapter 6) that he proceeded, immediately afterward, to give his first teaching on how his own body, so soon to be slain, would be given till the end of the world for the soul's nourishment. The teaching that his body would be the bread of souls he gave in Capernaum. He prefaced it by a miracle about bread—the feeding of the five thousand—and by a miracle about his body—the walking on the water.

Feeding of Five Thousand

The first of these is the only miracle that we find in all four Gospels. Jesus had said to the apostles: "Come apart into a desert place, and rest awhile." They crossed the northern corner of the lake by boat, and came to a place with hills sloping to the water a few miles beyond Bethsaida. It was "a desert place" indeed, but they did not rest "awhile". The crowds, whose urgency had driven Jesus and the apostles to the last gasp of exhaustion, saw where the boat was going and followed round on foot—it would not have been more than seven or eight miles from Capernaum.

Once more the sight of the crowd was too much for Jesus' resolution. Compassion brought him down to them. Once more the teaching and the healing began and went on steadily through the day. By the end of the afternoon they were still thronged about with people—five thousand of them ("besides women and children", adds Matthew, who as a tax collector had been accustomed to counting heads).

Read Matthew 14, Mark 6, Luke 9, and John 6 for the detail of the miracle that followed. Jesus decided to feed them there on the spot. The food available was five loaves and two fish—Andrew had somehow discovered that there was a boy in the crowd thus provided. Jesus fed them all, the five thousand men plus the women plus the children, with the boy's provisions.

Mark, giving us Peter's memory of the great day, makes the scene most vivid. Jesus had the people sit down on the grass: then he *gave thanks*—"eucharisted" is John's word—*blessed* and *broke* the loaves (Mk 6:41). And the Twelve distributed, and distributed, and distributed, till no one could eat any more. It is Peter who remembers that the grass was of the light green color of spring; and that the groups sitting in their many-colored robes looked like beds of flowers (but you have to go to the Greek to find that).

Observe how strange a miracle it was. Jesus did not simply hand out the five loaves and the two fish to the first few people, and then create further loaves and further fish for the rest. In some mysterious way he fed everybody with *those* five loaves and *those* two fish. The food left over at the end was the remains of the original supply — "they filled twelve baskets with *the fragments of the five barley loaves*" (Jn 6:13); "and when they took up the broken pieces, and what was left of the fishes, they filled twelve baskets with them" (Mk 6:43).

Jesus performed the miracle solely because he wanted to. It was a convenience to the crowd, of course, to have food provided on the spot: otherwise they would have had to walk the few miles to Bethsaida, or the even fewer miles to villages closer still. But it was no more than a convenience, the walk would not have been a great hardship. When Saint John tells us that the first teaching on the Blessed Eucharist was so soon to follow, we see a reason why Jesus should have wanted to work this particular miracle at this precise moment.

Christ Walks on the Lake

The miracle completed, he told the Twelve to get into the boat, and make their way back across the lake. He himself would dismiss the crowds. These, indeed, wanted to make him King. It would be interesting to know just how he dissuaded them. All we do know is that he went up into the mountain, alone, to pray.

Meanwhile the Twelve were having difficulty in rowing the boat back against the wind. By about three in the morning they had still made only three or four miles. From his hilltop Jesus saw them and came to them — walking on the water (Mt 14:22–33).

When they saw him, they thought they were seeing an apparition — a spirit good or evil. They were in the sort of panic in which, had they known about the sign of the cross, they would certainly have made it. They cried out in their fear; and Jesus answered: "Be of good heart: it is I, fear ye not."

And now, for the first time since the apostles were chosen, Peter emerges from the anonymity of the group. We have grown to think of Peter as talking ahead of the others, acting ahead of the others, more or less accepted by them as their spokesman. But, in fact, till this moment there had been nothing, in the nine months since the apostles were chosen, to single him out from the rest. The manner of his emergence was characteristic. As so often afterward, hot courage landed him in a situation in which he had not the cool courage to maintain himself. Matthew tells us the story.

Jesus had said, "Be of good heart." Peter, for the moment, was of very good heart indeed. He said, "Lord, if it be thou, bid me come to thee upon the waters" and, at our Lord's single word "Come", Peter got out of the boat and began to walk across the water toward his Master. Then, seeing (what had been apparent all the time) that the wind was strong, fear overcame him and he found himself going under. But if his courage had lost its fine edge, faith had not wholly gone. He cried, "Lord, save me." With the single comment "O thou of little faith, why didst thou doubt?"—our Lord took him by the hand and both entered the boat.

The wind ceased at that moment. And those in the boat fell at his feet and said, "Thou art indeed Son of God."

Mark, writing Peter's memory of the scene, leaves out the whole episode of Peter's excess of nerve leading to break of nerve. But he adds (6:52) a surprising comment on our Lord's walking on the water and the reaction of those in the ship: they were astonished beyond all measure, "for they understood not concerning the loaves: for their heart was blinded". (Read that, as Peter would have said it, with "we" and "our" instead of "they" and "their".) Later (Mark 8:17) Jesus would talk of blindness of heart in his followers: but here one of themselves says it. And the one who says it is Peter, Mark's Gospel being his.

Of all the group in the boat, Peter had the most to be astonished about. His mind must have been in a chaos after what had just happened to himself. Yet the explanation he gives for their bewilderment may bewilder us—"because we did not understand *concerning the loaves*". What had they failed to understand about the loaves? They had seen the miracle happen: they were no less overwhelmed by the superhuman power displayed than were the crowds who wanted to make the wonder-worker King. What, exactly, had they not understood? And what bearing had their failure to understand upon their astonishment at their Master's walking on the surface of the water?

The truth is that the feeding of the five thousand differed from every miracle they had so far seen our Lord work in one most important respect. Perhaps they did not see it. Perhaps we do not, either.

It seemed to contain in itself, as earlier miracles did not, sheer contradiction. To order devils out of a man, to order disease out of a man, to order a storm to cease—these meant power, yet they are in a sense quite straightforward. And it may well be that the apostles had seen simply one more example of the same kind.

We remember that the feeding was with those five loaves. We speak of the multiplication of loaves. But the Gospels make clear that the loaves themselves were not really multiplied at all: there were five of them at the end as at the beginning, the same five, but now in five thousand stomachs and twelve baskets. It was their presence that was multiplied, the number of parts of space they occupied at the same time. Multilocation of loaves would be more precise than multiplication. It looks as if each loaf was broken into a few pieces: each piece was nourishing one man here, and in the very same moment nourishing another man there, and another man elsewhere, up to hundreds of men. And after all these thousands had been fed, the quantity left over was fantastically greater than when the meal began.

That, I say, is how it looks. By all that the apostles, or anybody else, then knew it was sheer contradiction, sheer impossibility therefore.

Peter, meditating long afterward, said that the Twelve "had not understood concerning the loaves". This, perhaps, was his way of saying that if their minds had really operated as they should upon what had just happened, they would have been prepared for all that followed—not only for their Master's body walking apparently weightless and Peter's own body seeming weightless too while his courage lasted, but also for the promise next day of Christ's body as food for men's souls. They had been given a chance to see—and would have seen if their souls had not been dulled by daily preoccupation with material things—that matter itself is more mysterious than matter's surface. They had been shown a distinction they had never dreamed of, between things in themselves and the ways in which they operate upon and react to their physical environment.

"I Am the Bread of Life"

When the boat brought them back to their own side of the lake, they were recognized and there was the usual throng of people to be healed—healed by his touch, healed even by the touch of the cloak he was wearing. And by the next day Capernaum was full of people who had returned from the place where all those thousands had been fed. They all pressed in upon Jesus even more insistently and tumultuously.

His reception of them was not that of a miracle-worker modestly receiving congratulations. As so often, he was the cool realist. He told them that they had come simply because he had filled their stomachs with bread.

"Bread" was to be the key word of the teaching he was about to give—as "birth" had been the key word in his talk to Nicodemus, and "water" in his talk to the Samaritan woman at the well. In all three instances, his hearers assumed that he was talking of the natural thing or event. Nicodemus had asked, "How can a man enter a second time into his mother's womb, and be born again?" The many-husbanded Samaritan had said, "Give me this water, that I may not thirst, nor come hither to draw." So now they said, "Lord, give us always this bread." They knew, at least, that it was not to be ordinary bread: but they had not got beyond the manna with which their fathers had been fed in the desert long ago. We must read the sixth chapter of Saint John's Gospel to see what Bread Jesus meant, and to see his audience not seeing it.

He begins the new teaching: "Labor not for the food that perishes, but for that which endures unto life everlasting, which the Son of Man will give you. He it is that God, the Father, has sealed." Fastening on the word "labor", they asked what work they should do to secure this food. Jesus' answer could not well be terser: the work they must do was to believe in himself, for God had sent him.

Their reaction to that almost takes our breath away: "What sign dost thou show that we may see and believe thee? What dost thou *work?*" considering that they had been there when he fed the five thousand with five loaves, and that in this very town of Capernaum he had worked miracles beyond number, one wonders what more they could possibly want. But their question had a real meaning.

That he had power beyond the human they did not doubt. But was his power from God? They wanted a sign from heaven, and by that they meant a sign from the sky—where God was!

Before God made his covenant with Noah, the heavens had poured down rain for forty days. When Moses went up to Mount Sinai to receive the Commandments, there was thunder and lightning, and the whole of Mount Sinai was wreathed in smoke "where the Lord had come down with fire about him". Elijah, the greatest of the prophets, had been carried up into the sky. But they had seen no sky-miracle from Jesus. Awhile before they may have noticed a great storm over the lake suddenly ceasing; but they had not heard Christ order it to be still.

So, when he now talks (Jn 6:27) of bread that should endure unto life everlasting, their minds went back to Moses and the manna God had given their fathers in the desert fifteen hundred years before (Ex 16). Would this bread be like that? But, said Jesus, Moses did not give bread from heaven. Manna came down, as we know, not from heaven, not even from the sky as perhaps his hearers thought, but only from trees. In any event, the sky is not heaven. Heaven is the seen presence of God. The bread he was now announcing was from heaven in that strictest, richest sense; and it would give life to the world.

Here for the first time we are hearing of the Blessed Eucharist, Christ's own Body and Blood to be received into man's body. This first promise only Saint John gives us. We remind ourselves that the other three Gospels, showing the institution of the Eucharist at the Last Supper, had been in the Church for a long generation before John wrote his. John does not tell the institution over again. Instead he, and he only, tells of the promise, showing it as being made a year earlier (though some wonder if John has not brought forward—in order to link it up with the multiplication of the loaves—words said by Jesus at the Last Supper itself). Read his sixth chapter carefully, especially verse 26 to the end.

We get the impression that Jesus began to talk of the Bread of Life in the street. But verse 60 says that he is in the synagogue. Perhaps the change, if change there was, is at verse 43. The synagogue, we remember, was the one built for the Jews by the pagan centurion, who had said, "Lord, I am not worthy that thou shouldst enter under my roof. Say but the word. . . . "

We return to verse 33 where Jesus had spoken of the Bread of God coming down from heaven. And the people said, "Lord, give us always this bread." Read the next six verses. Jesus says, "I am the Bread of Life"—to people, remember, to whom he had not yet said who he was, or what he was, in his very self. He says that whoever comes to him shall not hunger, whoever believes in him shall not thirst. He says explicitly that he has come down from heaven, sent by his Father: and everyone who believes in him, the Son, shall have life everlasting, "And I will raise him up in the last day."

His hearers found these the hardest words they had heard from him yet. He had said sufficiently startling things about himself. But the claim that he had come down from heaven was just too much. After all, they knew his father and mother! Nazareth was a bare twenty miles away. Some of them might have known him as a baby, might have seen his Mother pregnant with him.

They "murmured", says Saint John. They knew perfectly well that he had been born like everybody else. What was this nonsense about coming down from heaven? Other claims may have sounded like blasphemy, this one sounded like mere raving. So did his claim to be bread—did he mean that men were to eat him? The murmurs, one imagines, swelled to a storm. But it was as nothing to the shock produced by the discovery that he did mean precisely that.

He deals first with the objection raised by his claim to have come down from heaven. Of that claim—the first explicit reference we have heard him make to his own origin—he modified nothing. Even Catholics may be surprised at what he said next. We all know that a year later, at the Last Supper, he said: "No man cometh unto the Father but by me." Here (in verse 44) he said something more startling: "No man cometh unto me but by the Father." Pause on that for a while. He went on to say explicitly that no man had seen the Father, but only himself, who was from God. But he still did not give any explanation of the mystery how one and the same Person, already existing with the Father in heaven, could have been born of Mary of Nazareth.

Then come the twelve verses in which he says what he had meant by the claim "I am the Bread of Life." Again and again in that brief compass, he said that he was to be eaten by men unto eternal life. The bread, of which he had said so much already, was his flesh. Half a dozen times he speaks of "eating" it, half a dozen times of everlasting life brought to men by the eating.

"Unless you eat the flesh of the Son of Man and drink his blood, you shall not have life in you. He that eats my flesh and drinks my blood has everlasting life: and I will raise him up in the last day. For my flesh is meat indeed: and my blood is drink indeed. He that eats my flesh and drinks my blood abides in me, and I in him. As the living Father has sent me, and I live by the Father, so he that eats me shall live by me. . . . He that eats this bread shall live forever."

There are those still who think he was using figurative language, and that all he meant to say was that to believe in himself and to receive into one's mind the lessons of his life and the lesson of his death would make for the soul's salvation. But figures of speech are used to make obscure ideas clearer. This would be a totally monstrous example of using figures of speech—"eat my flesh", "drink my blood"—to make clear ideas totally incomprehensible! His hearers anyhow did not attribute to him a teaching method so strange.

Many Disciples Leave Jesus

Catholics, who have been receiving the Blessed Eucharist ever since they reached the age of reason, can hardly begin to imagine what these words meant to those who heard them uttered for the first time. Whether they believed in Jesus or not, the shock was the same. In all the books of the Jewish people there was nothing—nothing literal, nothing figurative—to prepare them for this talk of eating his flesh. And given that Jews were forbidden to eat meat from which the blood had not been drained out, the talk of drinking his blood was even worse. It sounded like an invitation to cannibalism and to orgies of all horror.

Many of those who had followed him thus far, followed him no further. This they felt was delirium, this was abomination. He did nothing to unsay what they had understood him to say. As against their finding incredible his claim to have already existed with the Father before he was born of Mary of Nazareth, he simply said: "So you are scandalized! Will it make any difference if you see the Son of Man ascend up where he was before?" Then came a profound phrase, adding a mystery to a mystery, yet luminous too. "It is the spirit that gives life, the flesh profits nothing. The words that I have spoken to you are spirit and life."

In the New Testament "flesh" usually stands for human nature and "spirit" is set over against it as the power of God operative in it. The phrase would thus mean that human nature avails nothing without the Holy Spirit. But "flesh" in this chapter has been so steadily used for his body, that it would be strange if it had not that meaning here too. If so, our Lord was making clear that he had not been speaking of the eating of dead flesh, the eating of himself dead: but of flesh with the spirit in it, himself utterly alive. He had not been talking of death, but only of spirit to be nourished by a contact never yet dreamed of, with himself who would be wholly life—a contact whereby man's own life should be lifted into his.

"Jesus knew from the beginning, who they were that did not believe, and who he was, that would betray him" (Jn 6:65). Thus the first mention of the treachery of Judas was linked with refusal to believe that men must eat Christ's flesh and drink his blood. Judas would have another year with the apostles before the actual betrayal. But it may have been this sermon in the synagogue which began the corroding of his faith.

It was not only the crowd, we are told, that could not accept the teaching, but many of his own disciples. It may not have been an absolute landslide, but enough left him to cause him to ask the Twelve if they were going too. Peter answered for them all: "Lord, to whom shall we go? Thou hast the words of eternal life." Peter could no more make sense of the eating of Jesus' flesh and the drinking of his blood than anybody else present, and he did not pretend to. What Jesus said might seem to him meaningless, or capable of no meaning that was not repulsive. But if Jesus said it, that was enough: "We have believed and have known that thou art the Holy One of God."

It is the first time we find Peter acting as spokesman for the Twelve, answering a question addressed to them all. He says "we". But was he in fact uttering the mind of them all? Of all but one, perhaps. For Jesus' comment was "Have I not chosen all twelve of you? And one of you is a devil." The others certainly did not realize that Judas was the one who was "a devil". Did Judas?

We cannot *know,* of course. But, if Judas already knew his own baseness and knew that Jesus knew it, it is hard to imagine his continuing in close companionship for another twelve months with the One who so thoroughly saw through him. He would surely have felt that situation intolerable. When at the Last Supper Jesus said that one of them would betray him, they all fell to asking, "Is it I, Lord?" They probably did precisely that, now. And Judas may have asked the question now, as he did then: but this time his question may have been quite genuine.

The refusal by Capernaum is the end of a chapter. Ten months earlier Jesus had moved to Galilee and made Capernaum his headquarters. In that ten months everything happens in or within reach of the city. When he does go as far in one direction as the opposite shore of the lake or in the other direction as Nazareth, he does not stay long. He comes back to Capernaum. In this period we find the Pharisees testing him and finally deciding against him: in Capernaum they plan for the first time to destroy him. Soon after we have the definitive calling of the Twelve and the Sermon on the Mount. In this same period we have the widow's son raised to life at nearby Nain and the daughter of Jairus in Capernaum itself. We have the day of parables.

Then, with the second Passover approaching, we have the murder of John the Baptist, the feeding of the five thousand, and the sermon on the Bread of Life. With this last the town of Jesus' choice was put to a supreme test, and failed in the test. It was truly the end of a chapter, the Capernaum chapter.

For another six or seven months—till the Feast of Tabernacles in the following October—the scene of his ministry would still be in the north, some of it in Galilee itself. But there would be a visit to Jerusalem for Pentecost; a visit to Phoenicia where he would cast a devil out of a Gentile girl, to the Ten Cities, and to Philip's Caesarea, very close to the border of Syria. There he would announce that Peter was the rock on which he would build his Church. A week after that comes Mount Tabor and the Transfiguration. Then south for the half-year that would bring him to Calvary.

26 *THE FATHER AND THE SON*

The promise of the Blessed Eucharist is in the sixth chapter of Saint John's Gospel. In the seventh, we find Jesus in Jerusalem for the Feast of Tabernacles. But that feast is in October, whereas John has told us in chapter six that the Passover was at hand—say late March. In the seven months that lie between these two chapters, many things happened. The first, perhaps, is the visit to Jerusalem described in chapter five, which many scholars think should come after chapter six instead of before it—though of course it need not. Then there are the happenings in Galilee, Phoenicia, the Decapolis, and Mount Tabor—described by the other three evangelists and not by John. Let us look at John's chapter five.

The Paralytic by the Pool

Jesus went up to Jerusalem for a feast day—perhaps the Passover, which John had said was near, perhaps Pentecost seven weeks after. Read the first eighteen verses of the chapter for the healing of the paralytic whom he found lying on a bed—a sort of mat or mattress—by a pool called Bethesda just outside the city wall near the Sheep Gate. It has certain resemblances to the healing of that other paralytic in Capernaum, the one who was lowered through the roof. To both men Jesus said, "Arise, take up thy bed, and walk." To the first he began by saying, "Thy sins are forgiven thee." To this later one, his last words were faintly ominous: "Sin no more, lest some worse thing happen to thee." They must have been rather different types of men!

Once again the Pharisees were in a rage, this time because it was the Sabbath day and the healed man carried his bed—even a dried fig must not be carried on that day. As when Jesus healed a crippled hand in Capernaum, so now the Jews of the stricter sort wasted no joy over the healing, their whole mind was on the legal question of work done on the Sabbath. They were furious with the man for carrying his bed, still more with Jesus for working his miracle on the day of rest.

The answer startled them more than the crime. Jesus said: "My Father works until now; and I work." There is an air of equality about this bracketing himself with God which is quite unmistakable and could only be maddening. God "works"—creates, conserves in existence the beings he has created, exercises his providence—ceaselessly, on the Sabbath as at all times. When good is to be done, his Son is no more bound by times and seasons than he. So we see his meaning. But to his hearers he seemed to be saying: "God breaks the Sabbath, I'm his Son and I break it too." They now had two causes of anger instead of one. Sabbath-breaking was bad: far worse, he claimed that "God was his Father, making himself equal to God." So they "sought the more to kill him"—as the Pharisees had, in Capernaum, nearly a year before (Mk 3:6).

Jesus answered with another of his discourses—like those with Nicodemus and the Samaritan woman, like the Sermon on the

Mount, the opening group of parables, and the sermon on the Bread of Life. But for the first time his discourse is of his Father and himself. Read it carefully (Jn 5:19–47). I can only summarize it here. It treats of himself as God, himself as man, and of his hearers in relation to him.

"Son of God"

He calls himself explicitly "the Son of God". He has already said that he works continuously as his Father does. He goes on to say that as the Father raises up the dead and gives life, so does the Son. Whatever the Son sees the Father doing, he himself does in exactly the same way. All should honor the Son as they honor the Father: to fail in honor to the Son is to fail in honor to the Father.

Thus there are clearly two distinct persons involved, one the son of the other, distinct yet equal. The Son receives his existence and his nature—all that he is and all that he has—from the Father, for that is what being a son means. But he receives *all* that the Father is and has in utter equality. So that the Son too is God. To the Jews listening, it seemed an assertion of two Gods, himself being one of them, blasphemy therefore and by Jewish law meriting death. Later (Mk 12:29) they would hear him affirm the oneness of God, but how reconcile that with this? In between the two statements, he would say, "I and the Father are one" (Jn 10:30). But this did not abate his claim about himself and seemed to his hearers no more than lip-service to the oneness of God: For how can a father and son be one? Can a father beget himself? Later, as we shall see, Matthew (11:27) and Luke (11:22) quote him as saying something even profounder about the Son's relation with the Father. If any of his disciples heard what he was saying now, it would have been *some* preparation for that.

We who know the doctrine of the Blessed Trinity know how, within the oneness of God, there lies a distinction of Persons which leaves God still utterly one. His hearers could have no possible notion of what he meant. But their horror at what he *said* poured out of them at his examination before the high priest.

Let us return to them as they listened to the carpenter thus incredibly defending himself against the accusation of one sin by admitting, or rather glorying in, sins even graver. So far, with his claims to equal power and equal honor with the Father, he had been speaking of himself as God. He went on—adding confusion to confusion, as unbelievers must surely feel—to speak of himself as God-made-man, still wholly God but now truly man. The key point here is that it was not his own will that was decisive for him, but the will of the Father who sent him.

Why had the Father sent him? For two things particularly. One was to teach the truth that gives life. "He that hears my word and believes that the Father has sent me, has life everlasting." The other was to judge, to judge especially at the end of the world. "The hour comes *and now is* when the dead shall hear the voice of the Son of God, and they that hear shall live"—this seems to refer not to those who have left this world but to those who are dead in sin and ignorance and error. But also, "All that are in the graves shall hear the voice of the Son of God—and they that have done good things shall come forth unto the resurrection of life; but they that have done evil unto the resurrection of judgment." This *does* refer to those who have left our world.

Then he comes to the most dramatic element in this strangest of apologias. He talks of his hearers' relation to himself, what it should be, what it is. They had begun by accusing him of breaking the law of Moses. He ends by accusing his accusers of not believing in Moses themselves.

Observe closely the line of his argument (Jn 5:31–47). The Baptist—"in whose light you were willing *for a time* to rejoice"—had given testimony of him. But Jesus had a greater testimony than John the Baptist's, the testimony of God himself, shown by the miracles which by God's power he worked. "The works themselves which I do give testimony of me that the Father has sent me."

He gives two reasons why, with such testimony from the Father, they do not receive him. "You have not his word abiding in you." And again: "You have not the love of God in you." It is an appalling double indictment. They had searched the Scriptures—that indeed was their lifework here below, upon which they relied for life everlasting. Yet all their study of Scripture had brought them neither knowledge of God nor love of God. Then the unkindest cut: "Think not that I will accuse you to the Father. There is one that accuses, Moses, in whom you trust. If you believed Moses, you would perhaps believe me also, for he wrote of me."

One can imagine them returning to their homes and going over the five books of Moses lynx-eyed, to see what he could have said that had any bearing on the carpenter from Nazareth with his monstrous claims. What phrases could they have overlooked which even hinted at the possibility that God might have a Son of his own, a Son who owed everything to him yet was totally equal to him? And as they read and reread, the one thing that must have emerged most certainly was that God was one, not two!

He had made Judea too hot to hold him. The Jewish leaders judged him worthy of death. In the end they would have their way, but he had work to do first. He returned to Galilee (Jn 7:1).

"Not What Goes into the Mouth"

After these shocks administered to the leaders of the Jerusalem Jews, we find Jesus again in Galilee. And again we find scribes and Pharisees, who had followed him from Jerusalem, arguing with him. For the present argument read the first twenty verses of Matthew 15 and the first twenty-three of Mark 7.

The discussion this time did not take in the larger issues. It was mainly about the rituals they had made into laws, beginning with a complaint that the disciples did not wash their hands before eating—a breach of the Law which the stricter sort of Pharisee seems to have thought worse than sinning with a harlot. We have heard Jesus refer to hypocrites before, leaving not much doubt whom he had in mind. Now for the first time we hear him say "you hypocrites" to actual individuals. Once more he hurls Moses at them—most of the ritual law was manmade, he says: all this business about washing was very recent indeed; meanwhile the commandments Moses had given were being dishonored in the name of rules of conduct Moses had never heard of.

He then laid down a principle which undercut what he obviously regarded as the ritual frenzy of the leaders—"Not what goes into the mouth defiles a man, but what comes out of the mouth" (Mt 15:11). The apostles, brought up from smallest infancy to venerate scribes and Pharisees, were obviously shaken to see their Master dismissing them thus totally. "Do you know", they asked him, "that the Pharisees were scandalized?" Considering what had happened already, "Do you know?" is rich! And Peter, acting as spokesman for the second time, asked him to explain what he meant about going into the mouth and coming out of it.

Jesus was as shocked at the disciples' failure to understand as they had been at his cavalier treatment of the scribes. Food, he says with a touch of impatience, goes into the stomach and through it, it makes the heart of man neither better nor worse. But what comes out of a man comes from the heart, and if it be evil thoughts, murders, adulteries, blasphemies, and such, it really does defile him. Compared with these things, to bother about washing the hands before eating—for fear that the (ritual) uncleanness of the hand should contaminate the (ritual) cleanness of the food—is mere frivolity.

27 OUTSIDE PALESTINE

He seems only to have passed through Galilee this time. Taking the apostles, he went on to Tyre. We are not told why he thus moved out of Palestine. But it may well have been to get away from the endless arguments. He had not been able to show his face anywhere in Jewish territory without a scribe coming at him. And he did want a little time for the formation of the Twelve.

The Canaanite Woman

In the region of Tyre the group found themselves pursued by a Gentile woman, a Canaanite, one of the original stock whom Israel had dispossessed. She hailed the rabbi as "son of David", calling upon him for mercy on herself and on her daughter, who was possessed by a devil.

Jesus said nothing. The disciples, their nerves racked by her pleading, wanted him to give her her miracle and get rid of her. He answered, "I was sent only to the sheep that are lost of the house of Israel."

Pause for a moment upon this phrase. He had come to save all mankind. He would commission his apostles to teach all nations until the end of time. But his own personal mission here upon earth was to the chosen people. They had been chosen by God for so high a double function—the preservation of monotheism, the expectation of a Redeemer. We remember Saint Paul's words: "God's fidelity demanded it; he must make good his promises to their fathers" (Rom 15:8). This Canaanite woman—what a pity we do not know her name—should be the patron of all who grow weary at prayer long unanswered. Her prayer, indeed, had not merely gone unanswered: it had been answered with a straight no. She kept right on. She was refused again.

By now we are accustomed to Jesus' speech being brief, to the point, unsentimental. But his second refusal of the Canaanite woman's plea still startles us. His first refusal had been on the ground that his immediate mission was to the lost sheep of Israel: if he cast an evil spirit out of this woman's daughter, Gentiles would pour in on him by the hundred and the thousand, bringing their sick. This second time, since she would not take a polite no for an answer, she gets an impolite one: "It is not right to take the children's bread and throw it to the dogs" (Mt 15:26)—the Greek word means small dogs, puppies, which does not seem to help.

The words sound like Jewish contempt for the Gentile carried to the highest point. But the woman wasted no time resenting the word "dogs": she wanted her daughter healed. "Ah yes, Lord, the dogs feed on the crumbs that fall from their masters' table."

And at that intensity of love for her daughter and faith in himself Jesus gave way. Her daughter was healed in that instant. We are not told if her husband was alive; but the apostles could hardly have heard the parable of the importunate widow (Lk 18) without remembering her.

Miracles East of the Lake

Jesus went hurrying on north before an avalanche of sick could crush him—he would in any event, perhaps, not want to work miracles where he had done no teaching. Near Sidon, he turned eastward, probably towards the foot of Mount Hermon where the Jordan starts, then south again to the east of the lake and the region of Greek cities known as the Decapolis, each autonomous, loosely under the control of the Roman governor of Syria. We do not know how long the journey lasted, but it was through country where he was not known, so that the Twelve could get his undivided, undistracted attention.

Somewhere in the region of the Greek cities he worked a miracle, unlike any he had yet worked, at least in the way he went about it. Only Mark tells it, which suggests that it had impressed Peter rather specially. He healed a deaf and dumb man, not by a word or a touch only. He put his fingers into the man's ears, put some of his own spittle onto the man's tongue. Jewish and pagan healers sometimes used their spittle and Jesus would do it once again: it is a symbolic way of associating the whole self with the healing action. Jesus said an Aramaic word which means "Be opened." Then, as later at the raising of dead Lazarus, he groaned. We are reminded once more that a miracle was not for him simply a wave of the hand or a wave of the will: power went out of him.

He also worked other miracles in this area, and Matthew tells us that the Gentiles "glorified the God of Israel". They glorified the carpenter too. Once more they thronged after him to a desert place, four thousand of them. Once more we read of his feeding the crowd with a handful of loaves—seven this time—and a few little fish. All four evangelists tell of the feeding of the five thousand; only two of them, Matthew and Mark, tell us of this later multilocation of loaves and fish. And they tell us that there was a more powerful reason for his feeding them on this occasion—they had been with him three days. As before there was a gathering of fragments, seven baskets (seven being, like twelve, a standard number).

Through Galilee to Bethsaida

The apostles went off in their boat, but this time Jesus went with them. They went to "the coasts of Magadan", says Matthew (15:39) to "the parts of Dalmanutha" (Mk 8:10). One of these may have been a village and the other a whole district, but no one now knows where either is or was. What is clear is that the group were back again in Galilee, and the arguing went on as before, but with one new element: for the first time we find those ancient enemies, the Pharisees and the Sadducees, sinking their differences to combine against him. They demand a "sign from heaven"—a miracle in the sky. Jesus "sighed deeply in spirit"—grieved, we may suppose, as he had been at the blindness of heart of the Pharisees after the healing of a withered hand on the Sabbath (Mk 3:5). And, as then, he was angry as well as grieved: "A wicked and adulterous generation seeks after a sign; and the only sign that will be given it is the sign of Jonah the prophet" (Mt 16:4). They must have scratched their heads over that: was he planning to be swallowed by a whale? And vomited up after three days?

Once more he left Galilee. As they crossed the northwest corner of the lake towards Bethsaida (Mt 16:5), Jesus told the Twelve to "beware of the leaven of the Pharisees and Sadducees", and of Herod too, adds Mark.

If we are to take this scene in the boat as a specimen class—with him as teacher and them as pupils—it is faintly depressing. They had been with him over a year, they had heard the parable of the leaven (Mt 13:33), yet the only thing the word "leaven" now suggested to them was bread. They thought he was in some way rebuking them for having set out on the journey with only one loaf among all of them. Once again his patience was tried. Why should they think he would be bothering them about loaves of bread—didn't they remember how he had fed five thousand with five loaves, and four thousand with seven loaves? By the leaven of the Pharisees and Sadducees, they should have known that he meant their doctrine, their whole attitude to life, the evil flowing out of what they did and said.

"Do you not yet understand? Have you still your heart blinded? Having eyes do you not see, having ears do you not hear?" (Mk 8:17–18). It sounds like a crushing examiner's report upon the men he had already sent out, two by two, to preach the Kingdom of God. It is troublingly like what he had said—to these very apostles—about the unbelieving Jews (Mt 13:13–15).

Having arrived in Bethsaida, he worked another miracle in which he used his own spittle—this time to heal a blind man. Like the earlier miracle of the same sort, this one is told by Mark only, which suggests that it must have made a powerful impression upon Peter. It has its own uniqueness, in that the healing is in two stages. After the first laying on of hands, the man said, "I can see men as if they were trees, but walking." After the second laying on of hands, he began to see clearly and soon recovered his sight completely.

"Who Am I, Do You Think?"

The group continued north, probably along the east bank of the Jordan, in the territory of Philip the Tetrarch, the milder brother of Herod Antipas. Two days' journey would have brought them to a town which had once been called Paneas, because of its shrine of the god Pan, but which Philip had rebuilt and named Caesarea, in honor of the Emperor Augustus. Visible for miles in every direction was a high rock upon which Herod the Great had built a temple to the god-emperor.

For some little time (Lk 9:18) Jesus was alone, praying, just as he had been before the choosing of the Twelve. Back with the disciples, he asked them what guesses people were making as to who he was. They gave a variety of the guesses they had heard— John the Baptist, Elijah, Jeremiah, "or one of the prophets" (had nobody said "Messiah" in their hearing?). Then he asked them a question which still has power to startle—who did they them-selves think he was? (Mt 16:15).

For every one of them, of course, it was the question of questions. It must have been the chief thing they talked about among themselves—who was he? what was he? But clearly, in all that year of companionship, these men who had committed their whole lives to him had not liked, or perhaps dared, to ask him. And he had chosen not to tell them. He had told the Samaritan woman (Jn 4:26), but not his own disciples. He waited for *them* to tell *him*. And now Simon Peter told him: "Thou art Christ, the Son of the living God."

These words produced a reaction which must have utterly shattered Peter and the others. "Blessed art thou, Simon son of John, for flesh and blood has not revealed it to thee, but my Father who is in heaven."

What was so special about the phrase of Peter that it should draw that response from his Master? Nathanael, at the first meet-ing with Jesus (Jn 1:49), and the Twelve in the boat when he came to them walking on the water (Mt 14:33), had told him that they knew him for Son of God, without drawing any comment from him at all. Peter's cry of faith was different. His own reasoning had not brought him to the certainty that the carpenter was at once Christ and Son of the Father, though it may have brought him to the threshold of certainty. Nor was it because he had heard the carpenter say such things and every human instinct told him to trust the carpenter. It was his Father in heaven who had illumined Peter's mind with this certainty of faith, with this splendor of vision.

Obviously Peter was not using "Son of God" as the Old Testament had used it of all sorts of people. That use would not have produced so extraordinary a response. He was using it as Jesus had just maddened the Pharisees by using it, giving himself a wholly unique relationship to the Father (Jn 5). He meant by it no less, certainly, than the high priest would mean when he put the fateful question to Jesus—"Art thou the Christ, the Son of the Blessed God?"—and accepted Jesus' acceptance as blasphemy (Mk 14:61–64).

"Thou Art Rock"

Peter had said, "Thou art Christ." Jesus balances that: "And I say to thee that thou art Peter." Peter had proclaimed Christ's office as Redeemer, Christ proclaimed Peter's office as Rock (not just a foundation built in, we notice, but very rock).

At their first meeting (Jn 1:42) Jesus had said: "Thou art Simon, the son of John: thou shalt be called Cephas" (the Aramaic word for rock). Simon must have been puzzled, for Cephas (scholars tell us) was not used as a man's name, and there seemed no point in calling a deepwater fisherman "Rock". Now, a year and a half later, Simon was to learn what the point was. And Cephas did indeed become his name—three times in the second chapter of Galatians Saint Paul calls him so.

Translating Cephas into Greek, one might have expected Simon to be called *Petra,* the Greek word for rock. But the word *petra* is feminine gender, and in Greek it was impossible to call a man by a feminine noun. If one wanted to call a man by a name meaning rock, one had to substitute the masculine ending and call him *Petros,* hence Peter.

There are those who think that this later part of Jesus' answer to Peter may have been said by Jesus on a later occasion—at the Last Supper, perhaps, or after the Resurrection—and inserted here by Matthew to round off the statement of Peter's official relation with his Master. To me this seems improbable, yet the *where* of the saying is not of first importance. Consider that Jesus said: "Thou art Rock, and upon this Rock I will build my Church." It is the first time we have heard "Church" on his lips—*Ekklesia,* from the verb "to call". (Northern Europeans have preferred words like "church", "kirk", based on *kyriakon,* "belonging to the Lord".) In the Old Testament the word *qahal,* it too from the verb "to call", had been used for all Israel in its worship of God.

But Jesus says "*my* Church". He was about to build something new, and upon this wholly improbable rock! As he uttered the words, the group may well have been looking at the rock upon which Herod had built his vast marble temple to the emperor-god Augustus. Any passing stranger might have found something comic in hearing a carpenter tell a fisherman that he would build a rock church mightier than Herod's rock temple. And comic it would indeed be, if it had not happened.

"And the gates of hell shall not prevail against it." In those days of walled cities where the gates mattered so enormously, "gates" was a normal expression for the city as a whole—Isaiah (3:26) had said of Zion: "Her gates shall lament and mourn." Jesus saw the city of hell at war with the city of God which now he was founding upon Peter, and he promised that hell should not have the victory. The war has never ceased—assault from without, fifth column within. There are moments—is the present one of them?— when the only hope Catholics can see lies in this assurance that hell *cannot* win!

"I will give to thee the keys of the kingdom of heaven." For hell, Jesus had used the figure of a walled city with gates. With the word "keys" he now used the same figure for the Church too. Whoever controlled the keys controlled the gates, whoever controlled the gates ruled the Church.

An odd, in fact meaningless, idea has grown up that Peter was given the keys of heaven itself. But the soul newly dead will not meet Peter at the point of arrival, unless of course Peter happens to be passing that way at the moment. The keys he was to have were not of "heaven" but of "the Kingdom of heaven", the Church on earth. The Son of David was promising him the key of David, of which Isaiah (22:22) had spoken: "He shall open and no man shall shut, he shall shut and no man shall open."

In the Kingdom that key could be possessed of right only by the Messiah himself, as Revelation tells us (3:7). It is surprising to hear Jesus entrusting it thus almost casually to Peter. And that is not the end. He proceeds (Mt 16:19) to underline and double underline what he had just said, by promising that whatever Peter should bind or loose—command or forbid—should be bound or loosed in heaven: God would ratify Peter's commands—Peter of all people!

That last phrase, one feels, must have occurred to some at least of the other apostles as the stupendous promises were made to Peter. Why would their Master himself not keep the keys and issue the orders? What would he be doing, while Peter lorded it over his Kingdom? And why Peter? We have heard nothing so far to suggest that Peter was to be the first among them, and no reason to think that they had, either. But of course we can only guess. We are not told here how the apostles reacted. That their reaction was not quite what we should have expected, we shall see later.

For Peter it could only have been a moment of intoxication. He may have been puzzled to hear that he was the rock upon which Christ would found a new Church—what that meant would take some thinking out, and Peter, though quick to act, was not a quick thinker. He may not instantly have remembered what Isaiah had said about the key of David; and he had not yet heard Jesus speak of that other key, the key of knowledge which the scribes had taken away (Lk 11:52). But the general sense of his Master's words was straightforward enough—the Kingdom of heaven here upon earth, himself with the keys which meant he was its governor, himself with the power to command and to forbid.

That was all glory. And Peter could do with glory just then. The immediate past had been so very inglorious. He must still have been feeling a fool over the fiasco of his walking on the water. Others of the Twelve—no-nonsense Thomas, perhaps, and sly Judas—would have reminded him of it every time they passed a sheet of water.

And their mockery would have been a smaller wound than the continuing memory of Jesus' words as he pulled him into the boat, "O thou of little faith, why didst thou doubt?" Nor was that the end of ingloriousness. Crossing the lake at the start of this very journey, Jesus had said to him, along with the rest, "O ye of little faith" and accused them all of blindness of heart and eye, of deafness of ear (Mk 8:18).

The moment at Caesarea Philippi must have seemed to Peter to mark the end of a depressing chapter. No more stupidities from himself, no more snubs from his Lord. But the exalted moment did not last. Within minutes Peter was to hear Jesus call him Satan. Read the next four verses of Matthew (16:20–23) to see how it happened.

Jesus Tells of His Death and Resurrection

Christ's first words after the great promises were a command to all of them "that they should tell no one that he was the Christ." We know that people's expectations of what the Messiah would do had to be corrected before it was safe to publish the news that the Messiah was already among them. And there may have been a further reason for this present veto—namely, that the Twelve did not yet know enough about who and what Jesus was, to be able to answer the questions with which they would certainly be flooded.

As yet not even Peter, certainly not the rest, understood this truth well enough to teach it to others. Jesus warned them against trying—"he commanded his disciples that they should tell no one that he was the Christ." Only after the descent of the Holy Spirit would they be ready to teach about Christ himself. Remembering the questions they had asked and were still to ask, we tremble to think of their doing so earlier. (In the Catholic Evidence Guild we do not allow beginners, even if they have been Catholics all their lives, to teach Trinity or Incarnation or redemption to street-corner crowds.)

Then, for the first time, he broke it to them that suffering at the hands of "the ancients and scribes and chief priests" awaited him, followed by his slaying, and on the third day his Resurrection. They seem hardly to have noticed the promise of Resurrection: their minds were wholly overwhelmed by the suffering and the death: so that was why he had appointed his successor!

Peter did not want power at that price. God's mercy must not let such things happen, he urged, they simply must not be. In the glow of the primacy just promised him, Peter drew Jesus aside and "scolded" him—that is what the Greek word means: "God be merciful to thee, Lord, this thing must not happen to thee." It was a cry born of affection.

Look closely at the reply.

"Get behind me, Satan": Jesus used the very verb with which he had ordered Satan himself away after the third temptation in the desert.

"Thou art a scandal to me": the Greek word *skandalon* meant an obstacle in the road, a stone over which one might stumble, even a trap set.

"Because thou savorest not the things that are of God, but the things that are of men": the phrase means that Peter's judgments, tendencies, almost instincts, were governed by purely human values: Saint Paul (Phil 3:19) uses a somewhat similar phrase for men "whose end is destruction, whose god is their belly and whose glory is in their shame".

Did Jesus ever utter harsher words to anyone not an avowed enemy? Satan, we remind ourselves, is a common noun meaning "tempter" as well as being the special name of the Tempter-in-Chief; but that could have been small consolation to Peter, especially when he heard the words that poured out after it. Since it seems that Peter spoke out of affection, why was the retort so violent? We may get a glimpse of an explanation if we go forward to the agony in the garden, and see Jesus' utter revulsion from what he had undertaken to suffer. The violence of "get behind me, Satan" is a first hint of the violence of the emotion which was to produce the sweat of blood. Peter's urging was well-meant, but it was in fact what Jesus called it—a stone in his path, making his path more difficult to tread.

Turning from Peter, Jesus told the disciples something, not more unexpected, but affecting themselves still more closely. He told them that *they* would be involved in suffering and death too: "If any man will come after me, let him deny himself and take up his cross, and follow me" (Mt 16:24). He had not actually said, and did not actually say now, that his death would be by crucifixion. But the word "cross" was about the most frightening word he could have chosen. The Romans had brought in crucifixion on a vast scale. When Jesus was a small boy, we remember, they had crucified two thousand men here in Galilee, and most of the apostles were Galileans so would have known about it.

Any pleased excitement they may have felt at hearing that the Kingdom of God was to be founded was dimmed in that instant. The Founder was to be tortured and slain. They themselves must follow him. Each of them must "carry a cross" (and they had seen men carrying their crosses!). The Kingdom, in other words, was not to mean anything that they had ever thought of as glory. And Jesus went on to draw a contrast between the transience of this life and the permanence of the next, with the trials of this life as a precondition of glory in the next, for which nothing in their training had prepared them.

The Old Testament had so little to say of splendor after death, and most of what there is comes in books which were in the Greek version of Scripture made by the Jews in Egypt, not in the Scriptures read in Palestine. There was a whole spiritual revolution in the phrase "What does it profit a man to gain the whole world and suffer the loss of his own soul?"

There was something else. They had already heard (Jn 6:40) that at the Last Day Jesus would raise up those who believed in him. Now he gave the first picture of the Judgment—"The Son of Man shall come in the glory of his Father with his angels." The prophet Daniel (ch. 7) had told of the coming of "one like the Son of Man", but that was a coming to the throne of God, this was a coming to this world to judge it.

And Jesus emphasized both that the world was to be judged by him—"He will render to every man according to his works"; and that it was to be judged *by its attitude* to him—"He that shall be ashamed of me and of my words, of him the Son of Man shall be ashamed."

28 *TRANSFIGURATION*

Gospel to the Dead

At Caesarea Philippi Jesus told the apostles that he would suffer and die and on the third day rise again. A week later, transfigured upon a mountain, he told Moses and Elijah.

Present when he told them were Peter and James and John, whom he had chosen to have with him when he raised Jairus' dead daughter to life, and whom he would choose to have nearest to him in Gethsemane. We tend to think of them as principals at the Transfiguration, almost as though the whole incident had been staged for their sake. Strengthened and comforted by it they certainly were; but they were not principals. Jesus conversed with Moses and Elijah: the three apostles were asleep part of the time and contributed nothing. Only one of them said anything at all: Peter said that it was a good thing they were there — they could make three shelters, one for Jesus, one for Moses, one for Elijah; but he himself tells us, through Mark (9:5), that he was too frightened to know what he was saying.

Let us glance quickly at what happened as told in the opening verses of Mark's ninth chapter and Matthew's seventeenth. Read especially Luke (9:28–36). He gives the most detailed account, and we wonder who was his informant. Of the three who were there, Peter tells us what happened through Mark (and we find it again in 2 Peter 1:17–18 — be sure to read it); James was long dead; could it have been John? Apart from "we saw his glory, the glory as of the only begotten of the Father", he says nothing of the Transfiguration in his own Gospel. It may be that Luke had already told all that John had to tell.

As at Caesarea Philippi, Jesus had climbed some way up a mountain to pray. As he prayed he was "transfigured" — the Greek word is "metamorphosed" — his face shining like the sun, his garments dazzling white, like snow. It is not clear at what point the three apostles went to sleep, but when they were fully awake they saw their Lord "in his glory", and Moses and Elijah standing with him, they too in glory. The three were speaking of the death that he would die in Jerusalem.

Moses was Israel's law giver, dead these fifteen hundred years. Elijah, greatest of prophets, had been whirled up into the sky eight hundred years before; and the prophet Malachi had said (4:5) that God would send him "before the coming of the great and awe-filled day of the Lord". Where had they come from?

Of Elijah the destiny is wholly mysterious. About Moses there is no such mystery. He was simply one of the greatest of those who had died at peace with God. Heaven was closed to these until

Calvary should expiate the sin of the race. The soul of Moses, and the souls of all of them, were in a place of waiting—limbo, the border region, we most often call it. Abraham's bosom, Jesus called it in the parable of Dives and Lazarus; paradise, he called it to the thief who appealed to him on the Cross.

Supremely Moses represented the Law, and Elijah the prophets. What happened on the mountain established the continuity between Israel of old and the Kingdom, now at last to be founded, in which Israel was to find its fulfillment. It seems strange that the representatives of the Kingdom were, as they would be likewise in Gethsemane, asleep part of the time, and frightened when they were fully awake. It was no very stimulating account Moses would take back to limbo of the men on whom the Kingdom was to be built.

But for these—long dead or newly dead—who had been waiting in all patience till the Redeemer should open heaven to them, Peter, James, and John must have mattered little compared with the news Moses brought back that their redemption was at hand and how it was to be accomplished. What Jesus had told at Caesarea Philippi to men living upon earth, he now told through Moses to the expectant dead. Through Moses the Law had been given to the children of Israel. Through Moses the Gospel, the good news, reached limbo.

As Peter finished his proposal to build three shelters, a luminous cloud overshadowed them, wrapping them round so that once again they were afraid. A Voice came out of the cloud saying: "This is my beloved Son, in whom I am well pleased: hear ye him." The last three words, establishing our Lord's authority as teacher, were new. All the rest had been said by the same Voice at Jesus' baptism in Jordan.

Peter, James, and John had been afraid—afraid when they saw Jesus and Moses and Elijah all white and luminous, afraid when the cloud wrapped them round, afraid when the Voice sounded from the cloud. With a touch of his hand and the words "Arise and fear not", he recalled them to the world they were used to.

As they raised their frightened faces, they saw "no one but only Jesus"! He told them to say nothing of what they had seen on the mountain till the Son of Man (still his own phrase for himself, used of him by none of them) should be risen from the dead. Among themselves, they wondered just what that "risen from the dead" might mean. They had seen the daughter of Jairus and the young man of Nain dead and alive again. But they could not imagine how all this could apply to him who had raised those two.

And there was another problem, which they did discuss with Jesus himself as he and they came down the slope next day. They had just seen Elijah, and with this talk of Jesus dying, they would remember that Elijah had not died like other men; and they would remember that Malachi had said that Elijah would return and restore a sinful people to virtue before the day of the Lord. It was all very puzzling, and they put the puzzle to their Master. His answer, to the effect that Elijah had already returned in the person of John the Baptist, might have been clearer to them, had they known what the angel had said to Zechariah in the annunciation of John's birth (Lk 1:17) — "He shall go before the Lord in the spirit and power of Elijah . . . to prepare unto the Lord a perfect people." At least they would have remembered that Elijah had lived in the desert, preached repentance, and rebuked rulers.

The Demoniac Boy

At the foot of the mountain there was a great crowd gathered, and in the middle of it the other apostles hot in argument with some learned men, scribes perhaps. From all we know of the apostles up to this point, we cannot feel that they were in any state to distinguish themselves in controversy with scribes, either about the great mass of scribal learning, or about the special question of Jesus as Messiah and Son of God.

But perhaps the argument was about something which concerned the whole crowd most particularly at that moment — the failure of the apostles to cast a devil out of a possessed boy. Read especially the account given by Mark (9:13-28). From the symptoms told us, the boy would seem to have suffered from epilepsy, with hysteria to make all worse: but we remember that the Gospels draw a clear line between natural illnesses and illnesses, apparently similar, caused by demons. This boy was a demoniac. And the apostles, fresh from the mission on which in the power of their Master they had indeed cast out devils, failed to cast out this one. They must have looked awful fools as the demon simply ignored their order to quit: and the crowd would have jeered maddeningly.

Jesus' impatience at their failure startles us—"O faithless and perverse generation, how long shall I be with you and suffer you?" (Lk 9:41). Peter, James, and John may have felt a little smug, since they had not been there when the failure had happened: but the words would have reminded them, as well as the others, that when he was crossing the lake he had said to them all: "O ye of little faith . . . hearts blinded . . . eyes not seeing . . . ears deaf" (Mk 8:17-18).

Faith, for Jesus, is the test, faith is the key. Miracles are not merely acts of superhuman power, but of power meeting faith, the faith of the sufferer or of those who love the sufferer: it is from the meeting that the miracle issues. The boy's father begins with a despairing appeal to Jesus—"Help us, *if you can!*" Stripped to its barest, the dialogue has the father saying, "Can you?" and Jesus answering, "I can if *you* can."

In other words, it was not a question of his power but of his questioner's, *not* can he heal the boy, *but* can the father believe that he can. Everything depended upon that. "If you can believe, *all* things are possible." Jesus' words lifted the man from the very edge of incredulity to one of the greatest cries of faith in the history of the human soul—"I do believe, Lord; help my unbelief." With that, Jesus ordered the demon out of the boy; and, with a final rending and tearing, the demon went out of him.

The Transfiguration, followed by the healing of the demoniac, we may place in early August. Ten weeks later, round the middle of October, Jesus was in Jerusalem for the Feast of Tabernacles. By then, the Galilean ministry based upon Capernaum, begun a year and a half earlier, was at an end. From the October till the Good Friday of his death he would be mainly in, or close to, Judea.

About the ten weeks that still remained of his time in Galilee we do not get much detail. Saint John tells us nothing at all. The other three tell only of Jesus doing his special work of preparation upon the Twelve—his concentration upon this may well have been his reason for not wanting all Galilee to know that he was there (Mk

9:29). There is only one miracle recorded—the catching of the fish with the tribute money in its mouth (Mt 17:23), but even that we may see as part of his instruction upon the headship of the Kingdom.

He gives the apostles a great deal of pastoral and moral teaching—on the Church principally, on humility, on mercy, and on this life as preparation for the next. But what strikes most of us most is the dimness of their understanding of what lay immediately before him. We, who know that he suffered and died and rose again, marvel that they should not have seen at once what he was foretelling. Perhaps our marvel contains a misunderstanding of our own.

After the healing of the demon-possessed boy, the apostles asked Jesus why they themselves had not been able to cast the demon out (Mt 17:18). "Because of your unbelief" was his answer. "If you have faith as a grain of mustard, *nothing* shall be impossible to you"—even the moving of a mountain! Jesus is not speaking here of the theological virtue of faith—of which all of us, we hope, have at least a mustard grain—but of trust in his power, operative in them. Perhaps it was now that the apostles said to him, "Increase our faith" (Lk 17:5)—echoing the words of the possessed boy's father, "I believe, help my unbelief."

A question remains. They had already cast out many devils: Why not this one? His answer may have been more enlightening to them than it is to us—"This kind is not cast out except by prayer and fasting." There is a suggestion here of higher and lower levels of demonic power. Yet it remains that even the highest is subject to those who have subjected themselves in total trust to our Lord.

More about Death and Resurrection

What may very well have kept their trust from reaching its last fine edge was their sheer failure to understand what he had told them about his death. Now he proceeded to tell them again. "The Son of Man shall be betrayed into the hands of men and they shall kill him; and after he is killed he shall rise again the third day" (Mk 9:30). They had heard him say all of it before—except about the betrayal: this they were hearing for the first time: Had Judas as yet the faintest suspicion that he would be the betrayer? Anyhow, Mark tells us that the Twelve did not understand what he had said, and that they were afraid to ask him.

What were they afraid of? It seems at least probable that what they really feared was what the answer might be: if the words meant what they seemed to mean, they would rather not know. Precisely *because* of their trust in him, they could go on persuading themselves that behind the dreadfulness of the words there was some less dreadful meaning—just as they hoped that there might be behind his talk of eating his flesh and drinking his blood. With the daughter of Jairus and the widow's son of Nain they had seen him show his dominion over death; how could death have dominion over him?

But, we say in our impatience at their slowness, he told them that he would rise again, so that they should have known that he would be overcoming death in himself as in those others. Here, perhaps, hindsight betrays us. We must not assume that they knew, as we do, what he meant by "rising again". The Pharisees taught (and the Sadducees denied) that *everybody* would rise again bodily—in the new age. Did the apostles grasp that they would meet him *here upon earth* three days after his death? There is nothing in the Gospels to make us think that they did. When death *did* take him, they were so far from expecting the Resurrection that they dismissed the first account of its actual happening as "idle tales" (Lk 24:11).

Why, we wonder, did he not tell them more? Having told them at all, why did he not tell them enough for comprehension? We get a glimpse, perhaps, of the answer when we find him saying at the Last Supper: "The Holy Spirit, whom the Father will send in my name, will teach you all things, and *bring all things to your mind, whatsoever I shall have said to you*" (Jn 14:26). He seems to be saying that while he had told them certain great truths, it would be for the Holy Spirit to make these come alive in their minds, giving their minds the light to understand them.

We remember how they had accepted, with no understanding at all, the teaching on the necessity of eating his flesh and drinking his blood. He left that truth unexplained then, just as he now left his Resurrection. These, and even mightier truths, were to lie, heard but uncomprehended, in the womb of their minds, until the Holy Spirit should bring them to birth. We might wonder why the words were not left unuttered until the meaning too could be shown. Yet we can see that it would be a great thing for the apostles, as the light fell upon truth after truth, to remember that these things had indeed been spoken in their hearing by the lips of Christ. As it is a great thing for us to hear him say them. That *he* said them is everything. The movement of the Holy Spirit, in their souls and ours, would meet more resistance if he had not.

29 ENDING OF THE GALILEAN MINISTRY

About the same time—that is, soon after the Transfiguration—we find another, simpler, example of the difficulty the apostles had in believing something they would rather not believe. We recall what had happened at Caesarea Philippi, when Jesus, using to Peter such words as had never been used by God to man, promised him that he should be the head of the new Kingdom. Yet we find the apostles, on their way back to Capernaum, "disputing among themselves which of them should be the greatest" (Mk 9:33). Back at the house where he lived in the town, he asked them what they had been talking about. They had the grace to maintain an embarrassed silence. He knew, of course—"He saw the thoughts of their hearts" (Lk 9:47).

"Servant of All"

When they had not known what he meant about his death and Resurrection, he left them in their unknowledge. But upon this matter of the government of his Church he spoke further to them—this was a practical question, which they needed to know about for the practical work they would soon have to do. Matthew, Mark, and Luke link up this dispute among the apostles with a whole set of teachings about the Church given by Jesus, perhaps, on various occasions but grouped together here.

He gave a lesson upon what headship of the Church means—"to be least of all and the servant of all" (Mk 9:32-34)—which remains to this day a final word to all who hold any kind of authority. Their duty is to give themselves wholly in the service of those under their command, themselves having no superiority whatever save a superiority in service: the work entrusted to them is of greater importance. Pope Gregory the Great was to summarize that lesson in one phrase, calling himself "servant of the servants of God". The phrase is often taken as proof of his humility, but we know from our Lord that it is a precise statement of fact: the Pope is there for our convenience.

Taking a small child in his arms, Jesus told the Twelve that the standard by which greatness in the Kingdom was to be measured was not the importance of a man's office, but a totally spiritual quality in the soul—like the "humility" of that tiny child. He chose humility, perhaps, precisely because the desire to be first which had led to the original argument among the apostles implied a degree of conceit and vainglory, and humility is at the opposite pole. He chose a child too young for conceit, one who had not passed the boundary between thinking his parents know everything and wondering if his parents know anything. That boundary, in any event, came later for Jewish children of that day than for the more cynical children of our own.

The moral, namely that spiritual quality, not high office, is the measure of greatness, the Church has never forgotten. Power may have gone to individual heads, but from the beginning until now the saint has been the chosen hero of Catholics: masses are offered almost daily in honor of saints, not of popes—unless a pope happens to have been a saint.

That, then, was rulership. Who was to be the ruler? Jesus' only comment recorded at this point was an underlining of the unique position among the Twelve of Peter. The underlining is very curious. The law of Moses provided that every adult male should make a small payment each year for the building of the tabernacle for the Ark of the Covenant. This had become a payment for the upkeep of the Temple. It was a tiny sum, half a dollar or less, a few shillings. It was most definitely a tribute paid to God. Further, though payment was expected, a man could not be legally compelled to pay. The collectors asked Peter: "Does not your Master pay the coin?" (Mt 17:23). Peter answered, "Yes", obviously thinking that there could be no question about it.

But there *was* a question, as Jesus reminded Peter. Monarchs do not exact tribute from their own children. Christ was Son of God, why should he pay tribute to his own Father? Peter had no answer. How *could* he, when he himself had so recently confessed that Christ was the Son of the living God? All the same, Jesus went on to say that he could not refuse the payment without giving scandal, since the collectors did not know of his unique relation to God the Father. He would pay, since the explanation called for would have been just too involved and difficult.

So he told Peter to go down to the lake, cast in a hook, and open the mouth of the first fish he caught. There he would find a coin sufficient to pay the Temple tribute not for his Master only but for himself as well. It looks as though he were definitely emphasizing a special relationship between himself and Peter. In fact the argument which was to be greatest did not die, as we shall see: we find the apostles still at it during the Last Supper.

Peter was to be head of the Church upon earth after Christ our Lord. But vast power was to come to the other apostles too. "I say to you, whatsoever you shall bind upon earth shall be bound also in heaven: and whatsoever you shall loose upon earth, shall be loosed also in heaven" (Mt 18:18). They *collectively* were to have the power to command and forbid upon earth which at Caesarea Philippi Jesus had promised to Peter *individually* (Mt 16:19). And just as the great promise to Peter was immediately followed by "Get thee behind me, Satan", so the promise just made to the Twelve would not permanently eclipse the memory of "You are the salt of the earth. But if the salt lose its savor . . . it is good for nothing but to be cast out and to be trodden on by men" (Mt 5:13). No matter how high the office, it carries no guarantee of personal holiness.

Jesus concluded the lecture with "Keep peace among you" (Mk 9:49). Those words tell us what we might anyhow have guessed, that the original dispute had not been peaceful. The Greek word (Mk 9:33) is used in the Epistle of Jude of a dispute between the archangel Michael and the devil. Perhaps Jude remembered that foolish argument in which he had been involved so long before.

"Forbid Him Not"

Our Lord had told the Twelve that they were to have the power of binding and loosing—commanding and forbidding (Mt 18:18). About this time we come upon the first recorded instance of their forbidding someone to do something. John, the beloved disciple, told Jesus that they had seen a man casting out devils in the name of Jesus, and had ordered him to stop, because he was not one of their company (Lk 9:49). But this time what they bound upon earth was *not* bound in heaven: their Master told them that they had been wrong.

The reason he gave may surprise us: "Forbid him not, for he that is not against you is for you." It sounds like a flat contradiction of that other phrase of his—"He that is not with me is against me" (Lk 11:23). But there is no contradiction. A man who was trying in the name of Christ to free the possessed from devils is not "against" our Lord: some belief he must have had.

But there is another principle involved too. A man who *teaches error,* even if he appeals to the name of Christ, must be resisted by the proclamation of the truth, for error is harmful, only truth sets man free. But if a man is simply trying to do good, why should he be stopped from doing it? We remember the name the Master gave John and his brother—Boanerges, Sons of Thunder. John's judgments still had too much element of the thunderous. And of course the Kingdom in which the apostles were to bind and loose had not yet been founded — any more than it had when they tried to stop the children coming to our Lord (Mk 10:13).

Last Teachings in Galilee

Christ goes on to give further instructions about their attitude to those whom they were appointed to serve. He does it first in terms of the child he had taken in his arms. Principally, he shows the identity of the Christian with himself: "Whoever receives this child in my name receives me: and whoever receives me receives him that sent me" (Lk 9:48). In these words we are already hearing an echo of a cry not yet uttered — "Saul, Saul, why persecutest thou me?" To persecute the Church is to persecute Christ: to receive in Christ's name even the smallest member of the Church is to receive Christ: the doctrine of the Mystical Body is here.

He speaks also of their duty to "the little ones", meaning now not simply children, but the unlearned, the insignificant. To scandalize one of these — that is to set his foot upon the road to hell — is a sin so grievous that it would be better to be hurled to death by drowning than commit it. Three times Mark has Jesus use that most mournful of all descriptions of hell — "where their worm dieth not, and the fire is not extinguished" (Mk 9:42–48).

To put the soul of one of these insignificant ones into peril is to imperil one's own. Even to despise one of them, to treat him with anything less than reverence, is a failure to realize the value of his soul in the eyes of God. To all, including the most seemingly valueless, God has appointed an angel, and that angel maintains his own unbroken gaze upon God's face (Mt 18:10).

This value attached to the valueless was so different from what the apostles were likely to have heard all their lives, that Jesus dwells upon it. He makes it the occasion of one of those very rare statements of his own reason for coming into the world — "The Son of Man is come *to save that which was lost.*" From this he proceeds to the parable of the lost sheep in which he extends his saving purpose even to those who shall stray altogether out of his Kingdom. His utterance of the moral of this parable is a charter of hope for all men, none excluded: "It is not the will of your Father in heaven that one of these little ones should perish."

The eighteenth chapter of Saint Matthew and the ninth of Saint Mark bring us to the end of our Lord's ministry in Galilee. They contain a mass of teaching, all based on one truth—that every soul matters immeasurably, because it matters to God. Nobody on earth is nobody. Children, the ignorant, apostates—every soul is of such value that it is glory for the ruler to be allowed to serve it.

Jesus applied this truth rigorously. The parable about the sheep that goes astray (Mt 18:12) and the shepherd who leaves the other ninety-nine and goes after it, states a principle that no religion had ever held—nor indeed would any religion ever find it easy to put it into practice.

The ruler must serve. That is what he is there for. If one of those committed to his care is rebellious, every effort must be made to win him to a better mind—by reasoning with him by himself, reasoning with him in the presence of others, summoning him officially before the Church (Mt 18:15). Only if he is still rebellious, excommunicate him. Other souls must be served too, and he is endangering them: a line must be drawn—but how slowly drawn, how reluctantly.

That is the guidance their Master offers to the apostles as rulers. After it, Matthew quotes guidance he offers to all. "If thy brother sin against thee, reprove him; and if he repent, forgive him." How often? "Till seventy times seven". These figures are a way of saying that there is no end to the possibility of forgiveness for the repentant. (Though I remember a heckler at a Catholic meeting who shouted, "Thou shalt forgive unto seventy times seven, saith the Lord, *and not once more!*")

This principle, too, Jesus applied rigorously. He told the parable of the high official who had converted to his own use the revenues of a whole province, was forgiven by the king, then had one of his own servants cast into prison for a trifling debt: and of what the king did about it (Mt 18:34). The parable is a frightening illustration of the words of the Our Father—"Forgive us our trespasses, *as we forgive those that trespass against us.*" We are so used to the words, that it is a shock to find that our Savior actually meant them: we shall be forgiven by God only in the measure of our forgiveness of damage done to ourselves. And what we owe God is immeasurably greater than what any man owes us.

Jesus was about to leave his own province, Galilee, which had been the center of his ministry for nearly a year and a half. He had gone there "in the power of the Spirit" (Lk 9:14), after the arrest of John the Baptist. Now he was to move south. The half year that still remained before Calvary he would spend mainly in Perea, Herod's other province, across the river Jordan from Judea.

We feel that he felt his work in Galilee had failed. "Woe to thee, Chorazin, woe to thee, Bethsaida. For if in Tyre and Sidon had been wrought the mighty works that have been wrought in you, they would have done penance long ago" (Lk 10:13). On Capernaum his word was worse: "If in Sodom had been wrought the miracles that have been wrought in you, perhaps it would have remained unto this day" (Mt 11:23). We have seen him at work in Capernaum and in Bethsaida. Of what he did in Chorazin, the four Gospels tell us nothing.

It must have appalled his Jewish hearers to have Jewish cities found wickeder than cities of the Gentiles. And Tyre and Sidon had not the infamy of Sodom, destroyed for its sins by brimstone and fire out of heaven. For Tyre and Sidon, even for Sodom, it would be more tolerable in the Day of Judgment than for the cities of Jesus' own province—not because these had refused to accept him, but because they had not repented their sins, in spite of the miracles by which God had surrounded and guaranteed the call to repentance.

30 *AT THE FEAST OF TABERNACLES*

Jesus Leaves Galilee

For what lay between the departure from Galilee in October, and the raising of Lazarus which more than any single thing triggered the catastrophe of Good Friday, we rely almost entirely upon four chapters of Saint John (8–11) and ten chapters of Saint Luke (9–18). Some little of what Luke has Jesus saying or doing, Matthew and Mark give in other contexts—the Our Father, for instance, is given by Matthew in the Sermon on the Mount. But Matthew and Mark take up the story again only when the Pharisees question Jesus about divorce and remarriage, and that is very near the end.

We study, therefore, Luke and John. We cannot always be sure of the order of happening. John, indeed, keeps a straight line, from the Feast of Tabernacles in mid-October, to the Feast of Dedication in late December, then to the going to Perea (Herod's other province), then to the raising of Lazarus. But Luke is not concerned with the order of time. Four times he has Jesus set out for Jerusalem, but only on the fourth does he bring him there. Evidently, from the people he tells us he consulted, Luke had learned of things done and said in this period; his informants either did not remember the when and the where, or perhaps differed among themselves. He simply recorded all of it. These things *were* said and done, that was what mattered.

As it happens, while vast things were *said,* there is not a great deal of actual incident. John has one single miracle, and the incident of the woman caught in adultery (though this may not have been originally John's: it reads like Luke); and he tells of twice when his enemies wanted to stone Jesus. Between the first and the second of these, Luke has the sending out of the seventy-two disciples, the visit to Bethany when Martha got the meal and Mary just sat, and the incident of the woman in the crowd who cried out, "Blessed is the womb that bore thee." After the second he gives us the healing of the ten lepers, the mothers who brought their children to Christ, and the rich young man. But what matters throughout this period is the teaching—especially the discourses in the Temple, the answers to opponents, and some dozen parables.

Advice from Jesus' Cousins

Saint John (8:2) begins the story of the last six months with a dialogue between Jesus and his cousins—not James and Jude, who were among the Twelve, but the rest, who seem to have stayed on in Nazareth. We have already met them (Mk 3:30); it was probably they who had wondered about the carpenter's sanity and thought he ought to be put under restraint in his own interests. That was eight months ago. Now John tells us that they still did not believe in him (7:5).

They knew that he could work miracles: but they did not believe he was sent by God: above all, they still assumed that they knew better than he what was best for him. It was a pity, they felt, to waste his gift of miracles in a backwater like Galilee. They urged him to go down into Judea, where he might exploit his power to some purpose—after all, they can hardly have been expected to have a deeper understanding of the true nature of the Kingdom he might found than the Twelve had. If he was ever to have a sensational success in Jerusalem, the Feast of Tabernacles provided the ideal setting.

The answer he gave they must have found as irritating as his whole attitude. He said that he would not go up to celebrate the feast, giving a reason which they could hardly have found luminous—"My time is not accomplished." What did he mean by his time? He had told them, but they had had no mind to understand. The world hated him, he said, because he told it so openly that its works were evil: men would kill him, therefore; but they would kill him in God's time, not theirs.

So the cousins went up without him for the festival, and were there for the solemn inauguration. Four days later Jesus himself went up, but not to take part in the festival—he arrived when it was half over. He went in order to do something for which the ritual of the feast made no provision, to utter the truth about himself to the vast crowds the feast had brought to the Temple.

Nor did he try for the sensation his cousins wanted. He worked only a single, quite unspectacular, miracle. He did not try to dazzle the crowds. He puzzled them.

The Feast of Tabernacles

The Feast of Tabernacles—the word means "tents"—was originally a kind of harvest festival. Israel's long wandering in the wilderness fifteen hundred years before had somehow become linked with it: in memory of the tents, it was the custom to make huts or cabins of boughs with the leaves on them and actually live in them for the seven days of the feast. On the eighth day, the huts were abandoned and the whole day given to carnival. Jesus decided to arrive in Jerusalem before it was over. He had one main purpose: "Now about the midst of the feast, Jesus went up into the Temple *and taught*" (Jn 7:14). It was his first teaching in the Temple.

Luke (9:51) describes the withdrawal from Galilee in words of great solemnity: "When the days of his taking up were drawing near, he steadfastly set his face to go to Jerusalem"—"set one's face" was a Jewish way of expressing an important resolution firmly made. The first part of the journey took Jesus and the Twelve through Samaria. He sent some of them on to a town unnamed, to make preparations for their lodging. But the centuries-old hatred between Samaritans and Jews broke out. The town would not receive the rabbi from Galilee. James and John, the Sons of Thunder, wanted him to allow them to command fire to come down from heaven and destroy the unworthy citizens. They were not far from the place where, twice, soldiers sent to arrest the prophet Elijah had been destroyed by fire from the sky.

Jesus rebuked James and John—he had come not to destroy but to save. They went on to another town. Nothing forbids us the pleasure of thinking this more receptive town may have been Shechem, where the woman lived to whom Jesus had spoken so profoundly at Jacob's well, and where he had stayed two days and won many to believe (Jn 4:40).

Pilgrims coming up for the feast arrived in groups, waving branches and shouting Hosannah: so, presumably, the cousins came themselves and would have liked the carpenter to come. In fact, he arrived "not openly, but as it were in secret" (Jn 7:10). In other words, he slipped in unnoticed, to find everybody wondering where he was—for at that moment he was the most talked-of man in Palestine. Opinion was divided. Some thought he was a good man, others that he was leading the people astray; all were conscious that you had to be careful what you said about him because you never knew who was listening, and the leaders of the people had made their own hostility plain.

First Teaching in the Temple

He did not remain unnoticed. At this point it would be wise to read carefully what he did and said on that earlier visit to Jerusalem described in the fifth chapter of Saint John. This present visit—described in the seventh, eighth, and ninth chapters—will be better understood if this reading has been done. His claim to equality with his Father is much more explicitly made in the earlier chapter—whatsoever the Father does the Son does in like manner; the Father raises the dead and gives life and so does the Son; the Son is to be honored as the Father is honored. On the later visit Jesus takes his Sonship for granted and concentrates upon what he had said on the earlier visit about himself as man. On both visits he accuses the Jewish leaders of being unfaithful to Moses and his law.

The first reaction this time is amazement that one who had never been to the schools of the rabbis should know so much. The answer they got went straight to the heart of the mystery: "My doctrine is not mine, but his that sent me." And how were they to know that his teaching was God's? The answer was hard: all who really wanted to do God's will would know whether the doctrine was from God, or merely the invention of a carpenter from Nazareth.

Then he asked the direct question: Why did they seek to kill him? And some of the listeners, strangers to Jerusalem evidently, thought he must be mad: What was this nonsense about people wanting to kill him? At that, Jesus spoke of the earlier visit, when those of the stricter sort had in fact tried to kill him—for healing a paralyzed man on the Sabbath.

At the end of the earlier visit to Jerusalem described by John in his fifth chapter, "the Jews sought the more to kill him, because he did not only break the Sabbath, but also said God was his Father, making himself equal to God." On the visit we are now considering, that second, greater, matter does not seem to have arisen. Although Jesus spoke again and again of being sent by his Father, of receiving his doctrine from his Father, and of his Father as bearing witness to him, "they understood not that he called God his Father" (Jn 8:27). In other words, one presumes, they knew that he was speaking of God, but not that he was claiming for himself a special sonship. Most of the attack this time was on the carpenter's breaking of the Sabbath, and upon other points that we should think even less important.

Jesus challenged his opponents at once, on their accusation that he sinned in healing a stricken man on the Sabbath. They themselves would circumcise a child on the Sabbath if that was when the eighth day fell: How dared they be angry at him for "healing the whole man on that day"? They simply had not understood Moses.

The crowds reacted variously. Some of them actually believed that he was the Messiah, moved by the miracles which had streamed from him ever since the baptism by John. Others, strongly attracted, were still bothered by what they knew of his origin. Some clung to the idea that the Messiah would come suddenly, as from another world: whereas Jesus had been among them for thirty years, they knew all about him. What stuck in other throats was his being a Galilean, the Messiah they knew must be born in Bethlehem—we note that Jesus is never quoted as mentioning his birthplace.

The Guard Sent to Arrest Him

There was another problem. Why, people asked, did the leaders allow him to speak openly in the Temple itself? Was it even possible that they themselves were beginning to wonder if he might not, after all, be the Christ? Why did they not arrest him? That last question, anyhow, the rulers of the Temple settled soon enough. Twice they sent the Temple guard to arrest him. The first time "no man laid hands on him, *because his hour was not yet come*" (Jn 7:30). In other words, God prevented them. But the second time they were prevented by a movement deep in their own souls. Observe what the officers of the guard said.

The chief priests, who were Sadducees, and the Pharisees—now solidly linked in face of a common danger—asked the officers why they had not brought Jesus. The officers answered in a phrase which has always held the forefront of the Christian mind: "Never did man speak like this man." The retort to this deserves close study. It was in two parts. The first: So he has seduced you too. The second: Who, anyhow, believes in the seducer?—not the men of power, the Sadducees, not the men of learning and piety, the Pharisees, only the mob—"this accursed multitude that knows not the Law" (Jn 7:49).

What effect this retort had upon the men of the guard we are not told. But the leaders now had someone of a very different caliber to answer. Nicodemus was one of themselves, a Pharisee, rich, learned. We remember how he visited Jesus by night and received the glory of the first recorded teaching on the new birth by water and the Holy Spirit (Jn 3). Now he intervened: "Does our law judge any man without first hearing him?" The intervention may seem to us mild enough: anything milder would have been no intervention at all: we feel that a little more boldness would have done Nicodemus credit. But in fact he was being very bold indeed, given the place and the time. As we shall soon see, from what happened within the next day or so to the man whose blindness Jesus healed, not to take one's stand against the seducer could mean excommunication.

Again the retort fell into two parts, like the retort to the officers. The first: "Art thou also a Galilean?" The second: "Search the Scriptures and see that out of Galilee no prophet rises." Nicodemus, of course, would have known that "a servant of the Lord, the prophet Jonah, son of Amittai, was born in Galilee" (2 Kings 14:25)—only a few miles from Nazareth, in fact. The other Pharisees would have known it too. The error could have been made only by Sadducees, who regarded the five books of Moses as the whole of Scripture and would not have taken Jonah so seriously.

31 *THE MAN BORN BLIND*

The Light of the World

We have seen Jesus' way of drawing timeless teaching out of some happening of the moment. We remember how a Samaritan woman came to draw water at Jacob's well, and he spoke of grace in the soul—"the water that I will give him, shall become in him a fountain of water, springing up into life everlasting" (Jn 4:14). It was after the multiplication of bread in the wilderness that he taught for the first time about the Bread of Life. The Feast of Tabernacles gave him two opportunities—the great candelabra lighted in the court of the women on the first night, and the procession to the pool of Siloam to bring back water which should be poured out before the altar of the Most High. He used them both.

On the first evening of the festival, golden lampstands were set up in the court of the women, a space open to everybody. These stands were enormous—150 feet high, we are told—and as the lamps were lit, there was singing of canticles and playing of musical instruments—the sound of the music could be heard twenty miles away in Jericho! Strangest of all to our taste, we read of a Torch Dance, with the highest dignitaries of Israel dancing to a set rhythm with lighted torches thrown high into the air and caught again. What was in every mind was the pillar of fire which had given light to the Israelites in the desert.

The hall of the treasury was in this same court. Here Jesus said: "I am the light of the world: he that follows me walks not in darkness, but shall have the light of life" (Jn 8:12). Light and life are the two key words of all these utterances. But what must have caught the attention, especially of his adversaries, was the word "world"—he was the light of the *world,* not of one people. They would have remembered a text of Isaiah (49:6), a text they were not much given to quoting: "I will make thee the light of the Gentiles, to carry my salvation even to the farthest parts of the earth."

Living Water

The procession to the pool of Siloam, which was outside the city, bringing back water in a golden pitcher to be poured out in libation, took place every morning. As the priest drew the water, the choir chanted from Isaiah: "You shall draw water with gladness from the fountains of salvation." We hardly need to be told that here was a symbol of the water gushing from the rock in the wilderness when Moses struck it with his rod. Jesus twice made his own use of the water of Siloam, once as a statement about himself, once in the healing of a blind man.

On the last day of the feast he stood up and cried out—"If any man is thirsty, let him come to me; if a man believes in me let him drink; as the Scripture says: Fountains of living water shall flow from his bosom" (Jn 7:37). It is very much what he had said of grace in the soul of the Samaritan woman—he was the rock from which the life-giving water would flow. Saint John adds his own explanatory comment: Jesus was speaking of the Holy Spirit which those who believed in him would one day receive—for as yet men's souls had not experienced the full power of his working in them "because Jesus was not yet glorified". The apostle is here applying what Jesus said to them all at the Last Supper—that unless he himself left this world and went to the Father in the glory of his death and Resurrection, the Spirit would not come to them.

Blind Man Healed

More striking, since it was not in word only but in act, was the part he had the pool of Siloam play a few days later in the healing of a blind man, the Light of the world giving light to blind eyes. It is the one miracle he worked on this visit, and it was very different from the spectacular miracles his kinsmen had been counting on. He spat on the earth, made clay with the spittle, and touched the man's eyes with it. It is doubtful if anyone but the apostles even noticed the incident. At his command, the blind man went to wash in the pool of Siloam. When his sight was actually restored, Jesus was not even there.

It was only gradually, indeed, that the realization spread that a miracle had been worked. And on the Sabbath! Scribes and Pharisees were frantic. They wanted to kill him, but they wanted even more to discredit him. If only they could prove that the healing had not happened! For their almost hysterical reactions, read Saint John's ninth chapter. As sheer reporting it is fascinating, no school of journalism should neglect it. For the first time the Pharisees tried to prove that a miracle had not happened: perhaps, they said, it was a different man; or, if it was the same man, perhaps he had not been blind from birth. They cross-questioned the man himself, his parents, the man again.

The parents were determined not to incriminate themselves: Yes, he was their son; yes, he was born blind; beyond that they knew nothing, had no opinions even. Better ask *him.* All this because the leaders of the Jews had agreed that anyone who affirmed that the carpenter was the Christ should be "put out of the synagogue". To be thus excommunicated would make life for a Jew in Jerusalem nearly unlivable.

The man himself made no effort to cover up. Of all the people healed by Jesus, he is the only one whose personality has come down to us. Who knows what kind of girl Jairus' daughter was? Was the widow's son of Nain a good son? We know nothing of any of them. But this man is a joy—alert, humorous, devastating in retort. He was much too delighted by the new gift of sight to worry about being excommunicated—

which of course he was. Read verses 35 to 38 for his act of faith in his healer.

Saint John places this episode at the end of the Feast of Tabernacles. It had been a trying time for the leaders of the Pharisees. They honestly saw this man from Galilee as waging war upon the religion of their people, and now for the first time he had brought the warfare into the very Temple itself. This was the last straw. The Sabbath rest had been broken twice—by the shaping of the clay, by the healing of the blindness. Then there was the sheer effrontery of sending the man to wash in the pool of Siloam, inviting comparison with the prophet Elisha, who had sent Naaman the leper to wash in the Jordan. And there was the beggar himself, known for years to every visitor to the Temple as a man born blind.

The Wife Caught in Adultery

It had been a trying time indeed for Jesus' opponents. He had brought his doctrines into the Temple, and they had confronted him. But they could not feel that they had come very well out of the confrontation. To every challenge, his answers were instant; and they were of two sorts: answers that they could not answer, answers that they could not even understand. Even in the second sort there was always something, something they could not laugh off or shrug off, a sense of depths beyond.

Just a little before the healing of the blind man, we find in Saint John's Gospel—it sounds more like Saint Luke and is sometimes attributed to him—a remarkable example of Jesus speaking with total clarity, and his hecklers reduced to silence. He had spent the night on the Mount of Olives—perhaps in the very cave where the Temple guard would find him on the night of his arrest. Early in the morning he came down to the Temple, took his seat and began to preach. "And the scribes and Pharisees bring unto him a woman taken in adultery." They had always found him much too kind to sinners, here was a chance to test him. The law of Moses had said that she ought to be stoned to death. What did he say? "But Jesus, bowing himself down, wrote with his finger on the ground"—that being a recognized way of indicating that one wished to take no part in the conversation, an invitation to the others to go away.

They did not go away. They kept on putting the same question. At last he spoke: "He that is without sin among you, let him cast the first stone at her"—then back to his finger-writing! This time they went, beginning with the eldest.

The sinning wife was alone with Jesus. He asked her if no man remained there to condemn her. She answered: "No man, Lord." He said: "Neither will I condemn thee. Go, and now sin no more." She was an adulteress, but he had not come into this world to judge and condemn individuals. When later (Lk 12:14) a man asked him to settle an inheritance dispute, Christ said: "Who has appointed me to judge over you?" He had not even, as John the Baptist had, publicly condemned Herod's sinful marriage with Herodias. When sinners claimed to speak in the name of God, he would brand them sinners. For the rest, he was here in this world as Redeemer, not Judge.

Harshness and Mildness

As an example of answers they could not even understand, consider this: "I go to him that sent me. You shall seek me and shall not find me. Because where I am, you cannot come" (Jn 7:33). What did he mean? That he was going to leave Palestine? That he was going to commit suicide? (Jn 8:22). Why, anyhow, should they seek him?—they felt they would be only too delighted if they never set eyes on him again.

We know that it was the Messiah they would be seeking— when Jerusalem was on the point of destruction—and that he was the Messiah. But they did not. *We* know that he was going to the right hand of the Father. They did not know that either. And he was at no pains to clarify. He was offering, not primarily a set of teachings, but himself. In Galilee he had announced the Good News. From now on he *is* the Good News. We shall hear him say: "I am the Resurrection." He could well have said: "I am the gospel."

Those who truly willed to do God's will would be given the grace to accept him (Jn 7:17). And they would accept what he taught, not because he proved it but solely because he taught it; not because they understood it, solely because he taught it. The failure of these men before him to accept him as Messiah was a sure proof to him who read their hearts that they willed their own will, not God's: "If you do not believe that I am he, you shall die in your sins."

Those—so numerous today—who say that Christ was not God but the perfect man should read again these chapters 7 and 8. One feels that they would not have enjoyed his company very much. The text just quoted is typical of his harshness with the religious leaders. But with the sinful and sorrowful he was never harsh. With the adulterous woman, for instance, there was no sentimentality certainly, but not a trace of harshness either, firmness only: she had been a sinner, she must abandon her sin: her lover must get along without her. His harshness was for those who had set their wills against his Father.

Stones to Stone Him

One interchange in particular we should read with care. It begins with Jesus saying: "If you continue in my word . . . you shall know the truth, and the truth will make you free." So far he was speaking to those who had come to believe in him. But others were listening, and they retorted angrily that they were free already, for they were children of Abraham: not only that, they were children of God. He swept aside both paternities with one of the fiercest things he ever said: "You are of your father the devil, and what your father wants you will do. He was a murderer from the beginning, and he stood not in the truth; because truth is not in him. When he speaks a lie, he speaks of his own: for he is a liar, and the father thereof."

To men enraged at this, Jesus said: "If any man keep my word, he shall not see death forever." Here, at least, they felt they had him trapped. Abraham was dead, the prophets were dead, who did he think he was, to offer freedom from death? Our Lord's answer must have seemed to them to go from one depth of monstrousness to one deeper still. The first depth—"Abraham your father rejoiced that he might see my day: he saw it and was glad." They asked how that was possible, given his age—clearly they had not heard the rabbinic idea that Abraham was given a vision of the future. It would not have helped if they had, for he proceeded to the second depth—"Before Abraham was made, I AM."

They took up stones to kill him. Why? A few minutes before, he had told them that they would crucify him—"When you have lifted me up, you shall know that I am he", the Messiah. "Lifted up", so scholars tell us, was a regular way of saying "crucified", very much as in our own day "to swing" can mean "to be hanged". Many of those who heard him must have rejoiced in the thought. Yet suddenly they could not wait, they must stone him to death there and then.

Stoning for blasphemy was rare: one remembers two instances in the Old Testament—an Egyptian whose mother was an Israelite and who had cursed the name of God (Lev 24); and Naboth on a false accusation of blasphemy plotted by Jezebel, the Herodias of her day (2 Kings 21:13). Why were they so set upon stoning Jesus?

He claimed to have existed before Abraham, before the founder of the Jews, before the first Jew. A man might be stoned for blasphemy, but was that blasphemy? Or were they wrought to the point of killing by the words "I AM"? They may very well have remembered that that was the name by which God told Moses (Ex 3:14) he himself was to be called, when Moses bore his message to his people—"I AM has told me." So they took up their stones, but he mingled with the crowd and went out of the Temple. It *was* to be crucifixion, after all.

The Good Shepherd

Saint John ends his account of what happened during and after the Feast of Tabernacles with Jesus' teaching about himself as the Good Shepherd. He had been talking of the Pharisees as "blind guides" (Jn 9:41). He went straight on to develop the ideas of blind guidance and right guidance. We have heard him describe his Kingdom as a walled city with a gate (Mt 16:18). Now he describes it as a sheepfold, with a door. The idea of God as the Shepherd of Israel appears constantly in the Old Testament. But it was never worked out so fully as here. Jesus was the door of the sheepfold. Many—the false Messiahs, for instance, who were constantly appearing—tried to get into the fold otherwise than through the door that was Jesus of Nazareth. Such men could lead the sheep only to destruction.

He was not only the door, he was the Shepherd. Reading quickly, we might wonder how the *door* of the sheepfold could be the *shepherd.* But Jesus was not under the mastery of his metaphor. He had called Peter (Mt 16:18) the foundation *and* the key-bearer—impossible in a building, but quite possible in a society of men, and that was what Jesus was actually talking about. So now he himself could at once be the door, the point of entry into the Christian flock, and the Shepherd, the guide and nourisher of Christians.

"I am the Good Shepherd": the contrast is now not with thieves and robbers, false Messiahs, but with men simply doing the job for pay, hirelings. They were entitled to be there, but they were not to be trusted. The prophet Ezekiel had said it long ago: "Woe to the shepherds of Israel, who feed themselves instead of feeding the sheep" (34:2). In the last chapter of the last Gospel, we find the Good Shepherd appointing Peter to be shepherd after him of the whole flock. A glance at the fifth chapter of Peter's First Epistle shows us how the scene we are at this moment discussing remained in his mind. He warns the men who, under him, are subshepherds of his own flock that they must not be hirelings, they must "feed the flock of God ... not for filthy lucre's sake but freely". And he goes on to speak of the Prince of shepherds, the One from whom he drew his own authority.

So far any Pharisee would have found in this talk of himself as the Good Shepherd only one more of those grandiose claims which the carpenter from Nazareth was so irritatingly fond of making. But suddenly he stabbed deeper than irritation, bringing the Gentiles in where no Jew could think they belonged: "Other sheep I have, that are not of this fold; them also I must bring, and they shall hear my voice, and there shall be one flock and one shepherd." So the pagans were God's sheep too, and they would jostle Israel in one same flock, be led to the same pasture, fed with the same food.

So much for his enemies as they listened. We may wonder if they even noticed the one phrase which, for us who believe, blazes out from the whole discourse. The rest of the parable is simply the background for "I lay down my life for my sheep" (Jn 10:15). In that one sentence are two things that we have not heard from his lips before—*I lay down* and *for my sheep.* Perhaps the Twelve had not, either.

For my sheep: twice in Galilee he had told the Twelve that his enemies would kill him. Already, on this present visit to Jerusalem, he had said that they would lift him up, and they knew that that phrase meant crucify. But there was as yet no hint that his death would be redemptive. He had spoken of death, violent and painful, inflicted upon him; but that it would be in some way of benefit to his followers, this we have not heard him say before.

So the sheep would be the gainers by the Good Shepherd's death. But *what* would they gain? What gain could compensate for the loss of the Shepherd? Surely they must have questioned him when they had him to themselves. If only we knew what they had asked, and what the answers had been. Peter and Andrew and John would have heard the Baptist say, nearly two years before, that he was the Lamb of God, who would take away the sin of the world. But how could he do that by being slain? They knew about sin-offerings, of course, with animals slain; but Jephthah's daughter was to the contrary, human sacrifice was not in the Jewish religion: it simply never occurred to the apostles that he could mean that.

I lay down my life: so far Jesus had spoken of being betrayed into the hands of his slayers. But twice in this discourse he uses words which suggested that he would be consenting to his death—and not consenting only, but somehow *actively* involved. He did not leave us with the mere suggestion. He said: "I lay down my life that I may take it up again. No one takes it away from me: but I lay it down of myself, and I have power to lay it down; and I have power to take it up again. This commandment have I received of my Father."

We shall never discover all the richness that is here, but let us make a beginning. Men could not kill him unless he chose to let them. Death is the separation of soul and body, and he whose soul and body were in question was God the Son. They were his, and no created power could separate them against his will. But, since the rulers of his people had determined to kill him, he would let them—for they would be serving not their own purpose but his. He would lay his life down—his human life only, the life of soul and body—but he would take it up again, for it was wholly his. He would die *in order to* rise again, because it was his Father's will that by his death and Resurrection men should be redeemed. It was not his Father's will only, but his own will too, and the Holy Spirit's: for there is but one will in that divine nature which all three Persons possess in utter equality.

There is mystery in the one Person possessing two natures, being true God and true man, uttering the divine nature which is his eternally, uttering the human nature which is his from the moment Mary of Nazareth conceived him, and uttering both with one same "I". As God, he was one with the Father in willing the command which as man he willed to accept in total obedience, knowing all that it would cost him. And his Father loved him for it.

I have called this only a beginning of understanding. Questions surge up in our minds, questions that only he could answer. Did the Twelve ask him? There is no hint that they were given to asking him doctrinal questions. For the first reference that any one of them is recorded as making to the Blessed Trinity we must wait till the Last Supper, when Philip asked: Show us the Father. Certainly the reaction of the apostles to his death and Resurrection when they came does not suggest that they had gone very far in understanding the text we have been considering.

We have come to the end of what Saint John has to tell us of the Feast of Tabernacles, which was celebrated round the middle of October. From there he goes straight to the Feast of Dedication. But that was in late December. For what happened in the two months between, we turn to Saint Luke—chapters 9:57 to 13:17. We are not told of much that he did, but a great deal of what he said—including forty wonderful words about his Father and himself.

32 FORMING THE NEW CHRISTIANS

In all the Gospels we hear only one man say that he would follow Jesus wherever he went. Who was he? "A certain man", says Luke (9:57). Matthew, who places the episode earlier (8:19), takes our breath away with the information that the man was a scribe, one of the most learned of the Pharisees, a member of the group which argued with Jesus most relentlessly and was foremost in planning his death. That scribe could not have uttered a more total renunciation of his own world for a world that he could as yet barely have glimpsed. His fellow scribes must have been as startled as Levi's fellow tax extorters on an earlier occasion!

The answer he got was: "The foxes have holes, and the birds of the air have nests; but the Son of Man has nowhere to lay his head." Only while he was actually out on the road could he have said this in Galilee: for there was the family home in Nazareth, and in Capernaum there was Peter's home, which he had made very much his own. But in Judea, where he now was, he had no home. There was a house in Bethany, where he would spend an occasional night. For the rest, he simply slept where he happened to be at nightfall: even when he was teaching daily in the Temple, we read of his spending the night on the Mount of Olives.

The Sending of the Disciples

Luke goes on to tell of two other men, willing to be disciples, but not quite yet!—one of them wanted time to bury his father (burial of the dead being with Jews, as it is with Catholics but even more so, a "corporal work of mercy"); the other wanted to say good-bye to his family (his wife, one supposes, would be worrying). We are at first startled at the rigor of Jesus' refusal of these modest requests. To the one he says: "Let the dead bury their dead: *you* go and preach the Kingdom of God." To the other he says that when a man starts ploughing, he must keep his eye steadily on the plough and on the end of the furrow; one who keeps looking back over his shoulder instead of concentrating on the work in hand is useless to serve the Kingdom of God.

I have said that we find this startling, because Christ allowed his ordinary followers—disciples, the laity so to speak—to live their ordinary lives, not calling on them to abandon everything to give themselves wholly to work for him. Perhaps these two are special cases, called not for a lifetime in the ministry, but for a particular, short-time job which had to be done at once. The mention to each of them of the Kingdom of God suggests what the job was. For he was just about to send out the seventy-two disciples to go ahead of him to every place where he himself was to come, bearing the message that the Kingdom of God was near (Lk 10).

The seventy-two disciples, mentioned so casually, are rather startling, too. Where have they been all this time, we wonder? We remember that, nearly a year and a half before, after a night in prayer, Jesus had "called his disciples to him, choosing out Twelve" (Lk 6:13). Though it is not talked of, a Christian community must already have been forming. Those who from day to day came to believe in him would naturally draw together—the greatest experience any of them had ever had would be a bond. They would talk of what they had seen and heard, would share the latest news of him. Some fell away after his talk of giving his flesh to eat and his blood to drink. But some remained and others joined.

How many disciples were there while our Lord was still upon earth? We tend to answer one hundred and twenty, because that number were in the Upper Room with Peter when one was chosen to fill the place of dead Judas (Acts 1:15). But those were probably only the believers who were in Jerusalem at the time. Saint Paul tells us (1 Cor 15:6) that between the Resurrection and the Ascension Jesus "was seen by more than five hundred of the brethren at once". The truth is that we have no notion how many disciples there were. But there must have been more than perhaps we thought, for him to be able to take so many men from their families, and from their daily work, whatever it was, and send them on a healing and preaching mission.

They were sent out very much as the twelve apostles had been. They were to go in pairs, make no provision for their daily needs, eat what they were given ("for the laborer is worthy of his hire"). They were being sent as lambs among wolves (the Twelve had been sent as sheep!). With the wolves they were to be not lamblike but very tough. Yet even to them they should announce that the Kingdom of God was at hand.

For that was what they were sent for—to heal the sick and tell of the Kingdom's nearness. As earlier, with the Twelve, we wonder how well they were equipped for teaching upon this of all subjects. They could not say when it was coming or what its structure would be; it is hard to believe that they had any greater realization than the Twelve of the place Gentiles would have in it. But they went their way with a guarantee not mentioned in the account of the earlier sending: "He that hears you, hears me; and he that despises you despises me. And he that despises me, despises him that sent me."

Clearly they ran into no difficulties in delivering their message. On their return their talk was not of questions they could not answer but of devils they had cast out. And Jesus told them that while they had been in action he had seen Satan falling, as lightning flashes down from the sky. The devil's doom was already written clear.

There was a lesson for the disciples too. Their joy in ordering out spirits mightier than themselves was natural. But the rage they had caused in the demons was a trifle, weighed against the joy they had caused in heaven. "Rejoice in this, that your names are written in heaven."

Jesus Rejoices

We have so far had only an occasional reference to what was going on inside Jesus, his moods and feelings. Here, for the first and last and only time, we are told that he was joyful—"He rejoiced in the Holy Spirit." At what? At the choice of these insignificant ones, to receive a revelation God had not given to "the wise and prudent"!

With Calvary—and Gethsemane—never out of his mind, this glory given to "little ones" could still bring him joy, a very ecstasy of joy in which he cried out the innermost truth of his own relation with the Father. "No one knows the Son but the Father; and no one knows the Father but the Son—and those to whom the Son shall reveal him" (Lk 10:22).

He was asserting equality with his Father, but *this* he had asserted already—he could do whatever the Father could do, he was entitled to the same honor (Jn 5:19, 23). Now we hear him speak of his own personal relationship with the Father, the life within the Trinity. It is by the way of knowledge that he proceeds from the Father, subsists within the Godhead as known by the Father, knows his Father and is known in total equality. Matthew (11:25) has our Lord say these words much earlier. If he did, then they might have had their effect upon Peter's "Thou art the Christ, *the son of the living God*" (Mt 16:16).

Saint John has no clearer statement of the Father-Son relation. And of that relation we are the beneficiaries. The Son will reveal the Father to us—if we will listen. At the Last Supper he was to say: "No one comes *to* the Father but through me." Here he says that no one comes even *to know who the Father is,* but through him. And it is true that outside Christianity there is not even a poor beginning of the doctrine of the Trinity, but only here and there a parody.

The disciples were to go "two and two *before his face* into every city whither he was himself to come" (Lk 10:1). If they had gone only to one place each, that would have been thirty-six places! They must surely have gone to many more. In the four months between the Feast of Tabernacles and the raising of Lazarus, Jesus must have gone into every town, townlet, village, in Judea and Perea. We know that midway in that period, he came to Jerusalem for the Feast of Dedication. For the rest, he must have been on the road continuously. Even if he had had somewhere to lay his head, he would have had no time to lay it there.

Martha and Mary

Jesus had rejoiced that the Father had shown truths to the disciples that had not been shown to the wise men, the learned men, the present teachers of the chosen people (Lk 10:21). Not only that: "Blessed are the eyes that see the things you see. Many prophets and kings have desired to see the things you see, and have not seen them; to hear the things you hear, and have not heard them." We come to one who really knew how blessed her eyes were. We hear of only one house that Jesus was in the habit of visiting, Martha's house in Bethany, a couple of miles from Jerusalem. There she lived with her brother Lazarus and her sister Mary. We meet them first as Jesus comes to the house, at some point between late October and late December, a few months before Calvary.

Luke's description of what happened has shaped countless lives. Yet the whole passage contains under a hundred words, and there is no way of expanding it, and nothing to be gained by expanding it.

Lazarus is not mentioned, only the sisters. Martha was on her feet, getting the meal ready, setting the table; Mary was at *his* feet, wholly absorbed in him. Martha was outraged. "Lord," she said, "*don't you care* that my sister is letting me do all the work? Do tell her to help me." That "don't you care?" we have heard before: Mark uses the identical Greek phrase for the apostles' appeal when their ship seemed to be sinking—"Don't you care if we perish?" (Mk 4:38).

That time he answered with a miracle and a rebuke. This time he answered with a rebuke, and words that have had more effect upon lives than any miracle: they are at the very heart of all Christian spirituality. "Martha, Martha, thou art careful, and art troubled about many things. But one thing is necessary. Mary has chosen the best part, which shall not be taken from her."

We shall meet Mary again—twice certainly, oftener if she was Mary Magdalen. When we first met her she was sitting at Jesus' feet; at the tomb of her brother Lazarus she fell at his feet; at Simon's banquet table (Jn 12:3) she anointed his feet.

Was Mary of Bethany Mary of Magdala? Bethany was in Judea, Magdala in Galilee. It is not improbable that a Galilean family should have moved to Judea, and it would be easier to account for Jesus' friendship if they were Galileans: Magdala is only a dozen miles or so from Nazareth. It is hard to believe that the Mary who was absorbed in contemplation of him in Bethany did not travel the two miles to be with him on Calvary. It is hard, too, to believe that the Mary who anointed his feet in Simon's house—"for my burial", our Lord said (Mt 26:12)—would not have been of the party that brought sweet spices to anoint Jesus in the tomb.

Beyond that we cannot go. If Mary of Bethany and Mary of Magdala *were* two and not one, they must have had wonderful conversations about the Christ they both knew better than any woman knew him except Mary of Nazareth.

Mary had chosen the best part—not that Martha had chosen evilly, what she was doing was necessary; her error lay in thinking that the contemplation of Christ was mere idling, whereas it is the highest activity of all. On two other occasions in this same two-month period, between the Feasts of Tabernacles and Dedication, our Lord emphasizes the primacy of grace over nature: the union of the soul with God is more important than anything, literally anything, that men can do.

More important than getting the dinner, obviously, as Martha was told. More important than casting out devils from the possessed, as the disciples had just been told (Lk 10:20). But more important even than being the Mother of God-made-man, as a nameless woman was soon to be told (Lk 11:27–28).

She had called out a blessing on the womb that bore the wonder-worker. And he had answered: "Yea, rather blessed are they who hear the word of God and keep it." To have conceived Christ in the womb was blessed; but holiness is more blessed still. And in holiness none have equaled his Mother. Saint Luke, who tells of this, has already told (2:51) how she "kept all these words in her heart".

The Two Great Commandments

Saint Luke devotes his chapters 10 to 13 to what happened between the time the Jews wanted to stone Jesus after the Feast of Tabernacles in October, and his return for the Feast of Dedication, late in December, when again they wanted to stone him. The evangelist brings together a mass of the Master's teaching, particularly on the spiritual and moral life of the Christian. "Yea, rather, blessed are they who hear the word of God and keep it." Doing God's will is the foundation. Without that, the rest is nothing.

At the lowest level, it is the plainest common sense to obey God. God's enemies will persecute the Christian, but these can destroy the body only, and then there are the long reaches of eternity which lie outside their power. Fear them, for the pain they can inflict: yet not with real fear, fear at the roots of your being. Only God can cast the sinner into hell (Jewish thought did not distinguish what God permits from what God positively wills): fear God therefore with real fear: for that is the beginning of wisdom.

But only the beginning. *Love* is the meaning of man's relation with God. In the Law taught by the scribes there were 613 commandments—248 of things one must do, 365 of things one must not do. To test our Lord, a doctor of the Law asked him which of these was the great one, the fundamental one. The carpenter had been too strong for the Sadducees; this Pharisee question would test not only his judgment of values but the extent of his learning as well. It was the kind of question that might, one imagines, have figured in an examination in any Jewish law school.

As always Jesus cut through to the very heart of the question. So much of the Law his questioner had in mind was manmade. But even the Ten Commandments given by God to Moses could be cut down to elements more fundamental still. There was a text in Deuteronomy (6:5)—"Thou shalt love the Lord thy God with thy whole heart, and with thy whole soul, and with thy whole strength." That, said Jesus, was "the greatest and the first commandment". Added to that, there was a text in Leviticus (19:18)—

"Thou shalt love thy neighbor as thyself." Jesus quoted that too, and then told his questioner: *"On these two commandments depend the whole Law and the prophets."*

It was one of the great moments in the history of mankind when man's whole duty was thus summed up in love of God and love of neighbor. The thrust of self against God may merit hell, but that is not the best reason for obeying him. *"If you love me,* keep my commandments", our Lord would say on another occasion. "Thou shalt not" has its place, but only as an outflow of love.

Marvelously the lawyer saw it, saw it instantly. He had begun as an opponent of our Lord, probing for a weakness. Now he repeated the two texts after him, and added: "To love one's neighbor as oneself is a greater thing than all holocausts and sacrifices." Jesus was not much given to praise, but this Pharisee he praised: "Thou art not far from the Kingdom of God."

For the Christian there is much teaching beside in these four chapters. There is, especially, teaching on prayer — the Our Father which Saint Matthew gives as part of the Sermon on the Mount, Saint Luke places here (11:2–4); we must pray with total confidence in our Father's love (11:9–13); we must not be discouraged when our prayer seems unanswered, we must keep asking, be importunate with God (11:5–8), refuse to take no for an answer — we remember the Syro-Phoenician woman whose importuning of Jesus himself had so got on the nerves of the Twelve (Mt 15:23).

Our confidence in God can be absolute, *if we do his will.* We must be obedient, we must be vigilant, not idly luxuriating in God's love and selfishly presuming on it. Temptation will be fierce and obedience may cause anguish. None the less, "Come unto me, all you that labor and are burdened, and I will refresh you. Take my yoke upon you . . . and you shall find rest to your souls."

33 *THE OPPOSITION HARDENS*

The weeks go by after the Feast of Tabernacles, through November, into December. In these first weeks Jesus was probably mainly in Judea; later he would cross the Jordan into Perea where Herod of Galilee had had John the Baptist beheaded. The miracles went on and the teaching—teaching direct, teaching in parables. Jesus was forming his followers, winning new followers. But his enemies were always there. Remember that to these last, it was he who was the enemy, the mortal threat to be met, with his plain denial of so much that their fathers in Israel had taught them as God's will for his people.

Three things particularly in these weeks increased the determination which Pharisees had reached in Galilee a year and a half earlier that he must be destroyed—the parable of the Good Samaritan, the charge that certain of his questioners blasphemed against the Holy Spirit, the listing of sins which stained the Pharisaism of that moment. Not once did he utter a word likely to diminish their conviction that he must die.

The Good Samaritan

Take first the parable of the Good Samaritan. The scribe who had accepted love of God and love of neighbor as the two great commandments (Mk 12:32) went on to ask: "And who is my neighbor?" (Lk 10:29). Jesus answered with this most famous of parables: "answered" is too weak a word—the Greek word means much more than that. Our Lord fell upon the question as if it had been the one question he was waiting for.

Only one who knows the Old Testament well can realize the shock to every Jew present. It was bad enough that priest and Levite should have failed to help the wounded man, for they were officials of the great Temple in Jerusalem, their lives bound up with the sacrifices by which Israel lived before its God. Yet his hearers must have been prepared for this, for Jesus had already taken his stand against the Establishment. But nothing had prepared them for the Samaritan.

Samaritans were the next-door neighbors to whom the Jews felt so very unneighborly. Hatred flowed steadily between the two peoples. Only a couple of months before the parable was uttered, the Samaritans had refused lodging to Jesus himself and the Twelve (Lk 9:53). And it was one of these that Jesus chose as the model of neighborliness.

With that he had gone to the limit. If a Samaritan could be listed among the neighbors whom the Jews must love as themselves, then no one at all could be excluded. If neighbor includes Samaritans, then neighbor includes all men whatsoever: there is no one who is not our neighbor, no one whom we are not called upon to love as ourselves. Observe, too, how Jesus answers more than the question that was actually asked. From "Who is our neighbor?" he advances to what neighborliness involves—"Go thou and do likewise."

The beloved disciple and his brother James must have felt the eyes of the other ten upon them as the story unfolded, for it was they who had wanted to command fire from heaven to destroy the Samaritan city which would not receive their Master. If they still had any tendency to take for granted that all Samaritans were inferior to all Jews, one more shock was awaiting them. *In the parable* a Samaritan had done the right thing when Jews had failed; soon they were to see a Samaritan do the right thing *in real life* when Jews had failed (Lk 17:12). Ten lepers, keeping the distance prescribed for men of their disease, begged Jesus for pity. He did not heal them on the instant, simply told them to go and show themselves to the priests—the Mosaic law required that cure of leprosy must be certified by a priest (Lev 14). As they went they found themselves healed. One of them returned to thank him, only one, and this one a Samaritan.

Blasphemy against the Holy Spirit

At the Feast of Tabernacles, his enemies had tried to discredit Jesus—"You are a Samaritan and have a devil" (Jn 8:48)—"devil"was hardly necessary, "Samaritan" was quite enough to destroy his credit totally: all the more because Samaritans were supposed to practice magic! But the maddening thing was that this subversive nobody could not be simply shrugged off: the crowds were too much impressed by the miracles he worked.

He worked one that time, and they tried to get rid of a fact so inconvenient by saying that it had never happened at all (Jn 9). He worked one this time, casting out a devil from a dumb man: they fell back upon what had been their second line, that he had a devil himself: "He casts out devils by Beelzebub, the Prince of devils" (Lk 11:15).

The accusation might have meant that the whole affair was a plot between all the devils of hell and this impostor, with laughing devils going through the motions of being cast out, in order to give him a prestige which would enable him more effectively to win Israel away from God. But his answer shows that what they were saying was that he was in alliance with the prince of devils against the others: hatred being the demonic rule of life, they hated one another, and their leader chose to humiliate the rest by subjecting them to the power of a mere man. It was a ridiculous idea. Hatred or no, the devils had to act together: as Jesus reminded his accusers—a kingdom divided against itself cannot stand.

What lay behind the accusation, as he saw, was a willed refusal of light: only by the power of God could the carpenter do the things he did; but if they admitted that, they would have to admit that the Kingdom of God had come upon them. So desperate a resort as accusing him of being in league with Satan meant a very profundity of sinfulness in themselves. He met it with a mysterious phrase (Mt 12:31–32): "There is pardon for all the other sins and blasphemies of men, but for him who blasphemes against the Holy Spirit there is no forgiveness, either in this world or in the world to come" (the last phrase is simply a Semitic way of indicating total neverness, it does not mean that other sins *can* be forgiven after death). We remind ourselves that the Holy Spirit *is* Love, that sins against love are the worst sins, and that the man who persists in the denial of love makes his own reconciliation with God impossible.

But the phrase remains mysterious: we may doubt if men have ever wholly fathomed its meaning. For his accusers anyhow the meaning was plain enough: they had accused him of diabolism, he accused them of blasphemy. "Holy Spirit" had not the same meaning for them as for us. The word "blasphemy" was the one that got through to them, the most appalling charge that could be made against a Jew.

He deserved death, obviously. But how could they make the common people see it while he went on working miracles? They demanded a sign — that is, a miracle in the sky. Such a miracle even they would have to admit was of divine origin. There was nothing winning in the manner of his answer — "An evil and adulterous generation asks for a sign." And there was nothing immediately convincing in the only "sign" he promised them, "the sign of Jonah the prophet", famous for his three days inside the big fish. Whatever they made of them at the moment, the words remained in their heads. For when he was in the tomb they asked Pilate to put a guard there because he had said that he would rise again after three days (Mt 27:63).

Dinner with a Pharisee

A Pharisee, possibly still not decided against him, invited him to dinner (Lk 11:37), and noted that he did not ask for the ritual washing before taking his place at table. The Pharisee was polite enough not to mention it, but Jesus read his mind, or perhaps his face, and launched into a fierce indictment of Pharisaism as he had seen it. This matter of washing, for instance, and their *formalism* generally. There was no sin in the precise observance of scores of minute rules, but it was no substitute for the love of God and the love of man. He went on to the *vanity* which led them to value first seats in the synagogue and deferential salutations in the marketplace — there was sin in that, though not of the worst sort.

But the third count in the indictment, corruption in the soul, was
the worst thing he had yet said against them; there is nothing
worse for anyone to say against them.

They were like graves that are not known to be graves, so that
the passerby is not aware of what is inside them (Lk 11:44). In a
much fuller indictment, which Saint Matthew places later, Jesus
works out this comparison with graves in case anyone might not
have got the point: "Woe to you scribes and Pharisees, hypocrites,
because you are like whitened sepulchres, which outwardly appear
to men beautiful, but within are full of dead men's bones and all
filthiness" (Mt 23:27). It is a horrifying description of inner
corruption. If only we could feel confident that it applied to none
but a handful of men long dead, our discomfort in it would be eased.

One of the guests, a lawyer, asked Jesus if lawyers were included
in the indictment. He drew upon himself nothing for his comfort —
Woe to him, said our Lord, and his caste, because they made all
sorts of observances binding upon others, while finding wholly
legal ways out for themselves; because they honored dead prophets,
whom their ancestors had killed, yet were themselves planning
the death of the greatest Prophet of them all, there present among
them; because they claimed control of the way to true knowledge
of God's law, but in fact they had remained outside it themselves,
and had kept others from it.

We have been witnessing one more, if a rather extreme, example of his almost unvarying harshness to scribes and Pharisees. We
remember the instructions he gave us not to judge others, lest we
should incur divine judgment upon ourselves. Is he breaking his
own rule? In fact the rule does not apply to him. Two things
forbid us to judge others, and neither of these is in him: we cannot
read their souls, where guilt and innocence lie, and he could; and
we ourselves are stained with our own guilt, and he was not.

He was justified in judging and uttering judgment. But we can
hardly be surprised that the judged did not see it so. We hardly
need Luke to tell us what their reactions were: they "resolved to
hunt him down mercilessly . . . they lay in wait for him, hoping
to catch some word from his lips which would give them ground
of accusation against him" (Lk 11:54). Mere abuse of themselves,

however violent, was not enough. They wanted him to say something which the law of Jew and Roman alike would see to be conclusive, to be punishable only by death.

"I and the Father Are One"

This was the position when he went to Jerusalem for the Feast of the Dedication, late in December. The feast had been established by Judas Maccabeus two hundred years before, when the altar of the true God, profaned by Antiochus Epiphanes, had been consecrated again. There was a week of pomp and splendor, with magnificent illuminations, so that it was called also the Feast of Lights. Saint John (10:22–39) takes all that as known. He is concerned with one thing only, Jesus' assertion of his divinity as he walked in the vast colonnade of the Temple named for Solomon, which faced across the valley of the brook Kidron to the garden of Gethsemane.

They asked him: "How long do you hold our souls in suspense? If you are the Christ, tell us plainly." It was the same demand for a categorical statement that the Baptist's disciples had made (Lk 7:19). This time, as then, no categorical answer was given: Jesus referred his questioners both times to the miracles he worked in the name of his Father as sufficient testimony. And then he made a claim compared with which the question—Was he the Christ?—was a mere trifle.

Anyone concerned to follow Jesus' teaching upon the relation of himself and his Father should reread John's report of those earlier feasts (chapters 5 and 7). Now he adds a phrase we have not heard from his lips before: "I and the Father are one"—the word "one" in Greek is neuter, "one thing". He and his Father are distinct persons—for a father and son are not simply two aspects of one person; but between them there is a profounder oneness than is known between created fathers and their sons. Yet he did not actually say, "I am God", just as a minute before he had not actually said, "I am the Christ." They were too wrong about the Messiah to be trusted with the one statement. They did not know enough about God to be trusted with the other.

What *did* they make of "I and the Father are one thing"? They saw rightly that he was making himself God, and would have stoned him to death. But what did they think he was actually saying? Not knowing the doctrine of the Blessed Trinity, they could see it only as a claim to be a second God. Without the doctrine, the "one thing" would have conveyed nothing to them at all.

What he did by way of calming their anger must, as so often with his answers, have seemed to them to make darkness darker. He reminded them of the verse of the eighty-second Psalm in which human rulers are called gods. Why, then, should he be accused of blasphemy—he "whom the Father had sanctified and sent into the world"—for saying, "I am the Son of God"? As so often, one feels that he is talking not to the questioners before him but to us. There is no immediate connection between the word "gods" as applied in the Psalm to men who are men and no more, and the word "God" as applied to himself. But there *is* a profound connection all the same. We have it in the Ordinary of the Mass—"that we may be made partakers of the divinity of him who did not disdain to become partaker of our humanity": men can be truly divinized only because God the Son became man.

None of this was evident to his audience. He returned to the point of "oneness", with the words "The Father is in me and I in the Father." With those words we hear the first sound of the formula of our salvation which he was to utter at the Last Supper—"I am in my Father and you in me and I in you" (Jn 14:20).

How did they receive that? "They sought therefore"—"therefore", note—"to take him; and he escaped out of their hands." It was the third time. Two months before, they had wanted to stone him to death in the Temple. Just a year before, his fellow citizens of Nazareth had planned to hurl him to his death over a cliff at the edge of the town. But his time had not yet come. They could not "take" him, he was keeping himself for Calvary, now only three months away.

34 MAINLY IN PEREA

Most of our account of the last three months of the public life we get from Saint Luke, chapters 13 to 18. There is not a great amount of incident reported—Jesus is told that Herod plans to have his life and he sends back a highly impolite message to Herod: "Go tell that fox . . ." He heals ten lepers. He meets a rich young man, who goes away sorrowful from the meeting. He takes little children in his arms. But the chapters are filled mainly with his teaching, teaching by parable especially.

Renewal of Parables

We cannot always be sure, as we have frequently had to note, of the order in which he did or said given things. But if we simply follow the order of the Gospels, we are conscious of a long unparabled gap. There had been the first group of seven parables, back in Galilee, recorded soon after the Sermon on the Mount, mostly by Saint Matthew. In the next fifteen months or so, to the Feast of Tabernacles, there is only one, the unmerciful servant. Between Tabernacles in October and the Dedication in December there are four, between Dedication and the raising of Lazarus in late February or March a dozen.

The three months between the Feast of the Dedication and the raising of Lazarus (Lk 13–18) contain the first outpouring of parables since the first group nearly a year and a half before. Both groups of parables are concerned with the Kingdom of God, but differently. For the phrase means wherever God is King, wherever his law is obeyed, whether in the individual soul, or in the society of men he has founded. The first group were primarily about the second of these, with the first as an overtone. In the new group the main concern is the individual soul. Only the parable of the great supper, near the beginning, and the laborers in the vineyard, with which this group ends, actually use the words "the Kingdom of God". In these two, any listener who knew the way Jesus' mind was moving might have seen the changed emphasis whereby Gentiles were to be full members of the Kingdom, with Jewish predominance lost.

It may be, also, that the principal theme of the prodigal son, Dives and Lazarus, the Pharisee and the publican, and the good Samaritan was the loss of Jewish preeminence and the emergence of Gentiles to take the place that the Jewish people were refusing. But of none of these four is that interpretation demanded, either by the story told, or the context in which it is told. All of them give rich teaching about the individual soul in its acceptance or rejection of God's Kingship. And this is quite clearly the theme of all the other parables of the group.

For us who take the universality of the Kingdom for granted, it is the teaching given by the parables about our own souls that matters most urgently. Reading them we come across way after way in which we ourselves have failed and will only too probably fail again.

But they do not give what Catholics call a general examination of conscience. There is not so very much about individual sins— sexual sins do not figure in them at all. One man fails to show to an inferior the mercy that has been shown himself; another strikes his fellow servants, eats and drinks with drunkards; the dishonest steward wastes his employer's goods; the prodigal son lives riotously, but we are left to fill in the details of his riotous living for ourselves; the wicked husbandmen beat a messenger from the lord of the vineyard and kill his son. The sins attacked come under the general heading of worldliness—greed for gain, for power, for glory in the eyes of men.

In other words, what Jesus is treating in the parables is not individual moral offenses, breaches of the Ten Commandments for instance; but the states of soul from which all sins flow, spiritual emptiness, spiritual excess. We meet men who listen to God's truth and do nothing about it, men who make a beginning but lack root, men who see what they should do but make excuses. At one end of the scale of defect are those who want to be honored for their virtues—honored not only by men, like the seekers of first places and respectful salutations, but even by God, like the Pharisee who lists his virtues and thanks God he is not as other men, or the prodigal's elder brother who is aggrieved at the younger's return to favor. At the other end there is a sort of fruitlessness: talents hidden, the gifts of God put to no use. One sin fills all the air we breathe in the parables—hypocrisy; one virtue—humility. And over all, the sheer foolishness of rating this life above the next.

We find a similar proportion in the teaching Jesus gives on the spiritual life when he is not using parables. In opposition to the Pharisees who made so much of ritual eating and ritual drinking, we have heard him teach that what comes out of a man defiles him much more than what goes into him: he lists among the things that come out of a man evil thoughts, adulteries, fornications, murders, thefts, covetousness, malice, deceit, lasciviousness, envy, blasphemy, pride, foolishness (Mk 7:21). Even one who acquits himself of all the other items on the list might not be sure about the last one.

Apart from that, there is not much detailing of individual sins: sexual sins, for instance, get nothing like the emphasis Saint Paul gives them. Hypocrisy Jesus constantly attacks. But nothing stirs him to real anger save the insulting of his Father—the profaning of his Father's house, of his Father's law, above all of his Father's image, which every man is.

Gentiles and the Kingdom

The three-month period Jesus spent almost entirely outside Judea. For most of it he was in Perea, Herod of Galilee's other province to the east of Jordan; but we find him on the border of Galilee and Samaria for the healing of the ten lepers. In Jerusalem and the country around, his enemies would certainly slay him. When the death of Lazarus called him back there—to Bethany, only a couple of miles from Jerusalem—Thomas reminded the other apostles, correctly, that he was going to his death.

Under Herod he was safe enough, for the tetrarch had no Jewish blood and therefore no sufficient interest in the teachings which the Pharisees hated so much; nor had the carpenter, as the Baptist had, attacked Herod's scandalous marriage to his brother's wife. In any event his beheading of the Baptist and the remorse that followed probably left Herod no stomach for killing prophets. Yet he might very well have felt happier to have Jesus preaching somewhere else.

This may have been behind the warning brought to Jesus by some of the Pharisees—"Depart, for Herod has a mind to kill you." They might have been happy enough to bring him a warning which would get him either back to Judea and death, or out of Palestine altogether. This reply opened with a phrase not often used to kings, even third-rate half-kings like Herod. "Go and tell that fox, I cast out devils and do cures today and tomorrow, and the third day I reach the end" (Lk 13:32). In other words, Herod need not worry, Christ would be in his dominions only a short while longer: then he would go, because only in Jerusalem should a prophet perish.

Meanwhile he was busy underlining those elements in his teaching which were most certain to madden the Pharisees. They had planned his death a long time: he gave them no excuse for a change of mind. Some of the things he said were harmless enough— like "You cannot serve God and money" (Lk 16:13)—harmful only because the Pharisees took it (with reason, according to Luke) as directed against themselves.

But there were more serious things. He went on healing on the Sabbath, for instance—that Sabbath on which the scribes taught that even God rested. He told the parable of the Pharisee and the publican, embarrassing to the Apostle Matthew who had been a publican, but infuriating to any Pharisee who took it for granted that he was not as other men.

It was a moderate parable, really, as we have already noted. The Pharisee was not described as a bad man, only as a man too pleased with himself. And Jesus did not say that he had gained condemnation by his visit to the Temple, only that the publican had been justified more (Lk 18:14). But even that was an intolerable insult, especially since he went on drawing publicans and sinners to him, went on receiving them and eating with them.

What was far worse was the reiteration of the teaching that the Jews had forfeited their place of eminence, and that Gentiles would be their equals in the Kingdom. The Qumran community have left a scroll—a sort of fighters' manual, Dr. Alexander Jones calls it—which expresses the bitterest hatred of all that is not Jew and outlines plans for vengeance. They were extremists, these, to whom even the Pharisees seemed lax. But in seeing the Gentiles as destined to a lower place, they were all one. There could hardly have been any phrase which more surely sealed Jesus' fate than: "There shall be weeping and gnashing of teeth, when you shall see Abraham and Isaac and Jacob, and all the prophets in the Kingdom of God, and you yourselves thrust out. And they shall come from the east and the west, and the north and the south; and shall sit down in the Kingdom of God. And they are last that shall be first; and they are first that shall be last" (Lk 13:28–30).

There may not have been weeping at this assertion that Gentile latecomers would not be the losers by their lateness, but teeth were certainly gnashed. The same truth was embodied in the parable of the laborers in the vineyard (Mt 20), with those who came in at the eleventh hour receiving the same payment as those who had been there from the beginning. In the Old Testament, we remember, the vineyard was the established figure of Israel, God's people on earth; and the Lord of the vineyard was God.

Yet even this parable did not carry the shock of one he was to give some weeks later (Lk 20, Mk 12, Mt 21). It told—and they knew that it told—how the Jews, with the vineyard left in their charge, had failed in their duty and ended by killing the Lord of the vineyard's Son. Just three days after the parable was uttered they *did* kill the Lord of the vineyard's Son.

Two Comments from the Twelve

What did the Twelve think, what did they feel, as these last months went by? We hear little of them, and into their minds we get hardly a glimpse. What we do hear is not very impressive. On two occasions we are told that they made rather obvious comments on what the Master had just said; on one occasion they intervened—he brushed their intervention aside; and there is a question by Peter on how their following of Christ would end. We shall glance at all these, beginning with the rebuke for interference.

Parents had brought their infants to our Lord that he might touch them. The Twelve tried to wave them away. "When Jesus saw this he was much displeased and said to them: Suffer the little children to come unto me, and forbid them not. For of such is the Kingdom of God. Then he took the children in his arms and blessed them" (Mk 10:16). The interference of the Twelve had been natural enough, given that their Master was constantly thronged about with people, and the bringing up of a pack of babies seemed to the apostles like a last straw. Their two comments were of the same naturalness, one on the episode of the young man who was very rich, one on the prohibition of divorce.

For the rich young man, we should read all three accounts, Luke 18, Mark 10, Matthew 19. Each has its own special touch. The man had asked what he must do to gain everlasting life. Our Lord told him to keep the commandments, linking with these the command to love his neighbor as himself, which was not one of Moses' ten but one of his own two. The young man felt he had met that condition anyhow, but he knew by some instinct that this was not all that Jesus had to say to him. "What is still wanting to me?" he asked. Our Lord, "looking on him, loved him", and said, "If you would be perfect, go sell all you have and give to the poor, and you shall have treasure in heaven: and come, follow me." At that, the young man went away sad: he did really want to be perfect, but he was so very rich.

Our Lord was sad too. For the only time we see his invitation "Follow me" refused. "It is easier", he said, "for a camel to pass through the eye of a needle than for a rich man to enter the Kingdom of heaven." It was at this that his followers made one of what I have called their two obvious comments. "Who then can be saved?" It drew the comforting answer: "To God all things are possible"—even the salvation of the rich!

Just before this episode, Mark (10:2) and Matthew (19:3) tell of the Pharisees' trying to break through Jesus' guard with a question about divorce. There were two schools of thought among them—the great Hillel had taught that divorce might be allowed for all sorts of reasons, Shammai only for adultery. What did the carpenter think? If, as seems probable, the question was asked in Perea, it was loaded: for Perea was Herod's. Jesus answered it strictly on its merits.

His answer went beyond Shammai and Hillel, even beyond Moses, who had allowed the wife to be divorced for "defilement" (Dt 24), back to the creation (Gen 2:24). When a man and woman decide to be husband and wife, it is God who makes them so. "Now they are not two, but one flesh [a Jewish way of saying 'one person']. What therefore God has joined together, let no man put asunder." To break a marriage was beyond man's power. Moses had allowed divorce, but only because his people had not the moral and spiritual strength for unbreakable marriage. Jesus was now restoring the first law, with divorce not possible on any ground.

Thus Mark, Luke (16:18), and Paul (1 Cor 7:10) record our Lord's teaching. Matthew alone inserts a phrase that might be taken as allowing one ground—"If a man divorces his wife *not on account of fornication* and marries another, he commits adultery." Is divorce then permissible, as Shammai thought, for adultery?

But the text does not say "on account of adultery". It says "fornication", which is the sexual sin of the unmarried and there-fore does not apply here: perhaps it has also some other meaning—marriage between people too closely related has been suggested, which is no marriage at all. It is an oddly-worded phrase which did not affect the certainty of Mark or Luke or Paul that divorce was absolutely forbidden. The Twelve were certain too. If a man is really tied to one wife whatever happens, they said, it is safer not to marry at all. Our Lord's answer was a mysterious word on those whom God calls to celibacy.

So in the period between the end of December and the raising of Lazarus in March, all we have of the apostles is a couple of comments made by them—it might be safer not to marry at all if there was no divorce; and who could be saved if the rich couldn't?—and one effort to do something. It was not much, this last; only an attempt to prevent mothers bringing their babies to Jesus. They were rebuked for it, as John and James had been for an earlier suggestion to bring down fire from heaven on the Samaritan city that did not want them.

A Question from Peter

What of Peter? We cannot, for instance, imagine that born activist doing nothing at all when twice our Lord's enemies were on the point of stoning him. Surely, we feel, he must have punched somebody. But then we remember how his nerve was to fail on the night when his Master was in the hands of the high priest. Jerusalem seems to have done something to Peter. In the period we are discussing, we hear his voice only once (Mt 19:27). The Twelve had given up all things to follow Christ; "What therefore shall we have?" he asks.

It was a reasonable question, not so much claiming a reward as wondering what the upshot was to be. Twice before they came south, they had heard their Leader foretell his own death—his Resurrection, too, but they did not know what he meant by that. In Jerusalem he had gone further with "I lay down my life for my sheep" (Jn 10:15)—he would be slain, but he would be consenting to the slaying, and his followers would be the gainers.

His talk was not only of catastrophe for himself, but for them too. Peter's question might very well have been the outcome of long discussions among the Twelve upon one special thing they had heard their Master say: "If any man come to me and hate not his father, and mother, and wife, and children, and brothers and sisters, yea and his own life also, he cannot be my disciple" (Lk 14:26). It was not the word "hate" that bothered them, for they had heard Jesus summarize all the duty of man in two commandments of love, and the word "hate" was only an idiom that they knew, a strong way of saying that they must love Christ above all. Saint Matthew, recounting the same episode, actually casts the condition of discipleship in the form of love, not hate.

What bothered them was the phrase "and his own life also", especially as the next words were "Whoever does not carry his cross and come after me, cannot be my disciple." They had seen enough crucifixions to know what carrying the cross meant. They had indeed abandoned their families to follow Christ—we never hear of their wives, never of their children. But was the reward of so much abnegation to be the cross?

Our Lord's answer to Peter's question was wonderful. They should be rewarded a hundredfold even in this life, and in the world to come they should have life everlasting. Not only that. "When the Son of Man shall sit on the seat of his majesty, you also shall sit on twelve seats judging the twelve tribes of Israel", ruling the new Israel as, before the kings, judges had ruled the old.

Yet how the splendor of this prospect was to be reconciled with the more than hint of suffering and death for themselves, and the plain statement of the death that awaited their Leader, he did not tell them. At least they no longer had any doubt that he was to be slain. There were not only his own words, but the intentions of the leaders of Israel were quite clear. They knew that he was safe enough in Herod's country. They could only hope that nothing would take him back to Judea.

And something did take him back. Lazarus "whom he loved" lay ill unto death in Bethany; Martha and Mary had sent our Lord a message. There were two towns called Bethany. This one was in Judea, less than two miles from Jerusalem, on the lower slope of the Mount of Olives. Even if Jesus had slipped into the town quietly, and left it quietly, he would have been taking an immense risk. He went in openly, and worked the most spectacular miracle of his life.

35 RETURN TO JUDEA

After getting the message from Martha and Mary, Jesus let two days go by. Then he said to the Twelve: "Let us go into Judea again" (Jn 11:7). They reminded him how recently the men of

Judea had sought to stone him. When he told them that Lazarus had died, they must have felt that there was now no point in his going to Bethany after all. Their relief did not last long. He was still bent upon going.

At that, Thomas said one of the great things: "Let us also go, that we may die with him." When the time came, Thomas ran with the others. But he meant it when he said it, and there was splendor in it—all the more, perhaps, because he did run later: courage costs braver men less! This is the first thing we have heard Thomas say.

The Raising of Lazarus

The story of the visit to Bethany and the raising of dead Lazarus is told in the first forty-four verses of Saint John's eleventh chapter. I shall comment only on certain elements in it, especially the reactions of Martha (who this time eclipses her sister), and what the miracle seems to have cost our Lord.

Martha came to meet him outside the town, with the words "Lord, if you had been here my brother would not have died. But I also know that whatsoever you ask of God, God will give you." That last phrase can only mean that there was a faint quiver of a hope in her that he might bring her brother back to life. Yet how could that have occurred to her, even as a possibility? Had she, perhaps, heard of the widow's son of Nain, or of Jairus' daughter, both raised from the dead in Galilee? Of course, if she and her family were Galileans, then she would certainly have known of the miracles, and might have known the girl, or the young man, or both.

But the hope, if it was there at all, could have been no more than the faintest stirring. For when Jesus said, "Your brother shall rise again", she did not take it as the answer to her hopes. She spoke as if he meant only that final resurrection of all men, which the Pharisees taught and the Sadducees denied (which, as we have noted, is what the Twelve probably thought he meant when he spoke of his own Resurrection).

Comprehension or no, it is Martha's abiding glory that Jesus' words, "I am the Resurrection and the Life", might never have been spoken but for her. Yet there was nothing in his next statement—that spiritual life was bound up with belief in himself—to indicate that he meant to bring her brother back to life in this world. And when, standing by the tomb, he told them to take away the stone, no hope seems to have stirred in her. She could think only of how very dead Lazarus must be by now: "Lord, by this time he stinks, for he is now four days dead." After all, Jairus' daughter and the Nain boy were barely dead, they had not yet been buried!

But the faint hope that had for one moment been there, however totally it had died in her, must have been revived by his answer: "Did I not say to you, that if you believe, you shall see the glory of God?"

Nothing is stranger in the story of the raising of Lazarus than Jesus' own reactions. There is nothing in the accounts of other miracles to parallel his weeping and distress, his sighing and groaning, over this one. We cannot hope fully to understand the emotions of a God-Man, but we must bring our minds to bear upon them: they are not told us for no reason at all.

When the news first came to him on the other side of Jordan that Lazarus was sick, he answered: "This sickness is not unto death, but for the glory of God: that the Son of God may be glorified by it" (Jn 11:4). When Martha wondered at his ordering the removal of the stone that closed the tomb, he said, "You shall see the glory of God." The raising to life, on Jerusalem's very doorstep, of a man four days dead, was no chance miracle, it was part of the divine plan for the showing of Jesus as what he was. Lazarus must die; but he died in order to be brought back to the life of earth by the Son of God.

As they were approaching the tomb, Jesus saw Mary weeping, and her friends with her, and he wept too. But his weeping, as the Greek verbs show, was different. Theirs was the sobbing and the wailing normal at a Jewish funeral, his was a shedding of tears, soundless. Why, we may wonder, did he shed tears at all, since he knew that he was so soon to work the miracle that would wipe away their tears? But tears are not for grief only. A revelation of the depth or splendor of human character can bring tears to the eyes, tears of joy at sheer human goodness. He might well have been weeping to see their love for the brother whom they loved, and whom he loved as he loved them (Jn 11:5).

Meanwhile he is having those strange reactions of his own of which we have already made mention, groaning in the spirit, troubling himself. There seems no doubt that he was praying to his Father for the power this miracle, of all miracles, needed; for when it was on the point of happening, he said, "Father, I give thee thanks that thou hast heard me." We are reminded of Saint Paul's "The Spirit himself intercedes for us with groans beyond all utterance" (Rom 8:26). Saint Paul seems to be saying that when man is asking for something intensely difficult, something that seems almost beyond reason, he must put his whole self into the asking, with an intensity of self-giving which would be beyond his power if the Holy Spirit did not pour his own power into him.

That, we may feel, may be all very well for *us* and our praying. But can it apply to Christ? We find the beginning of an answer in the Epistle to the Hebrews (5:7): "Christ, during his earthly life, offered prayer and entreaty to the God who could save him from death, not without a piercing cry, not without tears." A prayer to save himself may have cost him much, a prayer to bring Lazarus from the tomb exacted its own price too. We have not to wait for Gethsemane to hear him pray with groaning.

Few miracles are led up to in such detail. But the miracle itself is told swiftly. Our Lord cried with a loud voice, "Lazarus, come here"—as it were, "come *to me.*" Lazarus emerged, still wrapped for his burial, and our Lord said, "Loose him and let him go."

Let us remind ourselves that this miracle was worked, quite explicitly, for the effects it would produce upon friend and enemy alike. It is the only time, to take one example, that Jesus actually says he is speaking aloud to his Father "because of the people who are standing near"—he *wants* them to hear. And many did indeed believe because of what they had heard and seen.

But it seems beyond doubt also that the effect upon his enemies was part of the purpose of the miracle. It made his death certain. The Pharisees had wanted him slain these many months. But with this miracle the Sadducees are brought to will his death for the first time. And it was they, with the high priesthood in their grip, who had the right—and the influence with the Romans—to bring it about.

Enter Caiaphas

In all his parables, there is only one character to whom Jesus gives a name—Lazarus, which means "God has helped". He, we remember, "died and was carried by the angels into Abraham's bosom"—a phrase for the place where the just of Israel waited till Christ's redeeming sacrifice should open heaven to men. We remember, too, how the rich man, "buried in hell", asked Abraham to send Lazarus the beggar to warn his five brothers still on earth of what might await them. Abraham dismissed the request—they would not believe even if Lazarus came back from the dead.

That was the parable. And now, in fact not parable, a man named Lazarus did come back from the dead, called by the carpenter of Nazareth. And they did not believe. Instead the leaders of the Jews decided to kill the carpenter. They planned to kill Lazarus too (Jn 12:10)—return him to Abraham's bosom, so to speak, from which he had been thus irregularly dragged.

We must try to follow the thought processes of the Jewish leaders. The Pharisees, we know, had long determined that the carpenter must die for the crime of contradicting the traditions which were the whole of religion to them. But the Sadducees had no special attachment to the traditions. These men were essentially power politicians, they had secured for themselves the high priesthood and the total control of the Temple, they knew how to handle their Roman overlords.

They would not have bothered about the carpenter's religious heresies—they thought the Pharisees heretical anyhow. But upsetting the Romans was a very different matter. The masters of the world were always on the watch for men who might lead subject peoples to rise in revolt. With the raising of a man from the dead on Jerusalem's very doorstep, the Sadducees suddenly saw Jesus as dangerous. It looked as if he was ready to make his bid for power. Even if he had no such intention, this was the sort of miracle that would have the Rome-hating crowds thronging after him. If that happened, or even if it was seen as a possibility, Rome might destroy the holy place, the Temple, and eliminate the Jews of Palestine as the national unit they had managed to remain.

Now we meet Caiaphas for the first time. He was high priest, son-in-law of Annas, the high priest Rome had deposed fifteen years earlier. With Sadducees and Pharisees gathered in council to think out what had best be done to save the Temple and the nation, Caiaphas touched off the discussion: "You know nothing. Surely you realize that it is best for us that one man should die for the people, and that the whole nation should not perish" (Jn 11:49–50). He only meant that if one man was a threat to national survival, then the obvious thing was to kill him. But the evangelist tells us that, unknown to himself, the high priest was prophesying that Jesus should die for the Jews, not only for the Israel of blood and race, but for the Israel of God—all men who should be united with God in Christ. It would have startled Caiaphas beyond words to know that that was what he was actually saying.

To have the Sadducees determined upon his death changed the situation considerably. They held the high offices in Judea, they were in daily contact with the Romans. They could get the Romans not only to consent to his death, though that was necessary, but actually to put him to death, thus saving themselves from the kind of odium that had clung to Herod of Galilee ever since the beheading of the Baptist. Romans could take odium in their stride, especially if they felt they were acting with strict legality.

36 *EPHRAIM TO BETHANY VIA JERICHO*

Following the decision, uttered by Caiaphas and accepted by Sadducees and Pharisees, that he must die, Jesus went to Ephraim—probably, though not certainly, a place fifteen miles from Jerusalem, on the edge of desert. The Passover was near, says Saint John (11:55), and he would be in Jerusalem at the Passover for his death. But how near was it? And what road did he take back? From the Gospels, we cannot be certain of the answer to either question.

It may be that he went north into Samaria, to the border of Galilee, before moving over to Jordan, and then south by way of Jericho and Bethany. If he did, then the healing of the ten lepers, with the Samaritan coming back to thank him, may have taken place at this time (Lk 17:12). This episode has one point of uniqueness: it is the only occasion on which our Lord mentions thanksgiving as a duty (a duty which only the Samaritan rendered). Otherwise he is silent about it—strangely, we may feel. Even in the Our Father, the prayer he himself gave us as a model, there is no clause in which God is thanked.

What we know for certain is that he did go through Jericho and Bethany on his way to Jerusalem, and a glance at the map suggests that he went to Jericho straight from Ephraim, where he may well have been for only a few days. On the first stage of the return journey Saint Mark tells us that Jesus walked ahead of the Twelve and that they were afraid. At last he was walking toward his death, and they felt him different.

Detailed Prediction of Passion

Then he gave them ground for their fear, with the fullest, most detailed prediction yet of his Passion and death and Resurrection. Here is how Mark (10:33) records Peter's memory of what he said:

"We go up to Jerusalem and the Son of Man shall be betrayed to the chief priests, and to the scribes and ancients, and they shall condemn him to death and shall deliver him to the Gentiles. And these shall mock him, and spit on him, and scourge him, and kill him. And the third day he shall rise again."

Considering the extreme clarity of this statement; considering the two earlier, quite clear though not quite so detailed, foretellings of the death and Resurrection that awaited him (Mt 16:21 and 17:21); considering that the leaders of the Jews had made their own intentions clear; considering that Thomas had expressed the mind of all of them when he said that if their Lord returned to Judea it would mean his death and the Twelve must be prepared to die with him—we may find Saint Luke's comment here rather puzzling: "They understood none of these things, and this word was hid from them" (18:34).

Soon after, Matthew and Mark have Christ saying, "The Son of Man is come not to be served but to serve, and to give his life a redemption for many": Daniel's Son of Man and Isaiah's Suffering Servant are one same person.

James and John Want High Places

Whatever sense the Twelve made of what they had just heard, two of them still counted on a happy ending. James and John, either on their own account (Mk 10) or letting their mother speak for them (Mt 20), made a claim to preferment in the Kingdom—that they might sit one on Christ's right, the other on his left. One thing they had not grasped, namely the nature of the Kingdom; one thing they had forgotten, namely that Peter had been promised primacy in the Kingdom.

Jesus' answer makes no reference to Peter, but contains its own kind of reminder of what the Kingdom was to be: "You do not know what you are asking. Can you drink of the chalice that I drink of, or be baptized with the baptism wherewith I am baptized?" What he meant may very well have been the humiliation and the agony of which he had just been speaking to them.

Whatever they thought he meant, the brothers answered in all confidence, "We can." To which our Lord answered, "You shall indeed"—James would remember that at his beheading by Agrippa, and John in his exile at Patmos: but, Jesus continued, the places of honor in the Kingdom, here upon earth or in the glory of heaven, were not for him to dispose of, but his Father.

We get the impression that the request had been made, sensibly we feel, at a moment when the other ten were not there. But they came to hear of it and "began to be much displeased at James and John" (Mk 10:41).

The journey from Ephraim was the last Jesus would make to Jerusalem, and Jericho and Bethany were its last stages. The Twelve felt in their bones that it was to be decisive (but what would the decision be?). The crowds knew it too—they must have been warned by the command issued by the chief priest and the Pharisees that anyone who knew where the carpenter was should inform them, that they might arrest him (Jn 11:56). Jesus knew he was walking to his death. The crowds knew it, which made them more anxious for a last look. Only the apostles (*not* Thomas, one imagines) clung to their own hope—with James and John, backed by their mother, applying for places on his right hand and his left: John and his mother would be on Calvary and would see who occupied those two places!

Blind Men in Jericho

They came to Jericho, twenty miles from Jerusalem. It was very much Herod the Great's city, he had largely built it and had died in it; his appalling son Archelaus had built himself a palace there. Near the city Jesus healed two blind men—Mark and Luke concentrate on one of them, the more trustful, as we may suppose; Matthew tells us of the other.

They remind us of two other blind men whose sight Jesus had restored (Mt 9:27), particularly in their persistence, and in their hailing him as Son of David. That title mattered more here in Jericho, with the Kingdom a vivid possibility in everybody's mind. The Twelve, and neighbors in the crowd, told them to stop their shouting. But Jesus called them, questioned them, healed them. They joined the group that straggled after him.

Conversion of Zacchaeus

Inside Jericho he once again converted a publican, Zacchaeus—the word means "pure", which taxpayers may have thought a name ill-suited to the chief tax collector of the region. He was a little man, too small to see Jesus over the heads of the crowd. So he climbed a tree. It is hard to imagine any prominent official doing anything so undignified today: it was just as improbable then. The people near the tree must have been as much interested in the tax collector up it as in the carpenter coming their way. Arrived at the tree, Jesus addressed Zacchaeus by name—he must have heard a dozen people saying the name at once—and said, "Make haste and come down; I am to lodge today at your house." So the tax collector dropped from the tree and was host to the carpenter.

Jesus seems to have had a way with tax collectors. There is so much in this incident that reminds us of the calling of Matthew—particularly the abruptness of the summons, with no explanation appended, and the going into a house no Pharisee would have dreamed of entering. Matthew became an apostle. Without doing that, for Jesus had not called him to it, Zacchaeus became a new man. "Here and now, Lord," he said, "I give half of what I have to the poor; and if I have wronged anyone in any way, I make restitution of it fourfold"—this last must have made a considerable inroad on the half of his fortune he was keeping for himself!

The stricter of the Pharisees, so concerned ritually about what might be eaten and with whom, spoke their criticisms of Jesus, just as the same sort of men had done in Capernaum outside the house of Levi who became Matthew. And that brings us to the final point of similarity between the two episodes. For, in explanation of his visiting Matthew, Jesus had said, "I am come not to call the just, but sinners to repentance" (Lk 5:32). And in explanation of his visiting Zacchaeus he said, "The Son of Man is come to seek and to save that which was lost."

We are not told what Matthew made of the incident, and he does not mention it in his own Gospel. Yet we may think about Matthew for a moment. No convert surely excited him so much as this one, a richer member of his own former profession. And Zacchaeus might have found his help useful in working out just how much he had in fact overcharged taxpayers! Judas—to glance at another of the Twelve who might have had a special interest in the richest "contact" since Nicodemus—might have been only too willing to advise about the distribution of all that money to the poor!

But there was no time for either Matthew or Judas to help Zacchaeus. Our Lord and his group were on their way to Bethany.

Parable of the Nobleman

The conversion of Zacchaeus is followed by what I feel as the strangest of our Lord's parables (Lk 19:11–28). The unjust steward, you think? No. That one is fairly straightforward. I mean the parable of the nobleman who went into a far country to receive for himself a kingdom.

The key words are "He spoke a parable because he was coming near to Jerusalem and because *they thought that the Kingdom of God should immediately be manifested.*" Throughout this last journey, the minds of his followers had been dominated by that thought (it, surely, had prompted the effort of James and John to bespeak for themselves the highest places—Mt 20:20). So he spoke the parable as a corrective. But where is the connection between the parable and their mistaken expectation?

In the word "immediately". They were expecting him to go the last twenty miles to Jerusalem and *there* be throned in glory. That picture he painted out. He told them that he must go "into a far country"—to the next world, as we know now—to receive his Kingdom, to be invested with the Kingship by his Father in heaven. On his return he would sit in judgment upon his servants, rewarding those who had diligently used the treasures he had left with them, while those who had neglected them would lose all.

So far there is nothing very strange: his Kingdom would be in this world, indeed, but not of it; we must all use sanctifying grace or lose it. The strangeness lies in verse 14: while he was in the far country his citizens, who hated him, sent an embassage after him, saying, "We will not have this man to reign over us." What happened to these rebellious ones, the parable tells in verse 27: "But as for those my enemies, who would not have me reign over them, bring them here and kill them in my presence." How, we wonder, could such an embassage be sent to heaven, the far country to which our Lord has actually gone? What can it conceivably mean?

Thirty years before, with Jesus still an infant, what we may call the framework of the parable had actually happened. When Herod the Great died, he left his eldest surviving son Archelaus as his principal heir. Archelaus went to Rome—a far country, a two-thousand-mile journey—to ask the Emperor Augustus to make him king, as his father had been: only Rome could give him the kingship. The Jews, hating him, sent fifty of their most important men hurrying after him to urge the Emperor not to make him their king, but to make Judea a Roman province under a governor. Augustus compromised. Judea was given to Archelaus, but not the title of king, only ethnarch. He returned, aflame with hatred, and he might very well have uttered the words of verse 27, whether or not he could carry them out. He was a very murderous man. His subjects finally had their way. After ten years of evil rule he was exiled by Rome, and Judea became a Roman province under a procurator.

Would our Lord, we ask ourselves, have used such a story for a parable about himself and his own Kingdom? If so, it would be perhaps the most striking example of a way he had of drawing comparisons from situations or episodes of which only some of the elements did in fact apply to himself and his dealing with men's souls: we cannot always follow any given comparison further than he himself took it.

Remember that it was his custom to utter his teaching in terms of something actually present before his hearers at the moment of utterance. He was in Jericho, where Herod had died. Archelaus would have begun the long journey to Rome from that very place. During his reign he had built a palace for himself in Jericho.

They might well have been standing in front of it as they heard the parable. The Archelaus incident would have been still alive in the minds of his listeners.

It would have been alive in his own mind too, for there was a pattern in it which was about to be completed. To save him from death at the hands of Archelaus, Joseph had not settled in Judea as he had intended, but had gone back to Galilee. And now he was to meet death in Judea after all—at the hands, not of Archelaus, but of the Roman procurator ruling in his place, and at the request of the successors of the men who had first asked for a procurator.

Anointing in Bethany

From Jericho Jesus went to Bethany. He was now within two miles of Jerusalem and a week of Calvary.

In Bethany we find him still with Lazarus and Martha and Mary. But this time the great scene is not in their house, but in the house of one Simon called "the leper". Why are we told this about him? Possibly because Jesus had healed him. On the evening of the last Sabbath before Calvary, Simon gave a banquet for our Lord, with Lazarus one of the guests, and Martha waiting at table. Once more Mary leaves Martha to get on with the serving and herself chooses the better part: she anoints Jesus' head and his feet with precious ointment, and wipes his feet with her hair, so that "the house was filled with the odor of the ointment."

There are three accounts of the scene, given by Mark (14:3–9), Matthew (26:6–13), and John (12:1–11). Read especially John's. He alone tells us that Lazarus was a guest, that it was Mary who did the anointing, that she anointed Jesus' feet, as well as his head. All speak of the indignation her act caused, but John alone tells us that Judas Iscariot uttered it and was rebuked by Jesus. It looks as if this was for Judas the last straw: a few days later he agreed to sell his Master for thirty pieces of silver.

Observe the reason Judas gives—"Why was not this ointment sold for three hundred pence, and given to the poor?"—three hundred pence would have supported a workman for a year. Observe John's comment: "He said this, not because he cared for the poor; but because he was a thief, and carried the purse"—he was treasurer for the Twelve, and had been dipping into the small treasury. There is no point in thinking up nobler reasons, as some have done, for Judas' handing over of Jesus to his slayers—as, for instance, that his sole desire was to force him to show his power and take over his Kingdom at once. John knew him. John said he was a thief.

It will have been noticed that Saint Luke, who does describe that earlier meal in Bethany at which Martha served and Mary adored (Lk 10), does not mention this one. But then Luke (7:36–50) is the only one to tell of an anointing by a sinful woman, as Jesus sat at table in Capernaum, the host, there too, being named Simon. Was that the same incident? We know that Luke is not concerned with strict chronological order. He might have had reasons of his own for describing the Bethany scene in among a series of happenings in Capernaum.

There are similarities, indeed, yet they read like separate incidents. In Capernaum, the host is hostile, or at least not friendly. He shows the bare civilities, none of the courtesies. In Bethany, Lazarus is a fellow guest and Martha helps with the serving—we cannot imagine any courtesy left unshown with Martha there. We note also the difference of the reactions to the extravagant gesture of the anointing. In Capernaum the criticism is of Christ—if he had been a true prophet, he would have known the woman's sinfulness and not allowed her near him. In Bethany, the criticism is of the woman—the money might have been spent upon relieving the miseries of the poor (true, but Jesus reminded them that they had himself only briefly, the poor would be there for their charity for the rest of their lives).

If there *were* two anointings, were there two anointers? Was Mary of Bethany the "sinful woman" of the Capernaum scene? And was either (or both?) Mary Magdalen? The Gospels do not answer one question or the other. One can only record an impression that the two anointings were the work of one woman: the similarities are too great for coincidence—especially the utterly improbable drying of his feet with the woman's hair. Even the alabaster vase of Capernaum was surely the one used in Bethany—

never to be used a third time for, as Mark tells us, Mary broke the neck of it before pouring out the oil of nard.

Was Mary of Bethany Mary Magdalen? Glance at Jesus' answer to the criticism of her extravagance: it is given slightly differently by Matthew, Mark, and John: but in all it linked her act with the anointing of his body for burial. And Mary Magdalen was one of those who brought the ointment to the tomb—the ointment they did not need to use. Here in Bethany was the anointing for the burial.

37 *PALMS AND A FIG TREE*

The Passover was only six days away, Jerusalem was crammed with people. All the talk was of the raising of Lazarus from the dead. Everybody wanted to meet the miracle-worker—everybody but the chief priests who had decided to kill Lazarus along with the carpenter who had brought him back from the dead.

Ride into Jerusalem

On the Sunday morning Jesus began on the last two miles, taking the shorter way from Bethany, over the Mount of Olives. For the first time we see him riding—he was on a donkey. His enemies in the crowd must surely have remembered how that other son of David, Solomon, promised the kingship by his father, had come riding into the city from this same Mount of Olives.

The roads would have been thronged with the pilgrims who poured into the city for the great feast, from all Palestine, from all over the Roman world. His followers spread some of their garments on the donkey and others in the road in front of him. The excitement spread. Pilgrims cut branches from the trees and strewed them in the road. Meanwhile the news that he was on his way brought crowds out from Jerusalem to meet him, carrying palms.

The excitement grew toward frenzy, with the crowd shouting, "Hosannah to the Son of David. Blessed is he that comes in the name of the Lord. Hosannah in the highest. Blessed be the kingdom of our father David which is now coming." The Kingdom was indeed coming; he who was to come—the Messiah—was coming. At last. But the donkey should have warned them that it would not be the kingdom of their dreams—he was coming peaceably, not as for war.

As he came to the top of the Mount of Olives, where the descent began, Jerusalem lay before him. For the second time we hear of his weeping, seeing it so glorious there, seeing all that God had meant it to be, seeing what the Romans would do to it forty years later—"leaving in you", he cried to the city, "not a stone upon a stone". And why? "Because you have not known the time of your visitation". He had wept for Lazarus, whom he loved. He wept for Jerusalem, for he loved Jerusalem too.

Meanwhile the Pharisees were at a high point of fury. They could hardly argue with the crowds—the noise was too great, and all passions were running his way. But twice they urged him to do something about an uproar so unseemly. The first time he answered that if the people fell silent, the very stones in the road would cry out. The second time was after he had actually reached the Temple. The men in authority showed their indignation at finding children too shouting "Hosannah to the Son of David." Children, they felt, should be seen and not heard. So at times they should. But not always: there are moments when even the children must speak. Jesus quoted a verse of the Psalms (8:3)—"Out of the mouth of infants and of sucklings thou hast perfected praise."

Among the crowds were Gentiles, who had come to Jerusalem for the feast, proselytes probably, men who accepted the God of the Jews but had not had themselves circumcised. They wanted to see the cause of all the excitement and they approached Philip—he had a Greek name, he was from Bethsaida, a town where Jew and Gentile mixed and mingled, he would have spoken Greek (Jn

12:21). Philip consulted Andrew, and they told Jesus. Did he give the Gentiles their interview? John does not tell us.

For the crowds, Palm Sunday had been a full and frantic day. For the Twelve, too. But especially, and very differently, for two of them. The sound of thousands of voices shouting "Hosannah to the Son of David" must have made Peter feel the Kingdom very close to its establishment, and of that Kingdom he, Peter the fisherman, had been promised the keys. Judas, torn two ways, isolated in his own bleak thoughts, could not have shared the emotions of the others. If they glanced at him at all, they could only have been puzzled to see his look grow darker in concentration on the problem he could share with none of them. But perhaps he went off by himself to fight his solitary battle.

Gethsemane Foreshadowed

What did it all mean to Jesus himself? The uproar, probably, not much. He knew people too well. When he had fed five thousand people with five loaves and two fishes, they had wanted to make him King: but when the same people heard his teaching on the Blessed Eucharist they walked no more with him. Now they were in a frenzy of excitement because he had raised a man to life in what was practically a suburb of Jerusalem, but he knew how much hysteria was in their excitement.

They were thinking of his triumph. So was he. But *he* knew in what it would consist—for himself, for those who should follow him. He tried to tell this to the apostles (Jn 12:23)—"The hour is come for the Son of Man to be glorified"; but the entry into glory involves dying: leave a grain of wheat lying about and it remains simply that, a grain of wheat: it must be buried in the earth if it is to bring forth abundance of new life. That, he tells them, is the law for them too. They must not love this earthly life too much, for it must surely end; and, if it alone is loved, it will have no sequel of glory. "If any man minister to me, let him follow me; and where I am there also shall my servant be."

In all that had happened so far, Jesus had been the self we know, calm at the heart of a whirlwind. Then it is as though the horror to come flooded in on him. For this instant his control seemed close to breaking. Reading the Gospels we have seen him angry, seen him compassionate, seen him sorrowful, seen him grieving, but always master. For the first time we feel the mastery waver. Gethsemane was anticipated.

It is all in a single verse (Jn 12:27). "Now is my soul troubled" (compare with "My soul is sorrowful even unto death"). "Father, save me from this hour" (compare that with "Father, if thou wilt, remove this chalice from me"). Then, this time as in Gethsemane, comes resignation. "But for this cause I came unto this hour"—his whole life would have been stultified had that petition of a moment ago been granted: he would have been a grain of wheat which remained only that. But in his death, he would be made life-giving.

"Father," he cried, "glorify thy name." We note that he does not say glorify *my* name but *thine*. The Father was to be shown glorious in the Son's glory. And a voice came from the sky: "I have both glorified it and will glorify it again." Our Lord's next words were all of triumph. The moment of crisis was at hand, the supremely decisive moment for the whole world, never one like it before, never again to be one. For Satan's time as world ruler would be ended, with Christ raised on the Cross to be the vital center of a new humanity. "Now is the judgment of the world: now shall the prince of this world be cast out. And I, lifted up from the earth, will draw all things unto me."

As Palm Sunday ended, Jesus went back to spend the night at Bethany. Of the next four days—until the night of Holy Thursday— Saint John tells us nothing; we read of them in the other three Gospels. Even as to Palm Sunday these give one episode not in Saint John's account of the day.

They describe the scourging of the moneychangers and the sellers of sacrificial animals out of the great courtyard of the Temple. Saint John had placed an episode exactly similar at the beginning of the public life, just after the marriage at Cana (Jn 2:15). Did Jesus cleanse the Temple twice, or was John tacitly correcting the other three by placing the episode, single and unrepeated, where it properly belonged? We cannot be certain. But it does seem at least probable that had so startling a defiance of constituted authority happened in the very week of Jesus' arrest, there would have been some mention of it when they were examining him: and the high priest would hardly have needed any other pretext for his arrest.

The Fig Tree

On the Monday morning, on the way into Jerusalem, he did something very puzzling. He was hungry, we are told (Mt 21:18); they came to a fig tree, green in its leaves but with no figs. And he laid a curse upon it—it should never again bear fruit. Immediately the tree withered away; when they passed that way the following morning it had dried up from the roots (Mk 11:20).

Even told thus, it seems an aimless display of power—hard on the tree's owner, hard to defend. But Mark adds a detail which might at first strike us as lifting the incident outside the borders of rationality altogether—he tells us it was not the season for figs! So feeling, we should be wrong. Jesus was teaching by parable, not telling it but acting it. The point of the fig tree parable is the damnableness of an outward show of religion with none of the fruit of religion, which is the love of God and man.

He was teaching not about fig trees but about men. And it is always the season for men. There is no off-season in which it would be against the order of nature for men to do their duty to God or their fellows. There is something here not altogether unlike the condemnation passed upon Satan after the Fall of our first parents— that henceforth he should go on his belly. How could a pure spirit go on his belly? But God was talking to Satan in serpent language. And our Lord is warning men in fig-tree language.

The Twelve could make nothing of the incident. Peter, for them all, asked what it meant. What Jesus may have answered as to the meaning, we are not told. Matthew and Mark simply record his promise that they themselves should do things more spectacular than willing a tree to its destruction, provided only that they had faith. A mountain would cast itself into the sea at their command, so long as there was no weakening in their faith—no

staggering in their heart, says the Douay version. We get this
phrase only in Mark (11:23): Mark got it from Peter himself, who
would never have forgotten how his own heart staggered so soon
after.

38 *PHARISEES, SADDUCEES, AND HERODIANS*

Between Palm Sunday and Holy Thursday, Sadducees, Herodians,
and Pharisees all intruded their questions into Jesus' teaching in
the Temple. They had decided on his death, but they must still be
at him.

Whose Wife Should She Be?

The incident of the Sadducees is curious. At a moment when they
had united with their enemies the Pharisees to bring Christ to
death, they put him a question about the resurrection of the dead,
a matter on which the Pharisees were against them and with Jesus.
Basing themselves on the Mosaic law (Dt 25:5) that if a married
man died without children, his brother must marry the wife and
beget a son who should count as the dead man's, they posed a
problem of seven brothers, six of them dying childless, so that all
seven had to marry the wife in turn. If there really was a resurrection (which Sadducees denied), whose wife should she be?

Jesus' answer to the immediate problem was that in heaven
there would be no marrying, no sexual union (this would have
startled a good many Pharisees): the citizens of heaven would be
immortal and would need no new generation to take their place:
in this matter, they would be as the angels (Lk 20:34–36). Saint
Luke seems to emphasize—with the words "They that shall be

accounted worthy of that world"—that Jesus is restricting his answer to the souls of the just. Nothing is said of the damned, and we are left wondering if in some way lust may continue to add one more horror to hell.

He answered not only the special problem, but the general question of resurrection—not only the manner of it (with his reference to angels, of whom also the Sadducees had their doubts) but also the fact of it. God had called himself "the God of Abraham and Isaac and Jacob" (Ex 3:6): the living God would not have proclaimed himself the God of three dead men, three no longer existent men, three memories. Some of the scribes among them—for the Sadducees had their scribes as well as the Pharisees— were moved to something that sounds like agreement.

Tribute to Caesar?

As hecklers, the Herodians, working closely with the Pharisees, were more on the spot. The Sadducees were really concerned with the doctrinal point, these others wanted "to ensnare him in his speech", to drive him into a statement for which he could be handed over to the Roman procurator. They began with a loaded compliment—that he might be relied upon to tell the truth without concern for whom he might offend or the cost to himself (Lk 20:21). Then came the question: "Is it lawful for us to give tribute to Caesar?"

Of all the questions ever asked him, this one had been chosen with the most care. If he said yes, then he would certainly alienate the mass of the Jews who, to the normal human dislike of paying taxes to anybody, added a patriotic loathing for having to admit the rule of foreigners by paying tribute. If he said no, then they could hand him over to Pontius Pilate at once, with the certainty that he would be put to death. Upon no subject were the Romans more sensitive.

Jesus refused the trap. He demanded that they show him one of the coins in which the tribute was paid. And when it was brought he made them answer his question—"Whose image and inscription does it bear?" There could be only one answer—Caesar's.

And it was a coin that all of them used, not the strictest of them dared face death by refusal of the tribute. Then came his summing up—"Render therefore to Caesar the things that are Caesar's and to God the things that are God's."

There are two elements here: an immediate element, and a profounder. Caesar was the ruler, hated but legitimate, of Palestine: even the Pharisees had asked for a Roman procurator instead of the murderous Archelaus. That was the answer to the question actually asked. But the words go far deeper. Caesar has powers, of course: he can take what he wants. But now we hear from the words of the Man who was God that Caesar has *rights.* Whatever the civil authority requires for the proper conduct of society, to that it has a right—Christ says so; in the truest sense, therefore, it is a divine right.

And this our Lord could say just a few days before Caesar crucified him.

By What Authority?

This time it was a powerful group—"the chief priests and the scribes, with the elders"—that publicly challenged Jesus in those last days before Calvary to tell by what authority he acted as he did (Mt 21:23, Mk 11:28, Lk 20:2). "Chief priests" means the most influential, not the high priest himself, but men who had held that office, along with members of the rich Sadducee families from whom high priests were chosen. We shall find the same group again—chief priests and scribes and elders—at the interrogation of Jesus on the night of his arrest, accusing him before Pilate and before Herod, deriding him on Calvary. He answered with a question which put them in the same kind of dilemma as the Herodians had meant to put him in. He asked them—was John's baptism from heaven?

The Baptist's popularity was vast, and they dared not say no at a moment when everything for them depended upon winning the people to their side. But they could not say yes without condemning themselves for not having accepted him and his baptism. There was only one possibility left: they said they didn't know. Jesus answered that if they would not tell him about John's authority, he would not tell them about his own. It was not simply an evasion. He was certain (and in this he could rely upon carrying most of the ordinary people with him) that it was only a willful refusal that kept them from admitting that John had been sent by God. His own sending was clearer still, for he had worked miracles, as John never did. There was no point in offering light to a blindness so determined.

But what he was suggesting about himself was not as disturbing as what he had to say about them, the rulers of his people. He followed their admission that they did not know about John's baptism by the parable of the two sons (Mt 21:28) who had been ordered by their father to work in his vineyard. One said he would not, but did, all the same. The other agreed at once, but did not. His hearers admitted that it was the first, for all his initial refusal, who did his father's will.

Then he said the most crushing thing yet: "The publicans and the harlots shall go into the Kingdom of heaven before you"— because these outcasts, the moral scum of Israel, the ones who had at first said No, had believed John, while the religious leaders neither believed him nor repented at his urging. Things technically worse than this Christ had said and would say, things that seemed to them blasphemous, whereas this was not blasphemy. But to place publicans and harlots before them was the ultimate in insult: there was no further for insult to go.

Jesus Tells His Slayers

Talking thus, he was rushing on his death. In the parable of the wicked husbandmen, *he* told *them* that they would kill him. Read the parable (Lk 20, Mk 12, Mt 21). In the one just quoted about the two sons he had spoken of the vineyard, a regular metaphor for God's chosen people. Yet the word need mean no more than a literal vineyard, a place where grapes grow. Now he uses vineyard again, but leaves no doubt that he is referring this time to Israel—he describes the hedge built round it, the place dug for the juice to flow, the winepress, the tower. It is almost a verbal quotation from Isaiah 5. So read that too. His hearers had read it. They knew that in the parable they were now hearing, the owner of the vineyard was God; they themselves, like their fathers before them, were the husbandmen, the vinegrowers to whom God has entrusted Israel.

Jesus told how the owner sent his servants from time to time: the vinegrowers began by beating and otherwise maltreating them, went on to kill them—the Old Testament has prophets slain by the Jews themselves. So the Lord of the vineyard said, "I will send my beloved son: it may be when they see him, they will reverence him." Him too they killed.

In the fifth chapter Isaiah gives as fierce an indictment of the leaders of the chosen people as any that Jesus was ever to utter.

"Alas," he says, "it is the house of Israel that the Lord called his vineyard; the men of Judah are the plot he loved so. He looked to find right reason there, and all was treason; to find plain dealing, and he heard only the plaint of the oppressed." The vineyard was growing not grapes, but wild grapes only. God's justice would visit the vineyard: "I mean to make wasteland of it; no more pruning and digging; only briars and thorns will grow there, and I will forbid the clouds to water it." God's justice would visit the men in charge of the vineyard: "The abyss hungers for you, opens its greedy jaws, till all alike, the nobles of Zion and her common sort, that boast and triumph now, go down to its depths."

Pharisees and Sadducees could read the chapter with reasonable calm—their fathers had sinned and been punished for it, but it was all eight centuries ago. Not so calmly could they listen to the parable. For the carpenter from Nazareth was applying it to themselves—"they knew that he spoke of them." A like doom, he threatened, awaited the Israel of now, their Israel. Their fathers had slain the prophets. That they did not deny. But Christ was claiming to be greater than the prophets, not God's messenger but God's own Son, and he told them to their face that they would slay him too.

Worse, he took two Old Testament prophecies in which especially they gloried, and applied these to himself, not to them. In each the word "stone" was the key word.

The first reference was to "the stone which the builders rejected" (Ps 118:22) but which became the cornerstone of a mightier building. In the Psalm it means the Jewish people, rejected by the Gentiles but destined to triumph over them. That particular Psalm was a song of victory, the last of those songs of praise which the Jews sang at the end of the Passover meal: Jesus and the apostles sang them as they left the supper room for Gethsemane. But he was clearly meaning himself as the stone that the Jews rejected, which would be the cornerstone of a building they had never dreamed of—the stone of Isaiah (28:16) which Qumran identified with the council of its own community. "The Kingdom of God shall be taken from you, and shall be given to a people which yields the revenues that belong to it"—the new people shall use their place in the Kingdom for God's profit, not their own.

The second of these infuriating references was to the "stone no hands had quarried" (Dan 2:34–45) which should grind to powder the empires of this world and bring into being "another empire, never to be destroyed, never to be superseded, conqueror of all those others, itself unconquerable". This, too, they had taken to be their own Israel: Christ is telling them that it is his new Kingdom, against which they themselves will come into conflict to their own undoing, and which will grind to powder those who finally reject it.

The Hostile Minority

When Jesus had finished the parable he asked the crowd a question. What would the Lord of the vineyard do?

The various answers are a reminder that the crowd contained many elements. For some answered (Mt 21:41) that he would bring the evil men to an evil end and give the vineyard to others, who would run it for the owner's profit. Clearly they had not realized that the vineyard was Israel itself—if they had ever read the fifth chapter of Isaiah, they had forgotten it. Those who did realize reacted very differently: on hearing from Jesus that the men in possession would be destroyed and the vineyard given to others, they cried, "God forbid." Yet those seem not to have questioned the justice of that doom.

There was a third element, the leaders—the chief priests who were Sadducees and the scribes who were mostly Pharisees. They knew exactly what he was saying about the vineyard, about himself, and about them. They would have arrested him there and then (Lk 20:19), only that they feared the crowd would not tolerate it. They must wait for a better occasion.

We should note the distinction, in this matter of hostility to Christ, drawn between the leaders and the Jewish people. The Sadducees, who held the high priesthood, were men of wealth and power, in numbers a tiny minority as the richest always are. The Pharisees were a spiritual elite, they also were small in numbers, as spiritual elites tend to be! The population of Palestine at that time may have been about two million. The Jewish historian Josephus says that the Pharisees numbered about six thousand. How many of these were really hostile to our Lord we have no means of knowing—Nicodemus was not, Joseph of Arimathea was not, and we know that a number of Pharisees became Christians. What is certain is that it was a very tiny percentage of the Jews of Palestine who determined that Jesus must die, and put pressure on Pilate to execute him.

Against this minority Jesus had spoken throughout his public career and seems to have spoken with special vehemence in these last days (though Matthew, who quotes his attacks upon them at greatest length, may here be putting together in one place things said by Jesus at different times). It was against the Pharisees that he raged. The eight woes he launches against them (Mt 23) remind us of the six woes of Isaiah in that same chapter 5. But Isaiah's were directed mainly against the rich and powerful, the sort of men, in fact, who would later be Sadducees. Jesus, on the other hand, has not much to say against the Sadducees. They seem to have been worse men, but not so dangerous, precisely because they were not much concerned with teaching: men of power are not in the long run as dangerous as teaching men.

As we read, we find the attack concentrated mainly upon pride and hypocrisy. What he is drawing is the classic portrait of the hypocrite wherever he may be found, and he tends to be found in all societies where religion is held in high honor. A century after this time, we find Pharisees themselves attacking the very faults in their members that Jesus stigmatizes here—some of them even use the phrase "pharisaic plagues". The Catholic Church too has had its share of them. Fortunate the religion that has not.

There is not so much here about Pharisaism as distinct from the sins of Pharisees, not as much as we have heard earlier from Jesus about the emphasis on the external and the verbal in itself, but only about its fantastic exaggerations. As an institution, he sees the Pharisees as keeping men out of the Kingdom of God, themselves not entering. In the best of them, as Paul says (Rom 10:2), there was zeal for God's honor; it was their understanding that was wrong. But there were among them men of no zeal: we have heard what Jesus calls them—"whitewashed sepulchres, which outwardly appear to men beautiful, but within are full of dead men's bones and of all filthiness".

39 *A CHAPTER OF ENDINGS*

The End of the Temple

We are still on the Tuesday of the first Holy Week. Jesus had uttered the decisive parable about the vineyard, Mark and Luke go on to the incident of the widow's mite. They show Jesus as sitting in an inner court of the Temple, facing the treasury. He watched rich and poor come in to make their offerings. One of these was a poor widow who cast in "two brass mites". Our Lord said, "This poor widow has cast in more than all of them. For all the others cast in of their abundance: but she of her want, and she has cast in all the living that she had" (Lk 21:3).

Matthew—shy about money, perhaps—does not mention this incident. Instead he gives that much lengthier outpouring against the Pharisees which we have already discussed. He concludes it with a phrase which Saint Luke placed earlier: "Jerusalem, Jerusalem, you that kill the prophets and stone those who are sent unto you, how often would I have gathered together your children, as the hen gathers her brood under her wings, and you would not have it. Behold, your house shall be left to you, desolate."

We are reminded of the tears Jesus had shed for Jerusalem on Palm Sunday morning, as he came over the brow of the hill from Bethany. So, probably, were his apostles: but what held their minds most strongly was the reference to the house—surely (as they felt) the Temple—which was to be left desolate.

On each of these last five nights Jesus left the city as the day was ending. This time he went to the Mount of Olives, intending to spend the night in the place where, two nights later, Judas and the Temple guard would find him. The apostles, still shaken by the threat to the Temple, begged him to look at it, as it stood there all glorious. Obviously they hoped that he would say that he had not quite meant that about its destruction. His answer left them no gleam of hope: "There shall not be left here a stone upon a stone that shall not be destroyed" (Mt 24:2).

The End of Jerusalem and the End of the World

Later, as he sat on the slope of the hill looking towards the city, four of the apostles—the inevitable three plus Andrew—asked him when this would happen, and what would be the sign that it was about to happen—and also, as Matthew tells us, the sign of his own Coming and "of the consummation of the world". As to "when", the answer was brief: "Of that day or hour no man knows, neither the angels in heaven, nor the Son, but the Father" (Mk 13:32). But upon the sign or signs which should herald it, Jesus gives one of his longest discourses, longest and most mysterious. Matthew, Mark, and Luke all give it. We shall follow Matthew (the whole of chapters 24 and 25). It would be well to read these chapters before reading the very sketchy commentary I shall make.

The first forty-four verses of chapter 24 which treat of the destruction of Jerusalem, our Lord's Coming and the end of the world, are the most difficult to sort out. After that, he talks of the preparation that each one of us must make for death (which is the end of our own private and particular world); then goes on to his judgment of the human race at the end of all. For the moment we must look at those troubling forty-four verses.

They have two main themes. One is the destruction of Jerusalem, the other is the end of the world, with the Coming of Christ linked to one or the other. Great scholars and great saints have differed as to where the division comes between one theme and the other; some indeed holding that there is no actual line of division, but that the themes are interwoven, with an occasional verse referring clearly to one of them, many verses referring to both at once.

The destruction of Jerusalem and its Temple Jesus clearly foretold—the Temple which Herod had begun in 20 B.C., fifty years before, and to which the last touches were not to be put till 64 A.D. Six years after that it was destroyed, and the city with it.

Jesus had another theme as he sat on the Mount of Olives looking towards the city. He spoke of the end of the world and of his own Coming. Again there are differences of opinion. What is meant by the end of the world? The Greek phrase could mean all that the English words suggest to us—the end of our whole cosmos; but could equally mean the end of the particular era in which men were then living, the final liquidation of the era of Jewish preeminence in God's plan. This latter possibility is at least hinted at by the phrase "All these are the beginnings of sorrows" (Mt 24:8)—because the word translated "sorrows" actually means "birth pangs", and suggests that a new era is being born.

The language Jesus used of his Coming suggests the end of the created universe—sun and moon darkened, stars falling from heaven, the Son of Man coming in the clouds with great power and glory, angels with trumpets, the elect gathered from the four winds. But in the Old Testament such splendor of language is normally used to describe any great intervention of God. Read indeed how Peter, quoting the prophet Joel, uses similar language when describing to the crowd to whom he preached on the day of Pentecost the great event of the Church's emergence—"Wonders in heaven above, and signs in the earth beneath, blood and fire and whirling smoke; the sun turned into darkness and the moon into blood" (Acts 2:19). His hearers did not turn their eyes upward to check Peter's statements: they knew about the language of prophecy.

There are those who think Jesus was speaking of his Coming at the end of the world to judge all mankind. There are those who think he was speaking of his coming to a new level of activity in his Kingdom on earth. Perhaps he meant both, the one fundamentally related to the other, the same principles in operation in each.

The End of Each Man's Life

With the end of his own earthly life so close, his mind was much upon endings. He had talked of the end of Jerusalem, the end of the age, the end of the world. He went on to talk of the end of each man's life. Death is for each of us an end of the world: and the things he says of the end for all mankind and the end for each individual are largely interchangeable.

What he has principally to say of our own death is that we should always be ready for it, for we never know at what moment it will come. That is the moral of the parable about the five sensible girls and the five silly ones. The story is based upon the wedding customs of that time and place. It is not easy for us to reconstruct; but, it being the custom for the bridegroom to come to the bride's house and lead her processionally to his own, it looks as if these girls were attendants on the bride, waiting with her. Something delayed the bridegroom, they all drowsed off: the lamps which they had to carry in the procession burned out. The five sensible girls had brought an extra supply of oil, the others had not: these others therefore could not go in the procession, and were excluded from the wedding feast.

The wedding merely provided a framework for the truths the parable was meant to convey. As a framework, it was soon discarded. Jesus is clearly talking of his own coming to the individual soul at death to lead it to the eternal banquet, and of the terrifying urgency for the soul that it be in a state of grace, and thus capable of banqueting with him. He had already, as we have seen, talked of himself as the Bridegroom (Mt 9:15): now he did it again. To any Jew, what he was claiming was quite unmistakable—for God himself was Israel's Bridegroom (note Isaiah 54:6).

What Jesus has to tell of the judgment—"when the Son of Man shall come in his majesty, and all nations shall be gathered together before him, and the sheep shall be separated from the goats"—is all to be found in the last sixteen verses of Matthew 25. These verses—with their "Depart from me, ye cursed, into the everlasting fire that was prepared for the devil and his angels"—could be discussed, inadequately, in a long book. Here we note one single thing: men shall be judged according to the way they have treated their fellow men. Indeed the good and the evil they have done to the very least of our Lord's brethren they have done to him. In some mysterious way he is present in all, treated rightly in all, maltreated in all. One other thing we may not have noted— for the first time Jesus speaks of himself as "the king".

The End of the Road for Judas

It was on the evening of the last Tuesday before Calvary that Jesus, before lying down to sleep on the Mount of Olives, talked so mysteriously of the end of Jerusalem and the end of the world. It may very well be that he was at the end of his own public ministry too. There is no suggestion that he came into the Temple on Wednesday. We get nothing at all about the happenings of Wednesday, except as they concern Judas. Matthew and Mark, indeed, tell the story of the anointing with precious ointment from the alabaster box, and the protest of Judas so instantly dismissed by his Master, immediately before telling of the betrayal which took place on the Wednesday. One imagines that Matthew and Mark put the story here in order to link Judas' resentment at the public rebuke with his betrayal of Christ, which *did* take place on the Wednesday. There was indeed a connection between the two, but there had been four days between, to allow the resentment to fester.

Matthew, Mark, and Luke all tell of the betrayal. The Passover was only two days away. The chief priests and scribes were in continual discussion as to how they might bring about the arrest and slaying of Jesus. Their problem was that he was so popular with so many of the people—not all, but enough to make a riot possible: they dared not act against him publicly, especially at a time when Jerusalem was crammed to bursting point with pilgrims who had come for the Passover. Yet it was precisely this massing together of people which would make it possible for Jesus to stir the sort of tumult that would bring the Roman soldiery into action—we know that the Romans increased their guards in the city every year at Passover as a normal precautionary measure.

Priests and scribes were talking in the palace of the High Priest Caiaphas, when there came to them a man who could solve at least part of their problem—the problem of arresting the troublemaker without causing a riot: for this man knew where Jesus would be spending the night!

What moved Judas to the act which has ensured that his name would be known till the world ends?—even enemies of Christ automatically call a traitor Judas. "Satan entered into him" (Lk 22:3)—which is consoling, as far as it goes; to see Satan bringing about the death which would be his own destruction is a reminder that he is not omniscient and can make the most startling misjudgments as to his own best interests, which are never our best interests. Apart from that we have Judas' resentment at the curt dismissal of his protest; and we have Saint John telling us that he was a thief, who handled—and therefore, one presumes, had mishandled—the small funds of the apostles.

All the same he remains profoundly mysterious.

Observe that the officials answered his question "How much?" by giving him "thirty pieces of silver". Exodus (21:32) had appointed this sum to be paid to the owner of a slave who had been gored to death by another man's ox—the penalty where a member of the family was slain was death: so that the price fixed now could hardly have been more contemptuous. And Judas took it. We are told that it was worth 120 denarii: and the vase of ointment whose waste had so upset Judas had been worth 300! If resentment was the motive, why did he so eagerly ask about the price he was to be paid? If he was small enough to sell his Lord for so little, how account for the remorse which led him to suicide when he realized that Christ was to be slain? The truth is that there is too much about Judas—the man of Kerioth, the only non-Galilean among the Twelve—that we do not know. So long before, Jesus had seen something in him that has not been shown to us, when he said (Jn 6:71), "I have chosen you Twelve, and one of you is a devil."

PART THREE

Redemption

"The Son of Man did not come to have service done him; he came to serve others, and to give his life as a ransom for the lives of many."

(Mt 20:28)

"I am come that they may have life and have it more abundantly."

(Jn 10:10)

40 *THE LAST SUPPER*

The Passover

On a Friday the Savior was crucified. On the Thursday night he celebrated the Passover with the apostles—"the first day of the unleavened bread when they sacrificed the Pasch", Saint Mark calls it; Saint Matthew uses a similar phrase; Saint Luke calls it "the day of the unleavened bread, on which it was necessary that the Pasch should be killed". For all three, it seems clear that the Passover was on Friday, beginning at sunset on Thursday and ending at the next sunset. The difficulty is that Saint John says that the Jews who were forcing Pilate to crucify their Master regarded the Passover as on Saturday, beginning therefore at sunset on the Friday.

Was the Passover, then, observed on different days, by different groups? It seems that this is a possibility. We know that Pharisees and Sadducees calculated Pentecost differently, the Pharisees beginning their count of fifty days from the day after Passover, the Sadducees from a Saturday, whether the Saturday of the Passover itself, or the first Saturday after it. The Sadducees held the high priesthood, and could issue the calendar for the year. It has been suggested that when the Passover fell on a Friday, they would move it to the Saturday, so that for that year at least they and the Pharisees would be celebrating Pentecost on the same day. Thus it may be that for the Pharisees the Passover began at sunset on Thursday, for the Sadducees one day later.

There are those who think that Galilee may have observed Passover a day ahead of Judea. And recently we read of the discovery of a calendar used by the Essenes. It was based on the sun, not the moon. If Jesus had used this, the supper would have taken place on the Tuesday, not the Thursday, leaving the Wednesday and Thursday for the examination and trial, with condemnation pronounced and sentence executed on the Friday.

All these seem possible explanations. We cannot be certain of any of them. Anyhow it is clear that what Christ himself and the Twelve celebrated on that night was the Passover, not any kind of ritual supper, but the Passover itself. Earlier in the day he sent Peter and John with the words "Go and prepare for us the pasch, that we may eat." The instructions must have struck them as mysterious—read them in Matthew 26:18, Mark 14:12–16, Luke 22:10–13.

They were to go into the city and meet a man carrying a pitcher of water. We might think the directions lacked precision; but in fact it was usually the women who carried pitchers of water, a man thus diminishing his dignity would be instantly observable. They were to give this man a message from their Master: "Where is my guest-chamber, where I may eat the pasch with my disciples?" And Christ told them that the man would show them a large dining room furnished, and there they would make the preparations. It seems clear that the man, though not known to the apostles, was a friend of their Master. Since we know that after the Ascension the apostles would meet in the house of Mark's mother, it seems not a fantastic guess that the man with the pitcher was a servant in her house.

The evening came and the thirteen gathered round the table. For Catholics, this meal stands out above all the meals that men have ever eaten together, because of the institution of the Blessed Eucharist, and because at it John shows Christ giving his fullest teaching on the Blessed Trinity and on the Church as his Mystical Body. But it is memorable also for the cold realism of his vision of the Church as a society of men, with all their failings thick upon them—yet loved by him.

All four evangelists give us an account of the Last Supper— Matthew 26:20–35, Mark 14:17–31, Luke 22:14–38, John 13–17.

Not one of them sets out to tell everything that happened. The first three total only fifty-six verses among them. Saint John adds thirty-eight verses of description, followed by three chapters of Christ's discourse. In fact each is writing his own Gospel; from the great mass of things said and things done, each makes his own selection of the handful that specially concern him as writer of his own particular book.

Nor are they concerned, at this point any more than elsewhere in the story, with the order in which things happened. Sufficient for them—and for us—that Christ did these things and said these things. In what I have to say of the Last Supper I shall be moving from one Gospel to another.

Saint John and Saint Luke introduce the meal most solemnly. Saint John says (13:1): "Jesus, knowing that his hour was come, that he should pass out of this world to the Father, having loved his own who were in the world, loved them to the end"—the Greek means not to the end of his life but to the limit of his loving power.

Saint Luke quotes Jesus as saying (Lk 22:15-16): "With desire I have desired to eat this pasch with you. From this time I will not eat it till it be fulfilled in the Kingdom of God...." In these words of our Lord there were depths and heights immeasurable. But for the moment the minds of the apostles were not upon them. He had used the word "Kingdom": and that word always touched a nerve in them. Their impatient expectation of the Kingdom's establishment had become an obsession.

Greatness in the Kingdom

The hearing of the word was enough to account for the surprising thing Luke tells us—"There was a strife among them which of them was to be accounted the greatest." The strife, indeed, may already have begun over the placing at table: to see John sitting next to Christ might well have reminded them of their fury at the demand for places on his right and on his left that John and his brother James (or their mother for them) had made so recently. There is something pathetic about such an argument among men who a few hours later would be running for their lives. But argue they did, and their Lord's reactions to their rivalry fill a great part of the meal.

The point actually at issue he settled once for all. Greatness would certainly be theirs: in the Kingdom allotted to him by his Father they should sit on thrones, judging the twelve tribes of Israel—that is, the Church, which Saint Paul would call the Israel of God (Gal 6:16). Through them he would rule his Kingdom. But to one was reserved the highest function, by which all should benefit.

"Satan", he told them, "has desired to have you that he may sift you as wheat"—run them through his fingers, leaving the winds of false doctrine to scatter them, the most disruptive of winds. Christ's answer to Satan's design for their scattering was Simon Peter. "Simon, Simon, I have prayed for thee that thy faith fail not: and thou, being once converted, confirm thy brethren" (Lk 22:32). God would guard Peter's faith, false doctrine would never come in through him; Peter's faith would support theirs.

The question who among them should be the first really was settled now. It never rose again. But Jesus was concerned with a profounder question—not only which of them should be the greatest but in what does greatness in his Kingdom consist. He had said it before, now Luke has him saying it again. Greatness was not splendor, not glory in the sight of men. In fact, it was not glory at all. It meant work to be done, a function to be performed necessary for the conduct of the Kingdom. The essence of the function was to serve. The leaders *must* see themselves as servants of the whole group down to its lowliest member, themselves valuable only in so far as they were good servants. He illustrated what he had been saying by a parable, an acted parable. He washed their feet (Jn 13:4–16).

He rose from supper, took off his outer garment, tied a towel about his waist, put water into a basin, washed their feet, and wiped them with the towel. It was the most servile action imaginable. Peter, of course, objected: "Thou shalt never wash my feet." The answer is terse, and, because terse, not easy to understand—"If I do not wash you, you shall have no part with me." The meaning perhaps is that unless Peter realizes that there is no service too menial for the ruler to perform, he is not fit to be ruler himself.

Peter instantly went to the other extreme—"Lord, not only my feet but also my hands and my head." Our Lord was again terse, but this time the meaning was clear. Peter should have washed himself properly before he came: only the sandaled feet could be excused for having picked up dust on the journey. Then, with one of those swift changes from one level of meaning to another level, he goes on: "And you are clean, but not all of you." He is not thinking of the body now, but of the heart. Saint John continues, "for he knew who he was that would betray him"—Judas, whose feet he had washed with the rest.

Judas Goes into the Night

All four evangelists tell us of our Lord's saying at the Last Supper that one of the apostles was about to betray him. He knew which of them it was. Judas knew. The rest did not. Nor did they get any immediate light. They saw that their Master was "troubled in spirit", so that clearly his talk of betrayal was not just a figure of speech which might turn out to mean something quite different.

The apostles—including Judas himself—asked, "Is it I, Lord?" With everybody speaking at once, it seems that none but Judas heard Christ's answer: "Thou hast said it." He would use those same words to the high priest asking him if he was the Christ, the Son of God, and to Pilate asking him if he was the King of the Jews.

To the whole group at the table he said that the traitor was "one of the Twelve, who dips his hand with me in the dish". There were a number of dishes on the table, containing the sauce of dates and raisins that ritual required—so those further down the table could breathe again. The traitor must be one of the three or four nearest to him. He went on: "The Son of Man indeed goes, according to that which is determined: but yet, woe to that man by whom he shall be betrayed." So reports Luke. Matthew and Mark add: "It would be better for that man if he had never been born."

It might indeed have been better for Satan, too, if Judas had never been born. He gained nothing but only lost by what he prompted Judas to do. Two years before, after his efforts at tempting Jesus in the desert, Satan "departed from him *for a time*", or better *"until the time"* (Lk 4:13). That time came (Lk 22:3) when

Satan entered into Judas and moved him to approach the chief priests with his offer to betray his Master.

Peter—anxious to know which of the three or four closest was the betrayer but not wanting to risk another snub (like the one he had had about the foot-washing) by asking Jesus—made a sign to John, to find out if he knew. Had Jesus been leaning forward, this particular piece of by-play could have happened behind his back. John, whose head was very close to our Lord's breast, asked him the question: "Lord, who is it?"

Jesus answered that it would be the one to whom he would offer bread dipped in the special sauce—one near him, therefore. It was, and still is, a way of honoring a guest in the East thus to dip bread or meat or herbs into sauce and offer the morsel to him. Jesus did precisely that to Judas, but only John read anything into the gesture. Even Judas, probably, did not grasp what it meant. But "after the morsel, Satan entered into him", and he went out immediately. As he went, Jesus said to him, "What you do, do quickly." The others heard the words, but thought only that Judas was being sent on some errand.

So Judas went out into the night. He had refused his last chance.

The Blessed Eucharist

"Judas went out immediately. And it was night" (Jn 13:30). Jesus seemed to feel that the room was better for his going. There is almost exultation in the words he uttered: "Now is the Son of Man glorified, and God is glorified in him." With the one hating element removed, he could say: "As I have loved you, do you also love one another. By this shall all men know that you are my disciples, if you have love one for another."

He could hardly have said that with Judas in the room. Yet how, we wonder, with the immediate future clear in his mind, could he have said it at all? Certainly he was in no doubt as to the way the men around him, the men he loved, were so soon to behave. As they were leaving the supper room he would say: "Tonight you will all lose courage over me; for so it has been written, I will smite the shepherd and the sheep of his flock will be scattered" (Mt 26:31).

Peter asserted that, whatever the rest might do, he at least would never lose courage—"Lord, I am ready to go with thee both into prison and to death." Mark, Peter's disciple, reports the answer he got: "Today, even in this night, before the cock crows twice, you will deny me thrice." The others were as vehement as Peter in their assertion that they would die with their Master rather than deny him. But, when the moment came, they all ran as they had been told they would; Peter denied him, as he had been told he would. And these were the men, so clearly known by him in their weakness, to whom he entrusted that very night the sacrament of his own Body and Blood. We read about it in Matthew, Mark, and Luke; and in Paul's First Epistle to the Corinthians (17:23–5), the first written account we have.

A year before in Capernaum, as Saint John tells us—do reread his sixth chapter before continuing with this—they had heard him say half a dozen times over that unless they ate his flesh and drank his blood they would not have life in them. "He that eats me", he had said, "shall live by me." Many of his followers left him at that, feeling that such talk was not only insane but, in so far as it had a meaning, was monstrous, revolting. Would the Twelve go too? Peter answered, "Lord, to whom shall we go? Thou hast the words of eternal life." It was sheerest, blindest faith. Peter had no more notion than anybody else what it might mean, this eating of their Master; but somehow it *could* not be insane, not be monstrous, not be abominable. Somehow.

But how? They must have talked about it among themselves, as about many things. But only one of their conversations in his absence has come down to us, and that, we feel, we would not have missed if it had not—it was about which of them should be greatest.

And now, here it was. He had said in Capernaum that they must eat his flesh: now he gave them bread he had blessed, saying: "Take and eat, this is my Body which is given for you." He had said that they must drink his Blood: now he gave them wine he had blessed, saying: "Drink ye all of this, for this is my Blood of the new covenant, which shall be shed for many unto the remission of sins." So the question *How* was at last answered. It was not monstrous, it was not abominable, but was it sane? Had it *any* meaning?

"This", he had said, "is my Body." It had been bread, it still looked like bread—tasted, felt, smelled like bread—but it was not bread any more. It had become Christ's Body. If he had said *Here* is my Body, there would have been no such difficulty: in some way that they could not see, his Body would have been there *too,* but the bread would still have been bread (very much Luther's consubstantiation, in fact). The word he used however was *This*—this that he held in his hand, bread if ever they had seen bread.

For them at this first hearing, as for believers ever since, the test of faith lay less in believing that his Body was there than in believing that bread was *not* there. Was it possible? Peter, at least, must have had his answer ready, for he had said it a year before: "Thou hast the words of eternal life." If Jesus said it, it was so. But this time there was something further—"Do this in commemoration of me." What he had done, they must do. They could hardly have been very clear yet what it was that he *had* done, that they must do.

For most of us, perhaps, the Last Supper means the establishment of the Blessed Eucharist. And, indeed, even if that were all, it would still be vast. But there was much teaching besides. Read most carefully chapters 14 to 17 of Saint John's Gospel. Not to have made them wholly ours is to have impoverished ourselves intolerably. Chapter 14 ends "Arise, let us go", which links with the opening words of chapter 18, "When Jesus had said these things he went forth with his disciples." There are scholars who think that chapters 15 to 17 contain teachings given by our Lord at various times and brought together here by the evangelist. If so, we can only rejoice at the inspiration which moved him thus to assemble them.

In the discourse as he records it, we find the greatest body of teaching Christ ever gave on the Trinity. This was especially to the point here, for two reasons—because the Holy Spirit was soon to be sent, and because the redemption was soon to be accomplished.

Neither the sending nor the redeeming would be comprehensible apart from the doctrine of the Trinity.

The Holy Spirit. The apostles were desolate as their Lord told them that he must leave them and go to the Father. They could hardly have found much immediate consolation in the reason he gave for going: "It is expedient for you that I go: for if I go not, the Paraclete will not come to you" (Jn 16:7). Only as they came to know the truth about the Trinity better would light come about the gain to their own souls from this replacement of the person they knew and loved by a person they had merely heard of. Could they even be sure that the Holy Spirit *was* a person?

The Redemption. At the Last Supper they were given the profoundest meaning of redemption — not simply the sacrifice *by which,* but the new order *into which,* men were to be redeemed — "I in my Father, and you in me, and I in you" (Jn 14:20). Built into Christ's humanity, men were to be united with the divine nature which was his, as it was the Father's and the Holy Spirit's. That is what it is to be redeemed.

But what does "built into Christ's humanity" mean? What does "you in me and I in you" mean? He had already talked of establishing a Kingdom, building a Church; but these phrases have no obvious connection with either Kingdom or Church. In chapter 15 we hear our Lord say: "I am the Vine, you are the branches", and in that we have a new relation of believers to Redeemer for which nothing has really prepared us. A kingdom has living members, so has a church. But a vine is a living thing. The branches of a vine are not like the branches of a business. A vine does not decide to found some branches and keep a protective eye on them. The branches are an extension of its own life, they live by one same life with the vine, so that it is necessary to the branches; they could not live without it. But also if it is to be a fruit-bearing vine, its branches are necessary to it.

Saint Paul was to work out the implications for us — the Church is in a mysterious sense Christ's own body, her members living with his life as the cells of a man's body live with his. "All you who have been baptized into Christ have put on Christ" — have clothed yourselves with him — "you are all one person in Christ"

(Gal 3:27, 28). That, to repeat, is what it is to be redeemed. But Paul had only to work out the implications—the truth is here: Christ says it—"You have only to live on in me, and I will live in you."

"This is my Blood of the new covenant", Jesus said. It is his first mention of a covenant. The first covenant (Ex 24) had been made on Mount Sinai. Jeremiah (31:31) had foretold another: "I will make a new covenant with the house of Israel." Now Christ makes it: the first had been sealed with the blood of calves, this with his own Blood. And he makes it with a new Israel, the Israel of God—"I in my father and you in me and I in you."

41 *AGONY AND ARREST*

From the supper room, they came down the hill to the brook Kidron, crossed it, and went up the Mount of Olives to Gethsemane— a half-hour's walk. The "garden" was a small plantation of olive trees containing an olive-press. Who was the owner? A friend of our Lord's, surely; Jesus would hardly have made the private property of a stranger a frequent sleeping place for himself and the Twelve.

Jesus in Agony

Leaving eight of them, he went deeper into the garden, taking Peter, James, and John. With these near him, he lived his agony. "My soul is sorrowful even unto death. Stay you here and watch with me" (Mt 26:38).

Falling flat on the ground, he prayed that, if it might be, the hour might pass from him—the hour of the birth pangs of the new humanity with which he was in labor. In his agony he prayed, "My Father, if it be possible, let this chalice pass from me. Nevertheless not as I will, but as thou wilt."

To death Christ had sacramentally bound himself at the Last Supper, as he spoke of his Body given for them and of his Blood which should be shed for them and for many, unto the remission of sins. So it was not from death that he was asking his heavenly Father to save him. Nor was the suffering from which he shrank only — or mainly — the bodily torments, scourging and tearing of flesh and nailing and death, which he knew already in every detail (Mk 10:34). It was far more than that. Men have known, men do know bodily torments as grievous. But the agony beginning in him no other man has known. The prophet Isaiah had foretold it (53:4–6): "Surely he has borne our infirmities and carried our sorrows. He was wounded for our iniquities, he was bruised for our sin. The Lord has laid upon him the iniquity of us all."

It was no token suffering that he was offering to God in expiation for the sins of all mankind. He not only took upon himself the suffering those sins have deserved in us who commit them. In some sense he also took the sins themselves, everything of them save their guilt. That is what Saint Paul tells us: "Him, who knew no sin, God has made into sin for us" (2 Cor 5:21). All the sorrow sinners ought to feel and have not felt came flooding in on him. That was the heart of his agony, that was the chalice which he prayed might pass from him. His Father sent an angel from heaven, not to lessen the agony, but to give him the strength to bear it, that he might not die of it there in the garden. It was after the coming of the angel that the agony reached its high point with the sweat of blood (Lk 22:43). We are here at the furthest point of his humiliation; he can never have looked less like God! This indeed may have been the reason why we do not find the angel and the sweat of blood in a number of important early manuscripts (including Vaticanus).

Through all this Peter, James, and John slept. A first time he woke them, reproaching Peter especially — "Could you not watch one hour with me?" He urged them to pray that they might not find temptation too strong for them: "The spirit indeed is willing, but the flesh is weak." They slept again, and again he woke them.

But the third time there was a difference: their waking or sleeping no longer mattered. Through the trees gleamed the torches of the Temple guard, brought by Judas to lay hold of him — his hour was come. And as we hear him speak, we already sense that the conflict within himself was over. The sufferings might intensify, but from now on he was master of himself and circumstance. The redemption was as fully and freely willed by him as the Incarnation by his Mother.

Jesus Arrested

Judas arrived, showing the way to a large crowd — Temple police, servants from the chief priests and the scribes and the elders (Mk 14:43) and Roman soldiers as well (Jn 18:12), with a senior officer in charge of them. There is significance in their presence. Christ's enemies had not dared to arrest him in daylight for fear of the crowds: even less would they have dared to execute him, whether or not they had the right, for fear of those same crowds. They wanted him dead, but somehow they had to get the occupying power to kill him. That, one imagines, is why, along with their own people, they had a band of Roman soldiers go there for the arrest. The mere hint that there might be a riot would have got them the soldiers.

Judas told those with him that the man he should kiss was the one they should seize. The word he used for "kiss" applied to the somewhat sketchy embrace normal where the kiss is equivalent to a handshake. But the kiss he actually gave the Lord he was betraying was (as Mark and Matthew tell us) the kiss of warmest devotion: and one marvels at the nerve of the man who so soon after would be driven by remorse to hang himself.

Jesus' response may startle us: "Friend, what have you come for?" It was not so long before that he had said of this same Judas, "I have chosen you Twelve, and one of you is a devil." All through the public ministry we have noticed in him a terseness which can rise to fierceness: his speech is seldom observably gentle, and never when he speaks to men hardened in evil. From now on we shall hear that tone in him no more. The words to

Judas are a reminder that he has entered into his victim condition, he goes to the slaughter lamblike: there is no rage in him, no judging even. He is wholly judged.

We see something of this when he presents himself to those who would seize him with the words "I am he." So much majesty was in him that "they drew back, and fell to the ground." In that moment he could have passed through their ranks, as once or twice before. But it was not his will. He let them take him. That was Peter's moment, the last moment of flashing courage he was to have till Jesus was dead. He had brought a sword with him from the supper room. Now he swung it wildly, and somehow swept an ear off Malchus, a servant of the high priest. There is something farcically irrelevant about the whole episode. If he had to take off someone's ear, why not Judas'?

As three times before on that one night, his Master corrected him: "Put back your sword where it belongs: for all that take the sword shall perish with the sword. Did you not realize that I could ask my Father and have twelve legions of angels?—but I have a chalice to drink, a death to die." And Christ restored the ear to its place—his last recorded miracle of healing.

With Christ's arrest in the garden of Gethsemane, the temptation he had urged them to pray against came upon the apostles. The flesh proved weak indeed. They took to flight, all of them. And this within an hour or two of their First Communion.

In the Hands of the High Priests

Between the delivery of Jesus to the high priest and his handing over to the Roman procurator, we cannot be certain about the exact order or the exact detail of what happened. We have already noticed more than once that the evangelists were not much concerned with the *when* of the things our Lord said and did and suffered. What mattered to them was that he *did* suffer and do and say these things. Twice in those hours Jesus confronted leaders of his nation, and what took place at one confrontation might easily have been transferred to the other, or the two run together as one questioning.

Further, Matthew and Mark devote only twenty verses to all these hours, and the other two evangelists are even briefer. Obviously all four omitted a vast amount, each selecting the tiny handful of things that seemed to him most necessary to tell. In such a forest of omissions by all of them, it is unsafe to argue from the omission by one of something said by another.

It is Saint John who tells us (18:13) that his captors took their prisoner first to Annas, only later to Caiaphas. Annas, we remind ourselves, had been high priest for some years, had been removed by the Romans, but managed these same Romans skillfully enough to have the high priesthood given to five of his sons, as well as to his daughter's husband, Caiaphas, who now held it. The Jews did not take kindly to Rome's high-handedness about the hiring and firing of high priests. For them, we may imagine, Annas remained high priest, no matter which member of his family he had managed to slide into office at any given time.

With the high priest were gathered "priests and scribes and ancients" (Mk 14:53). This does not seem to have been a meeting of the Sanhedrin, the Jewish Senate, to which the Romans allowed so much administrative and judicial power. We have met "chief priests and scribes and ancients" before, heckling Jesus in the Temple (Mt 21:23, Mk 11:27, Lk 20:1). They were the hard core of his convinced enemies in the Sanhedrin. The moment they heard of his arrest, they, of all people, would have moved in on him, to continue the heckling—but with more abandon, now that he was alone and in their hands.

That night's meeting was not in any sense a trial. It was an informal gathering of men who knew what they wanted— ultimately Christ's death, immediately the evidence which would convince next morning's meeting of the full Sanhedrin that he deserved to die. There was a searching about for men to witness against the prisoner. But those they managed to find and bring in contradicted one another. Both Matthew and Mark mention two of these witnesses who spoke of that saying of his—"Destroy this Temple and in three days I will rebuild it." But each witness had his own way of misreporting the actual words, and both treated it as a threat against the Temple which was the center of Jewish worship, not realizing that Christ was speaking of that temple of the Holy Spirit which was his own body.

At some point Annas proceeded to question the prisoner about his teaching, but got no answer to his purpose: "Why do you ask me? Ask those who have heard what I have spoken in the synagogue and in the Temple. They know what I have said." One of Annas' servants struck Christ for daring to answer the high priest thus, and unanswerably Jesus said: "If I have spoken evil, give testimony of the evil; but if well, why do you strike me?" There was no anger in this, only rationality answering men enraged.

Annas should have rebuked the servant, but did not. Thus he gave the cue to those in whose charge Jesus was left for the rest of the night. They had their own sport with him. "They spat in his face, and beat him"—blindfolded him and slapped his face, challenging him to prove himself a prophet by saying which of them had done it. He must have passed a grim night.

So, indeed, must Peter, who, while all these things were happening, had denied again and again that he knew the prisoner. There was one appalling moment: Jesus was being led past him and he found the eyes of his denied Lord looking straight into his own.

At sunrise Jesus' captors brought him before the Sanhedrin. For what purpose? Not for trial, certainly. Had this been a trial at which he was sentenced to death, the evangelists—the three Jewish ones at least—would hardly have made so little of it. Matthew and Mark mention that it happened, but give no detail; John does not even mention it. It is only Luke, the Gentile, who gives anything at all of the proceedings—two questions asked and answered, and the answers taken as decisive.

In fact there was not even the semblance of a trial. And we can imagine the reason. They had not dared to arrest him in daylight (Mk 14:2); still less would they have dared to try him and sentence him and execute him themselves. There was too much possibility of immediate riot and abiding odium. They thought him a mortal peril, and they wanted him dead. But the occupying power must slay him.

Before the leaders could hand him over to death at the hands of the Romans, the whole Sanhedrin must be convinced that he deserved to die. That some of them were convinced of it, we have already seen—Pharisees because of teachings contrary to things they held sacred, Sadducees because he threatened their position, both with the Roman rulers (Jn 11:48) and with their own people (Lk 20:19). But men of the caliber of Gamaliel, for example, would have to be shown better evidence than reports at second or third hand, and better reasons than self-interest, for sending a fellow Jew to death.

There would be similarities between the two meetings—the night meeting of Christ's enemies trying to gather the evidence, the morning meeting of the full Sanhedrin at which the evidence was used. All the questions calculated to bring answers from the prisoner which would settle his guilt would have been asked at the first. Only those which had drawn such answers would be asked again at the second. There was one question in particular: Was he the Christ, the Son of God? (Mt 26:36, Mk 14:61). If only he could be got to give the same answer before the Sanhedrin, the leaders knew he was lost. Luke shows him giving it.

At the sunrise meeting, he told them that hereafter the Son of Man would be sitting on the right hand of the power of God (Lk 22:69). It was a fearful claim for any man to make, putting himself thus beyond all men that ever had been or ever would be. Yet was it blasphemy? The next question was the one that mattered.

"Art thou then the Son of God?"

"You say that I am."

He was saying yes, evidently. And yes they took to be evident blasphemy. But why? What indeed had they meant by the question?

The phrase "sons of God" had been used in the Old Testament concerning those God favored—the angels, the Jewish people, the judges of Israel; and in some of the apocryphal books—Enoch, for example, and 2 Esdras—it had been used for the Messiah. But in the Old Testament no single individual had actually been called "a son of God"—least of all by himself! Yet Christ had gone beyond even that barely tolerable limit by calling himself *the* Son of God. It was monstrous, as was his claim that he would be at the right hand of God. But it *might* leave him still within human bounds. What made it blasphemy were claims he had associated with the title Son of God as applied to himself, especially at the previous Pentecost here in Jerusalem.

John tells about them in his fifth chapter. It was after the healing of the paralytic at the pool by the Sheep Gate. Jesus had said that he works continuously, as his Father does; that as the Father raises up the dead and gives life, so does the Son. Whatever the Son sees the Father doing, he himself does in exactly the same way. All should honor the Son as they honor the Father: to fail in honor to the Son is to fail in honor to the Father. It was a claim to be God. And as his hearers knew nothing of the Blessed Trinity, they could see it only as an assertion of two Gods. That was blasphemy indeed, and by Jewish law merited death. Some members of the Sanhedrin might have been there when he said these things; all must have studied reports of the most shocking words ever uttered by a Jew. That was what the high priest meant by the question.

The admission that he regarded himself as the Son of God—taken with the claims to equality with the Father which he had so recently attached to that title (Jn 5)—settled the question for the Sanhedrin. He deserved death. The phrase we translate "guilty of death" is meaningless as English and does not represent the Greek, which means "liable to" or "deserving of", as Jesus himself uses it of the man who "calls his brother a fool" (Mt 5:21–22). It was not a judicial formula. For reasons we have seen, the Sanhedrin did not sentence our Lord themselves. But now, with the authority of the Sanhedrin behind him, Caiaphas could demand his death of the Roman procurator.

42 *TRIAL BY PONTIUS PILATE*

Pilate

All four evangelists give their own account of the trial by Pontius Pilate (Mt 27, Mk 15, Lk 23, Jn 18). As in their account of what followed the arrest, each gives a brief summary only, omitting a vast amount, selecting the things that seemed to him most necessary to tell, concerned with what was said and done but not so very much with the order of the saying and doing.

In all four, however, Pilate's opening question is "Are you the King of the Jews?" For the Sanhedrin, "Son of God" had been the fatal phrase. For Pilate, Christ had to be shown as a threat to Roman rule. Luke (18:2) lists three items in the indictment Caiaphas and the others laid against him—perverting the nation, forbidding the payment of tribute to Caesar, saying that he is Christ the King. Two elements in Jesus' answer (Jn 18:33–38) convinced Pilate that this was no case for his intervention. "My kingdom is not of this world", the revolutionary said! And again, "For this was I born, for this I came into the world, to give testimony to the truth."

"Truth!" exclaimed Pilate. "Is that all?" The Roman Empire, especially at its Eastern end, was littered with philosophers and sophists, mystics, and mystagogues. The Roman civil service was trained to treat them with a sort of contemptuous tolerance—there might even be something in the stuff they were talking, but nothing that interested practical men, above all nothing that threatened Roman dominion. The Jesus whom they wanted him to kill for them was evidently one of that mystical sort.

Pilate was no fool. He saw that the Jewish leaders clearly had reasons of their own for so passionately wanting the man dead. The powers Rome allowed the Sanhedrin varied under different rulers, and as things were they could not put a man to death. Pilate must oblige. Why did he not simply play along with them? We know enough about Pilate to make a reasonable guess. They wanted him to do their dirty work, so he felt, and he resented it.

Not because the work was dirty—there was too much blood on his hands for that. What he must have resented was being used as a convenience. Above all by the Jewish leaders. He disliked Jews. His patron in Rome, the Emperor's minister Sejanus, was strongly anti-Jew, had in fact been behind the expulsion of Jews from Rome in 19 A.D. Pilate had had three major conflicts with them. Two of these had been settled in Judea, with Pilate winning one and forced to yield ignominiously in the other. The third had gone to Tiberius Caesar himself. Pilate again lost and was censured by the terrifying little man in Rome.

Three times or four Pilate told the leaders that he could find no case for the death sentence against Jesus. But they kept the pressure steadily on him. We cannot be certain, within a year or two, of just when Jesus was tried. If it was as late as the year 31, Pilate would have had a special reason to avoid the Emperor's notice; in October of that year his patron, the great Sejanus himself, was executed by Tiberius, and many of his friends in Rome committed suicide to avoid worse. But, even before that, the high priests knew, and Pilate knew that they knew, that he would do a great deal to avoid their reporting him again to Tiberius. Yet he must have loathed the notion of being pushed around by them. He saw two loopholes, and tried both—an appeal to the crowd, and a transfer of the whole case to Herod the Tetrarch.

There had been a stream of people coming up to the fortress, in the courtyard of which the trial was conducted. They were there to put in their plea for the release of a prisoner—it being Pilate's custom to free one every year at the Passover (that feast, we remember, commemorated the release of the whole Jewish people from captivity in Egypt). Pilate hoped that they might choose Christ if he made the suggestion. The name of Barabbas was shouted—he was a murderer, says Peter (Acts 3:14); he had been arrested "with the rebels who had been guilty of murder during the rebellion", says Mark (15:7). Enough of the crowd took up the shout to ensure that Pilate could not use that way out. Later he asked the crowd what he should do with Christ. Someone shouted, "Crucify him", and that shout was taken up too. How large was the crowd? We have not a notion.

Herod Antipas

Meanwhile there was Herod. A man of no particular religious views, he followed the family custom of paying honor to the national religion whenever it was not inconvenient. So he had come up from Galilee for the Passover. Pilate, having learned that Jesus was a Galilean, thought that it would be a nice compliment to Herod and a solution to his own problem to hand the case over to him. Nor, one imagines, did the Jewish leaders mind. After all, Herod had put that other nuisance, John the Baptist, out of circulation in a dungeon at Machaerus. The great thing was to be rid of Jesus once and for all. The "chief priests and the scribes" went dutifully along, and accused Jesus all over again—"loudly", says Luke (23:10). But Herod was not playing either. He sent Jesus back to Pilate.

Herod had not got the entertainment out of the prisoner that he had expected—not a single miracle, not so much as a spoken word. It was probably for entertainment, otherwise lacking, that this retarded adolescent mocked Christ's claim to kingship by putting a bright robe on him (possibly an old one of his own—for he had wanted to be king himself).

Back to Pilate

It may have been this that put it into the heads of Pilate's soldiers to carry the kingship mockery to the limit. They put a purple robe on the prisoner, and a reed in his hand for a sceptre, and thorns twisted into a crown on his head. It was robed thus, crowned thus, and pouring with blood from the scourging, that he was shown by Pilate once more to the chief priests and their servants, with words for which Pilate will be remembered till the end of time— "*Ecce homo.*" We cannot read Pilate's mind. But the words sound like—"Look at him now!" It may have been one more effort to get Christ's enemies to see that there was no danger in this bleeding figure of mockery, no point therefore in going on to the kill.

If so, it failed. They wanted him dead, because he claimed divine honors for himself. They wanted Pilate to kill him, to save them the trouble and the odium. They tightened the screw. If Pilate would not have this claimant to kingship executed, then he was not Caesar's friend; for whoever calls himself a king speaks against Caesar. The threat was naked. They would report him to Tiberius. Pilate remembered the last time they had done that, and the censure that came upon him, although that time he had been acting to show honor to the Emperor. Pilate might hate the Jewish leaders very much as they hated the prisoner they wanted him to slay for them. His wife might urge him to mercy, with talk of a dream. He might even have come to a certain awe of the prisoner: when he reminded Jesus that he had the power to crucify him or let him go, the answer had come as from one sitting in judgment: might there be something supernatural about him? But Pilate dared not carry resistance beyond a point.

As we read of the things that were done to Jesus between his arrest at Gethsemane and his sentencing to crucifixion, we get the feeling that in some way he stood outside them. As prisoner on trial for his life he was the central figure; but he seemed not to belong to the circle in which these other men moved around him. The Sanhedrin passed him on to Pilate, Pilate to Herod, Herod back to Pilate. They mocked him and scourged him. He gives an effect of almost total passivity, furiously acted upon, hardly reacting at all.

The truth is that he was the central figure, but of a far wider action than his tormentors knew. For he was redeeming the whole human race, his tormentors included. He was active as no man has ever been, wholly given to the greatest thing that has been done upon earth.

It was a tragi-comedy of cross purposes. *They* saw themselves engaged in the trial of an individual blasphemer, whereas *he* was celebrating a cosmic religious rite — reality rather, in which all rites find their meaning. Of what was actually happening they knew nothing — least of all that he was dying to redeem *them!* Yet in the redemptive sacrifice they too had their function.

In the Temple sacrifices, only the priest could do the offering, the oblation; but the slaying of the victim, the immolation, often was done by the Temple servants. In the sacrifice of man's redemption, Christ as Priest *offered* the Victim, but he did not *slay* the Victim: Calvary was not suicide.

The chief servant of the Temple, the high priest, insisted on making the slaying his own personal concern. He and those with him would force the pagan procurator to have the Victim crucified. Thus, while Christ's mind was concentrated on the offering, theirs was on the slaying. The oblation was his action wholly, the immolation wholly theirs. He allowed the slaying, accepted it, offered it, but did not do it. They could torment his body, and he missed no throb of the pain. But, compared with the mighty thing he was doing, the torments were only a distraction, more intolerable as distraction even than as torment.

Nor did he complain. He had accepted victimhood, and it was not for the victim to lay down the conditions of his slaying—the sacrificial animals had never been consulted either. A complaining victim would have shadowed the majesty of the sacrifice.

The leaders, demanding his death with such passionate persistence, were serving an end they did not know. But serving it they were. "I, if I be lifted up," he had said, "will draw all men unto me." They saw to it that he should be lifted up.

Pilate yielded. The crowd—small crowd? large crowd? a tiny fraction, anyhow, of the Jewish people, representing nobody but themselves—had said, "His blood be upon us and upon our children" (Mt 27:25). Pilate washed his hands of the whole business—in real water!—and sent Christ for crucifixion. As the reason for execution to be attached to the cross, he wrote the words "Jesus of Nazareth, King of the Jews". The leaders were annoyed, and wanted him to insert that that was only what the criminal claimed. Pilate stood firm. It was the last spurt of temper. They had won the major victory. He planted his small barb, and retired with such dignity as could be salvaged from so sorry a wreck. A few years later he *was* summoned to Rome—Samaritans complained of a massacre he had ordered—and that is the last we hear of him. His niche in Roman history is tiny: Tacitus mentions him (*Annales* XV) as having put Christ to death!

43 *PRIEST CRUCIFIED*

The Road to Calvary

Following the usual custom, the cross was laid on the prisoner's shoulder. But it was soon clear that, with that weight on him, he would never reach the place of execution alive. So the soldiers seized a passerby, Simon of Cyrene, and made him carry the cross instead. "He was followed by a great multitude of the people and also of women, who beat their breasts and mourned over him"—to these he spoke serious words of no comfort.

As we read the Gospel account, we miss one familiar figure—for Veronica was not to arrive for a good many centuries yet! And we meet two whom we do not usually see pictured in the procession—two "evildoers", guilty of banditry probably, were being led to crucifixion with him (Lk 23:32). Having arrived at Calvary—the word means skull, the shape of the hill perhaps suggested the name—Jesus was stripped of his clothes and nailed to the cross, with one crucified bandit to his right, the other to his left.

His enemies, we realize, saw him only as the victim and knew nothing of the Priest. We know, of course, about the Priest. But we also are in danger of *seeing* only the victim, to such a point do his sufferings afflict us. We miss too much of the meaning of Passion and death if we do not realize that it was as celebrating Priest that our Lord carried the Cross, hung on the Cross, died on the Cross.

The Voice from the Cross

The Gospels record seven things he said in the three hours he hung there—three of them about others, four about himself. In none of them must we fail to hear the Priest speaking.

The first—it was spoken before the soldiers proceeded to divide his clothing among themselves—was clearly redemptive: "Father, forgive them, for they know not what they do." He was dying to win forgiveness for the sinful race of man, and his first word of forgiveness concerned his slayers, all of them. Peter (Acts 3:17) makes the same excuse for them—"Brethren, I know that you, like your rulers, acted in ignorance"—Peter did not forget that he himself had had less excuse of ignorance for denying Christ than they for crucifying.

Another thing that Christ said was redemptive, too. When one of the bandits reviled him, the other made the most astounding of all death-bed repentances—if we consider the bed on which he was dying, and the condition of the One in whom he made his act of faith. What he said to the man nailed to the next cross was: "Lord, remember me when you come into your kingdom." And Jesus answered his prayer: "*This day* you will be with me in paradise."

One third thing he said about others, which does not appear instantly to have to do with redemption, yet most profoundly has. To his Mother, who was standing before the cross with Saint John, he said, "Woman, behold your son." And to Saint John, "Behold your mother." On the surface it is a purely personal, purely domestic remark. But the surface meaning will not do. If he had merely wanted to arrange for someone to look after his Mother once he had left the world, he had had plenty of time to do it in the months before. It was not a sudden idea, come to interrupt the offering of his redemptive sacrifice. If he chose to say it at this moment, it was because it belonged to the redemptive process.

The Church sees it as more than the provision of a home for his Mother. Mary was being given as Mother not only to John but to all the children of Eve. The redemption Christ was winning for the race as a whole must be applied to each man individually. In the application, Mary was to play an essential part.

John must have wondered what it meant to be given a new mother. So must the mother who bore him. For she was there too. It had been a day of misery for Salome. It had begun with her learning that her sons—for whom she had demanded places on Christ's right and left when he should come into his Kingdom— had run with the rest when the soldiers took him. On Calvary she saw what looked like the end of the road for their King, saw too who were on his right and on his left, and in what posture. Now one of her sons was handed over to be someone else's.

Beside our Lady and John and Salome, who were at Calvary? Mary of Cleophas, who was related to our Lady, and Mary Magdalen, out of whom the dying man had cast seven devils. Other of his friends were there, unnamed. But his enemies were there in force, especially "the chief priests and scribes and ancients". They had heckled him in the Temple courtyard and been answered. They had continued with heckling and accusation in the high priest's house, Herod's court, Pilate's court, and been totally ignored: "He had answered them nothing."

The time for heckling was over. But there was still mockery: "This Christ is king of Israel, let him come down from the cross and show us!" (Mk 15:32); "He trusted in God, let God now deliver him if he wants him" (Mt 17:43).

None of this meant a great deal to the Priest on the Cross, concentrating his mind on the Father to whom, and on the race of man for whom, he was suffering the redemptive sacrifice. His mockers had no more claim on his attention than any other of the myriads whose sins he was dying that he might expiate. He heard them, of course, but as a priest at the moment of Consecration might hear people talking or a baby crying at the back of the church. They were on the periphery only: even the measureless agony of his nailed Body was peripheral: the Center was drawing his whole being to itself.

His enemies did not expect him to answer them. Nor *did* he, precisely. But suddenly they heard a great voice crying out: "My God, my God, why hast thou forsaken me?" (Mt 17:46). And again: "I thirst" (Jn 19:28). In the first phrase, they recognized the opening words of Psalm 22, the psalmist crying out that God is not helping him against his enemies. Hearing them, they would have been as automatically reminded of the whole Psalm of which they were the opening, as we by "Out of the depths have I cried unto thee." For those who knew the Psalm from end to end, the reminder must have been sobering.

So much was in it of what they were now seeing. "They have torn holes in my hands and my feet." "All my bones are dragged about." "They cast lots for my garments." These men of learning would have found the other cry too. "I thirst": for the Psalm has "Parched is my throat like clay in the baking, and my tongue sticks fast in my mouth."

They would have found their own selves in the Psalm: "All those who catch sight of me fall to mocking, mouthing out insults while they toss their heads in scorn, saying, 'He trusted himself to the Lord, why does not the Lord come to his rescue and set his favorite free?'"

For the moment too, they must have felt the chill of uncertainty. In spite of the desolation of its opening, the Psalm ends in triumph. "My cry for help did not go unheeded." Was there a threat there? Would he, after all, thrust their taunts down their throats by a last-minute descent from the Cross?

Once the idea had thus been forced on them that what was now before their eyes had been described so many centuries before, they would hardly have failed to be reminded (by something else that happened) of Psalm 69: "When I was thirsty they gave me vinegar to drink." That, anyhow, the soldiers did. After his cry of thirst, they soaked a sponge in sour wine and lifted it to his mouth. Like the wine and myrrh which he had refused just before he was crucified, this was meant to deaden pain.

It was after tasting it that Jesus cried, "It is consummated" (Jn 19:30). What he had become man to do was now done: expiation had been made, sufficient and overflowing for the first sin which had made the breach between God and the human race, and all the sins by which the breach had been widened. This was atonement. Disguised by our pronunciation, the meaning of the word is at-one-ment. God and the human race had been at-two: now, and forever, they would be at one. Individual men might still separate themselves from God, but no one could separate the race of man.

With his work completed, our Lord let this earthly life pass from him. "Father," the voice rang out, once more with a quotation from a Psalm, "into thy hands I commend my spirit" (31:6). The centurion in charge of the execution squad said, "Indeed this was the Son of God."

Laid in the Tomb

Matthew, Mark, and Luke all tell us that the sky had been darkened for the hours Jesus had hung upon the Cross. Only Matthew speaks of the earthquake and the splitting of rocks and dead men rising. But all three again tell that, at the moment of death, the veil of the Temple was rent. We do not know if this was the curtain that hung before the sanctuary, or the inner one closing off the Holy of Holies. We feel that its rending may have had something to do with the "great multitude of the priests" who joined the Church (Acts 6:7).

It was late on the Friday afternoon. The bodies must be disposed of, they could not simply hang there on the Sabbath. Before the first stars appeared they must be buried.

The Jewish officials asked Pilate for permission to dispose of them. Soldiers were sent, and broke the legs of the thieves, apparently to finish them off. But Jesus was so obviously dead that they did not go through this routine with him. "One of the soldiers with a spear opened his side, and immediately there came out blood and water." Saint John sees this as of immense importance—blood, the sacrifice by which we are saved; water, as so often, the spirit Jesus was to give men, the life in which salvation consists.

Ordinarily, Jesus would have been buried with the other two in the kind of pit used for criminals. But somebody else had gone to Pilate, and asked for the body of Jesus. He was Joseph of Arimathea, a town close to the Samaritan border (it may have been near there that Jesus healed the ten lepers, one of whom returned to say thank you). He was a member of the Sanhedrin, and "already a disciple, but secretly for fear of the Jews" (Jn 19:38). He decided to lay the body in a new tomb which he had prepared for himself. It was close to Calvary, and there was no time to take the body further.

He had approached Pilate "boldly", says Mark. There is a kind of splendor in his finding the courage to profess his faith in Christ at a moment when Christ seemed to have gone down in total failure. What is equally remarkable is that that other cautious member of the Sanhedrin, Nicodemus, found *his* courage in the same bleak moment. Joseph provided fine linen for the shroud, Nicodemus brought "a mixture of myrrh and aloes, about a hundred pound weight".

The myrrh and aloes were not for the embalming of the body. They would be scattered over the shroud, and over the ledge on which the body would be laid. The spices and ointments for the embalming were being prepared by Mary Magdalen and others of the women who had followed their Master from Galilee, to be used at the less hasty entombment which could follow the Sabbath. As we know, they did not need to use them.

Joseph had a stone rolled to close the entrance to the sepulchre. The leaders of the Jews remembered something that had come to their ears about Jesus rising on the third day. To make sure that his followers did not steal the body and pretend that he had risen from the dead, by arrangement with Pilate they put guards to watch the entrance, and sealed the stone.

That, they felt, was that. His disciples must have felt it, too. One of them, John, at least had something to occupy his mind. For our Lady had been given to him as his mother, "and he took her to his own". What the relationship must have meant to him over the years we get some notion from reading his Gospel. He had not been given to her merely to make her old age comfortable, and her loneliness bearable. She would have done more for him than he for her.

Their table conversation would not have been only about the people next door. They must have discussed the Son whose place was now John's. Sonship, in fact, had special interest for both Mary and John. We have already reminded ourselves that she was the only person who could say to God the Father "Your Son and mine". Does anyone who believes in the Trinity imagine that Jesus' Mother did not know from her Son of his own procession from the Father? And if she knew it, it is hard to think that she did not talk of it with the new son her Son had given her. John had a living woman in his home, not two dogmas and a statue.

But the flood of light that has poured for the whole Church from their relation did not begin that first night. What Mary knew about the immediate future of her Son we have not been told: everyone will make his own guess. But we do know that John was as startled as Peter and the rest to find that the tomb was empty.

"He Descended into Hell"

Descent into hell sounds an odd way of carrying out the promise Jesus had made to the repentant thief—that he would be with him in paradise that day. But the word "hell" was used in earlier English as the word "inferus" was used in the Latin of the Apostles' Creed, for everything in the next world that was not heaven. Where, then, did our Lord go in that time when his disciples were mourning him dead? He visited the souls of those who had died in the love of God but must wait until the sacrifice of redemption opened heaven to the fallen human race. Jesus had spoken of their waiting place as Abraham's bosom, naming it thus after that one of the great dead who mattered most to the Jews; to the thief he had called it paradise, because there was no pain but the pain of waiting, and that in the certainty of redemption.

Peter has another word for it, "prison", which emphasizes the longing to be gone (1 Pet 3:19). "Being put to death in the flesh, but enlivened in the spirit, in which also coming he preached to those spirits that were in prison"—the Greek word for "preached" means "heralded": it is used of Jesus preaching the gospel, the good news, in the synagogues (Mt 4:23). Since the Transfiguration, the expectant dead had known from Moses and Elijah that the moment of release was near at hand, and that their redemption would be brought about by Christ's death in Jerusalem. Now he came to them himself, new from death. The companion he had with him would have shocked some of them inexpressibly while they still lived on earth.

So "the Gospel was preached to the dead" (1 Pet 4:6). They were the first to have contact with the Savior after Calvary.

44 *RESURRECTION AND ASCENSION*

Easter Morning

The third day he rose again. No one saw him rise. The tomb was found empty, but no one saw him emerge from it. For forty days he was among them once more—"We ate and drank in his company after his rising from the dead", so Peter told Cornelius (Acts 10:41). Imagine how a mythmaker would have spread himself on the emergence from the tomb: but not a word. Not a word, either, on the dead body stirring to life: simply, the Father raised Jesus from the dead (1 Th 1:10).

The earliest written statement that has come down to us about those who saw him, we owe to Saint Paul. That he wrote it we owe to the chance—the fortunate chance, I almost said—that there were heretics in Corinth who asserted that the dead did not rise again. Paul based his answer to them (1 Cor 15) on the fact of Christ's Resurrection.

That had happened about the year 30. Paul had been converted perhaps five years after that. Writing from Ephesus, round 57, he reminded the Corinthians of what he had taught them half a dozen years before: "The chief message I handed on to you, as it was handed on to me, was that Christ, as the Scriptures had foretold, died for our sins; that he was buried, and then, as the Scriptures had foretold, rose again on the third day. That he was seen by Cephas, then by the eleven apostles, and afterward by more than five hundred of the brethren at once, most of whom are alive at this day, though some have gone to their rest. Then he was seen by James, then by all the apostles; and last of all, I too saw him."

We turn now to the evangelists. All four of them tell of the empty tomb and of Christ risen—Matthew and Mark briefly (20 verses each, though some of Mark's account may have gotten lost), Luke and John at more length. As usual each made his own selection—Matthew says nothing of the appearances to the apostles in Judea, Luke nothing of those in Galilee, John alone has both. No effort was made to harmonize their stories. The writers, or their informants, remembered certain things as having happened, clearly as to the fact, less clearly in detail, cloudily as to the order. We have already noted more than once that they were concerned with *what* was said and done, not much with *when*.

All four begin with the decisive fact: on Easter morning the tomb was empty. The women who had prepared spices came to anoint the body, and went into the tomb. The body was not there. An angel (two, says Luke) told them, "He is risen." Matthew alone tells how an angel rolled back the stone—"His countenance as lightning, his raiment as snow", and how "for fear of him the guards were struck with terror and became as dead men." Guards and women each reported the disappearance of the body.

The guards told the chief priests, says Matthew, and were given money to say, "His disciples came by night, and stole him away when we were asleep." To be asleep on duty carried the death penalty as a matter of course. The guards were reassured about that—"If the governor shall hear of this, we will persuade him and secure you": the Greek word for "persuade" was quite regularly used for "bribe". It was not much of a story—one has only to look at it to see one vast gaping hole in it—but there was no time to think up a better.

The news was brought by the women to the apostles, who did not believe it—"These words seemed to them as idle tales." Evidently they had taken all their Master's talk of Resurrection as meaning no more than that resurrection of all the dead which Pharisees taught and Sadducees denied. They were utterly unprepared for a return of Jesus to this earth. Peter and John went anyhow to look: and, belief or no belief, they ran! And the tomb *was* empty—they saw the shroud and the headcloth folded, but no body. They went back to tell the rest. It is typical of the evangelists that they do not bother to tell us what Joseph of Arimathea thought.

The first appearance of the risen Jesus, Mark tells us, was to Mary Magdalen (who does not figure in Saint Paul's list). Mark tells us nothing of what passed between Jesus and Mary Magdalen, only that she went and told the disciples, whom she found mourning and weeping for his death, "and they did not believe."

It is to Saint John that we owe the details. Read verses 11–18 of his twentieth chapter. We observe two things, perhaps, especially. The first is that she did not at once recognize him. The second is his mysterious opening word to her: "Do not cling to me, for I am not yet ascended to my Father." Scholars have wondered at the connection between the two clauses, and indeed it does not leap instantly to mind how one follows from the other. I can only report my own liking for one possible solution. Jesus was telling her that this was no momentary apparition of one who had died and gone to heaven: if it had been, anyone who loved him might indeed have clung despairingly to him. But he had not yet ascended to his Father: he would be here upon earth for a while yet: she would see him again.

There are stories of gods and demigods, dead men returning, living men bilocating. But there is nothing even remotely like the Resurrection of Jesus. In the forty days, he came and went by some rhythm of his own. He passed through the stone that sealed his tomb—it was not to let him out that the angel rolled away the stone, but to let the women in. He passed through the closed door of the Upper Room, in which the apostles were gathered. He rose into the sky at his Ascension.

He was concerned to prove that he was not a ghost—"See my hands and feet, that it is I myself; handle and see: for a spirit has not flesh and bones as you see me to have" (Lk 24:39). He had a real body, but it was a glorified body, the kind we ourselves hope to have at the resurrection. (Read 1 Cor 15:35–50.) It was a body wholly subject to the soul, to which the matter of our world was no longer a hindrance. Its *raison d'être* was to extend the soul's power, not to limit it, as our bodies so often do.

Yet it puzzles us if we theorize too confidently about what a glorified body can or should do, just as the agony in Gethsemane puzzles those who theorize too confidently on what the direct vision of God means to the soul of one still living here upon earth. Just what did his eating and drinking mean to a glorified body, what bodily need did food and drink meet?

On the Way to Emmaus

Two of the disciples were on their way to Emmaus (Lk 24:13–32). They had been with the rest when the women arrived with the report that the tomb was empty and that angels had told them Jesus had risen; and had been there still when Peter and John returned with the news that the tomb was indeed empty. As they walked, their talk was all of hopes and fears. Jesus joined them, went all the way with them, and only at the end did they recognize him—as he blessed bread and broke it and gave it to them.

Why did they not recognize him? Partly perhaps there was a difference in himself: may not all he had gone through have shown in his face, so that he was like the Jesus they knew, but not wholly like? But there was more in it than that. "Their eyes were held", says Luke. "He appeared in another shape", says Mark, which Monsignor Knox translated as "in the form of a stranger". We remember that Mary Magdalen had not known him at once— she thought he was a gardener. On the mountain in Galilee, most of the apostles adored—but some doubted if it were really Jesus.

Clearly it went with the glorified body that he was not at the mercy of men's eyes but could control what they saw of him, be seen as he chose and not as they chose, could be visible or invisible at will, could even perhaps be seen by some and not by others. As Saint Peter told Cornelius, "God granted the clear sight of him, not to the people at large, but to us" (Acts 10:40).

For his conversation with the two disciples, read Luke. One phrase stands out for us: after rebuking them for their failure to grasp what the prophets had spoken of him (which he then proceeded to elucidate), he said: "Ought not Christ to have suffered these things, and so to enter his glory?" We look long at "ought": we look long at "so"—this word is not in the Greek, but Jerome was surely inspired to insert it!

In the Upper Room

The two returned to Jerusalem to report to the apostles "and those that were with them", only to learn that their risen Lord had already appeared to Peter.

Then suddenly Jesus was in the room. At this time occurred the reassurance he gave them that he was no apparition: we have already noted it. All this is in Luke. John, writing long after, filled out the details of this meeting, and we begin to see what lay behind the forty days in which he came and went among them. He was teaching them, but not now of Trinity or his own Godhead or redemption. "He was telling them about the Kingdom of God" (Acts 1:3). He was completing their preparation to be rulers of the Church founded by his death and Resurrection. There are four main meetings, this one in Jerusalem, two in Galilee, the last meeting of all on the Mount of Olives before his Ascension.

There is something dramatic about the first meeting. The last time they had all been together, they had been arguing which of them should be first in his Kingdom: at his arrest, they had run. They might have been waiting with some nervousness for his opening words. These were "Peace be to you." Then the greatest commission ever given to men — "As the Father has sent me, I also send you." And "he breathed on them and said, Receive ye the Holy Spirit." Only once before has Scripture a divine breathing — when God formed man of the slime of the earth and breathed into his face, and man became a living soul. Calvary had been for the redemption of our sinful race. Now Jesus gave these first rulers of his Church power to forgive sins or withhold forgiveness.

There was another meeting in Jerusalem. It was a sort of pendant or postscript to this one, at which Thomas had not been present. That sturdy individualist was unimpressed by the story the others told of Christ's rising. He had to see for himself. "Unless I shall see in his hands the print of the nails, and put my finger into the place of the nails, and put my hand into his side, I will not believe." A week later Jesus invited Thomas to do precisely that, which means that in the glorified body the wounds were still present: they are eternally present. Thomas said, "My

Lord and my God"—for the first and only time we are hearing Jesus addressed as "God". Jesus' acceptance has in it the tone of that earlier time—terse, matter-of-fact, no softness in it. "Because you have seen me, Thomas, you have believed: blessed are they that have not seen, and have believed." There is a deeper ground for faith than a seen miracle.

Appearances in Galilee

At the meeting on the mountain in Galilee, he dotted the i's and crossed the t's of that earlier phrase about his sending them as he himself had been sent: "All power is given to me in heaven and on earth. Going therefore, teach all nations; baptizing them in the name of the Father and of the Son and of the Holy Spirit; teaching them to observe all things whatsoever I have commanded you. And behold I am with you all days, even to the consummation of the world." It is the very blueprint of the Church.

Catholicity is in it, for "catholic" means "universal", a word which brings together the two ideas of "all" and "one". Here is the threefold "all"—all nations, all teachings, all days—brought into "one" in him.

At the Last Supper he had answered a question of Thomas with the words "I am the Way and the Truth and the Life." Now he entrusts to the Church he is founding the teaching of the truth, the dispensing of the life into which baptism admits us—the two conditions without which we cannot walk the way, which is himself, to the goal which is his Father. They were a strange lot, these Eleven; they would be succeeded by men stranger than themselves. He who had foreseen Peter's denials and the flight of the men he had chosen, also foresaw popes like Benedict IX and John XII, foresaw whole hierarchies moving into heresy or cowering before rulers; he foresaw you and me. Yet this was his choice—the gifts of truth and life should come through these men and their successors; in union with them, we are in union with him all days until the end of the world.

There is one phrase which, as we ordinarily translate it, might mislead us—"Baptizing them in the name of the Father, and of the

Son, and of the Holy Spirit." The Greek does not mean "in the name", but "into the name". In other words, Jesus was giving not just the formula of baptism, but the purpose and effect of baptism: by baptism we are consecrated to the Blessed Trinity. Baptized into Christ Jesus, we are brought into life-giving relation with the divine Person that he is, and so with Father and Holy Spirit.

He had one last word to say to the man he was leaving as head of his Church. He said it on the shore of the lake. Peter and half a dozen others had gone fishing—at Peter's suggestion—and, as on a previous occasion, they had caught nothing. Read the story. It is in that twenty-first chapter of Saint John's Gospel which seems to have been added as an afterthought to a Gospel the writer had thought he had ended.

We find Jesus preparing a meal for them. As they sat eating it, "none of them dared to ask him, Who art thou? knowing that it was the Lord." They might well know that it was he, since they had just had one more immense catch of fish at his command. We can ponder on the fear that made them unable to ask him who he was, and the strange reason—namely that they already knew! The risen Lord was different.

At the Last Supper, he had foretold their scattering by a text from the prophet Zechariah (13:7): "I will strike the shepherd, and the sheep of the flock shall be dispersed." Now he tells of the new order, still in terms of a flock and a shepherd. From Peter he draws three utterances of love to parallel the three denials. He tells Peter to feed his flock, his whole flock. He was himself the Good Shepherd. He was about to leave this world. He made Peter to be shepherd in his place. With occasional waverings, Peter was a good shepherd. He has been followed by shepherds, good and less good. But the flock somehow survives.

Jesus went on to "prophesy the death Peter was to die", so very much the death he had himself died; "When you have grown old, you will stretch out your hands, and another shall gird you, and carry you where you go, not of your own will." Then comes a flash of the language we came to know so well in the public life. Peter asked what was to happen to John, and was told that it was no affair of his.

Christ Ascends into Heaven

In Acts, Luke tells us that Jesus was with them forty days, before he ascended into the sky, and a cloud took him from their sight. If we had only his Gospel, we might very well think that our Lord ascended on the evening of his Resurrection; and we might get the same idea from John (20:17) where, on the morning of his Resurrection, he tells Mary Magdalen to tell his brethren: "I ascend to my Father and to your Father, to my God and your God." But Luke in Acts makes it clear that the rising into the sky, seen by the Eleven, took place after forty days: none of which gives us any indication of what other contact there may have been in that period between the risen Lord and his Father in heaven.

The Ascension was from the Mount of Olives. The very last words the apostles said to him were: "Wilt thou in this time restore the kingdom to Israel?" It is the old obsession. They needed the Holy Spirit. And the Holy Spirit did come upon them, as our Lord had told them. Pentecost was ten days after.

45 *AT THE RIGHT HAND OF GOD*

The Redeeming Sacrifice

Resurrection and Ascension are not simply there as happy ending to a story of suffering and death. Of this the Ordinary of the Mass twice reminds us: the Mass commemorates not the death only, but the Resurrection and the Ascension as well. They are essential parts of the sacrifice of our redemption, not a sequel to it.

It was after the return to Judea toward the end of the public life that Jesus first told the apostles that the death he was to die was not simply a yielding to the violence of his enemies, but had a purpose in relation to men: "I lay down my life for my sheep" (Jn 10:15). Calvary was very close when he said: "The Son of Man is not come to have service done him; he came to serve others and to give his life as a ransom for the lives of many" (Mt 20:28). And at the Last Supper: "This is my blood of the new testament which shall be shed for many unto remission of sins" (Mt 26:28)—the "many" is a Hebraism: Jesus died for all men.

We observe that he never actually uses the word "sacrifice", although the meaning is clear. For the word, we go to Saint Paul—"Christ our Pasch is sacrificed" (1 Cor 5:7); "Christ has loved us and has delivered himself for us, an oblation and a sacrifice to God" (Eph 5:2).

The sacrifice our Lord offered was wholly in his humanity, so that it might be applied to the sins of men; but he who offered it was God, so that it had a value no purely human sacrifice could have. It was wholly effective in redeeming men from sin. But we never hear him mention Adam's sin—the sin of the world which John the Baptist, hailing him as the Lamb of God, said that he would take away.

Once again we owe so vast a clarification to Saint Paul. "It was through one man that guilt came into the world; and, since death came owing to guilt, death was handed on to all mankind by one man" (Rom 5:12). The sin of the representative man had made a breach between the human race and God. Paul goes on: "In this, Adam was the type of him who was to come. Only, the grace which came to us was out of all proportion to the fault. If this one man's fault brought death on a whole multitude, all the more lavish was God's grace, shown to a whole multitude, that free gift he made us in the grace brought by one man, Jesus Christ. . . . The sentence which brought us condemnation arose out of one man's action, whereas the pardon that brings us acquittal arises out of a multitude of sins."

Consider what sacrifice is. It is a public act, not just a private devotion of the priest; the people are passionately involved. In every sacrifice the victim was slain that it might be offered to God, offered to God that it might be accepted by him. If he did not accept, slaying and offering had accomplished nothing. In most sacrifices, only slaying and offering were visible—"public", so to speak—acceptance was not. Yet more than once in the Old Testament (Lev 9:24 and 2 Chr 7:1), acceptance too was shown— God sending down fire from heaven, to the measureless joy of priests and people: for it sanctified the victim, not only *making* it God's but *showing* it as God's. In the one perfect sacrifice of our redemption, of which all others were only figures, the Father showed his acceptance—and this time really, not only in symbol. By the Resurrection he glorified the victim.

What had the sacrifice, thus totally accepted, accomplished? The healing of the breach between the race and God, the opening of heaven to members of the so-long-sundered race; sin and death overcome—they would still continue, but their dominance was gone; Satan's head crushed.

For Christ himself, death and Resurrection meant glory. It is not simply that his glory was now shown forth. He was made glorious in himself, enriched in his very manhood. "He was established Son of God *in power*"—*dynamis*. *Dynamis* he already had: we remember the power he felt going out of him when he healed the woman with the issue of blood. What was the new power that came to him from death and Resurrection?

On the last day of the Feast of Tabernacles he had said of the Messiah: "Fountains of living water shall flow from his bosom." John adds the comment: "He was speaking here of the Spirit . . . the Spirit which had not yet been given to men, because Jesus had not yet been raised to glory" (Jn 7:39). Before his Resurrection he could bring dead men back to life, but he could not yet give men the Holy Spirit. That ultimate power, in which redemption lies, must await his glorification.

Jesus had not passed through the fearful experiences of Passion and death only to emerge exactly as before, as though nothing special had happened. "From the things he suffered," says the Epistle to the Hebrews (5:8), "he learned obedience"—he who had from the beginning made obedience the very principle of his life. There are depths too deep for us in that, depths deeper still in the next words of the Epistle—"He reached his full achievement." He was at last established in the existence as man which was proper to the only begotten Son of God. Thus fulfilled in himself, "he wins eternal salvation for all those who render obedience to him." From him and the Father, the Holy Spirit proceeds within the Godhead. Now he can give the Holy Spirit to those who are built into his risen body. At his first meeting with the apostles after the Resurrection he could breathe on them and say: "Receive ye the Holy Spirit."

Observe what the fact of the Resurrection means to us and to all men. In the fifteenth chapter of the first Epistle to the Corinthians, Saint Paul, answering heretics who denied that the dead rise again, founds everything upon the Resurrection of Christ: "If Christ has not risen, all your faith is a delusion; you are back in your sin. It follows, too, that those who have gone to their rest in Christ have been lost.... But no, Christ has risen from the dead, the first fruits of all those who have fallen asleep . . . just as all have died with Adam, so with Christ all will be brought to life."

Christ died not only to expiate sins, but to reconcile sinful men to God and lift them into a new order of existence. "Christ was delivered up for our sins and *rose again for our justification*" (Rom 4:25)—the same life-giving act that had raised him, raises us. God, "in giving life to Christ, gave life to us too" (Eph 2:5). It is in the risen Lord that we live. Members of his Mystical Body, we are built into his humanity, the humanity in which he lived among men, died and rose again from death. "The first Adam was made into a *living* soul: the new Adam was made into a *life-giving* spirit" (1 Cor 15:45). The second Person had come down to man's level that he might raise men to his. "We are made partakers of his divinity", says the Roman Missal, quoting 2 Peter 1:4, "who of our humanity did not disdain to share".

With the Resurrection God showed that he had accepted the Sacrifice, by glorifying the Victim. With the Ascension, God showed that he had accepted the Victim. This was a new element. In the symbol sacrifices of the Old Testament, there was no question of it. What could God do with a roasted bull or a slaughtered goat? They were slain as a way of giving up men's own use of them, a way of showing that they, like all created things, belonged to God. Now for the first time a real, not a symbolic, offering was made. The Priest had offered to God the Man that he himself was, the flower and perfection of the race for whom he was offered. The Victim was not only accepted, taken to himself, by God, but, as the perfection of sacrifice as a public act required, the acceptance was visibly expressed. That is the point of the Ascension.

To the apostles, sorrowing that their Lord was to leave them, he had said at the Last Supper: "It is better for you that I go, for if I do not go the Paraclete will not come to you. But if I go, I will send him" (Jn 16:7). Ten days after the Ascension, on Pentecost Day, the Church was indeed baptized with the Holy Spirit and with fire.

"Standing as a Lamb slain"

What is Christ doing now? The question sometimes startles. There are those who think his work was finished when he died on the Cross, just as there are those who think our Lady's work was finished when she bore him. They both had a great work still to do. It is his that concerns us here.

He sits at the right hand of God (Col 3:1). But sitting is not doing. What does he do? One thing we know he does and it concerns us supremely.

He had redeemed our race, but that redemption has to be applied to each individual. We read (Heb 9:24): "He has entered heaven itself, where he now appears in God's sight on our behalf"—that is, his presence in heaven continues to serve us, we are the gainers by it. Our individual salvation is bound up with his presence before God. "Jesus continues forever, and his priestly office is unchanging; that is why he can give eternal salvation to those who through him make their way to God" (Heb 7:24). Then come the words which surprise us if we attached too final a meaning to the "It is finished" that he uttered on the Cross. "He lives on still to make intercession on our behalf."

The Epistle has shown that this intercession consists essentially in his appearing in God's sight. The last Book of the New Testament adds the one elucidation needed. "I saw . . . a Lamb standing, as it were slain." Christ our Lord is in the presence of God with the marks of his slaying still upon him, his redemptive sacrifice presented everlastingly. We remember that even in the glorified body after the Resurrection, Thomas could have put his finger in the mark of the nails, put his finger into Christ's side. They are splendid, those wounds; but wounds they are, pleading irresistibly for the salvation of every one of us.

In heaven, then, Christ presents himself, once slain, now Lord over death, to God for our redemption. In the Mass this breaks through to the altars of earth. The same Christ, through the priest he has empowered, offers the same self once slain now truly present on the altar, to the same God, for the redemption of all. And in this action, all the members of his Body are privileged to have their part.

Index

MAP OF
PALESTINE
AT THE TIME
OF CHRIST

SCALE OF MILES

0 5 10   20   30

SIDON •

Mt. Libanus

ABILENE

• DAMASCUS

ZAREPHATH •

Mt. Hermon

SYRIA

DAN •

TYRE •

• CAESAREA PHILIPPI
  (PANEAS)

ITUREA

PHOENICIA

COROZAIN •
CAPERNAUM •
• BETHSAIDA JULIAS
BETHSAIDA •

TRACHONITIS

Plains of
Gennesaret

GAULANITIS

MAGDALA •
• KURSI

GALILEE

Sea of Galilee

ZIPPORI •

TIBERIAS •

• CANA
NAZARETH •
• NAIN

Valley of Esdraelon

• GADARA

DECAPOLIS

Range of
Carmel

CAESAREA •

Mt. Gilboa

• SCYTHOPOLIS

SAMARIA

• ENNON

Plain of Sharon

• PELLA

River Jordan

GERASA •

SAMARIA •

Mt. Ebal

Mt. Gerizim

• SHECHEM
  (JACOB'S WELL)

PEREA

JOPPA •

• ARIMATHEA

JUDEA

BETHEL •

• EPHRAIM

• PHILADELPHIA

Philistine Plain
Shephelah

• JERICHO

• BETHANY

NABATEA

• EMMAUS
• BETHPHAGE
JERUSALEM ◎ • BETHANY
AINKARIM • • BETHLEHEM

Wilderness of Judea

Dead Sea

• MACHAERUS

• GAZA

IDUMEA

• BERZABEE